Impermanence

Impermanence
Exploring continuous change across cultures

Edited by Haidy Geismar, Ton Otto and
Cameron David Warner

First published in 2022 by
UCL Press
University College London
Gower Street
London WC1E 6BT

Available to download free: www.uclpress.co.uk

Collection © Editors, 2022
Text © Contributors, 2022
Images © Contributors and copyright holders named in captions, 2022

The authors have asserted their rights under the Copyright, Designs and Patents Act 1988 to be identified as the authors of this work.

A CIP catalogue record for this book is available from The British Library.

This book contains third-party copyright material that is not covered by the book's Creative Commons licence. Details of the copyright ownership and permitted use of third-party material is given in the image (or extract) credit lines. If you would like to reuse any third-party material not covered by book's Creative Commons licence, you will need to obtain permission directly from the copyright owner.

This book is published under a Creative Commons Attribution Non-commercial Non-derivative 4.0 International licence (CC BY-NC-ND 4.0), https://creativecommons.org/licenses/by-nc-nd/4.0/. This licence allows you to share, copy, distribute and transmit the work for personal and non-commercial use providing author and publisher attribution is clearly stated. If you wish to use the work commercially, use extracts or undertake translation you must seek permission from the author. Attribution should include the following information:

Gesimer, H., Otto, T. and Warner, C.D. (eds). 2022. *Impermanence: Exploring continuous change across cultures.* London: UCL Press. https://doi.org/10.14324/111. 9781787358690

Further details about Creative Commons licences are available at
http:// creativecommons.org/licenses/

ISBN: 978-1-78735-871-3 (Hbk.)
ISBN: 978-1-78735-870-6 (Pbk.)
ISBN: 978-1-78735-869-0 (PDF)
ISBN: 978-1-78735-872-0 (epub)
ISBN: 978-1-78735-873-7 (mobi)
DOI: https://doi.org/10.14324/111. 9781787358690

Contents

List of figures	vii
List of contributors	xiii
1. Introduction *Haidy Geismar, Ton Otto and Cameron David Warner*	1

Part 1 Living with and against impermanence

2. Heavy curtains and deep sleep within darkness *Tsering Woeser*	25
3. Disinheriting social death: towards an ethnographic theory of impermanence *Carole McGranahan*	28
4. Atheist endings: imagining having been in contemporary Kyrgyzstan *Maria Louw*	47
5. Encountering impermanence, making change: a case study of attachment and alcoholism in Thailand *Julia Cassaniti*	65
6. Holding on and letting go: Tanzanian Indians' responses to impermanence *Cecil Marie Schou Pallesen*	83

Part 2 States of being and becoming

7. A Melanesian impermanence *Joe Nalo*	109
8. 'We are not an emblem': impermanence and materiality in Asmat lifeworlds *Anna-Karina Hermkens and Jaap Timmer*	110

9. The unmaking and remaking of cultural worlds: reinventing ritual on Baluan Island, Papua New Guinea   131
   Ton Otto

10. 'Do what you think about': fashionable responses to the end of Tibet   155
    Cameron David Warner

Part 3 Structures and practices of care

11. Negotiating impermanence: care and the medical imaginary among people with cancer   183
    Henry Llewellyn

12. Caring for the social (in museums)   205
    Haidy Geismar

13. Transitional sites and 'material memory': impermanence and Ireland's derelict Magdalene Laundries   226
    Laura McAtackney

14. Photos and artist statement   245
    Alison Lowry

Part 4 Curating impermanence

15. 'Neurosis of the sterile egg' – permanence and paradox: museum strategies for the representation of Gustav Metzger's auto-destructive art   251
    Pip Laurenson and Lucy Bayley

16. Culturing impermanence at the museum: the metabolic collection   272
    Martin Grünfeld

17. Screenshooting impermanence   292
    Winnie Soon and Sarah Schorr

18. 'Museum of Impermanence': the making of an exhibition   305
    Ulrik Høj Johnsen, Ton Otto and Cameron David Warner

19. Epilogue: self unhinged   334
    Caitlin DeSilvey

    Index   342

List of figures

5.1.   'Charming life: The secret of a happy life is to accept change gracefully'. The cover of a notebook at a bookstore in Chiang Mai. In addition to textual Buddhist teachings, an awareness of change permeates popular culture in Thailand, creating a general social orientation toward impermanence. Photo: Julia Cassaniti.   66

5.2.   A friend in 'Mae Jaeng' gets ready to send off a paper lantern *krathong*, in a ritual symbolising the letting go of attachments as they float away in the night sky. 30 December 2007. Photo: Rosalyn Hansrisuk.   73

5.3.   After Sen's visits to the hospital, his family decided to put up this portrait of the famous Northern Thai monk Khruba Siwichai in the shop, in the spot where they used to sell whiskey. 30 December 2007. Photo: Julia Cassaniti.   75

6.1.   The number of people of Indian origin in Moshi has been declining since independence. Moshi, Tanzania, 2016. Photo: Cecil Marie Schou Pallesen.   86

6.2.   Many nationalised houses are marked with the National Housing Corporation's logo. Moshi, Tanzania, 2016. Photo: Cecil Marie Schou Pallesen.   93

6.3.   The houses are female spheres but at the same time they are men's domains. Moshi, Tanzania, 2016. Photo: Cecil Marie Schou Pallesen.   100

7.1.   Joe Nalo (b. 1950), a painter from Manus, Papua New Guinea, who lives and works in Port Moresby, provides his vision of impermanence that includes the environment, plants, animals, humans, spirits, artefacts and technology.   109

8.1.	*Bisj* festival in the village of Biwar Laut on 24 September 2018. The public presentation of the *bisj* poles in front of the *jeuw* (meant to initiate revenge) was tuned to the visit of an organised tour of American tourists and some carvers were expecting tourists to purchase the poles. Photo: Jaap Timmer.	112
8.2.	David Jimanipits and the corpus, as well as the Last Supper, that he is carving. Ewer village, 19 September 2018. Photo: Jaap Timmer.	122
9.1.	Sakumai Yêp is pulling the rope attached to the pigs while supported by his son and his patrilateral cross-cousins. Baluan Island, Papua New Guinea, 2011. Photo: Ton Otto.	136
9.2.	Sakumai Yêp with the *kup* of six large pigs in front of him. Baluan Island, Papua New Guinea, 2011. Photo: Ton Otto.	137
9.3.	Some of the crowd watching the *yiwan kup* ritual performed by Sakumai Yêp. Baluan Island, Papua New Guinea, 2011. Photo: Ton Otto.	139
10.1a. and 10.1b.	*Trukcha* on blankets and *trukcha* on items at Munsel's store in Chengdu, 2018. Photo: Cameron David Warner.	162
10.2.	Nyedron recommended this particular photograph for the Moesgaard exhibition because the young woman also wears this silk necklace while performing *nangma*, professional singing and dancing at bars. The shape calls to mind Pema Dolkar's amulet case. Nyedron viewed this as symbolic of cultural loss over time. The outer form still exists in a diminished way, while the inner significance has been lost entirely. Photo: Nyema Droma, 2018, from the Precious Relics Project Collection.	163
10.3.	A women's jacket from Hima Ālaya with a design based on a Tibetan *chuba*, as displayed in the 'Museum of Impermanence' exhibition, 2019. Photo: Sarah Schorr.	165
10.4.	The opera mask hoodie featured in the '1376' rap of Tibet Cypher's video, purchased from the 1376 store (left) together with Rewa's formal *chuba* (right) in the 'Museum of Impermanence' exhibition, 2019. Photo: Sarah Schorr.	170

12.1.	Job advertised in the lobby at Bayeaux detailing the social skills needed for the position. Photo: Haidy Geismar.	214
12.2.	Analogue and digital practices at Bayeaux. Photo: Haidy Geismar.	217
13.1.	Remnants of the laundry room attached to the women's dormitories at Sean MacDermott Street, September 2020. Photo: Laura McAtackney.	235
13.2.	A scene from the laundry room at Donnybrook, June 2018. A large plinth featuring a statue of the Sacred Heart of Jesus sits beside a small fan located directly above two industrial laundry pressing machines. A large crucifix hangs over the doorway. Photo: Laura McAtackney.	239
14.1.	'Instead of the fragrance there will be stench; instead of a sash, a rope; instead of well-dressed hair, baldness; instead of fine clothing, sackcloth; instead of beauty, branding' (Isaiah 3:24) (cast glass, found objects, human hair, 2019). Photo: Alison Lowry.	246
14.2.	'The Cardigan' (a cast glass children's cardigan inspired by the poetry of Connie Roberts, 2019). Photo: Alison Lowry.	247
15.1.	Mona Hatoum, 'Performance Still', 1985–95, Tate. © Mona Hatoum.	252
15.2.	Marina Abramović, 'Rhythm 0', 1974. Installation view Tate Modern. Photo: Sculpture Conservation Tate © Marina Abramović.	253
15.3.	Gustav Metzger, 'Recreation of First Public Demonstration of Auto-Destructive Art', 1960, remade 2004, 2015. © Gustav Metzger. Photo: © Tate.	254
15.4.	Gustav Metzger at his first lecture demonstration at the Temple Gallery, possibly by John Cox, for Ida Kar, 2¼-inch-square film negative, June 1960. Purchased 1999. Photographs Collection, NPG x199033 © National Portrait Gallery.	258
15.5.	Gustav Metzger practising for a public demonstration of auto-destructive art using acid on nylon, possibly by John Cox, for Ida Kar, 2¼-inch-square film negative, 1960. Purchased 1999. Photographs Collection, NPG x134796 © National Portrait Gallery.	258

16.1.	Photograph from the collections at Medical Museion taken in 2019. Photo: Martin Grünfeld.	277
16.2.	Thomas Feuerstein, 'One and No Chair', 2002–8. Made of timber *Serpula lacrymans*, plexiglass, stainless steel and aluminium, 170 x 65 x 65 cm. Created with the support of Christian Ebner, Institute of Microbiology, University of Innsbruck.	283
17.1.	The screenshot of a dirty screen with a mobile phone, 2017. © Winnie Soon.	294
17.2.	The installation view of 'Unerasable Images', 2019. © Winnie Soon.	297
17.3.	The Lego reconstruction of the 'tank man' scene, 2018. © Winnie Soon.	297
17.4.	Nine selected images from 'Unerasable Images', 2018. © Winnie Soon.	298
17.5.	Sarah Schorr applies a tattoo during a performance and exhibition at Galleri Image in Aarhus, Denmark, 2019. © Sarah Schorr.	300
17.6.	Sarah Schorr's screenshot temporary tattoos are installed in the gallery to mimic the practice of putting butterflies in cases, 2019. © Sarah Schorr.	301
17.7.	Participants record their tattoos as they fade and email them to Sarah Schorr to be included in the exhibition, 2019. © Sarah Schorr.	302
18.1.	View from the Tibet section. Photo: Media Moesgaard, Søren Vestergaard, 2019.	312
18.2.	View from the Papua New Guinea section. Photo: Media Moesgaard, Søren Vestergaard, 2019.	312
18.3.	People watching a video presentation. Moesgaard Museum. Photo: Ton Otto, 2019.	313
18.4.	Morning *puja* in the Kwa Bahal temple in Patan. Photo: Media Moesgaard, Søren Vestergaard, 2019.	314
18.5.	The sand maṇḍala under glass. Photo: Media Moesgaard, Michael Johansen, 2019.	316
18.6.	Visitors and lamas collaboratively finishing the sand maṇḍala and closing the exhibit. Photo: Sarah Schorr, 2019.	318
18.7a.	Silk appliqué *thangka* of Goddess Tara by Tenzin Nyima, 2019. Photo: Cameron David Warner.	319
18.7b.	Hand-painted *thangka* inspired by a mural in Lo	

	Munthang by Dawa Thondup, 2019. Photo: Media Moesgaard, Søren Vestergaard.	319
18.8.	The 1376 'Museum of Impermanence' store. Photo: Media Moesgaard, Søren Vestergaard, 2019.	320
18.9a.	Pema Dolkar's amulet case. Photo: Media Moesgaard, Michael Johansen, 2019. Courtesy of the National Museum of Denmark.	321
18.9b.	Pema Dolkar's coral headdress and other jewellery. Photo: Ton Otto, 2019. Courtesy of the National Museum of Denmark.	321
18.10a.	The old Green Tara. Photo: Media Moesgaard, Søren Vestergaard, 2019.	323
18.10b.	Bekha Maharjan's new Green Tara. Photo: Media Moesgaard, Søren Vestergaard, 2019.	323
18.11.	The Nepalese section in bird's-eye perspective. Photo: Moesgaard Museum, Ulrik Høj Johnsen, 2019.	324
18.12.	The festival scene with video installation, dancing beam and large log drum. Photo: Media Moesgaard, Søren Vestergaard, 2019.	327
18.13a.	Original Manus skull in wooden bowl. Courtesy of Museum of Cultures, Basel.	328
18.13b.	Replica of the Manus skull in another wooden bowl, Moesgaard Museum. Photo: Media Moesgaard, Michael Johansen, 2019.	328
18.14.	Two houses, two different graves. Photo: Media Moesgaard, Søren Vestergaard, 2019.	329

List of contributors

Lucy Bayley is a Postdoctoral Research Associate at Tate.

Julia Cassaniti is Associate Professor of Anthropology at Washington State University.

Caitlin DeSilvey is Professor of Cultural Geography and Associate Director for Transdisciplinary Research in the University of Exeter's Environment and Sustainability Institute.

Haidy Geismar is Professor of Anthropology and Curator of the Ethnography Collections at UCL.

Martin Grünfeld is Assistant Professor of Metabolic Science in Culture at the Center for Basic Metabolic Research and Medical Museion at the University of Copenhagen.

Anna-Karina Hermkens is a cultural anthropologist and Lecturer at the School of Social Sciences, Faculty of Arts, Macquarie University.

Ulrik Høj Johnsen is Museum Curator in the Ethnographic Department of Moesgaard Museum and Adjunct Lecturer in the Department of Anthropology, Aarhus University.

Pip Laurenson is Head of Collection Care Research at Tate in the UK and Professor of Art, Collection and Care at Maastricht University in the Netherlands.

Henry Llewellyn is a medical anthropologist and Research Fellow in the UCL Division of Psychiatry.

Maria Louw is Associate Professor at the Department of Anthropology, Aarhus University.

Alison Lowry is an artist who lives and works from her studio in County Down, Northern Ireland.

Laura McAtackney is Associate Professor in the Department of Archaeology and Heritage Studies, Aarhus University.

Carole McGranahan is Professor of Anthropology at the University of Colorado, Boulder.

Joe Nalo is a freelance artist and former Curator at the Papua New Guinea National Museum and Art Gallery.

Ton Otto is Professor of Anthropology at Aarhus University and James Cook University.

Sarah Schorr, PhD, is an American photographic artist, researcher and educator.

Cecil Marie Schou Pallesen holds a PhD in Anthropology and is employed as Postdoctoral Fellow and Curator at Moesgaard Museum.

Winnie Soon is an artist and Associate Professor of Digital Design and Information Studies at Aarhus University.

Jaap Timmer is Associate Professor of Anthropology at Macquarie University and Senior Fellow at the Aarhus Institute of Advanced Studies.

Cameron David Warner is Associate Professor of Anthropology and Director of the Anthropology Research Program, Aarhus University.

Tsering Woeser (*tshe ring 'od zer*) is a Tibetan writer and activist who lives in Beijing.

1
Introduction: thinking about impermanence across cultures

Haidy Geismar, Ton Otto and Cameron David Warner

In the Tibetan diaspora, a family struggles with the loss of their reputation and the death of their social standing – from being close to the Dalai Lama to living in relative obscurity in exile. Can there be such a thing as social rebirth following social death? When something that is gone returns, did it never leave or is the return itself evidence of impermanence?

In London, museum practitioners and artists recognise that all artworks are underpinned by social networks and intangible skills, as well as an ever-shifting material infrastructure. They wonder if the object regimes of the museum can expand to include care for the precarious networks of skill and the unceasing obsolescence of technologies that are constantly changing and cannot be owned by the museum.

In Kyrgyzstan, a new generation of younger adults form communities centred on atheism and the rejection of the notion that there is any kind of life after death. These young people, grappling with the complex legacies of both socialism and resurgent Islam, use atheism as a way to break with the past through the establishment of practices, such as cremation, that take place after death and signal a resistance to participating in increasingly constrained religious hegemony.

These instances, and the others detailed in this volume, recount emerging and culturally located strategies that deal with impermanence, understood as both a common condition for all human beings and a point of tension and negotiation with the desire for permanence and fixity. Human bodies grow old, are prone to illness and unavoidably die, in old age or before. Our precious possessions do not last forever, despite our personal and collective efforts to protect and preserve them. Equally, our social status and distinct cultural practices are subject to continuous change, even as we attempt to eternalise them through language, law and tradition. Our natural environments are also always changing to an ever-growing extent as the result of our own activities. We may perceive the impermanence of these forms gradually, barely noticing change, or we may perceive change through shocking moments of recognition: the precipitous death of a glacier or a monument thrown to the bottom of a river.

The concept of impermanence allows us to sit within the uncomfortable tensions and paradoxes that emerge from our lived experiences and material engagements with the institutional, ideological and philosophical concepts that structure our understanding of the world. Impermanence is, by definition, a temporal frame that enables us to resituate our subjectivity away from fixed and solid points of knowledge and experience and acknowledge ongoing transformation and material flux. In this volume, we are concerned with how this condition unfolds and is reflected upon in different places and within different cultural traditions. Despite its overwhelming universality, human beings generally seem to resist impermanence rather than embrace it. Many ritual practices aim to create lasting identities for the person, the community or the nation. But there are also alternative conceptual and practical traditions that emphasise impermanence, such as the Buddhist ritual of making and unmaking a sand maṇḍala (see Chapter 18). The ancient Buddhist tradition of philosophical reflection and meditation on impermanence represents a potentially affirmative attitude toward impermanence (see Chapter 10) and is a key source of inspiration to our thinking here. Building on this particular cultural perspective on impermanence, we develop the concept of impermanence as a prism through which to analyse and compare different theories and practices dealing with transience and disintegration alongside aspirations of certainty for the future. In short, impermanence opens up a range of timely questions and discussions that speak to our shared experience of transformation – local and global, cultural and natural.

Until relatively recently, dominant strands of social theory were reliant on notions that imply some kind of permanence, such as structure, culture, identity, tradition and heritage. Only recently have concepts of decay, loss, rupture and ending become more prominent in Western social theoretical discourse, in part inspired by other cultural traditions such as Buddhism. This volume highlights strands of thinking across a range of different places and periods in which ideas about change, ending, transience and uncertainty are foregrounded as ways to understand the past, present and future. We bring together perspectives on impermanence in religious and secular settings from many different parts of the world, emphasising how studies of religious practices, rites of transition, museum collections and institutional practices of care collectively demonstrate the value of impermanence as a concept. The comparison between religious and secular institutional worlds enables a grounded reflection on the presence of impermanence in social structures as well as in doctrine and dogma, daily practice and lived experience.

This volume emerges from a symposium entitled 'Inevitable Ends: Meditations on Impermanence', held at Aarhus University in May 2019, and an accompanying exhibition at the Moesgaard Museum, 'Museum of Impermanence: Stories from Nepal, Papua New Guinea and Tibet' (on display from 9 February to 19 May 2019). The symposium drew together scholars of anthropology, archaeology, philosophy, heritage and museum studies, visual arts, and Buddhist studies, who work in dialogue with interlocutors in Europe, North America, East Africa, the Himalayas and Tibet, Central and Southeast Asia, and Melanesia. The exhibition aimed to visualise experiences and expressions of impermanence, using old and new museum collections as well as extensive photographic and video material based on three case studies: the global Tibetan community, Kathmandu in Nepal, and Manus in Papua New Guinea (see Chapter 18). This rich comparative framework forms both the theoretical and empirical scaffolding of the volume. In this introduction, we lay out the groundwork for our perspectives on impermanence. We begin by tracing the discourse of impermanence as it has emerged in Buddhism, and then move on to juxtapose this with other discourses in which impermanence emerges as a culturally specific way of understanding change in the world. Through the concept of impermanence, we aim to decentre Euro-American and Anglophone influences on contemporary social theory by linking social theory to other genealogies of thought, most especially those drawn out of Buddhist philosophy and practice, with the explicit intention of developing a more global and comparative analytic.

Theories of impermanence from Buddhism

Buddhism contains a rich narrative and literary tradition dating back around 2,500 years to the time of the historical Buddha Śākyamuni, often in the form of parables of the earliest converts and their discourses with the Buddha. One of the most harrowing is the story of how Kisāgotamī, a young woman, became a *therī*, a leader among Buddhist nuns. Kisāgotamī desperately wished to have a child – and she did, a boy, 'tender to [her] as [her] own breath' (Walters 2017). But the baby soon died. Distraught and grief-stricken, Kisāgotamī wandered from village to village with her dead baby. When she asked the Buddha for medicine to bring her son back to life, he said, 'Bring me a white mustard seed, collected from whichever home where death is unknown.' Eventually, Kisāgotamī came to the realisation that everyone is bereaved. In response to her realisation, the Buddha says to her:

> Better than a hundred years' life,
> not seeing how things rise and fall,
> is living for a single day,
> seeing things rise and fall.
>
> Not the condition of the village, or the town,
> and also not the condition of one clan.
> This is the condition of the entire world
> with its gods: the impermanence of all that is.

(*Therī-Apadāna of the Khuddaka Nikāya*, verses 719–20)

Here, Kisāgotamī represents all humans who have struggled to accept impermanence. It is natural to crave stability and be shocked when things change.

Impermanence serves as a cornerstone of most Buddhist ontologies and is taught to adherents as necessary for developing a beneficial perspective on life. Like other religions, Buddhism has spread and evolved into a wide variety of lineages, schools and denominations with a panoply of texts, ritual practices and social formations. But Buddhist proponents from nearly all times and places have returned to certain core principles that define what it ought to mean to call oneself 'a Buddhist'. One of the most common articulations of that core, both historically and in contemporary globalised Buddhism, is that of the 'Four Seals' – the four characteristics (or three characteristics in Theravāda contexts) that need to be reflected in any philosophy or doctrine in order for it to be considered Buddhist:

1. All compounded things/conditioned things[1] are impermanent.
2. All contaminated phenomena[2] are suffering.

3. All phenomena are empty and devoid of self.[3]
4. Nirvāṇa is peace.

Buddhists begin by recognising that the phenomena we experience are always changing and that the other cornerstones of a Buddhist approach to the world are interrelated with that truth.

For Buddhists, impermanence should be actively contemplated. Traditionally regarded as the Buddha's first and final teachings, in the *Sutra on Impermanence* (Skt. *Anityatāsūtra*; Tib. *Mi rtag pa nyid kyi mdo*), the Buddha taught his disciples:

> Good health is impermanent,
> Youth does not last.
> Prosperity is impermanent,
> And life, too, does not last.
> How can beings, afflicted as they are by impermanence,
> Take delight in desirable things like these?[4]

Overcoming suffering – the main concern of Buddhist thought and practice – is concomitant with a realisation that much of one's suffering arises from a hopeless desire for stability in a world that is fundamentally unstable. At both macroscopic and microscopic levels, the Buddha warned his followers that change was inevitable and potentially led to suffering. In gross and subtle ways, our bodies, our mental states and even our identities are inherently impermanent. This is due to observable phenomena being compounds of other compounded phenomena in ever-changing interdependent relationships with each other. For example, a bicycle is a conventional designation for an assemblage of parts – made of various materials, each of which interacts with the environment in its own way – that should all be expected to break down. Likewise, the sense of being a mother does not exist independent from having, for example, a daughter, but that sense of motherhood, how it is defined and the degree to which it occupies one's present identity is constantly shifting in relation to incalculable intersubjective factors.[5] The key point is that one of the more prevalent ways that suffering is produced is by wilfully ignoring change, by intentionally neglecting or avoiding a truth that no one needed to tell.

Impermanence is not simply defined through the lens of suffering. Ultimately, impermanence is also a liberating notion, for Buddhists and others, because it means that depression, illness and even authoritarian regimes will not last forever. In the case of Kisāgotamī, she not only came

INTRODUCTION   5

to accept that her son was dead because his life was impermanent; she also realised her state of grief was impermanent, as was her role in society. Instead of continuing as a bereaved widow and mother, she took up monastic vows and became a leader among Buddhist women. In that sense, impermanence is not merely something to accept in the sense of resignation to an unwanted and unfortunate truth but is actually something to rely on, to hope for and to use. Tibetan fashion designers, such as Anu Ranglug, and European artists, such as Gustav Metzger, strategise with impermanence in mind (Chapters 10 and 15). Even social death can be overcome through social rebirth, as discussed by Carole McGranahan in this volume (Chapter 3). When compared to what is conventionally described as European social thought, a Buddhist view of impermanence, with its simultaneous foci on gross and subtle forms, can serve as a bridge between discourses on permanence and change (decay, ruins or waste, for instance) and discourses on intersubjectivity (care, gender or ethics).

The ubiquity of discourses on impermanence across Buddhist times and places indicates the complexity and profundity of the concept, not its ease. In numerous interviews, the Dalai Lama has stated that he meditates on impermanence more than once every day. In another example, Gaton Lekpa Rinpoché (1864–1941), a well-known Tibetan yogi, spent 15 years in solitary retreat. During that time, he devoted an entire year to meditating solely on impermanence (Jackson 2013, 16). In short, Buddhists have long identified a mature acceptance of impermanence, defined as recognising the instability of all phenomena, as key to overcoming suffering, while at the same time acknowledging the immense difficulty of attaining that state.

We would also be remiss not to point out that, just as European social theory has more sporadically (and especially relatively recently) accounted for impermanence, at certain times and places, Buddhists have also articulated soteriological visions encompassing permanence. For example, in the same body of texts that celebrate Kisāgotamī, *nirvāṇa* is likened to the blowing out of a candle (that is, a complete cessation of suffering, leading to a permanent state beyond the cycle of rebirth and death, *parinirvāṇa*). In the Pure Land tradition of Buddhism, devotees focus their practices toward being reborn in a Buddhist heavenly realm, from which they progress toward full Buddhahood without again undertaking rebirth in the human realm. For Buddhists, therefore, impermanence in human life is a prerequisite for the permanence of enlightenment.

There seems, then, to be an inherent paradox: acceptance of instability serves as the only means of achieving stability, which is prefigured as one's ultimate goal. Does impermanence thus presuppose permanence? This apparent paradox is not an issue for Buddhist exegetes for they accept *a priori* a nondualist perspective, defined as remaining within the unresolved tension between monism and dualism (Venkatesan et al. 2013, 302). Specifically for Buddhists, non-dualism holds that certain phenomena are inseparable but without claiming that they are the same kind of thing (Venkatesan et al. 2013, 330). While Buddhists have written a variety of expositions on nonduality, their premise begins from a commitment to what they term a 'middle way' position that avoids the extremes of essentialism (things exist) and annihilationism (things do not exist). Some Buddhist schools, notably those that study Yogācāra texts, also reject subject–object duality. In that line of thought, there is no difference between the person who perceives an object and that very object. If there were a difference, then both the person and the object would have to have their own independent essence, and hence there would be dualism. In summary, within different Buddhist schools of philosophy, impermanence interacts with other doctrines, especially nonduality and subjectivity, in ways that demonstrate that Buddhists, themselves, have attempted to resolve the apparent paradoxes and tensions of attempting to disentangle impermanence from permanence.

Impermanence, temporality and materiality

In this Introduction, we build on this paradox and analytic tension in how we bring Buddhist-inspired understandings of impermanence into dialogue with strands of thought from other bodies of social theory, more mainstream within our academic disciplines. Inspired by the Buddhist tradition, we take impermanence as a starting point for our theoretical exploration, as well as the recognition that impermanence is fundamentally entangled with ideas and experiences of permanence. By looking at some key areas of social theory and our ethnographic case studies, it is clear that impermanence has emerged as a useful analytical focus across a range of cultural traditions and academic perspectives. In the following paragraphs, we will briefly outline a series of conceptual tools that complement the insights on impermanence drawn from a Buddhist framework. First, we excavate how impermanence may be studied and compared as a form of temporality, a commentary on the passing of time, and a form of historicity that varies across different cultures. Next, we consider how theories of world-making present an alternative perspective on the issue of impermanence and continuity. Finally, we recognise a convergence of several trends in social theory that focus on the materiality of decay, ruination, rupture and becoming.

Temporality and historicity

By starting within the Buddhist tradition and then seeking discourses of impermanence elsewhere, it became clear to us how much discussions of impermanence are *de facto* grappling with the question of the nature of change *over time*. In much of the so-called 'canon' of social theory, notions of permanence have been strongly aligned with temporal continuity – for instance, underpinning ideas of heritage, history and culture. Yet, logically, the assumption of continuous change lays claim to the existence of a permanent condition, whereas the embrace of universal and constant laws cannot explain how things change in a radical way (Prigogine 1997). Hence the paradox of impermanence, as a form of continuity, and permanence, as a phenomenon that is always subject to change, emerges everywhere. Rather than reifying a divide between Buddhist ontology and social scientific theories of change over time, the concept of impermanence, in fact, allows us to highlight how different understandings of time and temporality lead to different experiences of change and continuity.

François Hartog (2015) develops the idea of varying 'regimes of historicity' to explore how temporality structures theories of being across European history, helpfully articulating how the entanglement of concepts and experiences of permanence and impermanence is also fundamentally a reflection on our relationship to both the past and the future. Hartog identifies several regimes of historicity in European history: evolving from an ahistorical or mythical temporality in Homeric Greece to the understanding of history as providing examples and standards for the present (*historia magistra vitae*) during the Middle Ages and Renaissance; continuing to the assumption of a clear break between the past and the unique present, around the time of the French Revolution; moving on to a focus on the future to understand the present (*futurism*) at the end of the nineteenth century and much of the twentieth century; and, finally, to the contemporary situation that he characterises as *presentism*, referring to a complex collapsing of notions and representations of future and past into an over-determining present. This historian's view of the past thus helps us to understand and contextualise how ways of dealing with impermanence/permanence change over time and are related to societal changes.

Hartog emphasises that the usefulness of the 'regime of historicity' concept is not limited to European history, and cites Marshall Sahlins' description of a heroic type of historicity in nineteenth-century Fiji as an example of how it can be applied elsewhere (Sahlins 1985, 32–72).[6] Hartog's work on historicity, as a link between changing social practices and notions of temporality, has been formative for our development of a comparative approach to globally diverging notions of impermanence and for contextualising emerging alternatives and transformations within a more globally oriented social theory. For example, Hermkens and Timmer (Chapter 8) argue that the traditional Asmat rituals involving headhunting and the destruction of ritual objects were a precondition for the maintenance of this people's cosmology of impermanence and renewal, which is now threatened by a different historicity promoted by the Christian missions, the state and museums that prohibit the taking of life and emphasise the preservation of artefacts.

World-making, autopoiesis and the pluriverse

Alongside Hartog's notion of historicity, another line of social theory that addresses the impermanence/permanence opposition directly, albeit not in these very terms, derives from a combination of phenomenologist philosophy and biological theorising about life and cognition. Through the philosophies of Heidegger, Husserl and Schutz, among others, the concept of 'world' or 'lifeworld' has become an important analytical tool for the social sciences to make a connection between subjective, lived experience and the socio-cultural environment (Desjarlais and Throop 2011). Understanding the intricate interdependence between an organism and its world has been an object of biological theorising since Uexküll (1909, 2010) and has received an intellectual boost in more recent neurobiological research (Thompson 2007). The merging of these strands of thinking has focused on processes of world-making that presume that the act of living involves the co-creation of a self and a corresponding world. Whereas the self (or subject or organism) pursues continuity, the way it accomplishes this is by continuous adaptation and change in correlation with its particular environment – its world. Therefore, sameness, as a continuing identity, is accomplished through change (Margulis and Sagan 1995, 31). This approach is explored in chapter 16, where Grünfeld discusses the concept of the 'metabolic' museum.

An important source of inspiration for this line of thought is the work of the Chilean neurobiologists Humberto Maturana and Francisco Varela, who have developed an alternative cognitive theory in response to the Cartesian dualist notion of knowledge as the representation of a pre-given world by a pre-given mind. In their view, cognition is an embodied action that brings forth both a subject and its world. This is a form of nondualism, steeped in biological theory and extending to phenomenology and theories of mind and culture (Maturana and Varela 1987; Varela et al. 2016). The central concept of their theory is *autopoiesis* as the key mechanism of life, which refers to the work of every organism or social unit to continuously adapt its composition and structure to maintain its existence as a distinct unit. Through the very act of living, an individual self (at different levels of complexity) and a corresponding world emerge and keep changing in continuous interaction. Varela co-founded the Mind and Life Institute, together with R. Adam Engle and the Dalai Lama, to promote dialogue between scientists and Buddhists.

Inspired by theories of autopoiesis, world-making and interdependence (among others from Buddhism), a significant and politically motivated contribution to thinking about change and continuity within the social sciences emphasises the concept of the 'pluriverse' (Escobar 2018; de la Cadena and Blaser 2018; Reiter 2018). Emerging during the 2010s and gravitating around Latin-American studies and scholars, the pluriverse can be described simply as the imagining of 'a world where many worlds fit' (according to a dictum of the Zapatistas in Southern Mexico). It is rooted in a deep critique of the philosophies and hegemonic practices of neoliberalism that have resulted in global economic and environmental crises and negate the right of otherness and alternative, autonomous but interdependent ways of being among indigenous and other disadvantaged populations. Gathering around the epistemological and activist vision of a 'political ontology' (de la Cadena and Blaser 2018), these scholars see the pluriverse as a political imaginary for analysis and intervention, where their collaborative research and actions constitute a factor of alternative world-making. The ultimate ambition is nothing less than to counter neoliberal economic and environmental collapse through a new ontology and style of world-making. Escobar (2018) argues that a design for the pluriverse can contribute to radically different forms of transformation that respect local worlds and their different knowledge practices. In this way, theories of autopoiesis, world-making and the pluriverse – like those of temporality – are helpful to bring together with Buddhist theorisations of impermanence, which, combined, give us a toolkit with which to understand continuous change in relation to different forms of continuity. Chapter 9, for example, investigates the transience as well as the resilience of traditional ritual practices in Papua New Guinea in these terms, and Chapter 18 shows how these same ideas informed the aforementioned exhibition on impermanence that was staged at Moesgaard Museum as part of the research leading to the present volume.

Decay, ruination, rupture and rhizomes

In addition to scholars working with phenomenologically and biologically inspired concepts of world-making, another body of work has emerged that is directly relevant for thinking through impermanence. Where the concepts of historicity, autopoiesis and the pluriverse focus on how we might conceptualise and understand impermanence as a social and biological force, this work centres more on the materiality of impermanence. Here, concepts such as ruination, decay and rupture intervene with the supposed permanence of heritage and culture to emphasise how they come hand in hand with the forces of impermanence. In *Overheating: An anthropology of accelerated change* (2016), Thomas Hylland Eriksen argues that interrelated crises of the environment, the economy and identity are perceived *locally* as out-of-control changes concerning a major facet of contemporary human life. Eriksen's grand synthesis of the contemporary experience of change builds on Anna Tsing's concept of friction as 'the "awkward, unequal, unstable, and creative qualities of interconnection across difference"' (Tsing 2004, 4) that underpins a body of social theory, simultaneously scaled to the ethnographic (grass-roots) and the global (see also Appadurai 1990; Marcus 1998). Drawing on work with environmental activists in Indonesia, Tsing explores how global capitalism and local 'nature' are entangled, with each producing 'friction' upon the other. Continuing this theme in later work, Tsing (2015) explores 'the possibility of life in capitalist ruins', understanding the unequally zoned and differentially experienced forces of global capital to be a precondition for nature in a post-industrial world. Across much of their work, Tsing and her collaborators see the possibilities for the paradoxical persistence of life in ruined landscapes (Tsing et al. 2017). Whether tracking Indonesian activists or matsutake supply chains, they focus on interdependence, precarity and uncertainty, resistance and fragmentation as hallmarks of the global condition.[7]

In a similar vein, Caitlin DeSilvey explores the possibilities for conservation and heritage when inherent impermanence and instability become the bedrock of practices and structures of care. In *Curated Decay: Heritage beyond saving* (2017), a text that informed the thinking behind many of the chapters in this volume, DeSilvey studies crumbling historical sites, such as the harbour at Mullion Cove in Cornwall. She argues for the potential positivity of instability and challenges the entire notion of heritage preservation with the questions, 'what happens if we choose not to intervene? Can we uncouple the work of memory from the burden of material stasis? What possibilities emerge when change is embraced rather than resisted?' (DeSilvey 2017, 4). In this volume, we explore how the decay of buildings, artworks and photographs extends the vocabulary of preservation to include deterioration and disappearance (Chapters 6, 12, 13, 15, 16 and 17).

Of the many recent theories of change, those of emergence and becoming relate to an understanding of impermanence and demonstrate its usefulness in this historical moment. Anthropologists have associated emergence and becoming with a Deleuzian approach to describing change (Hamilton and Placas 2011). Recently, the term 'emergence' has been used to describe how rhizomatic networks articulate transformation over concerns for more fixed structure and agency (Jensen and Rödje 2009); in these cases, attention is paid to continual acts of creative invention and resistance to overly determined forms and positions. Rhizomes, like the matsutake mushroom described by Tsing (2015), spread both under- and overground as complex assemblages, highlighting material interdependence. It is hard to identify where the tree root begins and the fungus ends. For Deleuze, the rhizome interferes with more static concepts of territory and objecthood, as well as life and death. Rhizomatic metaphors work in similar ways to a concept of impermanence in that both recognise that change often persists unnoticed until it flares up in a mere moment and erupts into our direct experience. Relational theories of subjectivities and social worlds inform ethnographies of becoming where the subjectivity of the individual engages with a state of continuous change, flux, unpredictability and openness (Biehl and Locke 2017).

One of the central aims of this volume is to facilitate a sustained dialogue between peoples from diverse places in ways that reveal and challenge local premises about continuity and change. This intercultural dialogue is an open investigation intended to compare epistemologies and ontological assumptions on the ground. As a whole, we intend this volume to draw together thinking from a number of different theoretical and empirical contexts to explore how impermanence might help us to move toward a more globally oriented social theory. The chapters that follow collectively describe the nature of impermanence, as a cultural value, a regime of historicity and a universal condition for human beings.

The structure of this volume

The volume consists of four sections that explore the scope of human action in relation to impermanence, asking how an awareness of impermanence has served, or could serve, for example, to liberate through religious attainment, draw greater attention to repair, care and conservation, or lead to the acceptance of the inevitable end as a paradoxical condition of ongoing being. The sections (Living with and against impermanence; States of being and becoming; Structures and practices of care; and Curating impermanence) are accompanied by a series of shorter essays and commentaries by visual artists, poets and practitioners who have experimented with impermanence as a means of communicating directly with audiences. Taken together, the sections also highlight our commitment to cross-cultural engagement and to presenting a polyphonic picture of how impermanence is understood and experienced.

Living with and against impermanence

The four chapters in this section all explore the social and embodied experience of living within worlds in which impermanence is powerfully inscribed in everyday life through religious doctrine. However, contrary to expectations, in all four cases, impermanence disrupts and challenges the ideologies and assumptions of the various religious practitioners and the scholars who study them. These chapters show how impermanence is experienced as a problem in visceral ways, inflecting social and political structures, but also how people's bodies become grounds for the tensions and paradoxes raised by more doctrinal understandings of permanence and impermanence. For example, Louw shows how young atheists in Kyrgyzstan are concerned that their atheist identity will be effaced by their families and community through burial practice at the time of death. While Buddhist beliefs and practices have elaborate ways of accommodating and dealing with impermanence, including self-effacement, McGranahan unpacks how the social death of an entire family and their efforts to reconstitute their standing demonstrate the impermanence of both identity and its loss.

The chapters in this section, such as Cassaniti's analysis of impermanence as an emic concept for a Thai Buddhist who nearly drank himself to death, reflect on the existential dilemmas that arise in relation to people's experience of impermanence in their lives. Schou Pallesen's description of Indian property owners in Tanzania, experiencing the loss of property and livelihood since the nationalist expropriation of their buildings, emphasises how impermanence provides insight into transnational and diasporic identities in which homes are both sites of longing and moveable economic identities. She shows how Indian Tanzanians assume a double strategy of stubbornly holding on while also strategically letting go and moving on (and away).

In this section, impermanence as a concept brings together a diverse set of critical concerns while drawing attention to aspects of the authors' projects that would have either gone unnoticed or proven difficult to voice without the concept. Impermanence gives name to the simultaneous concern for the suffering attached to change and the *promise* of change, with a particular focus on the person-centred, affective and phenomenological experience of that dynamic.

States of being and becoming

What does impermanence contribute to our understanding of human lifeworlds, including their materiality? The chapters in this section focus on rituals of transition and renewal, on artistic creativity and on the ephemerality of material objects, whether they pertain to rituals, fashion or museum collections. Many human rituals deal directly or obliquely with issues of impermanence, such as transitions from life to death, changes in social position or the transfer of social status from one generation to the next. Rituals are a means of world-making that invoke and reinforce cultural statuses as well as sentiments and perceptions of reality (Geertz 1973; Seligman et al. 2008). As such, they help create and recreate continuity in ever-changing environments. Dealing with a rare, partly reinvented ritual in Manus, Papua New Guinea, Otto shows how rituals themselves are transient – as are the worlds they help sustain – due to changing political, ideological and economic circumstances. Nevertheless, there also appears to be a remarkable resistance to complete obliteration, which may be partly explained by the inertia of some of the components that are involved in world-making practices, such as structures and logics of language, habitual social relations, and material objects, all of which were used and reproduced in the rituals discussed by Otto.

In their description of impermanence and materiality in Asmat lifeworlds (in Papua, Indonesia), Hermkens and Timmer elaborate how it is precisely the ephemerality of certain material objects and their creative destruction in rituals that produce their world-making effect by signifying balance and continuity in people's social lives through ancestral connections. Hermkens and Timmer also investigate what happens when these same objects change status by becoming museum objects or art commodities, which takes them out of meaningful cycles of destruction and renewal. In some museums in Melanesia and the wider Pacific, new relations of makers, collectors and institutions are being experimented with that allow for continuing social use combined with curatorial care and the acceptance of inevitable decay and need for renewal.

While rituals may exercise a conservative force on societies, even when they embrace the condition of impermanence – such as in the Asmat case or the Tibetan Buddhist ritual use of sand maṇḍalas – there is always an aspect of creative renewal in their execution. Warner's chapter explores how Tibetan fashion designers self-consciously choose to highlight the liberative potential inherent in impermanence. Through reinterpreting tangible and intangible heritage, they attempt to overcome the pessimism so prevalent in the discourses around them in China. Their designs weave the new and the old together in original and forward-looking ways. Thus, the inherent temporalities of impermanence differ between and within societies – something that is clearly borne out by all chapters in this section.

Structures and practices of care

In this section, we explore whether a better understanding of impermanence might help to understand and restructure institutional practices (for example, in healthcare or heritage conservation). The concept of care has emerged as both a practice and a theory of relational being, which acts on both the social and the material. In a recent volume, *Matters of Care*, Puig de la Bellacasa (2017) links Bruno Latour's 'matters of concern' to a feminist ethics of care. Following Tronto's influential rendition of care as 'everything that we do to maintain, continue and repair "our world" so that we can live in it as well as possible . . . in a complex, life-sustaining web' (1993, quoted in Puig de la Bellacasa 2017, 217), the concept of care has emerged as a paradigm through which to reimagine relationships and the constitution of ethical forms of subjectivity. The feminist notion of care has been used to challenge the ethics and politics of care as a top-down form of governmentality or as a form of biopower. For Puig de la Bellacasa, care is an affective state and a material relation that deals with the anxiety of impermanence while also signalling the politics of hierarchy, authority and governmentality that may prefigure the mobilisation of matter into states of being that must negotiate with both permanence and impermanence. Cook and Trundle (2020, 179) argue for an understanding of care practices as 'unsettled', defying 'easy categorisation as effects of political forces or as socially unmoored affective experience' (Cook and Trundle 2020, 178).

Care – of people, objects and our environment – may be seen as a commentary on impermanence and a model for new forms of imagining the future. Practices of care, from the domestic to the institutional, signal the articulation of political economy on the body of both people and things (Tronto 2015). In this section, we use the rubric of care to explore how ideas about impermanence are materialised and developed as forms of practice or intervention. How care is established and implemented, and how it is experienced and imagined, is crucial for our understanding of the finitude and future of palliative care in hospitals and hospices, for the preservation or maintenance of artworks in collections and for the constitution of new heritage sites within communities. In each of these instances, care signals a disciplined form of attention, a politics of recognition and a localised lexicon of materiality.

Llewellyn explores competing philosophies and practices of care for terminal cancer patients that each internalise understandings of permanence and impermanence. Oncology works with the premise of hope for a cure, right up until the final moments of life, whereas palliative care accepts the inevitability of death and impermanence, to make the remaining time bearable and meaningful. McAtackney explores the grass-roots movement and archaeological interventions in Dublin to have one of the Magdalene Laundries registered as a site of conscience and memory. While one site, in particular, was earmarked for preservation, McAtackney focuses on other laundries, which have been allowed to decay but whose material presence in neighbourhoods still leaves indexical traces of the labour of women, often forcibly confined. The affective geography of Dublin therefore oscillates between practices of care that are being institutionalised into heritage and public memory, and those that remain obscured and hidden within communities. Similarly, Geismar explores the tensions around care that emerge in a museum project to understand contemporary art photography in the context of the network of skills and materials that enable the work of both artists and conservators in museums. This perspective on photographs, which focuses less on their material form and more on the ever-changing material and social infrastructures that produce them, changes our understanding of museum practices and of the definitions of care and preservation that underpin them.

Curating impermanence

This final section of the volume focuses on how impermanence may be used as a curatorial strategy within museums to display both cultural concepts about change and actual material transformation. For example, in Denmark, experiments are being carried out with museum collections exploring the transience of collectables. Grünfeld, working at the Medical Museion, Copenhagen, addresses the temporal regime and historicity of museums. He asks whether their primary function is to attempt to hinder the metabolic life-processes of their collections and thus freeze time, turning the apparent impermanence of museum objects into an illusion of permanence or, at least, delayed impermanence. Instead of a regime of 'conserved permanence', Grünfeld suggests that we experiment with 'cultured impermanence', dealing with collections as living ephemeral assemblages.

The challenge of curating impermanence highlights its elusiveness as an everyday experience. We are somehow aware of it, at least occasionally (and mostly in the back of our minds, except for more or less disastrous events of loss), but we are still able to elide impermanence as a conscious presence because we tend to focus on the materialities and regularities around us that suggest and evoke continuity. In other words, our everyday involvement in the present makes us myopic with regard to the longer-term processes of change. For example, Schorr and Soon reflect on the impermanence of images in the digital age, using the technique of what they term 'screenshooting' to make installations that simultaneously embody the seemingly permanent presence and the impermanence of digital imagery. Soon shows how the unlimited reproducibility of digital images, which are transient themselves, creates a strong and persisting sense of presence. For example, although the Chinese government censored the Lego 'tank man' image of the Tiananmen uprising shortly after it was uploaded onto the Internet, it still appeared in Google image-searches many years later. Schorr investigates how digital images and print-outs of screenshots used as temporary tattoos interact with the physical world and the human body, revealing the difficulty of preserving digital remains as technologies constantly change and become more personalised and embodied in our post-digital world.

INTRODUCTION

Here, the work of images and ephemeral objects, such as temporary tattoos and digital screengrabs, helps us to keep a longer-term perception of flux and transformation. But it does not always work this way. The preoccupation with heritage and conservation as ways to preserve the past in the present may also, paradoxically, create an illusion of unceasing presence (Hartog 2015), unless the visualisation and remembrance of decay are explicitly a part of the display.[8] The very task of cultural historical museums is to preserve artefacts, to stop their natural metabolism and decay and, thus, make them an eternal part of the present. This leveraging of the past into the present, and the future, struggles with discourses of impermanence (see Harrison et al. 2020).

The threat of impermanence to museum conservation practices is described by Johnsen, Otto and Warner, who reflect on their work as curators of the 'Museum of Impermanence' exhibition. The extreme, albeit understandable, protectionism of museums from which they had requested objects for the exhibition made it very difficult (and, in a number of cases, financially prohibitive) to integrate the objects in a meaningful setting for the public. The use of heavily protected showcases did nothing to facilitate the sensory exhibition display they were striving for and, in some cases, the use of replicas appeared to be the only – and probably also best – solution. But how should impermanence be shown in an exhibition that can only actually show things that exist, many of which are precious artefacts cared for by conservators? The curators opted for different kinds of juxtapositions, of old and new artefacts, video installations and objects, moving soundscapes and, not least, ritualised happenings as part of the museum experience.

Finally, Laurenson and Baley explore how Tate Gallery has worked with the impermanent artworks of Gustav Metzger. They highlight the tensions between Metzger's practice and his participation in an art world that transforms ephemeral work into collectable forms of museum property, and explore the implications this has for curatorial strategies into the future.

Towards a comparative and global approach to impermanence

Based on the work conducted for the symposium and the exhibition, we are convinced that the concept of impermanence provides a valuable tool for breaking new ground, both theoretically and in applied settings. All of the chapters in this volume grew out of discussions where the question of impermanence gave language to intuitions, conversations and insights previously unarticulated by the authors and their collaborators. In one sense, impermanence emerges as a poignant hermeneutic for our time. The case studies, practitioner commentaries and exhibitions presented in this volume largely derive from contexts where forms of permanence have been either presumed or desired. Impermanence can constitute an ameliorating intervention on a variety of worlds if it means, for example, a transition from the value of oncology to that of palliative care, from iconoclasm to innovation, or from the preservation of artefacts to the curation of exhibitions that include metabolism and change.

This volume has drawn together multiple trajectories of what we are presenting as an emerging globalised social theory of impermanence. In this Introduction, we have outlined three key threads that weave together across the volume: the longstanding Buddhist tradition of thinking about the dissolution of the world; the notion of impermanence as an alternative poetics and temporality in the context of concepts such as heritage, historicity, identity, autopoiesis and world-making; and a final strand of synthesis drawing together theories of material rupture, decay, emergence and care. Alongside these interwoven threads, the other key contribution of this volume is the exploration of the notion of impermanence through in-depth case studies of practices and beliefs in different cultural worlds, articulating how impermanence provides a significant and illuminating cross-cultural analytical perspective. Rather than simply presenting theories of impermanence as culturally located, by working across the range of examples and perspectives presented here, we have come to see the remarkable presence of impermanence as a conceptual provocation, a methodological tool and an embodied experience across time and space.

Acknowledgements

We gratefully acknowledge constructive criticism of earlier drafts of this introduction by Martin Grünfeld, Joanna Cook, Martijn van Beek and an anonymous reader for UCL Press. Thanks also to all of the participants of the Inevitable Ends symposium for their engaged contributions and for shaping the volume overall.

Notes

1. *Saṅkhāra* in Pali or *saṃskāra* in Sanskrit (conditioned or compounded things) are, to Buddhists, phenomena that encompass subject and object, and, as such, can include both physical and mental phenomena, such as a tree, time or thought. They do not possess an independent essence of their own and consist of a multitude of other phenomena.
2. By 'contaminated phenomena', Buddhists refer to how actions, emotions and thoughts tend to be tainted with selfish hate, greed or ignorance. This comes from seeing oneself as separate from other things and having a naturally self-oriented concern.
3. Phenomena have no independent existence of their own; they only exist relative to other phenomena.
4. There are many canonical Buddhist texts on impermanence in a variety of liturgical languages. For example, there are two sutras on impermanence in the Tibetan canon, Toh. 309 and 310. This quote comes from Toh. 309, Degé Kangyur, vol. 72 (*mdo sde, sa*), folios 155.a–155.b, publicly available at http://read.84000.co (last accessed 1 November 2021).
5. The most famous example of this argument comes from *The Questions of King Milinda (Milinda Pañha)*, in which the Buddhist monk Nāgasena used the simile of the chariot and the self as both being compounds of other compounds in temporary configurations (Rhys Davids 1890, 40–5).
6. For additional examples and arguments for the comparative value of the concept of historicity, see also Hirsch and Stewart (2005) and Koselleck (2004).
7. Many of these projects are presented in the web publication *Feral Atlas* (https://www.feralatlas.org).
8. For instance, in the case of the *Gedächtniskirche* (memorial church) in Berlin, which is preserved in its ruined state indexing the bombing of World War II.

References

Appadurai, Arjun. 1990. 'Disjuncture and difference in the global cultural economy', *Public Culture* 2(2): 1–24. https://doi.org/10.1215/08992363-2-2-1.

Biehl, João, and Peter Locke, eds. 2017. *Unfinished: The anthropology of becoming*. Durham, NC: Duke University Press.

Cook, Joanna, and Catherine Trundle. 2020. 'Unsettled care: Temporality, subjectivity, and the uneasy ethics of care', *Anthropology and Humanism* 45(2): 178–83. https://doi.org/10.1111/anhu.12308.

de la Cadena, Marisol, and Mario Blaser, eds. 2018. *A World of Many Worlds*. Durham, NC, and London: Duke University Press.

DeSilvey, Caitlin. 2017. *Curated Decay: Heritage beyond saving*. Minneapolis, MN: University of Minnesota Press.

Desjarlais, Robert, and C. Jason Throop. 2011. 'Phenomenological approaches in anthropology', *Annual Review of Anthropology* 40: 87–102.

Eriksen, Thomas Hylland. 2016. *Overheating: An anthropology of accelerated change*. Chicago, IL: Pluto Press.

Escobar, Arturo. 2018. *Designs for the Pluriverse: Radical interdependence, autonomy, and the making of worlds*. Durham, NC, and London: Duke University Press.

Geertz, Clifford. 1973. 'Religion as a cultural system'. In *The Interpretation of Cultures: Selected essays*, 87–125. New York: Basic Books.

Hamilton, Jennifer A., and Aimee J. Placas. 2011. 'Anthropology becoming ...? The 2010 sociocultural anthropology year in review', *American Anthropologist* 113(2): 246–61.

Harrison, Rodney, Caitlin DeSilvey, Cornelius Holtorf, Sharon Macdonald, Nadia Bartolini, Esther Breithoff, Harald Fredheim et al. 2020. *Heritage Futures: Comparative approaches to natural and cultural heritage*. London: UCL Press.

Hartog, François. 2015. *Regimes of Historicity: Presentism and experiences of time* (translated by Saskia Brown). New York: Columbia University Press.

Hirsch, Eric and Charles Stewart. 2005. 'Introduction: Ethnographies of historicity', *History and Anthropology* 16(3): 261–74.

Jackson, Michael. 2013. *Lifeworlds: Essays in existential anthropology*. Chicago, IL: University of Chicago Press.

Jensen, Casper Bruun, and Kjetil Rödje, eds. 2009. *Deleuzian Intersections: Science, technology, anthropology*. New York: Berghahn Books.

Koselleck, Reinhart. 2004. *Futures Past: On the semantics of historical time* (translated and with an introduction by Keith Tribe). Cambridge, MA: MIT Press.

Marcus, George E. 1998. 'Ethnography in/of the world system: The emergence of multi-sited ethnography'. In *Ethnography through Thick and Thin*, 79–104. Princeton, NJ: Princeton University Press.

Margulis, Lynn, and Dorion Sagan. 1995. *What is Life?* Oakland, CA: University of California Press.

Maturana, Humberto, and Francisco Varela. 1987. *The Tree of Knowledge: The biological roots of human understanding*. Berkeley, CA: Shambhala.

Prigogine, Ilya. 1997. *The End of Certainty: Time, chaos, and the new laws of nature*. New York: Free Press.

Puig de la Bellacasa, María. 2017. *Matters of Care: Speculative ethics in more than human worlds*. Minneapolis, MN: University of Minnesota Press.

Reiter, Bernd, ed. 2018. *Constructing the Pluriverse*. Durham, NC, and London: Duke University Press.

Rhys Davids, T. W. 1890. *The Questions of King Milinda. Translated from the Pāli*. Oxford: Clarendon Press.

Sahlins, Marshall. 1985. *Islands of History*. Chicago, IL: University of Chicago Press.

Seligman, Adam B., Robert P. Weller, Michael J. Puett and Bennett Simon. 2008. *Ritual and Its Consequences: An essay on the limits of sincerity*. Oxford: Oxford University Press.

Thompson, Evan. 2007. *Mind in Life. Biology, phenomenology, and the sciences of mind*. Cambridge, MA: Harvard University Press.

Tronto, Joan C. 2015. *Who Cares? How to reshape a democratic politics*. Ithaca, NY: Cornell University Press.

Tsing, Anna Lowenhaupt. 2004. *Friction: An ethnography of global connection*. Princeton, NJ: Princeton University Press.

Tsing, Anna Lowenhaupt. 2015. *The Mushroom at the End of the World: On the possibility of life in capitalist ruins*. Princeton, NJ: Princeton University Press.

Tsing, Anna Lowenhaupt, Heather Anne Swanson, Elaine Gan and Nils Bubandt, eds. 2017. *Arts of Living on a Damaged Planet: Ghosts and monsters of the Anthropocene*. Minneapolis, MN: University of Minnesota Press.

Varela, Francisco, Evan Thompson and Eleanor Rosch. 2016. *The Embodied Mind: Cognitive science and human experience* (revised edition). Cambridge, MA: MIT Press.

Venkatesan, Soumhya, Michael W. Scott, Christopher Pinney, Nikolai Ssorin-Chaikov, Joanna Cook and Marilyn Strathern. 2013. 'The Group for Debates in Anthropological Theory (GDAT), the University of Manchester: The 2011 annual debate – Non-dualism is philosophy not ethnography', *Critique of Anthropology* 33(3): 300–60.

von Uexküll, Jakob. 1909. *Umwelt und Innenwelt der Tiere*. Berlin: J. Springer.

von Uexküll, 2010. *A Foray into the Worlds of Animals and Humans*. Translated by Joseph D. O'Neil. Minneapolis, MN: University of Minnesota Press.

Walters, Jonathan S. (trans.). 2017. *Legends of the Buddhist Saints: Apadānapāli*. Walla Walla, WA: Jonathan S. Walters and Whitman College.

Part 1
Living with and against impermanence

2
Heavy curtains and deep sleep within darkness

Tsering Woeser (ཚེ་རིང་འོད་ཟེར་)

1.
My Jowo Buddha sat
cross-legged in the seething
and ardent chaos of fire.
No time to write a poem, cry,
or even allow me to search for the countless treasures
behind those hurriedly hung curtains,
even though the ultimate truth
is actually impermanence
as personally manifested by Jowo Rinpoche.

2.
Those heavy curtains are a metaphor.
On the second day after the fire
they took a piece of yellow silk
covered with red flowers,
almost without a wrinkle,
cut without a trace,
and draped it behind what was reportedly
the 'completely intact' body
of Jowo Śākyamuni.
It seemed like a dense and seamless wall.
Who knew what was behind it?
Or what could still be there?
Those who persevere, you actually know

that invisible fire has been burning unabated,
and those heavy curtains
concealed the world
long ago.

3.
Deep sleep within darkness.
One cannot but sleep deeply within darkness.
One cannot but rely on a dream
in deep sleep within the darkness . . .
But isn't darkness also diverse?
It's like these words (was it me who said them?):
'You may think there is darkness in this world,
but in fact, darkness does not exist.'
And so, you can try and describe
different forms of brightness—
glimmering light, dim light, brilliant light . . .
soft light, warm light, intense light . . .
as well as the flash of light,

> that time the light extinguished
> > more quickly than lightning,
> > > did you see it?

as well as the flaming light,

> that time the unquenched light

> > burned longer than fireworks,

> > did you see it?

Suppose there is no eternal light, then what?
Suppose there is not a single ray of light, then what?
Slowly entering sleep? Gradually dying?
And how, in this endless bardo,
can one be spared
the invisible temptations of every wrong turn?
A single drop of water falls on the eyelid
of the one who is fast asleep.

A single teardrop in the darkness laments
the death of the soul that lost its mind.
But some people say, as if in the whisper
of a country a lifetime ago:
'If you want to know how much
darkness there is around you,
you must sharpen your eyes,
peering at the faint lights in the distance . . .'

(Tsering Woeser, Beijing 2018, translated by Ian Boyden)

3

Disinheriting social death: towards an ethnographic theory of impermanence

Carole McGranahan

This ethnographic world was never only human. It was that and more. It *is* that and more. It is a world of spirits and deities, of animals and other sentient beings, of creatures seen and unseen. This ethnographic world is one of wonder but also of suffering. This world is one of many worlds, simultaneous but also sequential. It is a world of relations and reincarnation, where inheritance is not so much a matter of legality as it is of acceptance and impermanence. That is not a contradiction. It is instead the start to the story of a family.

*

'Did you hear that they tried to kill me?' I had heard. I heard it first from an old man in Kalimpong who sat me down and told me stories non-stop for weeks on end. I heard it again from people in Darjeeling, in Dharamsala, in Kathmandu. It was not an easy story to tell. It was sad and controversial and unresolved. People told it shaking their heads as they spoke, saying *snying rje* in Tibetan or 'poor things' in English. After others had told the story to me, I sat in Seattle with the woman whose story it was. Her name is Pangda Wangmo. In her own words, she told me how they had tried to kill her. What she said was this:

> Did you hear that they tried to kill me? [My father] went to Tibet. They said that I'm a communist too. [They said,] 'We must take away all their belongings and money and stuff.' They said that the

Pangda family must be wiped out from the Tibetan race. This was started by Gyalo Thondup [the Dalai Lama's elder brother] . . . It was someone's fantasy. So I went to Dharamsala and saw His Holiness the Dalai Lama. His Holiness was quite against all that happened in the past. So, such things happened. So with our family, they either wanted to kill us or put us in jail.

'They either wanted to kill us or put us in jail.' This is not hyperbole. No one would accuse her of exaggerating. Others would agree; others do agree. For her family, assassinations, assassination attempts, imprisonment and deportations were a reality. While much of the twentieth century was politically tumultuous in Tibet, not all families have the stories to tell that her family does. Then again, not all families were the Pangdatsang family.

The Pangdatsang family were traders from the eastern region of Kham. In the span of one generation, they grew from important regional traders to the wealthiest family in all of Tibet. Pangda Wangmo's father was Pangda Yamphel. He was the head of the family trading business, a patron of the major monasteries, and also a government official. Along with the family's wealth came power, and with both came complications and enemies. As with so many things, the Pangdatsang family's ascent to power would not be permanent. The making of the family ended up being their undoing. Following the Dalai Lama's escape from Tibet to exile in India in 1959, Pangda Yamphel became a political rival of the Dalai Lama's older brother Gyalo Thondup – a conflict that would end his career and impact his family. At that time, his daughter Wangmo was, herself, the mother of two young girls. In the Indian towns of Darjeeling and Dharamsala, she was verbally and physically attacked on the street by other Tibetans while she was out with her daughters. As she would later tell me, people wanted the Pangdatsang family dead. Or, at the least, wanted them *socially* dead, 'wiped out from the Tibetan race'.

Social death is a structural or metaphorical removal from society calculated to have political, economic and social repercussions. The academic literature on social death dates to 1982 and sociologist Orlando Patterson's introduction of the concept in relation to African slavery. Real-world experiences precede social theory, thus making Patterson's concept of social death one that is painfully applicable across societies. It is a concept that is, at once, provisional and precise, both mobile and locally grounded (Stoler 2016, 19). Useful here is ethnographic theory – the anthropological project of growing theory from 'the field' or from people's lived experiences and conceptual worlds, in all their clarity and contradictions (Lambek 2018; McGranahan 2012; Otto and Willerslev 2013; Steedly 1993; Tsing 2005). Social death is an ethnographic category as well as an analytic one, used by scholars to understand the removal of some people from society as a specific experience with worldwide resonance.

The Pangdatsang family's experience of social death was intimate and uneven across family members and generations. Temporally, their story took place during a period of transition: for Tibetans, it occurred at the same time as the loss of their sovereign country, of home – a period of displacement and uncertainty and of shifts in what could or should constitute the modern (Jabb 2015; McGranahan 2007, 2010). For the world, it occurred as newly hegemonic ideas of the nation-state were playing out against a backdrop of decolonisation, independence and the Cold War (Kwon 2010; Yoneyama 2016). But this story is as cultural as it is historical. It takes place in a Tibetan framework of possibility. It belongs to certain people from different worlds within the Tibetan community. Ironically, perhaps, it is this specificity – the details of this situation and of these worlds coming together – that opens this account to universal questions about impermanence as a component of being and becoming. This dispute between two men impacted many people. Sixty years later, a blow that seemed so final in its execution is still unfolding. This social death is not yet over.

Sinking into the possibilities of life after death feels deeply Buddhist. The Tibetan practice of reincarnation means that death both is final and is not. Life continues. Vertical relations in one's own series of reincarnations are paired with horizontal ones in the conceptual form of interdependence. Meaningful relations also exist across worlds – human, animal, deity, demon and spirit – that are, themselves, not singular (Bhutia 2018, 2019; Blaser and de la Cadena 2018; de la Cadena 2014, 2015; Karmay 1996; de Nebesky-Wojkowitz 1956; Ortner 1978; Pommaret 1994). Impermanence is an important part of this worldview. For Pangda Wangmo and her family, concepts of impermanence co-exist with other realities, both worldly and not, human and not, including ideas that resonate or dominate across divergent communities. Therefore, our efforts to think through globally available or shared concepts of impermanence – for example, ruins, nostalgia or legacies – must include attention to precise and local reckonings. In the Tibetan context, impermanence sits at the very centre of cultural and religious frameworks for turning fear of death into acceptance of it.

Impermanence

The *Oxford English Dictionary* (OED) defines impermanence as 'not permanent or lasting; unenduring; transient'. This definition requires a second one, that of the word 'permanent'. The OED definition for this is 'continuing or designed to continue to last indefinitely without change; abiding, enduring, lasting; persistent'. These ideas exist in Tibetan society and can be applied to things, to relationships, to properties and more. But the Tibetan word for 'impermanence' both does and does not correspond with the English word and its definitions. Hence, 'impermanence' in a Tibetan idiom defies attempts at word-for-word translation. Instead, it takes us into the world of ethnographic translation. In Tibetan terms, neither death nor social death is permanent. I mean this in the sense of impermanence as not lasting. In the Tibetan context, all sentient beings are reincarnated, life after life, until they achieve enlightenment. Reincarnation means that the death of the body is not the death of the *sems* or the heart-mind that transitions to a new life. Impermanence is thus not so much an ending as a continuum.

Nothing is permanent. The idea of impermanence, or *mi rtag pa*, is a core idea in Tibetan Buddhism. There are two types of impermanence: gross and subtle. Gross impermanence is visible change, of the kind that happens over a long period of time. Subtle impermanence is momentary change, the idea that inner, invisible changes of mind and matter take place in the smallest fraction of a second. We are aware of gross changes but cannot perceive subtle changes. This concept does not stand alone but is part of a conceptual universe of being and possibility. In Tibetan Buddhism, there are three principal characteristics of existence: (1) phenomena are impermanent (*anitya* in Sanskrit), (2) phenomena exist in a state of suffering or unsatisfactoriness (*duhkha* in Sanskrit), and (3) phenomena have no self, lacking an inherent substance (*anatman* in Sanskrit). Realising these three characteristics brings one to the goal of peace/*nirvana*. The Buddha taught that the four things most cherished in this world – good health, youth, prosperity and life – are all impermanent. None of these is stable, despite our efforts to make them so. In a Tibetan Buddhist sense, a three-pronged argument accompanies this: death is certain; the time of death is uncertain; and, at the time of death, only dharma or religion can help us. The specific aspect of dharma that will help is meditating on impermanence.

Meditating on impermanence helps individuals comprehend the transitory nature of reality and, thus, prepare for death. Grappling with this philosophical idea is the responsibility of all, but especially the responsibility of Buddhist monks and nuns, whose lives are devoted to the practice of religion. Lay people also meditate on impermanence, and, as with all religious concepts, impermanence shapes their lives and ideas. Existing in human form is a precious rebirth in a Tibetan sense, one that should not be wasted. Meditating on impermanence and death is thus key, providing a reason for spiritual practice and a path toward enlightenment. Many highly realised Tibetan Buddhist masters give teachings on this. Lama Zopa Rinpoche (1974) explains to students the importance 'of remembering the impermanence of life and death' so as to be happy at the time of death. He continues, advising that one should not be scared at the time of death but think of it like returning home or going on a picnic.

It is one thing for lamas and rinpoches (reincarnate lamas) to meditate on impermanence and to focus their lives on the path to enlightenment, but another for lay people to do so. People who are not monks or nuns or lamas are not able to devote themselves to this practise in the same way, often waiting until they are older and can retire from the obligations of work and family. In the meantime, they practise religion in a range of ways – going for *skor ba* or walking meditation, reading scripture, making offerings, practising compassion, accumulating merit, asking monks or nuns to do prayers on their behalf, and so on. In this way, people live concepts of impermanence such as *mi rtag pa* in their everyday lives (Cassaniti 2006, 2015, this volume). The concept of impermanence informs social worlds and possibilities, providing concrete structures for action and thought. One Tibetan friend explained it this way: '*Mi rtag pa* is part of our life. It is one of the Four Principles of Suffering – suffering, impermanence, emptiness and selflessness. I read this scripture every morning. I read about *mi rtag pa*. I read it out loud, not silently. It is important to read with body and speech not just with mind.'

In Buddhist society, there are many ways to prepare for death and reincarnation. But how does one prepare for social death? For example, if meditations on impermanence prepare one for death, can they also be useful for something less predictable, for the possibility of social death?

On luck and *las*: the Pangdatsang family

In the first half of the last century, the Tibetan merchant class was carving out a new bourgeois social space in Lhasa's aristocrat-dominated society. Many were trading families from Kham, and their efforts were a challenge to rigid hierarchies of regional status and social class in a national imaginary that privileged the Central Tibetan aristocracy. In Lhasa, genealogy trumped wealth, but financial success was beginning to infringe on the bastions of social prestige. Thus, although ascribed status still prevailed over achieved status, Tibet's new bourgeoisie did enjoy success stories. In Kalimpong, the Pangdatsang family and the Reting and Surkhang trading firms were remembered as 'the sun, star, and jewels of Tibet'.[1]

The family patriarch, Pangda Nyigyal, had moved to Lhasa in the early twentieth century. He became close with the thirteenth Dalai Lama and began to expand his business and the family name on a national scale. In 1921, he was dramatically murdered during a summer festival in Lhasa. While he was gambling and drinking beer in a tent with the sides rolled down, a storm brewed outside. As the story goes, he was shot at the precise time of a clap of thunder, so no one knew he had been shot until the tent was illuminated by lightning and people saw he had been killed. His killer escaped through the back alleys of Lhasa, and the murder remains unsolved to this day (McGranahan 2002). After his death, the story of the family continued with his three sons.

The three Pangdatsang brothers were often controversial figures associated with power and dissent. According to local gossip, the family had entered the Tibetan aristocracy through the *ltag sgo* or back door. Yamphel was the eldest, and became head of the family after his father's murder. Rapga was the middle brother, the intellectual, the dreamer, founder of Tibet's first political party, and a rebel intellectual who schemed with both Chinese and Indian nationalists to try to envision a modern Tibet (McGranahan 2005, 2017). Tobgyal was the youngest brother, the one who stayed at the family estate in Kham, chief of the region, swashbuckling rebel, and regional power figure.

Having great sympathy for the family, the Dalai Lama gave them sixth-level aristocratic rank and continued to grant the family trade concessions. It was unusual for a new family to be added to the aristocracy. The families on the roster of who comprised the aristocracy had been in place for centuries. The only regular admissions to the aristocracy were the families of each new Dalai Lama. Next, the Dalai Lama raised the

Pangdatsang family's status even higher by granting their trading firm full government agency to buy wool.[2] This monopoly was unprecedented. Other traders and governments formally protested the monopoly, but the Dalai Lama stood his ground, and the family's wealth and power skyrocketed. On 17 December 1933, the thirteenth Dalai Lama died. Amid the government corruption and conservatism following his death, Tobgyal and Rapga Pangdatsang led an armed revolt against Tibetan Government troops. By November 1940, they had reconciled with the interim Tibetan Government. As part of the reconciliation, Yamphel was given fourth-level aristocratic ranking, coupled with the posts of Tibetan Trade Agent and Governor of the border region connecting India to Lhasa, Tibet's capital.

These posts allowed Yamphel to fully control trade between India and Tibet, levying and collecting taxes and creating and lifting various trade restrictions. In 1948, he was a member of the four-person international Tibetan Trade Mission. This mission embodied Tibet's attempt to strengthen its economy and to bolster political relations with the United States (US) and England, especially as the civil war in China continued. Pangda Yamphel's goals were to import American goods, to ensure that Tibetan wool had a market in the US, and to acquire gold for himself and for the Tibetan government.

The mission partially fulfilled its goals. Economically, it was a success; politically, not so much. On his return to Tibet, Pangda's power continued to grow, but by now, Mao Zedong's communists had defeated Chiang Kai-shek's Nationalist army. China was now the People's Republic of China, and one of the first actions Mao undertook was to invade Tibet. The 1950s were a time of political chaos and uncertainty in Tibet. Yamphel continued in his post as Tibetan Trade Agent, and, in November 1956, was awarded third aristocratic rank, even further increasing the family's social standing. As the situation with China deteriorated, Yamphel decided to escape to India. He did so just ahead of the Dalai Lama's escape in March 1959.[3] Here is when his luck or *las* (karma) – repercussions of actions from past lives – began to turn.

The Dalai Lama's brother: power, patronage and resentment

For two generations, the Pangdatsang family had enjoyed close relations with the Dalai Lama's family, who are referred to as the *yab gzhis* family. This was a culturally structured relationship of patronage. In Kalimpong, for example, the best room in the Pangdatsang house was reserved for the Gyalyum Chenmo, the Dalai Lama's mother. Pangda Yamphel was the personal courier of the fourteenth Dalai Lama, bringing the young boy gifts from India and throughout Tibet, such as toys, apples and Lhasa Apso dogs.[4] He also paid school expenses for the Dalai Lama's siblings in India, and arranged and paid for their lodging when they were in China.[5] Not everyone appreciated this. One person who particularly did not appreciate it as time went on was the Dalai Lama's elder brother, Gyalo Thondup. He was educated in China and possessed modern political sensibilities he considered incompatible with certain elements of traditional Tibetan beliefs and practices. Gyalo Thondup was 28 years younger than Pangda Yamphel but, because he was the Dalai Lama's brother, he had power well beyond his years or accomplishments. Over the ensuing decades, he would consolidate his power but also be surrounded by controversy as well as fear.

The Dalai Lama's brother was not the best person with whom to pick a fight. Then again, Pangda Yamphel was not the one who started the conflict. In the early 1950s, Gyalo Thondup attempted to recruit Rapga and Yamphel into his political group but neither of them joined him (Knaus 1999, 122). Relations deteriorated from there, with disagreements generally centring on issues of gold, money and power – including the Dalai Lama's national treasure, which was stored in a monastery in Sikkim.[6] The two men argued over the treasure, and Gyalo Thondup had the government of India deport Pangda Yamphel. He accused the capitalist businessman of being a Chinese communist sympathiser, and Pangda's associates were similarly accused. As a result, the government of India imprisoned many of his immediate circle in Rajasthan in the same prison camp where over 3,000 Chinese-Indians were jailed following the 1962 border dispute between India and China. In addition to Pangda Yamphel's deportation from India, Gyalo Thondup's actions also constituted the social death of the family.

Yamphel's daughter and his brother Rapga were not deported, but this does not mean social death did not impact them or other family members. It did. On 25 August 1962, Rapga went for a stroll down Kalimpong's main street, calling in at the popular Eng Son shoestore to buy a pair of shoes. A young Tibetan came into the store, pulled out a pistol and fired. Luckily for Rapga, the man missed his target, instead hitting the Chinese shopkeeper in the foot.

In 1965, Pangda Yamphel's daughter Wangmo was 'struggled against' in the streets of both Darjeeling and Dharamsala. Other Tibetans physically and verbally abused her in public, a Tibetan exile version of the

Chinese communist practice of *'thab 'dzing* or 'struggle session'. Pangda Wangmo also stopped using the Pangdatsang family name. Although Tibetan women traditionally do not take their husband's name at marriage, she took her husband's family name and resettled outside of India. Rapga's family also never again used the family name, and even registered property in his wife's name so as not to lose their land and property to the government of India. As recently as 2015, some residents of Kalimpong did not know that Rapga's descendants, who still live in the town, were members of the Pangdatsang family. 'That explains it,' one man said to me after I gave a public presentation in Kalimpong on the family's history. 'I never understood how they had such a nice, old house on prime real estate in the centre of town.'

For their part, the family live quietly, careful not to discuss family history, given the criticisms they have received for being 'communist sympathisers', as Gyalo Thondup had declared. Yamphel's many properties and land in India – homes, warehouses, land, the Kanchan cinema in Kalimpong, and so on – were abandoned. Squatters took over the land and the buildings, and the Pangdatsang family lost control over it all. As individuals in both India and Nepal said to me, 'That family is no more' or, 'They are finished.' People say this, they insist upon it, and yet there are still Pangdatsang family members living around the world: in Tibet, in India, in China, in Switzerland and in the US. Given that they are still very much alive, what does it mean to proclaim the social death of the family?

Social death: concepts, realities, contexts

Social death is a concept and practice found around the world. It is linked to, but distinct from, expulsion, banishment, exile, ostracisation, deportation, isolation and exclusion. Of these terms, banishment has a long history as a legal punishment in Tibet. All of these practices have histories in Tibet. Giving someone a bad name, or a 'black' name, was also a known Tibetan social practice. However, losing one's family name, being excommunicated from society, being 'finished' as a family was an extreme and particular form of violence. This did not have a name per se, but everyone knew a social death had taken place. Social death was an open secret, an unnamed but known practice.

As a working concept across multiple disciplines, social death has several facets. There are three related ways to think of social death: as the loss of social identity or connection; as removal from society; or as the loss of fully human status. Social death can be collective or individual, and, as some scholars emphasise, does not always signify a lack of agency. Instead, for instance, groups or individuals who have removed or recategorised themselves may refuse dominant versions of what constitutes social (or even physical) death. For example, this might involve moving away from Dalit/untouchable status through conversion to Christianity; practices of not deadnaming someone who has transitioned to a new gender or sexual identity, so as not to mark a 'before' or 'after'; or even those individuals who choose a 'good' death, preferring isolation rather than being surrounded by family and friends. In most other instances, social death is a practice whereby a group or individual is excluded in some way, from community, from society, from humanity. But social death as exclusion is not always total or totally debilitating; or, at least, it might not be forever.

In the scholarly literature, social death appears in four main contexts. As noted earlier, Orlando Patterson, historian of slavery, was the first to propose the concept of social death in 1982. He argued that slaves were treated by society as socially dead, 'utterly alienated and with no social ties recognised as legitimate or binding' (Patterson, in Brown 2009, 1232–3). For Patterson, metaphorical social death was the condition of slavery, a relation of domination that existed in a context of no possible freedom or agency. Scholars from across the disciplines build on Patterson's work. Philosopher Claudia Card argues that social death is central to the evil of genocide. Social death means the end of social vitality, of the contemporary and intergenerational relationships 'that create an identity that gives meaning to life' (Card 2005, 63). Sociologist Lisa Marie Cacho uses social death to refer to how society measures the worth of certain individuals and finds they come up short; that is, some people are considered unworthy of belonging to neoliberal, heteropatriarchal society, such as those who are imprisoned, deported or deemed illegal (Cacho 2012).

In the medical field, the concept of social death arises for a range of reasons: longstanding requirements of objectivity toward and anonymity of patients, specific diseases such as Alzheimer's and dementia that dull one's social life, and degrees of sedation and 'being kept alive'. In her research on organ transplants, anthropologist Margaret Lock (2002) argues that social death may precede physical death using the example of how decisions are made regarding the use of CPR or other forms of revival on patients. For example, a patient 'considered to be socially "as good as dead" is unlikely to receive the same treatment as a patient who is considered to still actively be part of other people's lives and to have a viable social identity' (Lock, in Borgstrom 2017, 6).

The difference between social and physical death is marked by race, class and other markers of inequality within societies as well as across them. Power and fear can force such inequalities to the surface. Pangda Yamphel's dispute with the Dalai Lama's brother, Gyalo Thondup, took place against the backdrop of one family being indebted to the other. Both men were from families that rose to vast social heights, yet one decided the other was a threat he could get rid of – so he did. But Gyalo Thondup did not just have Pangda Yamphel deported from India; he also let it be known, in that subtle/unsubtle Tibetan way, that the Pangdatsang family was over. Returning to Card's arguments about social death in the context of genocide, she is careful to speak about other political situations, too. In specific reference to deportation – the modern state's form of banishment – she claims that it 'begin[s] to get at issues of disrupting social existence', but that it lacks 'the comprehensiveness of social death' (Card 2003, 77).

Social death is, indeed, comprehensive. The Pangdatsang family lost their name. They lost their homes. They were rebranded as Chinese communist sympathisers, which, in the Tibetan community, is one of the worst insults that one could use. This is not just the past, not just politics from the 1960s, but things people still say today. Social death for the Pangdatsang family was experiential and narrative; it was a redirecting of their lives and a rewriting of their history. It was part of a cultural relationship they had consented to for a long time: they submitted to cultural requirements and regulations to use their money to be patrons for the Dalai Lama's family and considered this an honour and an opportunity (McGranahan 2020). They showed deference and respect to a young Gyalo Thondup. They played by the cultural rules of patronage. The honour of serving the *yab gzhis* family, the Dalai Lama's family, is religious service that, in a Tibetan Buddhist context, is also part of karmic merit-making. This brings us back to the conceptual world grounding these experiences of impermanence.

Impermanence as preparation for death

How does one prepare for social death? In many ways, the same way you prepare for physical death. Through meditations on impermanence. Through religious practice in general. In addition to being patrons for the Dalai Lama's family, the Pangdatsang family were sponsors of the major monasteries of Tibet, including those of Ganden, Drepung and Sera. They were also directly connected with the Sakya tradition, one of the four main schools of Tibetan Buddhism.

Rapga, the intellectual of the brothers, read *dpe cha*, or Buddhist scripture, every morning and evening, including both Sakya and Nyingma texts, as well as histories and hagiographies, and meditation and philosophy texts. On his bookshelf in Kalimpong, he also had a text on the making of sand maṇḍalas. This Buddhist practice is often held up as an exemplar of the Tibetan idea of impermanence, as the making of a sand maṇḍala always also includes its ritual unmaking (Johnsen, Otto and Warner, this volume). Ideas of *mi rtag pa* and meditation on impermanence help with preparation for death and for survival after another's death.

After being deported from India, Yamphel looked for a home elsewhere. He went to England but could not stay there or immigrate to the US because Gyalo Thondup had told the US government that Pangda was a communist sympathiser. He went to Hong Kong but could not reside there permanently. He turned down offers to move to Bhutan and Taiwan. In the end, he returned to Tibet but only after receiving Chinese communist permission to do so. He joined his younger brother Tobgyal who was now living in Lhasa. During the Cultural Revolution, Tobgyal was arrested, tortured and struggled against. The Chinese government used religion as a way to shame and humiliate him: he was paraded in the streets dressed as the Sakya *'bag mo*, the witch who was one of the family's protector deities. Under the orders of Chinese Premier Zhou Enlai himself, Pangda Yamphel was not struggled against but was made to watch Tobgyal being tortured. Both brothers died in Lhasa, Tobgyal of a stroke and Yamphel of a heart attack. In Kalimpong, Rapga lived out his days quietly, and, aware of his brothers' deaths and struggles, is said to have lost his spirit. He died on 26 February 1976. This family, which had risen so high in such a short period of time, was finished.

The social death of this family was felt by others in the community. People positioned themselves in relation to it, to hedge against or reconfigure social, political and religious possibilities. The assassination attempt on the middle brother, Rapga, was reported in the Calcutta and Darjeeling newspapers. The 8 September 1962 edition of the Tibetan newspaper *Rangwang Sarshog* discussed the shooting in an editorial: 'This activity is stupid and very bad. It would be good if we could [find] and arrest the criminal, because as we say, "One bad person causes trouble for the whole community, and one bad piece of food causes trouble in the whole body." This one bad person has made all Tibetans in Kalimpong feel ashamed.'[7] As with the 1921 murder of Pangda Nyigyal, the question of who was behind the assassination attempt remains unsolved. Privately, however, people confess that they know who was involved – the head, the middleman and the gunman. People whisper that Gyalo Thondup was responsible. But everyone who was there at the time, including the family, fears political repercussions from naming him. Fear drives silence. Fear compels compliance. Fear is the exact thing that meditating on impermanence is supposed to prevent. It is also supposed to prevent shame.

Contemplating the transient nature of life is a way of making merit for one's next life. It is part of the long path toward enlightenment. Such practices are also part of being a moral person, the social work of biological and spiritual being. As explained by Lamo Yongzin Rinpoche, 'Not preparing for death is a shameful act. Even if you do not die, having prepared for death rids you of shame' (Somtsobum 2019, 7). Here is the starkest difference between physical death and social death: the source of shame. Shame is a foundational concept in Tibetan society. Shame, or *ngo tsha*, meaning a warm or hot face, grounds morality, sociality, humanity. To have shame is to act morally, to behave well, to be respectful, to know one's place. Shame is both public and hierarchical (Lau 2008). Not preparing for death is shameful. Being the subject or target of social death is to be shamed. The disjuncture between doing and having something done to you is also an issue of both *las*/karma and political consequence.

Consequences: spiritual, political, other

Politics often involves taking a vow, swearing an oath or committing oneself in some way. These actions take place in front of a witness and they require a relationship. One must be in relation with the witness. In exchange for the vow, something is offered in return: protection, guidance, learning, inspiration. But this relationship is not just transactional; it is not simply an exchange. Relationships with deities, both enlightened and worldly, can be affirming forms of care. They can suffuse one's everyday life, the way we move through the world, the way we respond to something like social death. In Tibetan Buddhism, for example, meditation is an active engagement with a concept, an engagement often facilitated in relation to a deity. Such relationships can be framed as ones of kinship (Joffe 2019) and, thus, of social practices informed by ideas independent of religion (Ramble 1990).

When Buddhism came to Tibet from India, Buddhist masters tamed local deities into becoming guardians of Buddhism. One example is the *srin mo*, a demoness whom Buddhist masters physically pinned down and thereby converted to a protector of Buddhism throughout Tibet (Gyatso 1987). Local deities became such guardians, but not only that (de la Cadena 2014, 2018). Some of them also remained local deities, too, spirits dwelling in mountains and rivers, and protectors of peoples and places and ideas. Over the course of a journey from Lhasa to Kalimpong on foot, travellers might make offerings to the local deities of passes they need to cross, ask for travel advice from their personal protective deity, or choose actions to avoid offending certain deities (such as, for example, boiling rather than roasting meat). Each year, people renew their relationships with the worldly deities closest to them. This practice can traverse animist, Buddhist and secular organisations of the world. None of these is singular. The rise and fall of the Pangdatsang family also traverses multiple worlds. Deities of all sorts were involved: protector spirits, witches, bodhisattvas and other enlightened deities. They are part of the story; but, given that this is evident for certain audiences, they are not always narrated as such. Some tellings of the story stay close to the secular, to this life and this world. But not all do.

Returning to 1921, the family's response to the murder of the patriarch Nyigyal is telling. Although the family suspected the aristocrat Tsarong, they chose to focus on sponsoring ceremonies for their deceased father rather than seeking revenge for his murder. For at least 11 years after his death, until 1932, they sponsored ceremonies on his behalf. Decades later, when Pangda Yamphel's daughter asked him about the murder, he told her not to think or speak about it. 'So many people were punished by the government that it is best not to talk about it, just to leave it as it is,' he would say.[8] He kept his word, for his daughter learned only later from friends that Tsarong was suspected of the crime. In the Pangdatsang household, at least between generations, the murder was not discussed. Punishments had already taken place, including of innocent men. Consequences also remained on the horizon, for justice is not determined by humans alone or distributed solely in the human world, or even just in this lifetime. Not only here; not only now.

Decomposition: an ethnographic theory of impermanence

'When you meditate on impermanence, that seed is planted. The minute a leaf is formed, its inevitable death is foretold. I find this reassuring. It gives me hope. I think of China and Tibet and I know Chinese rule there can't last. It, too, is impermanent. This gives me hope.' We were sitting outside in the mountains when K shared these thoughts with me. We were talking about impermanence and art and politics and the world. The spiritual and the worldly are intertwined in his practice, not easily separated, for separating them would not necessarily make sense in a Tibetan context. Impermanence is about how to be in the world. Impermanence is not simply about change, nor about a beginning with an inevitable end. Its temporality is without beginning or end. To use language from a different tradition, impermanence parallels philosopher Isabel Stengers' critique of modern practices as surviving, and even thriving, on borrowed time (2018, 92). An anthropology of impermanence bypasses modern impatience and the claims to truth and fixity that bolster such fleeting senses of time and being. In this global time of change, of loss, with its sense of unravelling and pulling at the seams of humanity, might a conceptual sitting-with-impermanence help us make sense of the world anew?

Our ethnographic starting points should not presume fixity or wholeness. Instead, how can we understand social death and other cultural practices as unstable or partial in their being? I think of this as similar to the disciplinary shift in anthropology from the ethnographic present to a notion of coevalness in historical time (Clifford 1983; Fabian 1983). Each of those shifts took place at a particular moment. What are the political requirements of this time? An anthropology of impermanence can challenge an unmarked sense of the ethnographic whole. By this, I mean positing not that things are falling apart now or even always, but that they were never whole or full in the first place. Thinking of culture as a series of lived contradictions may help, especially in grappling with the cultural work people do to hold to notions of impermanence in situations that feel particularly dire and immediate. Such contradictions compose the cultural frameworks of meaning that make social death possible.

Social death is a disciplinary tactic that can be used across classes, bringing down those who were once powerful or keeping down others who lack power. Practices and experiences of social death in different historical and social contexts are linked in some manners. These matter broadly in terms of our understanding of dehumanisation and exclusion as human possibility; and yet unmarked theory, dislodged from the location and conditions of its (usually Christian, European) production, can only get us so far in terms of comprehension. Ethnographic theory starts with the local concepts that organise life and how to live it, such as impermanence. Ethnographic theory also acknowledges that communities around the world organise themselves prior to, and independent of, a

European Christian modernity, rather than only in relation to it. We see this in the Americas; we see this in Africa; we see this in Asia.

What might concepts of gross and subtle impermanence, and also Buddhist notions of interdependence, open up in this conversation? Returning to the Buddha's teaching on good health, youth, prosperity and life as not-lasting, we can understand impermanence as a practice in addition to a condition, a state of being and a process. But notions of impermanence are not just for highly trained religious masters. As anthropologist Sara Lewis argues in her work with Tibetan torture survivors, the lived reality of impermanence enables individuals to choose to let go of suffering and thus be content in an unstable world (2020, 160). As a practice for people at different stages of their lives, both this one and as lived over multiple reincarnations, meditating on impermanence is an example of a concept at work in locally concrete and globally possible ways. Such meditation may be of the mind or the body or both.

One can meditate through visualisations of death, through the immersion of one's hands in soil, or through compassion in moments when someone is in pain or close to death. Thinking with, and about, impermanence also takes us out of capitalist expectations of 'productive' lives and worlds. One working concept intimately related to impermanence is decomposition (Bennett 2010; Lyons 2016, 2020). Anthropologist Kristina Lyons explains via her work with farmers in Colombia (2016, 59): 'What I learned was that rather than on productivity – one of the central elements of modern capitalist growth – the regenerative potential of these ecologies relies on organic decay, impermanence, decomposition, and even a robust fragility that complicates modernist bifurcations of living and dying.'

As anthropologists, attention to such concept-work in practice, to how people structure and live ideas of change, of decomposition, and of how becoming is also always undoing, might be what is needed now. This is so even – and especially – when such work takes place amid claims to truth, stasis and fixity.

The ends of inheritance

Pangda Wangmo did not use the Pangdatsang family name for almost 50 years. About a decade ago, however, she told me she was reclaiming it. She was going to legally change her name back to Pangdatsang. She is now, once again, a Pangdatsang in public. Several years following this, she made another decision: she travelled to Kalimpong, hired an attorney, and is seeking to reclaim some of the family properties. After submitting for decades to a social death that she had inherited generationally, she has moved into a new space. She has disinherited shame. She has reclaimed the family name. She is returning home. She is going, finally, on a different sort of picnic.

Acknowledgements

My deep gratitude to members of the Pangdatsang family for sharing their family history with me and trusting me with these stories. Thank you also to colleagues in Boulder, Paris, Stanford, and from the 'Impermanence' conference at Aarhus University for their suggestions and critiques, as well as to volume editors Haidy Geismar, Ton Otto and Cameron Warner.

Notes

1   Interview, Dawa Dhondup, 24 March 1998, Kalimpong.
2   British Library, IOR L/P + S/10/1088, Weir to Foreign Secretary, Government of India, 6 August 1930.
3   Interviews with Phurpu Tsering, Kalimpong, 29 June 1999, and Gyato Kelsang, New York, 24 June 1998.
4   Interviews, Wangmo Yuthok Pangda, Seattle, June 2000; Manang Sonam Tobgyal, Luzern, July 2000. In his autobiography, the 14th Dalai Lama writes, 'I was very fortunate in that I had quite a good collection of toys. When I was very young, there was an official at Dromo, a village at the border with India, who used to send up imported toys to me, along with boxes of apples when they were available' (Gyatso 1990, 25). The unnamed 'official at Dromo' was Pangda Yamphel.
5   Diary of Rapga Pangdatsang, 13 December 1948. Pangda Rapga arranged and paid for the lodging of the Dalai Lama's elder brother, 'yab gzhis sras.
6   Interviews, Gyato Kelsang; Wangmo Yuthok Pangdatsang; Manang Sonam Tobgyal; and Tsongkha Lhamo Tsering 1992, 181–2.
7   'The troublemaker for peace in society', *Rangwang Sarshog*, Darjeeling, 8 September 1962.
8   Interview, Wangmo Yuthok Pangdatsang, 2 June 2000.

References

Bennett, Jane. 2010. *Vibrant Matter: A political ecology of things*. Durham, NC: Duke University Press.

Bhutia, Kalzang Dorjee. 2018. 'Foxes, yetis, and bulls as lamas: Human–animal interactions as a resource for exploring Buddhist ethics in Sikkim', *The Journal of Buddhist Ethics* 25: 45–69.

Bhutia, Kikee D. 2019. '"I exist therefore you exist, we exist therefore they exist": Narratives of mutuality between deities (*Yul-lha Gzhi Bdag*) and *Lho-po* (Bhutia) villagers in Sikkim', *Folklore: Electronic Journal of Folklore* 75: 191–206.

Blaser, Mario, and Marisol de la Cadena, eds. 2018. *A World of Many Worlds*. Durham, NC: Duke University Press.

Borgstrom, Erica. 2017. 'Social death', *QJM: An International Journal of Medicine* 110(1): 5–7.

Brown, Vincent. 2009. 'Social death and political life in the study of slavery', *American Historical Review* 114(5): 1231–49.

Cacho, Lisa Marie. 2012. *Social Death: Racialized rightlessness and the criminalization of the unprotected*. New York: New York University Press.

Card, Claudia. 2005 [2003]. 'Genocide and social death'. In *Genocide and Human Rights: A philosophical guide*, edited by John K. Roth, 238–54. Basingstoke and New York: Palgrave Macmillan.

Cassaniti, Julia. 2006. 'Toward a cultural psychology of impermanence in Thailand', *Ethos: The Journal of Psychological Anthropology* 34(1): 58–88.

Cassaniti, Julia. 2015. *Living Buddhism: Mind, self, and emotion in a Thai community*. Ithaca, NY: Cornell University Press.

Clifford, James. 1983. 'On ethnographic authority', *Representations* 2: 118–46.

de la Cadena, Marisol. 2014. 'Runa: Human but *not only*', *HAU: Journal of Ethnographic Theory* 4(2): 253–59.

de la Cadena, Marisol. 2015. *Earth Beings: Ecologies of practice across Andean worlds*. Durham, NC: Duke University Press.

de la Cadena, Marisol. 2018. 'Earth-beings: Andean indigenous religion, but not only'. In *The World Multiple: The quotidian politics of knowing and generating entangled worlds*, edited by Keiichi Omura, Grant Jun Otsuki, Shiho Satsuka and Atsuro Morita, 21–36. London: Routledge.

de Nebesky-Wojkowitz, René. 1956. *Oracles and Demons of Tibet: The cult and iconography of Tibetan protector deities*. The Hague: Mouton & Co.

Fabian, Johannes. 1983. *Time and the Other: How anthropology makes its object*. New York: Columbia University Press.

Gyatso, Janet. 1987. 'Down with the demoness: Reflections on a feminine ground in Tibet', *The Tibet Journal* 12(4): 38–53.

Gyatso, Tenzin, His Holiness the 14th Dalai Lama. 1990. *Freedom in Exile: The autobiography of the Dalai Lama*. San Francisco: Harper.

Jabb, Lama. 2015. *Oral and Literary Continuities in Modern Tibetan Literature: The inescapable nation*. Lanham, MD: Lexington Books.

Joffe, Ben. 2019. 'White robes, matted hair: Tibetan tantric householders, moral sexuality, and the ambiguities of esoteric Buddhist expertise in exile'. PhD thesis, Department of Anthropology, University of Colorado.

Karmay, Samten. 1996. *The Arrow and the Spindle: Studies in history, myths, rituals, and beliefs in Tibet*. Kathmandu: Maṇḍala Book Point.

Knaus, J. Kenneth. 1999. *Orphans of the Cold War: America and the Tibetan struggle for survival*. New York: Public Affairs.

Kwon, Heonik. 2010. *The Other Cold War*. New York: Columbia University Press.

Lambek, Michael. 2018. *Island in the Stream: An ethnographic history of Mayotte*. Toronto: University of Toronto Press.

Lau, Timm. 2008. 'Understanding Tibetan shame and hierarchy through emotional experience in fieldwork'. In *How Do We Know? Evidence, ethnography, and the making of anthropological knowledge*, edited by Liana Chua, Casey High and Timm Lau, 157–78. Cambridge: Cambridge Scholars Publishing.

Lewis, Sara. 2020. *Spacious Minds: Trauma and resilience in Tibetan Buddhism*. Ithaca, NY: Cornell University Press.

Lock, Margaret. 2002 *Twice Dead: Organ transplants and the reinvention of death*. Berkeley, CA: University of California Press.

Lyons, Kristina. 2016. 'Decomposition as life politics: Soils, *selva*, and small farmers under the gun of the U.S.–Colombian war on drugs', *Cultural Anthropology* 31(1): 56–81.

Lyons, Kristina. 2020. *Vital Decomposition: Soil practitioners and life politics*. Durham, NC: Duke University Press.

McGranahan, Carole. 2002. '*Sa spang mda' gnam spang mda'*: Murder, history, and social politics in 1920s Lhasa'. In *Khams pa Local Histories: Visions of people, place, and authority*, edited by Lawrence Epstein, 103–26. Leiden: Brill.

McGranahan, Carole. 2005. 'In Rapga's library: The texts and times of a rebel Tibetan intellectual', *Les Cahiers d'Extrême Asie* 15: 255–76.

McGranahan, Carole. 2007. 'Empire out-of-bounds: Tibet in the era of decolonization'. In *Imperial Formations*, edited by Ann Laura Stoler, Carole McGranahan and Peter C. Perdue, 173–209. Santa Fe, NM: School of American Research Press.

McGranahan, Carole. 2010. *Arrested Histories: Tibet, the CIA, and memories of a forgotten war.* Durham, NC: Duke University Press.

McGranahan, Carole. 2012. 'Mao in Tibetan disguise: History, ethnographic theory, and excess', *HAU: Journal of Ethnographic Theory* 2(1): 213–45.

McGranahan, Carole. 2017. 'Imperial but not colonial: British India, archival truths, and the case of the "naughty" Tibetans', *Comparative Studies in Society and History* 59(1): 68–95.

McGranahan, Carole. 2020. 'Intimacy of details: A Tibetan diary of dissent'. In *The Intimacy of Dissent,* edited by Tobias Kelly, 151–71. London: UCL Press.

Ortner, Sherry. 1978. 'The white-black ones: The Sherpa view of human nature'. In *Himalayan Anthropology*, edited by James F. Fisher, 263–85. Berlin: Walter de Gruyter.

Otto, Ton, and Rane Willerslev. 2013. 'Introduction: "Value as theory": Comparison, cultural critique, and guerrilla ethnographic theory', *HAU: Journal of Ethnographic Theory* 3(1): 1–20.

Patterson, Orlando. 2018 [1982]. *Slavery and Social Death: A comparative study.* Cambridge, MA: Harvard University Press.

Pommaret, Françoise. 1994. 'On local and mountain deities in Bhutan'. In *Le culte des montagnes sacrées dans l'aire tibétaine et tibéto-birmane*, 39–56. Paris: HALS Archives Ouvertes.

Ramble, Charles. 1990. 'How Buddhist are Buddhist communities? The construction of tradition in two Lamaist villages', *JASO* 21(2): 185–97.

Rinpoche, Lama Zopa. 1974. *Impermanence and Death.* Kathmandu: Kopan Monastery.

Somtsobum. 2019. 'Buddhist identity in the advice of a contemporary non-sectarian master in Amdo'. MA Paper, Department of Religious Studies, University of Colorado.

Steedly, Mary. 1993. *Hanging without a Rope: Narrative experience in colonial and postcolonial Karoland.* Princeton, NJ: Princeton University Press.

Stengers, Isabelle. 2018. 'The challenge of ontological politics'. In *A World of Many Worlds*, edited by Marisol de la Cadena and Mario Blaser, 83–111. Durham, NC: Duke University Press.

Stoler, Ann Laura. 2016. *Duress: Imperial durabilities in our times.* Durham, NC: Duke University Press.

Tsing, Anna. 2005. *Friction: An ethnography of global connection.* Princeton, NJ: Princeton University Press.

Tsongkha, Lhamo Tsering. 1992. *Bstan rgol rgyal skyob, deb tang po, sku'i gcen po llha sras rgya lo don grub mchog gi thog ma'i mdsad phyogs dang gus gnyis dbar chab srid 'brel ba byung stang skor* (Resistance. Volume I. The early political activities of Gyalo Thondup, older brother of H.H. the Dalai Lama, and the beginnings of my political involvement [1945–1959]). Edited by Tashi Tsering. Dharamsala: Amnye Machen Institute.

Yoneyama, Lisa. 2016. *Cold War Ruins.* Durham, NC: Duke University Press.

4
Atheist endings: imagining having been in contemporary Kyrgyzstan

Maria Louw

Introduction: on pork, alcohol and biodegradable urns – and the liberating potentials of impermanence

Dastan[1] had asked me to meet him and the other core members of the association for atheists and agnostics in Kyrgyzstan at a cafe in one of Bishkek's big shopping malls on a spring day in 2017. The place was bursting with life and the cafe was rather packed, but we managed to find a table out on the terrace where we introduced ourselves and started flicking through the menu cards. Discovering a note pointing out that the cafe only served halal food, Dastan, Nazgul, Maksim, Sergey, Gulnara and Damira – one after the other – jumped to their feet and grabbed their belongings, loudly declaring that they wanted pork and alcohol. They then headed for the neighbouring pizzeria. Here, drinking cocktails and surrounded by cigarette smoke, I was interrogated about what it was like to be an atheist in Denmark and the possibility of being cremated upon death. Nazgul said that she dreamt about migrating to Canada because she had heard that it was a rather liberal country and because cremation was allowed there. Damira had heard of the idea of a biodegradable urn that would turn the deceased into a tree – a thought she found very appealing. But cremation was not yet a possibility in Kyrgyzstan.

The concern with death and funerals among Kyrgyz neo-atheists – which first struck me during this encounter and I have often come across since, in face-to-face conversations as well as discussions on social media – puzzled me for a long time. Most of the neo-atheists I have met up with in Kyrgyzstan are in their twenties or early thirties, and their deaths are most likely not impending events. While, among Muslims in Kyrgyzstan, one is expected to start pondering life's end around the time of retirement, and while funeral and memorial rites – as I will expand on here – are central to communal life and historicity, most people in their twenties are certainly not particularly concerned about their funerals. And they are not *supposed* to be concerned: they are supposed to indulge in life, creating lives, continuing the family line, taking over where others left – to focus on continuities rather than endings. Furthermore, it puzzled me that it would matter to an atheist what happened after her death when, according to atheist views, death would mean the end of her existence.

This chapter represents my attempt to understand this concern. In more abstract terms, I will address the relationship between finitude, care and community, and present the argument that a focus on the impermanence of the human body as it is experienced, reflected upon and dealt with may be a way into exploring the ethics of 'being-with' as a fundamental, albeit shadowy, aspect of human existence. My interest in finitude – the state of having a limit or end or, if you like, being impermanent – stems from a broader interest in how moral community is lived and experienced as an existential question, demand and burden. It also stems from a desire to explore what Hayder al-Mohammad has termed 'the with of being' (al-Mohammad 2010), the interconnection and interdependency that characterise (human) life and how it is experienced. As al-Mohammad has remarked, 'the way in which life is possible only through and with other beings, tends to recede into the background of our habituated daily engagements such that persons can come to think of themselves as separated off from the world and others. However, in certain situations, the "with" of struggling, of being, can become somewhat explicit' (al-Mohammad 2010, 434).

Building on this insight, in this chapter, I will argue that questions about moral community – about what we share with each other, how we are linked to each other – come up with a particular intensity in relation to (experiences of) finitude such as those related to birth and death. Deaths continually disturb individual and social life, and new indeterminate lives perpetually cut into the set ways of an 'old' world, with the effect that this perpetual birth of the new opens rifts of indeterminacy – possibilities for imagining new forms of community and new moral worlds as well as possibilities for confirming and reinforcing old ones. Since Robert Hertz published his classical study *Contribution à une étude sur la représentation collective de la mort* (Hertz 1907), anthropologists have studied death as a social event – how communities transform individual deaths into assertions of continuity, whether the continuity of the family, of the community or of the nation. Philosophers, on the other hand, have often approached the death of the Other as an experience that prompts one to respond and to care (Blanchot 1988; Levinas 2000).

In this chapter, I will also switch the gaze from acts of responding to death, whether as a community or as an individual, to the more pathic experience of leaving oneself (or being left) to the responses or the care of others – whether relatives, strangers, community, the state, God or ancestor spirits. I will also explore the reflections and feelings that accompany this experience – or, as in this case, the *anticipation* of this experience: how the care of others is imagined, and how it is imagined to transform (or preserve) one's very self upon one's death. In particular, I will draw on the work of philosopher Hans Ruin and his recent book *Being with the Dead: Burial, ancestral politics, and the roots of historical consciousness* (Ruin 2018). Here, Ruin builds on a reading of Heidegger's concept of *having-been* to argue that human relations with the dead may be seen as an existential a priori, out of which the basic forms of historical consciousness emerge. Starting out from this insight, I will argue that, in a context like the Kyrgyz one – where the having-been of the ancestors plays a central role in everyday life as well as in conceptions of community and historicity, continually linking the here and now with what was before – for people who feel at odds with community, there may be a liberating force, a sense of possibility, to be found in impermanence. In other words, cremation, in a context where it is disapproved of because it is thought to do damage to the continuity of self as well as the continuity between self and community, may become the purposeful destruction of self in order to preserve identity and singularity, an act of world-building at the end of one's world.

Before I develop this argument, however, let me return to the Kyrgyz neo-atheists and the context in which they seek to live atheist lives and form atheist communities. I will start by zooming in on the experiences of Nazgul, one of the neo-atheists I met at the Bishkek cafe in 2017, and situate them in the broader landscape of religion and atheism in present-day Kyrgyzstan.

(Neo-)atheism in Kyrgyzstan

The young atheists I focus on make for a very diverse group.[2] Some are devoted to a 'scientific' worldview, seeing it as incompatible with a religious worldview; others are feminists or LGBTQ+ activists who have been led to atheism primarily because of the gender inequality and/or the homophobia they see as central to religion in general, and Islam in particular. Some link their atheism with a Marxist or socialist ideology; some are mainly inspired by neo-atheist literature such as the works of Richard Dawkins or Christopher Hitchens, and yet others are primarily led to atheism through personal experiences of ethical transgressions related to religion or representatives of religions. For all their diversity, however, one thing most have in common is that they distinguish themselves from the older generations' perceptions and practices of atheism, which they consider to be mere default positions adopted to adapt to the political reality of the Soviet era,[3] rather than being based on personal conviction and knowledge.[4]

After the meeting at the cafe, I joined Nazgul for a walk in a neighbouring park. During our walk, she told me that the main reason she saw herself as an atheist was the way Islam tended to repress and restrict women. Her father-in-law always emphasised that he was a *Hajji* (a person who has performed *Hajj*, the pilgrimage to Mecca) to gain her respect; and, she said, he never wasted a chance to scold her in an attempt to make her live a more pious life. 'But fuck him!' she said, laughing, telling me that she had always had strained relationships with men because she was independent, 'not like other Asian girls'.

Like most people, Nazgul occasionally had to act pragmatically, compromising her values. Nevertheless, what was so noteworthy about her was the determination and energy with which she strove to transcend the identity and roles that had been imposed on her by others, to create a personally meaningful and viable environment and to traverse it in the pursuit of her own life-project (Rapport 2003, 3). This was characterised by the effort to cultivate a buffered autonomous self in a society where she felt there was very little room for individuality – a buffered autonomous self that remained autonomous even after she handed it over to the care of others upon her death. These days, she strove for economic independence. She recalled that, around the time her daughter was born, her husband twice went bankrupt. There was no food in the house and she ended up losing 30 kg. Now she was determined never to find herself in a similar situation again. She had found a new job in a private company that paid better than her previous job as a newspaper journalist and tried to save up to fulfil her goal of moving to Canada 'before Kyrgyzstan turned into a caliphate', as she put it. Here, she was referring to the increasing visibility of Islam and the increasing popularity of conservative and scripture-based interpretations of Islam, which had made such things as gender separation, the wearing of *hijab* and the abstinence from alcohol quite common among her contemporaries. What she loathed, in particular, was the hypocrisy she had seen accompanying the turn to piety. For example, she recounted that one of her classmates from school had embraced a conservative interpretation of Islam, growing a long beard and wearing long, loose clothes, but during weekends would nonetheless indulge in drinking and visits to prostitutes. Nazgul found his behaviour to be depressingly typical: Bishkek, a city with a previously rather liberal reputation, had become a gigantic religious theatre play in which many people only engaged in outwardly pious behaviour because it had somehow become fashionable. She felt an urgent pull to de-mask the hypocrisy but also felt that she was up against a machine that was larger than she could contend with.

Like Nazgul, the young neo-atheists in Kyrgyzstan I have come to know seek to live atheist lives and form atheist communities in a context that has undergone a profound religious revival in recent decades. When the Soviet Union dissolved in 1991, there was a sense among large parts of the population in the region that 70 years of Soviet rule had made them forget what it meant to be Muslim and, correspondingly, there was great interest in exploring it. During this period, many commentators talked about an Islamic 'resurgence' taking place, evidenced by, for example, an increase in the number of mosques and the activities of missionaries from other Muslim countries. While many citizens continued to lead a rather secular life, others began to observe rituals openly, such as the five daily prayers or the fast during Ramadan, or – in the case of women – the wearing of the hijab. Some began to call for a greater role for Islam in social and political life. Some started following and promoting 'universalist' or 'scriptural' interpretations of Islam, while criticising traditional popular practices and beliefs, such as visits to, and veneration of, sacred places and the importance ascribed to ancestor spirits. Others would criticise these 'new' Muslims for promoting versions of Islam that are foreign to the Kyrgyz, advocating, instead, forms of Islam grounded in local practice (Isci 2010; Louw 2011; McBrien 2017; Montgomery 2016; Nasritdinov and Esenamanova 2017; Pelkmans 2017).

In this period, atheism went from having a very prominent presence in public space during Soviet times to being virtually invisible – from being the default position taken by most people, at least in public, to being highly controversial. Within this context – dominated by heated debates about what kind of Muslims the Kyrgyz should be, with rarely any questioning of the idea that the Kyrgyz are, in fact, Muslims – it is relatively uncontroversial to declare oneself an atheist if one grew up during Soviet times (in retrospect, it was seen not as a personal choice to become one but a necessary adaptation to the political situation, and many still refer to themselves as 'atheists' to refer to their Soviet upbringing). But it is a very different matter to be young – that is, born after, or just before, the dissolution of the Soviet Union – and atheist. As religious life in Kyrgyzstan is closely bound up with family and community events that mark important moments in the life of a Muslim (circumcision, marriage and death, for example), declaring oneself an atheist is not merely seen as a personal rejection of religion but more broadly as the rejection of community and the values and practices that underpin it.

Like others among my atheist interlocutors (Louw 2019a), Nazgul spoke of community life conjuring up images of something so powerful and inflexible that the only choice was between fitting in, on the one hand, and being destroyed, on the other: 'When you become a *kelin* [daughter-in-law]', she explained, 'you should put on a headscarf and bow your head. You should just do what you are told and not think yourself. If you don't bow your head, others will bow your head for you.' And, although she seemed very much at ease among her atheist friends and joined the others in their vocal expressions of dissatisfaction at the absence of pork and alcohol on the menu of a cafe that prided itself on serving only halal food, more often, she would keep a low profile, living her atheist and liberal self discreetly. She did have conflicts with her parents-in-law but she also had to maintain a fairly good relationship with them, to be able to live the life she wanted. Her husband worked in St Petersburg; she was alone with their five-year-old daughter and she was thus dependent on her parents-in-law to take care of the little girl when workdays were long or when she wanted to go out with her friends in the evening (her own parents lived far away from Bishkek). When it came to religious rituals that were part of family and communal events, she would most often just participate while trying to distract herself by thinking of something else (Louw 2020). Her own wedding had also been blessed by an imam. But when it came to her own finitude – to her death and what would happen around it – she seemed much more uncompromising.

Being with the dead in Kyrgyzstan

Referring back to Nazgul's concerns that Kyrgyzstan was showing signs of becoming a 'caliphate', I asked her why she had set her eyes on Canada and she replied that she had never been there but had heard a lot of good things about the country: that it was liberal and, not least, that it was possible to be cremated when one died. Like many other atheists of the younger generation in Kyrgyzstan, Nazgul had an intense wish to determine the manner in which her remains would be handled after death. Specifically, she wanted to be cremated and have her ashes spread. More generally, and similar to atheists and humanists in other parts of the world (see, for example, Engelke 2015 on humanist funerals in the UK), Nazgul and other neo-atheists wished for a funeral that would emphasise the fact that death meant one's self had come to a definite end. Some, though, wanted to emphasise how their own biological life was intimately entangled with other forms of life. There was Damira, for instance, who, as we saw at the beginning of this chapter, liked the thought of having her ashes buried in a biodegradable urn, or Gulnara, another of my interlocutors, who said that she wanted to 'become fertiliser for trees and plants' upon her death, stressing the interconnection between human and other kinds of life. Some mentioned the possibility of donating their bodies to science or donating functioning organs to others. But most, like Nazgul, viewed cremation as the best and most rational choice and, furthermore, saw the choice of cremation as an important atheist statement because it is considered *haram*, forbidden, in Islam.

Islamic practice requires that the deceased be cleaned, shrouded, prayed for and buried with the head facing Mecca. In Kyrgyzstan, cremation is not an option: there are no crematoria in the country. But, even if there were, it would be difficult for atheists to persuade their families to perform a funeral rite that, in their view, would not only put the resurrection of their loved ones at risk but also very likely cause uproar in the community. Maksat, a man in his twenties, recounted how, when his grandfather passed away, he was the one to take care of his funeral as he was his closest relative. Like Maksat, his grandfather was an atheist. Before he passed away, he asked to be buried without any religious 'tinsel', and Maksat was determined to ensure his will was respected. At the cemetery, however, neighbours and distant relatives started crowding around the coffin, and when Maksat announced that the funeral was to take place in a secular manner, they created a commotion, yelling and harassing him. Some of them began to pray. When the coffin was buried, the gathered crowd became even more upset as they realised that no memorial ceremony would be held afterward and that no food would be distributed. Looking back at the incident, Maksat was furious at the disrespect people showed his grandfather and his wishes, becoming agitated when telling me about the incident in retrospect.

The question of how to deal with community expectations and social control was also brought up in the aforementioned atheist cafe encounter. Dastan and Gulnara, much to the amusement of the others, recounted how they had lied and told their relatives that their wedding had been blessed by an imam, when this was not, in fact, the case. But what to do about one's own funeral? One of the participants brought up the question of whether it would somehow be possible to legally oblige relatives to refrain from conducting any religious ceremonies around their deaths, fearing that they would not respect her wishes. The others were unsure on this point, but Dastan jokingly suggested that she should warn her family that if they did not follow her requests, her spirit would continue to haunt them: that, he reasoned, would probably be far more efficient than any legal obligation. Standing up against the force of community was very difficult, they all agreed.

Among Kyrgyz Muslims, funerals and memorial ceremonies are seen as central to community life. Like in Islam more generally, worldly life is seen as a mere prelude to, or preparation for, the afterlife in which every person will be judged by God (Smith and Haddad 1981). While lurking in the background during the whole life of a Muslim, the eschatological dimensions of Islam become more foregrounded as one ages. When people get older, they are expected to start thinking more about, and preparing for, their death and posthumous existence. They may start praying more regularly and – in the case of men – attending the mosque. When a person has passed away, performing a funeral and, later, memorial rituals in the proper manner is seen as particularly important, both for the afterlife of the deceased and for the family and community, whose lives move on without him or her. Funeral rituals are often long, elaborate and expensive; they involve the participation of hundreds of guests and the exchange of gifts and hospitality (Hardenberg 2010; Jacquesson 2008; Kuchumkulova 2007, 190).[5] 'Death sets society in motion', as Roland Hardenberg put it, in a discussion of Kyrgyz funeral rituals (Hardenberg 2010, 37).

After the funeral, there follows a series of memorial rituals. Of particular importance is the *ash*, usually but not always performed a year after a person's death. The *ash* is highly significant as it marks the transformation of the soul of the deceased into an ancestor spirit (*arbak*) and renews the links between the living and the ancestors as well as those between the living themselves (Jacquesson 2008, 282). Participation in mortuary rituals is seen as a means to enjoy good relations with the ancestor spirits and secure a peaceful transition to the afterlife for the deceased. Among the Kyrgyz, the *arbak* remain involved in the world of the living, following the lives of their living relatives and often seeking to interfere with them (Dubuisson 2017; Louw 2010, 2019b and forthcoming). They also play a central role in how Kyrgyz people practise Islam: many Kyrgyz people's relationship with the Qur'an, for example, is limited to the verses that are recited on their ancestors' memorial days or those they might recite themselves when their ancestors, as it is believed, visit them in their homes on Thursdays or Fridays, to see how they are faring.

The beliefs and practices related to *arbak* have increasingly come under attack from people who have adopted a more scripturalist version of Islam, but they nevertheless continue to be of major importance to many. There are a number of spaces in which 'ancestors can communicate with the living and where a mutual relationship of care and guidance is actively enacted in the world', as Eva-Marie Dubuisson has aptly put it (Dubuisson 2017, 4–5). One of the most important such spaces is dreams (Louw 2010). Even if the *arbak* might not show themselves directly, Kyrgyz people often interpret voices, images and feelings experienced in dreams as *ayan*, signs, from *arbak*, which often bring omens. If, for example, a person dreams that an ancestor walks away with a living person, it is usually interpreted as a sign that this person will soon die or fall seriously ill, whereas when a person receives something from an ancestor in the dream, it is usually considered a good omen (Bakchiev and Egemberdieva 2007). *Arbak* remind people about things they have forgotten, reprove them if they have done something wrong, warn them if they are about to make a wrong decision, but also lend courage and moral authority to undertake acts that other people may deem morally dubious. Ancestor spirits, in short, care for, and about, the living – and the living should care for, and about, the ancestor spirits by including them in their worlds: reading the Qur'an for them, lighting candles for them or cooking *boorsok* (deep-fried bread, the smell of which they are said to appreciate). If a person ignores them, however, they may haunt his or her dreams, appearing as suffering and uncared for, and eventually they may turn against him or her, becoming vengeful and causing harm.

'Death sets society in motion', to quote Hardenberg's apt phrase again, but it also brings up the question of the *with* of being. Matters concerning how people are entangled or connected with each other tend to become more intense or involved in relation to human finitude: deaths, like births, open possibilities for imagining new forms of community and new moral worlds as well as for confirming and reinforcing old ones. The ruins of a person, as it were, become the building-material for moral worlds of different kinds and open up the question of the *with* of being for the dying as well as for those who care for him or her. Let me dig a little deeper into that argument.

Caring for the dead

In his recent book, *Being with the Dead: Burial, ancestor politics, and the roots of historical consciousness* (2018), philosopher Hans Ruin revisits the analysis of finitude and the death of the other in Heidegger's *Being and Time*. Dwelling, in particular, on the concept of *having-been* (*da-gewesen*)[6] and drawing on the works of, among others, Derrida, Patocka and Levinas (whose attempts to develop an understanding of finitude take Heidegger as the primary reference point) as well as archaeological and anthropological sources, Ruin presents the argument that the ways humans relate to the dead as a present absence, or as spectral being, may be seen as a primordial form of historicity. He observes: 'Even though historicity is a category that is applicable to the living, it is the dead, in the peculiar existential mode of having-been, that are the source of the meaning of the historical, precisely by virtue of not being simply past but constituting a middle region of perfective or perhaps ancestral being' (Ruin 2018, 31). The predicament of historicity, Ruin argues, is connected to a responsive acting with regard to the dead; the historical in life emerges as an inner opening in the direction of the demand of the dead other, and the act of burial becomes 'the exemplary expression of how the past as the domain of life having-been can lay a claim on the living' (Ruin 2018, 39).

But what kind of claim the having-been can lay on the living, and what it takes to care for the other in and across death (Ruin 2018, 9), are fundamentally uncertain matters: we can never know what we owe to the dead or what they demand from us:

> What we find when we trace the question of the dead and being with the dead to the core dynamic of human historicity is not just a purified and authentic individual and collective resoluteness as suggested by Heidegger's analysis. Instead, we are led to a contested space of conflicting loyalties where the subject is always already called to respond to the dead – indeed where its historical belonging and historicity can be thought only within the larger existential domain of a being-with that it can never fully master but only hope to inhabit in a responsible way (Ruin 2018, 24).

Ruin takes as a point of departure the classical tragedy of Antigone by Sophocles, as recounted in Hegel's *The Phenomenology of Spirit*, to bring us into this existential domain that cannot be mastered and remains subject to conflicting claims. Antigone, for him, represents 'an exemplary necropolitical heroine' who is led by loyalty to her ancestors rather than complying with the juridical–political power of the king, being firmly committed to tending to her dead brother, who has been refused burial by King Creon as punishment for having conspired against the state. Defying the king's orders and under the threat of the death penalty, Antigone strews earth on her brother's dead body (Ruin 2018, 2–6). To Ruin, the tragedy stands as 'a paradigmatic necropolitical situation . . . where the fate of the community becomes concentrated in a dispute of how to care for its dead' (Ruin 2018, 6).

Hence, as the editors of this volume also point out in the Introduction, impermanence – in this case, human finitude – is both 'a common condition for all human beings and a point of tension and contention'. Anthropology is, indeed, full of stories about how the fate of the community becomes concentrated in a dispute of how to care for its dead. An obvious example to mention in this particular context is Katherine Verdery's now-classic study, in *The Political Lives of Dead Bodies: Reburial and postsocialist change* (Verdery 1999), of how the dead bodies of political leaders, as well as more humble people, were exhumed in the years following the end of Communist Party rule in Eastern Europe. Reburied in new gravesites, they came to play new roles in revisiting the past and reorienting the present. Also interesting in this connection, because it deals with alternative forms of being-with that develop around the death of people marginal to community, is Jarrett Zigon's recent book, *A War on People: Drug user politics and a new ethics of community* (Zigon 2019). In one of his chapters, Zigon meditates on the difference between a Memorial Day ceremony held in Copenhagen by the Drug User Association in Denmark to honour those drug users who had died during the previous year and those Memorial Day ceremonies that are held to honour those who died in, for example, wars that are recognised by the state. While official Memorial Day ceremonies transform the singular 'death of an individual into a foundational ground for a totalized and individualized community as nation' (Zigon 2019, 77), the deaths of drug users are not similarly recognised and are not grieved by the state. Nonetheless, Zigon argues, alternative forms of non-totalised communities, or what he terms 'communities of those without community', come into being around the deaths of drug users.

Here, he builds on the insights of Jean-Luc Nancy and his claim that 'community is revealed in the death of others' in the sense that the experience of death discloses one's existence as always already outside of oneself, exceeding the subjective boundaries of the body and ego (Zigon

2019, 81). Zigon also draws on the critical reading of Nancy by Maurice Blanchot, who argues that what is missing from Nancy's account is the demand that the death of the other places upon us. It is the experience of dying-with an other, not the awareness of one's own eventual death, that provides the ecstatic experience of finitude that grounds an open community – that is, a community that is open to anyone who arrives (Zigon 2019, 82). The community on which Zigon focuses, then, is a community of people who have nothing in common but their shared being-toward-death, 'the recognition of which discloses their essential being-with and the obligation to offer the gift of attuned care' (Zigon 2019, 83). The term 'attuned care' refers to a form of care sensitively aligned with the singularity of a person (Zigon 2019, 134) rather than a totalising attempt at normalisation: an open and liberal kind of community, not unlike what the young neo-atheists in Kyrgyzstan were longing for.

Building on these insights, I will now switch the gaze from acts of responding to death, whether as a community or as an individual, to the experience (or, more particularly, the anticipation of the experience) of leaving oneself, or being left, to the responses or care of others – becoming part of the having-been.

Care and world-building at the end of worlds

Let us return to the idea that questions about how humans are entangled or connected with each other – the 'with of being' – become more intense or involved in relation to human finitude. For Nazgul, for example, the experience of community as 'machinery' that allowed no space for her individuality became particularly intense when she pondered her finitude. And vice versa: the intense feeling of being suffocated by the demands of community made her ponder her finitude and plan her future, contemplating the kinds of finitude it offered. Nazgul did not fear nonexistence. What she feared was that her body, upon her death, would be left to others who would bury it and let it decompose while celebrating the community she had tried to escape. She feared that her ghost (notwithstanding the fact that she did not believe in her own spectral existence upon death) would continue to inhabit the worlds of the living. And she feared that the care of others for that ghost would ritualistically transform her – or the ruins left of her – into the foundational ground of a community (Zigon 2019, 77) whose ideas and values she found appalling.

The concept of care connotes a broad range of experiences and practices, from the more pathic experience of being moved by or concerned with something – and thus involved – to efforts at making that something into what one thinks it should be. Arthur Kleinman and Sjaak van der Geest expressed a similar spectrum, from the more technical meaning of care as carrying out activities for others who may not be able to perform them alone to the more emotional meaning of concern, dedication and attachment (Kleinman and van der Geest 2009, 159). But, basically, it is a concept that puts 'emphasis on interconnection and interdependency' as 'the ontological state in which human beings and countless other beings unavoidably live', as María Puig de la Bellacasa puts it (Puig de la Bellacasa 2017, 4), based on the premise that 'we are, above all, relational beings and that our very survival, as individuals and as a species, depends upon giving and receiving care' (Mattingly and McKearney, forthcoming).

Care, as I have argued elsewhere (Louw, forthcoming), always comes with a 'world' – a world that is moral, in the sense that it comes with a larger context or horizon of meaning to which it seeks to connect the object of care. This is not necessarily a clear and coherent worldview; very often, it is something fuzzier or a sense that something is wrong, that a world needs repair, rather than a clear idea of what has to be done in order to repair it. Sometimes, the very act of caring may even bring up the nature of such a 'world' as a pressing existential question, for the care-giver and care-receiver alike. In that sense, care is world-building and world-repairing, and very often world-questioning, and, as such, there is always a kind of subjunctive quality to it, even in its most ordinary forms, as a way into the space where the actual meets the possible. Caring for someone implies an idea, however vague and incoherent, of what that someone is or should be; and that idea does not necessarily match easily with what that someone thinks he or she is or should be. There is always the risk, as Emmanuel Levinas has taught us, that, in responding to the ethical demand of the other, one reduces them to a token or type, doing violence to their singularity (Levinas 1969; see also Rasanayagam 2017). And just as the *absence* of care may undo (Puig de la Bellacasa 2017, 1), denying the presence of a person in a world, care itself may be destructive of agency and selfhood, giving presence to a version of a person that that person cannot identify with and a 'world' in which they do not want to live. Care can do good – *and* it can oppress and convey control (Puig de la Bellacasa 2017, 1). We exist (socially) through acts of care but we may also be destroyed through acts of care; and, sometimes, the distinction between what makes us exist and what destroys us is not very clear at all. In the case of Nazgul, her very individuality rested on her in-laws, whom she also perceived to be the greatest threats to her individuality.

In a discussion in a Facebook group for Kyrgyzstani atheists, a young Russian man, Andrey, proposed that caring about how one's body would be handled after death was fundamentally 'anti-atheistic' – thus giving voice to what had initially also been my thought about a logical inconsistency in the concern with funerals among young atheists. Andrey, furthermore, made the argument that such concerns were expressions of anxiety imposed by religion, which resides in people subconsciously, no matter whether they are religious or not. His argument was quickly shut down by others, however. 'What about love for your body?', one person replied, and another asked the question, 'what do you care about?', suggesting, perhaps, that the concern about the handling of the body upon death is linked not to religion but to the broader question of what matters in life.

What do you care about? I think this question points to what is, indeed, a key to understanding the concern among young atheists about their deaths and funerals. Precisely because questions about being-with intensify in relation to finitude – because finitude presents us with openings that prompt people into efforts at world-building through care – for people who are concerned with building social and moral worlds different from those prevalent in society (worlds attuned to the singularity of each individual), death, paradoxically perhaps, presents itself both as a unique threat and a unique opportunity. It poses a threat because any attempt at cultivating an atheist identity and living an atheist life may be overruled as one leaves oneself to the care of others upon death and one is ritualistically transformed into the foundational ground of a community one experienced in life as repressive. It also constitutes a unique opportunity to leave a mark on the world: designing and organising one's departure becomes an act of world-building, and imagining it becomes the imagining of the kinds of worlds one would like to live and die in – the imagining of atheist utopias. These might be liberal worlds attuned to the singularity of each individual, as Nazul dreamt of, or worlds that emphasise the intimate entanglements of all living beings, as imagined by some of my other atheist interlocutors and implied in their reflections on biodegradable urns and the transformation from human into fertiliser upon death.

Just as Nazgul was concerned about her physical remnants, she was also concerned about her digital legacy. Like many other young neo-atheists, she was very active on social media, embracing them as a much-appreciated means of creating encounters with like-minded others. New media such as websites, blogs and online fora have played a significant role worldwide in creating new forms of interaction and communication between atheists, sometimes across national boundaries. This has been particularly important in places where atheism is seen as controversial and where atheists may feel isolated in their communities (Cimino and Smith 2014), such as in the case of Kyrgyzstan. For the younger generations of Kyrgyz atheists, Facebook, in particular, is used as a medium for networking, discussion and the sharing of information and experiences. Nazgul, in many ways, felt that she could live a truer version of herself through social media: they offered hope and possibilities for experiencing community, for world-building. But, like several other of my interlocutors, the initial relief she felt when discovering a group of like-minded individuals soon gave way to more ambiguous feelings as she discovered that the motives of other atheists in embracing atheism were sometimes quite different from her own. For example, she discovered that being atheist did not necessarily imply being feminist or tolerant of other ways of life, and that what she had hoped was a liberal haven was filled with jokes mocking women wearing burqas (Louw 2019a).

In the case of funerals in Kyrgyzstan, there was at least a known script for converting the ruins of a person into the building-blocks for community, whereas the fate of one's digital heritage was less clear. On the one hand, social media offered 'me-centred' or individualist social formations that sat well with the values Nazgul held; on the other, they allowed a picture of a burqa-clad woman to become the building-block for a world that was not hers, and so Nazgul was very concerned about how her profiles would be handled after death. She wanted them to be shut down immediately in a way that, similar to the cremation of her body, would emphasise the absolute end to her existence. She did not want the ruins that were left of her – whether physical or digital – to be cared for by anyone else.

Conclusion

What I have sought to demonstrate in this chapter is that, for people like the Kyrgyz neo-atheists – a group who find themselves on the margins of community, experiencing it as suffocating in its social control – what impermanence offers is opportunities to define oneself as singular, finite and irreplaceable in a society that tends to emphasise the value of community and family lines over the individual, and the relative unimportance of this life in relation to the afterlife. To the Kyrgyz neo-atheists, cremation – and the deletion of one's digital heritage – presents itself as a possibility for a purposeful destruction to preserve identity: the destruction of a potentiality (the ruin of a person, as it were) that may be used by others for other purposes. Cremation becomes an act of world-building at the end of one's world. More generally, I have argued that a focus on the impermanence of the human body as it is experienced, reflected upon and dealt with may be a way into exploring the ethics of being-with – the ways in which beings become entangled with the lives of other beings, and the complexities of these entanglements – as a fundamental, albeit shadowy, aspect of human existence.

Notes

1   All names used in this chapter are pseudonyms.
2   This chapter is based on ongoing fieldwork on young neo-atheists in Kyrgyzstan and their efforts to live atheist lives, crafting atheist selves and communities of atheists in face-to-face interaction as well as on social media. The project is part of a larger cross-disciplinary research project, 'Ethics after Individualism: Phenomenological Explorations of Moral Community', which explores how human beings in different contexts and circumstances experience their involvement or entanglement with each other – and the ethical concepts involved in their ideas about community. The project is funded by the Danish Research Council for the Humanities. My fieldwork in Bishkek has been funded by the Danish Institute in Damascus.
3   In the Soviet Union, the promotion of atheism and restrictions on religious practice were central aspects of government policy, and the Sovietisation of Central Asia involved a massive assault on Islam. Anti-religious campaigns were launched, including mass rallies where women were encouraged to burn their veils, which, for the Bolsheviks, were icons of Islamic tradition associated with repression, ignorance and religious fanaticism (Kamp 2006; Northrop 2004). Religious property was confiscated, mosques and *madāris* (the plural of *madrasah*, religious schools) were destroyed, the *ulamā* (religious authorities) were persecuted and Soviet Muslims were isolated from the rest of the world. The number of mosques permitted to operate was relatively small and people were discouraged from attending them (Keller 2001; Ro'i 2000). As a result, for many Muslims, the practice of Islam was largely confined to the performance of lifecycle rituals such as weddings, circumcisions and funerals. To some extent, Islam was rendered synonymous with tradition – a marker of national identity (Khalid 2007).
4   For more about Kyrgyz neo-atheists and their reasons for embracing atheism, see Louw 2019.
5   For rich and elaborate descriptions of Kyrgyz mortuary rituals, see Beyer 2016; Hardenberg 2010; and Kuchumkulova 2007.
6   While Heidegger emphasised death as final and nonrelational and something each individual must confront and deal with in the quest for existential authenticity, Ruin's argument in the book is that Heidegger, with the concept of *having-been*, 'in his own way also opens the door toward an exploration of a peculiar and irreducible intersubjective ontology of a being with the dead' (Ruin 2018: 29).

References

Al-Mohammad, Hayder. 2010. 'Towards an ethics of *being-with*: Intertwinements of life in post-invasion Basra', *Ethnos* 75:4: 425–46.

Bakhiev, Talantaaly, and Aida Egemberdieva. 2007. 'The role of initiation in the Kyrgyz world'. In *Mazar Worship in Kyrgyzstan: Rituals and practitioners in Talas*, edited by Gulnara Aitpaeva. Bishkek: Aigine Cultural Research Center.

Beyer, Judith. 2016. *The Force of Custom: Law and the ordering of everyday life in Kyrgyzstan*. Pittsburgh, PA: University of Pittsburgh Press.

Blanchot, Maurice. 1988. *The Unavowable Community*. Barrytown, NY: Station Hill Press.

Cimino, Richard, and Christopher Smith. 2014. *Atheist Awakening: Secular activism and community in America*. Oxford: Oxford University Press.

Dubuisson, Eva-Marie. 2017. *Living Language in Kazakhstan: The dialogic emergence of an ancestral worldview*. Pittsburgh, PA: University of Pittsburgh Press.

Engelke, Matthew. 2015. 'The coffin question: Death and materiality in humanist funerals', *Material Religion* 11(1): 26–49.

Hardenberg, Roland. 2010. 'How to overcome death? The efficacy of funeral rituals in Kyrgyzstan', *Journal of Ritual Studies* 24(1): 29–43.

Hertz, Robert. 1907. 'Contribution à une étude sur la représentation collective de la mort', *Année Sociologique* 10: 48–137.

Isci, Baris. 2010. '"Proper" Muslim against "authentic" Kyrgyz: The formation of Islamic field and secular challenges in Bishkek, Kyrgyzstan'. PhD thesis, Washington University in St Louis.

Jacquesson, Svetlana. 2008. 'The sore zones of identity: Past and present debates on funerals in Kyrgyzstan', *Inner Asia* 10: 281–303.

Kamp, Marianne. 2006. *The New Woman in Uzbekistan: Islam, modernity, and unveiling under communism*. Seattle and London: University of Washington Press.

Keller, Shoshana. 2001. *To Moscow, Not Mecca: The Soviet campaign against Islam in Central Asia 1917–1941*. Westport, CT: Praeger.

Khalid, Adeeb. 2007. *Islam after Communism: Religion and politics in Central Asia*. Berkeley, CA: University of California Press.

Kleinman, Arthur, and Sjaak van der Geest. 2009. 'Care in health care: Remaking the moral world of medicine', *Medische Antropologie* 21(1): 159–68.

Kuchumkulova, Elmira M. 2007. 'Kyrgyz nomadic customs and the impact of re-Islamization after independence'. PhD thesis, University of Washington.

Levinas, Emmanuel. 1969. *Totality and Infinity: An essay on exteriority*. Pittsburgh, PA: Duquesne University Press.

Levinas, Emmanuel. 2000. *God, Death, and Time*. Redwood City, CA: Stanford University Press.

Louw, Maria. 2010. 'Dreaming up futures: Dream omens and magic in Bishkek', *History and Anthropology* 21(3): 277–92.

Louw, Maria. 2011. 'Being Muslim the ironic way: Secularism, religion and irony in post-Soviet Kyrgyzstan'. In *Varieties of Secularism in Asia: Anthropological explorations of religion, politics, and the spiritual other*, edited by Nils Bubandt and Martijn van Beek, 143–62. London: Taylor and Francis.

Louw, Maria. 2019a. 'Atheism 2.0: Finding spaces for atheism in contemporary Kyrgyzstan', *Central Asian Affairs* 6(2–3): 206–23.

Louw, Maria. 2019b. 'Aging in the absence of the young and in the presence of the ancestor spirits'. Blog post, Central Eurasian Studies Society. https://www.centraleurasia.org/2019/aging-in-the-absence-of-the-young-and-in-the-presence-of-the-ancestor-spirit/ (last accessed 30 October 2021).

Louw, Maria. 2020. '"It is just doing the motion": Atheist time work in contemporary Kyrgyzstan'. In *Time Work: Studies in temporal agency,* edited by Michael G. Flaherty, Lotte Meinert Berghahn and Anne Line Dalsgård, 121–38. New York and Oxford: Berghahn Books.

Louw, Maria. Forthcoming. 'Virtuous aging in uncanny moral worlds: Being old and Kyrgyz in the absence of the young'. In *Imagistic Care: Growing old in a precarious world*, edited by Cheryl Mattingly and Lone Grøn. New York: Fordham University Press.

Mattingly, Cheryl, and Patrick McKearney. Forthcoming. 'The ethics of care'. In *The Cambridge Handbook of the Anthropology of Ethics and Morality*, edited by James Laidlaw. Cambridge: Cambridge University Press.

McBrien, Julie. 2017. *From Belonging to Belief: Modern secularisms and the construction of religion in Kyrgyzstan*. Pittsburgh, PA: University of Pittsburgh Press.

Montgomery, David. 2016. *Practicing Islam: Knowledge, experience, and social navigation in Kyrgyzstan*. Pittsburgh, PA: University of Pittsburgh Press.

Nasritdinov, Emil, and Nurgul Esenamanova. 2017. 'The war of billboards: Hijab, secularism, and public space in Bishkek'. *Central Asian Affairs* 4(2): 217–42.

Northrop, Douglas. 2004. *Veiled Empire: Gender and power in Stalinist Central Asia*. Ithaca, NY: Cornell University Press.

Pelkmans, Mathijs. 2017. *Fragile Conviction: Changing ideological landscapes in urban Kyrgyzstan*. Ithaca, NY: Cornell University Press.

Puig de la Bellacasa, María. 2017. *Matters of Care: Speculative ethics in more than human worlds*. Minneapolis, MN, and London: University of Minnesota Press.

Rapport, Nigel. 2003. *I am Dynamite: An alternative anthropology of power*. London and New York: Routledge.

Rasanayagam, Johan. 2017. 'Anthropology in conversation with an Islamic tradition: Emmanuel Levinas and the practice of critique', *Journal of the Royal Anthropological Institute* 24: 90–106.

Ro'i, Yaacov. 2000. *Islam in the Soviet Union*. London: Hurst and Co.

Ruin, Hans. 2018. *Being with the Dead: Burial, ancestral politics and the roots of historical consciousness*. Redwood City, CA: Stanford University Press.

Smith, Jane Idleman, and Yvonne Yazbeck Haddad. 1981. *The Islamic Understanding of Death and Resurrection*. Albany, NY: State University of New York Press.

Verdery, Katherine. 1999. *The Political Lives of Dead Bodies: Reburial and postsocialist change*. New York: Columbia University Press.

Zigon, Jarrett. 2019. *A War on People: Drug user politics and a new ethics of community*. Oakland, CA: University of California Press.

5
Encountering impermanence, making change: a case study of attachment and alcoholism in Thailand

Julia Cassaniti

'I just want things to *stop*,' my friend Sen said, looking at me blurrily, the whiskey he'd been drinking taking effect. 'I want things to be the way they *were*.' He seemed emphatic when he spoke but also disoriented, as if he knew he couldn't keep changes from happening around him but wasn't able to feel any other way. He excused himself from the desk to go to his room at the back of the house, and when he returned a few minutes later his eyes were even more glazed over than before, his breath smelling even more strongly of the cheap rice whiskey he'd been drinking more and more of lately. 'Before, friends would stop by, we'd travel around – around town, around Chiang Mai, on the empty streets,' he went on, glancing at the mountain by his house in Mae Jaeng, beyond which Northern Thailand's main city of Chiang Mai lay, a few hours away. 'In the red car, with the windows open, smoking cigarettes. I wanted it to just go on and on that way, forever. But now they're busy . . . Look at this road,' he gestured to the small street in front of us, where a steady stream of four-wheel pickups and motorbikes were passing by. 'It's so crowded, you can't even walk across the street without stretching out your neck to see, one way, the other way . . . Everyone's coming and going. I just want to *be* here.' He glowered and reminisced as he told me about life when he was a teenager, as he had often done in the many conversations we had had about his past. I was in town for the year doing anthropological research on conceptions of change in Thailand, and, in between the more formalised ethnographic interviews I was collecting, I would often stop

5.1 'Charming life: The secret of a happy life is to accept change gracefully'. The cover of a notebook at a bookstore in Chiang Mai. In addition to textual Buddhist teachings, an awareness of change permeates popular culture in Thailand, creating a general social orientation toward impermanence. Photo: Julia Cassaniti.

by and chat with him.[1] I would sit with him quietly, both of us thinking about change.

As a Buddhist living in a predominantly Buddhist community, Sen was familiar with the teaching of impermanence: impermanence is understood to be one of the central facts of life, and recognition of its truth is understood to help decrease suffering. Others around Sen were certainly familiar with the teaching, and they grappled with it in their own ways. Most of those around him seemed to be able to handle changes in their stride. Sen seemed unable to do so, and in the end it almost cost him his life. Everyone struggles with change, but most people are able to come to terms with it, more or less. In spending time with Sen, I found myself wondering: how does someone who has a hard time dealing with change manifest that struggle in their body and mind? And how does coming to terms with impermanence stand to help not just one person but all of us? I wondered, in other words, how an acceptance of impermanence doesn't just represent a kind of giving up, a passive helplessness in the face of the inevitable, but instead create change and help – as the bookstore notebook in Figure 5.1 put it – to live 'a happy life'. In sketching Sen's personal struggles with attachment and alcohol, leading up to and following a series of hospitalisations, I address these questions and suggest some of the lessons that impermanence offers for a small community in Northern Thailand, and potentially for us all. His case reveals avenues by which we can apply the lessons of impermanence, which can be read in different ways as a Buddhist concept, a universal concept and a local concept.

The Buddhist teaching of impermanence is well known in Mae Jaeng. It is referred to through the formal Pali term *anicca*, one of the Three Characteristics of life as expressed by the Buddha, along with *dukha* (unsatisfactoriness) and *anatta* (non-self). More colloquially, it is expressed in phrases incorporating ideas of *mai tiang* (instability) and *kwam mai nae non* (uncertainty). '*Anicca* means impermanence, transiency, the state of coming to life and eventually perishing; physically apparent change,' reads the highschool textbook *Religion and Society* in Thai that Sen's brother Noi was learning from at the time, and which Sen most likely learned from too. 'Uncertainty:', it continues, 'That which arises, must pass away. Instability'. When Noi was ordained as a novice monk, he and 99 other novices being ordained with him chanted about impermanence in Pali texts based on the Saṃyutta Nikāya (SN) 22.7–9 sutta, as all do for officially recognised ordinations in Thailand (Vajirañāṇavarorasa 1973). And when the head monk of a nearby monastery passed away, villagers gathered to hear chants about impermanence from the Mahā Parinibbāṇa Sutta (the last words of the Buddha), which is a common practice at Thai funerals. People chant at night about impermanence before sleeping, reading from chanting books commonly found in monasteries, libraries and convenience stores. They learn about impermanence at the many monasteries that sparkle with gold along the valley floor, where they gather to hear *dhamma* teachings from monks, and outside the monastery in movies, social media, political messages and public service announcements.

Impermanence seemed to be everywhere. Given the many religious teachings about impermanence circulating in Northern Thailand, at first I was surprised that it was not just Sen who didn't talk much about it. When I first started learning about it in Mae Jaeng, I expected that when I asked about it people would talk about it familiarly and emphatically. I thought they would tell me about impermanence in the kinds of abstract terms that I encountered in the chants around them, or from other similar teachings found throughout Theravāda Buddhism's sacred texts. Instead, when I asked about impermanence, few people seemed to have much to say about it at all. They said that they didn't know much about the concept, and that I should go talk to the monks to hear about such a philosophical topic. When I asked the monks, I was told generally the same thing: 'we're just trying to take care of the novice [monk]s here, go talk to the monks in Bangkok.'

After an early generation of Buddhist-studies scholars were intrigued that Buddhists would apparently live by such a difficult set of truths (such as the teaching of *anatta*, that one has no essential self) (Rahula 1967; Almond 1988), a second generation of scholars pushed back against the idea that Buddhists follow Buddhist teachings unproblematically, pointing to the many differences between doctrine and practice (Cassaniti 2006, 2015; Collins 1998; McDaniel 2011). The teaching of impermanence was a prime suspect for this anti-doctrinal move. After all, Buddhist teachings are hard to understand and even harder to live; this is why the monastery was created, as a place for refuge from a chaotic world. For lay followers, impermanence could perhaps be seen as an abstract, rather than a pragmatic, truth.

Yet I came to realise that people in Mae Jaeng had been hesitant to talk about impermanence not because it was irrelevant to their daily lives but because it was both too profound and too obvious to mention. They didn't want to risk saying something incorrect about a formal teaching to a foreign researcher or state something so obvious that it barely needed elaborating at all. The more time I spent in Mae Jaeng, the more I started to hear about impermanence in everyday settings, not in abstraction but practically, in times of challenge. It was raised especially in terms of helping people feel better about what was happening around them. 'I had a bad crop this year because of the rain,' a farmer named Aeh told me, sitting on her mat on the ground next to fields of rice, 'but I think about how things are *mai nae non*; we can't be sure. Sometimes we'll have a good year, sometimes we'll have a bad year. I think of how everything changes, and I feel better.' My host sister Goy told me about her father, who had been sitting with the family around a campfire just a few months before, when he had a heart attack and died almost immediately. 'It was a lesson for me', Goy said thoughtfully 'that things are *mai tiang* – not stable.' Impermanence was everywhere, and was useful.

An excess of attachment

For my friend Sen, though, change felt insurmountable. He understood the teaching of impermanence in a general sense but he didn't do anything to practice it, as far as I could tell. Though Buddhist like almost all of the others in town, Sen did not chant before sleeping, or meditate, or visit the village monastery, even for his brother's ordination. He himself had never been ordained as a monk, unlike virtually all other Buddhist males in this overwhelmingly Buddhist country. 'I respect the Buddha . . .', he told me, pausing thoughtfully, 'but I don't know about the monks.'

I had got to know Sen when he still seemed fine, before alcohol overtook his life. His welcoming smile and genial attitude readily brought friends to him, and, more often than not, he could be found drinking and relaxing with them in the evenings after running the family store during the day. Sen had gone to highschool in Chiang Mai, and lived there with his grandmother, Yeki. It was during this period, he told me, when he was 15, that he started drinking, and now, at 34 years old, he was living at his parents' home back in Mae Jaeng, along with Yeki, his 12-year-old brother Noi, his 32-year-old sister Gaew, and her new husband, Ton. On the outside, Sen seemed to live a fairly pleasant and unproblematic life: his was one of the richer families in town, and they ran the local convenience store in a casual, familial way, with different members taking over at the main counter when they felt like it, and everyone contributing to the many tasks of the business. Sen would sit at the front of the shophouse for most of the day, greeting friends and watching the world go by, as he sold ice and snacks to people in town. But over the last few years, a series of problems had begun to crop up, compounding each other to drive his drinking and his feeling of unhappiness.

Following the Northern Thai tradition of new husbands moving into their wife's natal home, the husband of Sen's sister Gaew had come to live with the family, but Sen and his brother-in-law didn't get along. Like the rest of the family, his brother-in-law was concerned about Sen's drinking and was more direct about it than Gaew or others were, or than Sen cared for. 'He told me that, once my parents die, he's going to kick me out of the house!', Sen once told me, indignant, 'and it's my house!' Typically, problems arising from the matrilineal housing pattern work their way out in Mae Jaeng when male members of the natal house themselves marry and move away, but Sen knew that wasn't going to happen. He had recently started a romantic relationship with his male friend Chai, who worked at the local hospital as a pharmacist. Although Thailand has a global reputation as relatively accepting of homosexuality, Sen felt it would be inappropriate to 'come out' to his family. 'Besides', he said, 'Chai's family is Chinese Thai, and he doesn't think they would accept him if he told them.'

Sen took these problems in his stride until the day his grandmother passed away. Yeki had raised Sen and was his closest friend. While I and my host family and the rest of the town were at the funeral with the family, Sen was nowhere to be found. A few days later, he still hadn't returned, and I asked Gaew where he was. After hesitating, she whispered, distraught, 'He's in his room. He hasn't left it for three days.' When he finally appeared, he seemed befuddled, and I found out from him later that he'd been drinking rice whiskey the whole time.

Sen's friends and family were worried about him, but they didn't know what to do. They felt that trying to get him to be a way he wasn't would not be good, because that represented attachments that would bring suffering, but accepting him as he was in his current addicted state also seemed like a bad idea. His mother admonished him and urged him to get help, ordering him to see a doctor for his increasingly jaundiced eyes and skin, but he refused, and she let it be: 'He has to *tham jai*,' she said, shrugging sadly, referring to the practice of 'making the heart' and coming to accept what is. 'He has to come to terms with it himself.' I also suggested he go see a doctor or go to the monastery, but Sen refused to go then, too, as he had done with others. I was worried about my friend, and, as a researcher interested in attitudes toward change, I was intrigued by the explanations that Sen and his family and friends gave for his condition.

They talked about the alcoholism that Sen was developing using the term *ditt lao* – 'to be attached', using the same word that people in interviews had been telling me represented attachments that needed surmounting through an attention to impermanence. One can become attached to alcohol like one can become attached to anything else, and attachments bring problems. It wasn't just that Sen was stuck on his whiskey, they told me; he was also stuck on a past that was inevitably gone. 'He's always been that way,' his sister Gaew told me, talking about her brother one afternoon while he was passed out on a bench near their house: 'He would have some idea in his head, and you couldn't get him to change it, no matter what.' One night, at a gathering in a restaurant by the river, Sen's friends discussed his situation. One of them, Jiew, explained how, 'a few years ago, it was different . . . we were young then. Now we have families of our own, we have responsibilities, we've grown!' Mae Jaeng had changed, but Sen hadn't changed with it.

A trip to the hospital and a return to impermanence

The situation continued to deteriorate, and I tried to help where I could, but eventually my time in Mae Jaeng was finished and I wished Sen well before returning to the United States. A year later, I visited again, but this time, Sen was nowhere to be found. Gaew hesitated when I asked where he was, and then whispered that he was in his room at the back of the house, motioning for me to go see him. I found Sen behind the house in the shed that served as his room, his skin a sickly yellow from jaundice, his stomach and legs bloated. He hadn't left the space in days, Gaew had told me, and he rarely ate. His family sometimes put food outside the door but he usually ignored it. As I massaged his calves and tried not to cry, Sen smiled weakly and told me he was OK, but it was clear that he wasn't. A hand appeared outside the window, and Sen reached out to take the plastic bag containing rice whiskey and a pack of cigarettes from his brother Noi.

The gradual change that Sen and his family were witnessing day-to-day was very different from the abrupt change I found in him now, after being away for some time. When I returned to the front of the house to tell his sister that Sen needed to get help immediately, she told me that we should wait until Sen was ready to accept that he had a problem – the same thing she and others had told me a year earlier. Her parents were away in Chiang Mai at a *Joh Rey* retreat (a Japanese Thai Buddhist tradition that Sen had told me had helped steer their father away from his own drinking) and Gaew didn't want to do anything drastic without them around. I could tell she knew the situation was very serious, though, and, after she had discussed it with her husband, the three of us agreed that Sen needed to be taken to a doctor immediately, even if he didn't want to go. We recruited a few of Sen's friends, along with the head of the Mae Jaeng Police, a childhood friend of Sen's, and went back to the house to force Sen to go to the hospital. When we got to the room, the door was locked, and when the police officer broke it down we found Sen sitting on his bed, bleary-eyed, holding a large kitchen knife. 'I'm *not* going to the hospital,' he said, raising the knife at us unsteadily, as his friends and the police officer slowly backed away. 'I'm staying right where I am.'

'Get the knife away and we can get him,' the officer told us as we exited the room, 'but otherwise we don't want anyone to get hurt.' That afternoon, I found Sen passed out on his bed, the knife inches from his hand, and slowly removed it and took it to the police. An hour later, we were in a car on the way to Chiang Mai, following the ambulance that carried Sen, who was now expressionless and disoriented.

A few weeks later, we were back in Mae Jaeng after a series of visits to Chiang Mai's Suan Prung psychiatric hospital, Nakhon Ping public hospital, and the Chiang Mai Ram private clinic. The doctors had told us that Sen had advanced cirrhosis of the liver and that he wasn't expected to live much longer. At the Mae Jaeng Hospital, where Sen was strapped to the hospital bed, mostly unconscious and artificially hydrated and fed, his friends gathered around him. Sometimes he would wake up, and alternately flail around trying to get up or yell '*Mat, Mat!*' ('Tie me down! Tie me down!') His parents visited the monastery to make merit, and a local *mor phi* (spirit doctor) visited his hospital room, waving leaves as he chanted and circled the bed. I was told that this was to cajole the spirits of alcohol away from him and detach them from where they had become 'stuck' or 'attached' to his *khwan*, his spirits of self. I was distraught, and said so to Mor Bom, the head doctor of the Mae Jaeng Hospital, who had previously spent many evenings out drinking with Sen. 'We should have gotten him help earlier!' I said. He looked at me: '*Anicca*, Julia. Have you heard of *anicca*? It means that everything is impermanent.'

Impermanence of, and for, Sen

I heard a lot of talk about impermanence in the days and weeks following Sen's trip to Chiang Mai. As he continued to lie unconscious in the hospital, people made merit to help his karma and talked about the importance of letting go. 'We have to *tham jai*,' his cousin said – in this case, coming to accept Sen's current dire situation rather than focusing on how everyone *wanted* the situation to be. 'We have to *ploy wang*,' his friend Jiew told me, referring to emptying the mind of emotional ties.

5.2 A friend in 'Mae Jaeng' gets ready to send off a paper lantern krathong, in a ritual symbolising the letting go of attachments as they float away in the night sky. 30 December 2007. Photo: Rosalyn Hansrisuk.

Sen's friends and family seemed calm, and this surprised me at first because I knew they cared deeply for him and I thought they would appear more upset. I realised, though, that it wasn't a casual or uncaring nonchalance that they were displaying. They were practising attuning their attention to the situation they found themselves in, and accepting it. A calm acceptance of the situation was understood to help it. I recalled people in Mae Jaeng telling me how doctor Mor Bom would tell them about an accident or a bad outcome of a loved one by asking them first to '*tham jai*', to 'make their heart'. In some ways, it was similar to the idea of mentally preparing to hear bad news, a little like being told, in my own cultural background, to 'have a seat' to prepare oneself before being given difficult news. His talk of impermanence and acceptance had, at first, struck me as a little fatalistic; everybody dies, he seemed to be saying, and the sooner we realise that the better we'll feel about dealing with death and other unwelcome changes around us. This is a similar strategy to the one the Buddha is reported to have told to Kisa Gotami (Thig 10; see also the introduction); in searching for a house free from mortality and drawing attention to the ubiquity of death, one is able to feel more connected to others and decrease the pain felt at one particular loss. But 'making the heart' is more than a coping strategy or a kind of resignation to the possible loss of a loved one. The heightened attention that people paid to impermanence after Sen's return to Mae Jaeng was meant to help them craft a psychological orientation to the truth of impermanence. This was understood to have the potential to create positive outcomes, to help themselves and to help Sen, too. It was about making change.

In part, this attention to impermanence was thought to help Sen spiritually if he did pass away then, because ties between people that last after death can be said to be the cause of existence on a spirit realm, where wandering ghosts (*phi*) are doomed to haunt the living. The suffering that can be brought on by the fact of impermanence in Buddhism transcends life and death. Yet in drawing attention to impermanence, Mor Bom and others were also working to create a more positive outcome for Sen's life itself. Sen was suffering from his attachments, whether these were understood to be to the past, to a wished-for way of relating to others, to alcohol or to the spirits of alcohol. Different people took different approaches but, for many, it was some combination of all these, connected through ideas about interpersonal, spiritual energies attuned to an impermanent reality. Sen's friends and family worked to attend to the fact of impermanence to create good effects by making use of Thai Buddhist theories of moral causation (*kamma*), which suggest that, when one does good (such as acting calmly and letting go of attachments), one will receive good effects, as will others. Here, to help Sen let go of his attachments and get better, people practised letting go of their own expectations of themselves and him.

'I wish I had made him go to the hospital sooner,' Gaew told me during a late-night conversation while Sen was in the town hospital, but then quickly changed her tone to talk about the future: 'I'm going to let go, start a new life. The store here hasn't been doing well for a while now. Once we stopped selling alcohol, people stopped coming in as much, and I hear a 7–11 [convenience store] is coming to town. I'm going to close down the store, open a noodle shop and live an easy life.' She knew that she had been carrying too many expectations of Sen, and that her expectations of him bothered her brother. She realised that, like Sen, she had been attached to a particular version of what she felt should happen, and that letting go of her attachment would help her live better. By letting go of her expectations of him, and of herself, she was helping to create an affective orientation to change that could create a positive outcome not only for herself but also, by extension, for Sen and the environment that Sen would be coming home to.

Others told me similar stories; making merit would help Sen, and accepting what had happened would, too. Sen's birthday fell soon after he returned to Mae Jaeng, and his little brother Noi's birthday happened to fall on the same day. After Sen's friends and family had visited him at the hospital, we went out to dinner to celebrate Noi's twelfth birthday. There, his father talked to Noi in a tone I wasn't used to hearing. Usually, he was either pithily casual or directive around his son, but now he seemed serious: 'Noi,' he said, 'I want you to know that you can do anything you want in your life. If you want to be a doctor, be a doctor. If you want to go study something, or do something else, or whatever you want, you can do it.' Sen's father was, in effect, telling his youngest son that he supported him no matter how he lived – and, in doing so, showed that he, like Gaew, had felt he had been too attached to an expectation of Sen that Sen was clearly unable to follow. In the build-up to the current crisis, they hadn't seemed to me to be too demanding of Sen, and I was surprised to hear these elliptical references at all. But I knew Sen felt they were, and it was clear that being more accepting was seen as the right approach.

I had thought that, when Sen returned to Mae Jaeng, his family would 'realise' that they had been too lax with Sen about his problems with alcohol, that they should have been more direct with him, following my own cultural logic of interventions, responsibilities and the talking out of feelings. Instead, they seemed to move even further away from these

5.3 After Sen's visits to the hospital, his family decided to put up this portrait of the famous Northern Thai monk Khruba Siwichai in the shop, in the spot where they used to sell whiskey. 30 December 2007. Photo: Julia Cassaniti.

ways of relating to someone, ramping up not their direct engagement but their 'letting go' in the face of the inevitable impermanence of Sen's life and their own. Significantly, instead of addressing impermanence as the root cause of stress and seeking to create permanence, they worked to put a wedge between their contact with change and the unsatisfactoriness that arises when one clings to that which will inevitably pass. An attention to impermanence became a catalyst for creating new outcomes.

After a week at the Mae Jaeng hospital, Sen was brought back to the family home, and spent the next year in bed as an invalid. Instead of staying in the back room, he was now placed front and centre in the upstairs of the house, but no one told him what to do, not even his brother-in-law. His old friend Chai rented one of the family's shophouses next door and visited now and then, though he was also busy starting a family of his own. Sen watched the world go by around him and, in his own way, he listened and learned from it.

After a year unable to get out of bed, Sen reached out to turn on a lamp, and, realising it was too far to stretch his arm, crawled over to it. Soon, he was tentatively walking, and a few months later he was able to get on a bicycle and wobble through town. In the face of impermanence, Sen had persevered. I had returned to Mae Jaeng again for my yearly visit, and stayed up late talking with him about his ordeal. He couldn't remember much of it, and he didn't particularly care to, but he did tell me he knew why he had got better.

'My sister thinks she's the reason,' he told me, 'going to the monastery to make merit. You think you're the reason I got better, getting me to the hospital. Everyone thinks they're the reason – people went to the monastery, the Christians down the road came and prayed – and they all helped. But really it's because of what I did.' He paused. 'I *ploy wang*. I let go.'

Over the course of the year, Sen had changed. He realised he had been stuck, wanting his life to be a certain way, and he let go of his attachments. He no longer talked about how he wished the past was still the present as much as he used to, and started talking about 'making the heart' with what is. He was happy when he saw his old friend Chai near the house, but didn't seem upset that his friend had moved on. He was glad when his brother-in-law moved to Chiang Mai to study for an MA degree at the university, but didn't become perturbed when he would come back on the weekends. He still missed his grandmother, but didn't get a dark look on his face when he talked about her. He noticed that others had changed, too, and spoke about it. He talked about his sister Gaew, especially: 'Look, she closed the shop and opened the noodle stand on the street, and she's happy now.' For her part, Gaew hadn't seemed unhappy before, but I could tell that she was happier now, after she had let go of the expectations she'd carried around of her brother and of herself. He laughed and started singing the chorus line to his favourite song, ไม่มีใครรู้ว่าพรุ่งนี้จะเป็นเช่นไร, '*mai mii krai ru wa prungnii ja pen chen rai*', by the pop band Peck: 'No one knows how tomorrow will be'.

It wasn't that accepting change meant resignation – not at all. It helped Sen move on from the past and it helped Gaew too: the new 7–11 branch was owned by their aunt, so the money stayed in the family, and they generated more income by renting out the shop than they had earned by running it. Those around Sen had succeeded not in getting him 'back' to some idealised way they wanted him to be, but by accepting him just as he was in the present. There was a kind of success, and liberation, in letting go. The Pali word for impermanence – *anicca* – translates in Thai most often to *kwam mai nae non*: 'uncertainty'; and becoming OK with uncertainty was an important emotional strategy for people in the community. A recognition of impermanence wasn't a giving up, it was the opposite: a way to create positive effects through a recognition of the power and presence of change.

On a recent visit, Sen surprised me by suggesting that we visit the monastery festival in town; it would be his first such visit in as long as any of us could remember. While we were there, he approached a line of small Buddha statues, each representing a day of the week; and, fishing around in his pocket, he quietly dropped a small coin into the pot in front of the statue that represented his birth day. He was making merit at the monastery, with the many ritual and philosophical meanings that come with it. A few days later, I was talking with him about my own worries about changes in my life, and he nodded thoughtfully, and said '*tham jai* . . . you have to make your heart – accept the present and prepare for whatever lies ahead.' In his own ways, Sen was grappling with the impermanence that his religion teaches to be inevitable.

The Buddhist, the global and the local in a Thai case of impermanence

Sen's problems with alcoholism, and his eventual (partial) recovery, highlight some of the lessons that an attention to impermanence can offer us all. For some of his family and friends, the teaching of constant change is a minor, almost taken-for-granted fact that informs daily life: it helps them feel better when something unexpected or unwanted happens, and it helps them recognise that, by holding onto expectations about the way things *should* be, one will inevitably suffer. Sen struggled with these lessons more than most, but, in the end, he persevered: he got better, and, in his own words, this happened because he learned to 'let go'. Alcoholism can be thought of as an extreme form of psychological and bodily attachment. By giving up on his addiction, Sen was able to give up his sense of wanting things to be a certain way and was able to create real change for himself. His case offers a pointed example of how impermanence doesn't necessarily mean a passive acceptance that one is not in control of one's own life; it suggests the opposite.

More broadly, Sen's case informs a wider scholarly enquiry into the role of impermanence in all our lives. It contributes to our understanding of impermanence as a Buddhist concept, a universal concept and a local one. It informs our understanding of impermanence as a Buddhist concept by showing us that, in Buddhist contexts (at least in Thailand), it is about letting go of attachments, and that doing so can help with psychological wellness and mental health. The sense that his family and friends had of Sen being ill because of being 'stuck' or attached (*dtit*) to alcohol and the past, and the importance of accepting (*tham jai*) and emptying the heart of expectations (*ploy wang*), are all part of interwoven Buddhist logics of meaning and causation. They connect to Buddhist conceptions of suffering (*dukkha*) as tied to this clinging, and to non-self (*anatta*) as a truth that becomes recognisable through an awareness that everything changes. These and other related Buddhist concepts – including moral efficacy (*kamma*), dependent origination (*paṭiccasamuppāda*) and others – create a meaningful spiritual orientation toward impermanence that forms part of Buddhist practices around the world. These Buddhist meanings of impermanence look different from other religious perspectives on change. They most directly oppose ideas of eternalism (*sassatavāda* in Pali) and a belief in an immortal soul (*ātmavāda*).[2] Even in religious and cultural contexts in which impermanence is emphasised and elaborated, the complementary meanings and the extension of impermanence to even the realm of consciousness set apart the Buddhist impermanence I have highlighted here as unique among world religions.

Sen's case also informs our understanding of impermanence as a universal concept because change is omnipresent in all our lives, whether religiously elaborated or not, and Sen's reactions to it represent human responses that are, in part, shared throughout the world.[3] When Sen felt stuck in his focus on the past, while those around him sensed the importance of letting go, they were grappling with a universal human struggle. Even in contexts that don't emphasise impermanence in philosophical and religious discourses, it can still be found infiltrating much of the social, existential realities with which we all must grapple. A neighbour in the United States recently had an old tree cut down in his property, and, while lamenting its passing, he said philosophically, 'Ah well . . . all things must come to an end.' Around the same time, in the midst of the COVID-19 pandemic, I heard on the radio that 'the one thing we can count on for sure is change.' Lessons of impermanence, though often not as elaborated as in Buddhism, may look similar to those I found in Mae Jaeng. Sen's case as an example of human struggles with transience helps us to counter a hegemonic emphasis on stability that dominates much of the discourse in the humanities and social sciences. His story helps to orient our attention more directly and comparatively to how change is dealt with in lives across time and space, and to the therapeutic potential of doing so. By this, we are laying the groundwork for an alternative ontological approach to time and self.

Finally, Sen's experience informs our understanding of impermanence as a localised religio-cultural phenomenon. Rather than seeing it as representing a reified, single *Buddhist* approach to transience, or as reflecting a universal truth experienced similarly everywhere, we can also learn from Sen's ordeal what impermanence looks like as part of particular social worlds.[4] As Cameron Warner, Carole McGranahan and others offering ethnographic accounts of Buddhist impermanence in this book and elsewhere can attest, the attentions to impermanence I have highlighted here are not exactly the same as those drawn on in other Buddhist settings. They are particular to a Northern Thai community at a particular time and place. The interpretation of the Pali term *anicca* as 'uncertainty', for example, may look different than its articulations in Tibetan, Japanese or even other Theravāda Buddhist settings. The 'spirits' that the spirit doctor worked to extract from Sen's body might be seen by some scholars not to relate to doctrinal interpretations of Buddhist teachings at all, but instead to reflect traditional ideas about spirits of the self called *khwan* that circulate in Southeast Asia and pre-date Buddhist influence (Formosa 1998; Cassaniti 2017). Yet they are also part of impermanence in Sen's community, as are the particular local practices of making merit, floating lanterns, articulating power and more. Society in Thailand is structured largely through *boon* (merit) or accumulated *barami* (a kind of charisma) that is thought to be developed by those who are able to demonstrate (or associate with those who demonstrate) a mastery of the Buddhist teachings, including mindfully gathering the mental resources to face impermanence (Cassaniti 2018). Monks in Thailand are sometimes seen to have acquired mystical powers through a mental mastery of the teaching (Puriwanchana 2011; McDaniel 2011), and, even without the mystical part of their powers, they are understood to have cultivated a powerful mental fortitude that is widely admired (Tiyavanich 1997; Jirattikorn 2016). Through a complex local logic that connects causation, karma and personhood, the 'technologies of the self' surrounding impermanence are understood to decrease personal and social affective stress and create powerful energies that inform the functioning of society across the region.

In the end, it may be the space between the universal and the particular that the Thai Buddhist case of impermanence I have drawn attention to here most helps to illuminate. Impermanence is enmeshed in a set of connected religious and social concepts about causation, personhood and much, much more, some of which translate to other Buddhist and non-Buddhist contexts, and some of which do not so easily connect. The study of impermanence suggests an exciting comparative project that is now being undertaken by ethnographically oriented Buddhist studies scholars (see the introduction; and Cassaniti and Chladek forthcoming). As with other concepts that come to be extracted from embedded cultural and religious meanings and re-articulated as universal ones, the Buddhist associations of impermanence that Sen and his family and friends help illustrate may not easily or unproblematically transfer to other settings – Buddhist or otherwise – where people have different ideologies and life goals.[5] Today, Sen still suffers from the lingering effects of his illness and still mourns the changes in his community from time to time. He still goes through phases of drinking, but less than before, and, with the support of his family, now seeks help for them. Overall, he is doing well, glad to be alive and generally content with his lot. As the head doctor, Mor Bom, said emphatically when I expressed my distress at Sen's illness, 'Impermanence, Julia, have you heard of that?' Sen's situation in a small community in Northern Thailand highlights how particular people deal in particular ways with a universal truth of impermanence.

Acknowledgements

I would like to thank Dr Richard Shweder, Dr Tanya Luhrmann and Dr Steve Collins for their contributions to this study. I would like to thank the Mellon Foundation, the Fulbright Foundation, a Century Fellowship at the University of Chicago, and a Culture and Mind Fellowship at Stanford University for the support that made this work possible. I would like to thank Cameron Warner, Ton Otto, Haidy Geismar and the participants of the 'Inevitable Ends' conference at the University of Aarhus, as well as the reviewers of this book, for their reflections on this chapter and their vision in drawing attention to this important topic. And I would like to thank my friend 'Sen' and all my friends and interlocutors in 'Mae Jaeng', whose experiences I have shared here.

Notes

1 Informant names (Sen, Gaew etc.) and place names (Mae Jaeng) have been altered to maintain anonymity. All quotes have been translated from Thai and *kam muang* (Northern Thai), unless noted otherwise. The case described in this chapter is elaborated in *Living Buddhism: Mind, self, and emotion in a Thai community* (Cassaniti 2015).
2 For example, the *Brahmajāla Sutta* (in the *Dīghanikāya*) and the *Saṃyutta Nikāya Sutta* 12.15. The direct oppositional interlocutors that the Buddha is said to be arguing against in these claims about impermanence are the ideas of a universal Soul, popular in contemporaneous Upaniṣadic conceptions of *ātman* (related to today's Hinduism). The idea of the eternal soul that Buddhist perspectives disagree with also pervades much of Western, Judeo-Christian philosophical traditions (Bayes 2010).
3 The Christian phrase 'Ashes to ashes, dust to dust' (Genesis 3:19) refers to the uncertainty and impermanence of life, as do the 'vanities' of the biblical Ecclesiastes (translated as *anicca* in Thai, Cassaniti 2015), according to my Christian Thai informants. The common Muslim refrain 'God willing' and the Qur'anic teaching that clinging to worldly permanence is dangerous (Shah-Kazemi 2010) do too. From Heraclitus (Graham 2008) and Marcus Aurelius (Hadot 1998) to Husserl (Hanna 1995) and Heidegger (1962) (as well as Deleuze, Varela and Maturana and many others – see Geismar, Otto and Warner in this volume), impermanence is elaborated in different ways in many different philosophic traditions.
4 Almond (1988), Hallisey (1995) and others have pointed out the constructed nature of a single global representation of Buddhism, and even of a single Theravāda Buddhism (Skilling et al. 2012; Collins 1990). Attempts to unify disparate branches of the religion can tell us as much about the powerful forces doing the constructing as about the religion itself.
5 An attention to impermanence may be helpful in developing alternative therapeutic interventions for addiction (Chen 2010; Marlatt 2002; Cassaniti 2019), but it is also the case that ideas about impermanence helped Sen because of its particular relevance in his community. An attention to it is positively reinforced, helping to create successful outcomes (Cassaniti and Luhrmann 2014) that may be experienced differently in different contexts. The global rise of mindfulness practices can serve as a useful example. While, in some ways, mindfulness highlights a universal capacity for mental development, Willoughby Britton and colleagues have reported psychotic breaks and other problematic psychological 'side effects' from extracting mindfulness meditation from its Buddhist roots (as popularised in twentieth-century Burmese vipassana movements, Braun 2013) and 'decontextualising' it into secular settings (Lindahl et al. 2017). Mindfulness's associations with other Buddhist perspectives are restructured when articulated in social environments with different views of the self and the good life (Cassaniti 2018), to different ends. The same may be true of impermanence.

References

Almond, Philip C. 1988. *The British Discovery of Buddhism*. Cambridge: Cambridge University Press.
Bayes, Jonathan. 2010. *The Apostles' Creed: Truth with passion*. Eugene, OR: Wipf and Stock Publishers.
Braun, Erik. 2013. *The Birth of Insight: Meditation, modern Buddhism, and the Burmese monk Ledi Sayadaw*. Chicago, IL: University of Chicago Press.
Buddhaghosa, Bhadantácariya, and Bhikkhu Ñāṇamoli. 1976. *The Path of Purification: Visuddhimagga*. Berkeley, CA: Shambhala Publications. Vis. Ch. xxi/p. 640.
Cassaniti, Julia. 2006. 'Toward a cultural psychology of impermanence in Thailand', *Ethos: The Journal of Psychological Anthropology* 34: 58–88.

Cassaniti, Julia. 2015. *Living Buddhism: Mind, self, and emotion in a Thai community*. Ithaca, NY: Cornell University Press.

Cassaniti, Julia. 2017. 'Wherever you go, there you … aren't?' In *Meditation, Buddhism, and Science*, edited by David McMahan and Erik Braun, 131–52. Oxford: Oxford University Press.

Cassaniti, Julia. 2018. *Remembering the Present: Mindfulness in Buddhist Asia*. Ithaca, NY: Cornell University Press.

Cassaniti, Julia. 2019. 'Keeping it together: Idioms of resilience and distress in Thai Buddhist mindlessness', *Transcultural Psychiatry* 56(4): 697–719.

Cassaniti, Julia, and Tanya M. Luhrmann. 2014. 'Cultural kindling of spiritual experiences', *Current Anthropology* 55(10): 333–43.

Cassaniti, Julia, and Michael Chladek. Forthcoming. 'Aimless agency: Religious engagement in an uncertain world', *Ethos: The Journal of Psychological Anthropology*.

Chen, Gila. 2010. 'The meaning of suffering in drug addiction and recovery from the perspective of existentialism, Buddhism and the 12-step program', *Journal of Psychoactive Drugs* 42(3): 363–75.

Collins, Steven. 1990. 'On the very idea of the Pali canon', *Journal of the Pali Text Society* 15: 89–126.

Collins, Steven. 1998. *Nirvana and Other Buddhist Felicities: Utopias of the Pāli imaginaire*. New York: Cambridge University Press.

Formosa, Bernard. 1998. 'Bad death and malevolent spirits among the Thai peoples', *Anthropos* 93: 3–17.

Graham, Daniel W. 2008. 'Heraclitus: Flux, order, and knowledge'. In *The Oxford Handbook of Presocratic Philosophy*, edited by Patricia Curd and Daniel W. Graham, 169–88. New York: Oxford University Press.

Hadot, Pierre. 1998. *The Inner Citadel: The meditations of Marcus Aurelius*. Cambridge, MA: Harvard University Press.

Hallisey, Charles. 1995. 'Roads taken and not taken in the study of Theravada Buddhism'. In *Curators of the Buddha*, edited by Donald Lopez, 31–61. Chicago: University of Chicago Press.

Hanna, Fred. 1995. 'Husserl on the teachings of the Buddha', *The Humanistic Psychologist* 23(3): 365–72.

Heidegger, Martin. 1962. *Being and Time* (translated by John Macquarrie and Edward Robinson). Oxford: Basil Blackwell.

Jirattikorn, Amporn. 2016. 'Buddhist holy man Khruba Bunchum: The shift in a millenarian movement at the Thailand–Myanmar border', *SOJOURN: Journal of Social Issues in Southeast Asia* 31(2): 377–412.

Lindahl, Jared R., Nathan E. Fisher, David J. Cooper, Rochelle K. Rosen and Willoughby B. Britton. 2017. 'The varieties of contemplative experience: A mixed-methods study of meditation-related challenges in Western Buddhists', *PloS ONE* 12(5): e0176239.

Mahaa-Parinibbaana Sutta (DN 16). 2013. Translated by Piyadassi Thera. In *The Three Basic Facts of Existence: I. Impermanence (Anicca). Access to Insight (BCBS Edition)*, 30 November.

Marlatt, G. Alan. 2002. 'Buddhist philosophy and the treatment of addictive behavior', *Cognitive and Behavioral Practice* 9(1): 44–50.

McDaniel, Justin. 2011. *The Lovelorn Ghost and the Magical Monk: Practicing Buddhism in modern Thailand*. New York: Columbia University Press.

Puriwanchana, Saipan. 2011. 'Following the Buddha's path: The Buddha's life story as the model for narrating the lives of *Phra Kechi Achan* (monks with mystical power) in Central Thailand', *Manusya: Journal of Humanities* 14(3): 1–20.

Rāhula, Walpola. 1974. *What the Buddha Taught*. New York: Grove Press.

Shah-Kazemi, Reza. 2010. *Common Ground between Islam and Buddhism*. Louisville, KY: Fons Vitae.

Skilling, Peter, Jason Carbine, Claudio Cicuzza and Santi Pakdeekham. 2012. *How Theravada Is Theravada? Exploring Buddhist identities*. Chiang Mai: Silkworm Books.

Tiyavanich, Kamala. 1997. *Forest Recollections: Wandering monks in twentieth-century Thailand*. Honolulu: University of Hawai'i Press.

Vajirañāṇavarorasa, HRH Supreme Patriarch Somdet Phra Mahā Samaṇa Chao Krom Phrayā, compiler. 1973. 'The ordination procedure and the preliminary duties of a new bhikkhu' (translated by Siri Buddhasukh and Phra Khantipàlo). Bangkok: King Mahà Makuta's Academy.

6
Holding on and letting go: Tanzanian Indians' responses to impermanence

Cecil Marie Schou Pallesen

In the years following Tanzanian independence, the rules for acquiring land were debated publicly. Instead of adhering to the pre-independence ideals of eliminating distinctions between 'natives' and 'non-natives', Saidi Maswanya, Minister for Lands, stated that African lands should be preserved for Africans and that Europeans and Asians could not acquire land 'in the tribal way without being [a] member of a tribe' (*Standard*, 18 June 1966, cited in Brennan 2012, 187). Maswanya's proclamation resulted from a growing resentment toward what President Nyerere called 'landlordism'. Indian houseowners, in Dar es Salaam in particular, were notorious for only renting out their properties to other Indians and not to *wananchi* ('indigenous'). Furthermore, due to a serious shortage of accommodation in the city, '[l]andlordism had been diagnosed as the principal evil of urban capitalism' (Brennan 2012, 190). Just two years after independence, in 1963, Nyerere proclaimed that private ownership of land was in conflict with the idea of *Ujamaa* or 'familyhood': the concept on which Nyerere based his vision of a socialist state. There was 'no room for the land parasites' (*Tanganyika Standard*, 16 April 1962, cited in Brennan 2012, 187). Thus, the Acquisition of Buildings Act of 1971 caused 2,482 buildings with a rental business or commercial property to be nationalised between 1971 and 1974 – 98 per cent of which were owned by Tanzanian Indians, many of whom held Tanzanian citizenship (Brennan 2012, 192). The nationalisations sparked a mass exodus of Tanzanian Indians. In 1962, there were 112,000 Indians in the country, falling to 85,000 in 1969 and 30,000 in 1984 (Oonk 2013, 219).

Based on 10 months of ethnographic fieldwork in Moshi, Tanzania, conducted between 2012 and 2016, this chapter takes its point of departure from the stories of two elderly Tanzanian Indian couples from the Jain community – Karan and Bhavana, and Manu and Deepa – whose lives were (and still are) deeply affected by nationalisations. Through their struggles to reclaim ownership of their nationalised houses, these couples, like many other Tanzanian Indians who stayed behind to look after their families' lost properties, fought a more fundamental battle to claim the legacy of the Indians in Tanzania, to honour their ancestors and to assert that Tanzanian Indians have the right to belong in Tanzania. But the struggle is also, as I show here, about securing and maintaining cultural purity in the Indian communities and not disappearing as a collective. And it is driven by an anxiety regarding permeability.

This chapter demonstrates how nationalisations triggered a fundamental change in the Tanzanian Indians' experience of time. Whereas the Indian communities settled permanently at the beginning of the twentieth century, built houses and established businesses, the time following the nationalisations was characterised by an experience of externally imposed impermanence and expectations that Indians' presence in Tanzania would come to an end. Tanzanian Indians responded to this new temporal 'horizon' (Koselleck 1979) with two parallel and somehow contradictory strategies: to claim their right to belong in Tanzania by holding on to their lost buildings, and to secure themselves by investing abroad, both socially and economically, and planning a potential future outside of the country. By holding on and letting go.

For Tanzanian Indians, Tanzania had, at the time of my fieldwork, become the only place where purity and 'Indianness' could be maintained and preserved, as India was seen as 'too developed' and the UK was a place of moral decay where one would 'lose the culture'. But Tanzania was also a nation that they felt they could not become legally part of; they were longing to be seen and accepted as good citizens who made a contribution to society. Thus, I argue, they were caught in a void where holding on meant staying in the position of undeserving 'foreigners', while letting go caused the cultural purity to crumble. And the nationalised houses had, at once, become physical monuments that witnessed the greatness and the fall of the Indian communities – concrete losses of value, heritage and legacy – and permeated personal places where anxiety and nostalgia quivered in the air. The houses embodied kinds of attachment that were simultaneously obstacles to progress and freedom as well as meaningful physical connections to a significant place.

Examining intimate experiences of the processes of holding on and letting go, this chapter foregrounds the intersections of postcolonial citizenship politics, transnational migrant mobility and the basic human longing for acceptance and recognition. It argues that the impermanence of the houses that physically attach Tanzanian Indians to Tanzania is painful because it is existential. The decay of the houses points to the disintegration of the communities and testifies to the making and unmaking of Indians as citizens of the nation-state.

Parasites

Indian merchants had been settling in East Africa since the mid-nineteenth century, when Omani rulers of Zanzibar invited them to stay (Heilman 1998; Burton 2013). A considerable number followed in the late nineteenth century when Gujarat was afflicted by drought and famine, and peasant farmers decided to try their luck across the ocean (Gregory 1993). The old trade ties made East Africa an obvious place to go (Bertz 2015). The Gujaratis first arrived in Madagascar, Zanzibar and Mombasa and slowly moved into the inlands of East Africa. They settled as *dukawallahs* (Hindi: 'shop owners') running small shops in villages and towns, and thus continued the merchant tradition of Indians in the region. In the transition from bartering to monetised transactions, which took place at the beginning of the twentieth century (Pandurang 2009, 50) and was encouraged by the British colonial administrators (Jones 2007, 18), the Indians played a central role. As the market was not very developed, it was a prosperous time for the *dukawallahs* to establish and expand their businesses (Burton 2013, 9–10). They became brokers with significant power, and, as their businesses developed, they became middlemen importing goods from Europe and India and selling them to Africans as well as Europeans (Pandurang 2009, 49). Qua their specific position in society, middleman minorities were able to support each other in ethnic networks and benefit from being 'strangers'[1] (Bonacich 1973; Brennan 2012; Kristiansen and Ryen 2002; Oonk 2013). In Tanzania, most Indians lived in close-knit religious communities and preferred to trade with community members or other Tanzanian Indians, and they continue to do so.

As 'father of the nation' (*baba wa taifa*) and 'teacher' (*mwalimu*), Nyerere launched his vision for a society built on the concept of *Ujamaa*, 'familyhood', in the Arusha Declaration of 1967 (Lal 2004, 1). His nation-building strategies and socialist convictions continue to be influential on

Tanzanian conceptions of belonging, morality and citizenship to this day (Fouéré 2014). At the core of *Ujamaa* was villagisation, the idea of a return to traditional African family and work structures, and an emphasis on equality and collectivity as national values (Fouéré 2014, 3). However, the aspirations of equality and collectivity appeared not to be capable of comprising all people living in Tanzania; and, in particular, the self-sufficient Indian communities were obstacles to the fulfilment of the vision. The nationalisations were partly a reaction to the Tanzanian Indians' role in society, which to a large degree was enforced by the British colonial administration (Brennan 2012). President Nyerere 'had no choice at [the time of] independence', he admitted in 1997. 'If he had left the economy to the private sector it would have become entirely Asian and there would have been racial conflict' (Tanzanian Affairs 1997).

In 1971, at the time of the nationalisations, John Mhaville, Minister of Housing, said, '(w)e must make a distinction between our enemies, who include all those who own buildings for exploitation, and their tenants who are among the people who are being exploited' (*Nationalist*, 23 April 1971, cited in Brennan 2012, 191). Meanwhile, Nyerere stated that 'landlordism is theft' (Nyerere's speech on building expropriation, 23

6.1   The number of people of Indian origin in Moshi has been declining since independence. Moshi, Tanzania, 2016. Photo: Cecil Marie Schou Pallesen.

April 1971, cited in Brennan 2012, 191). Landlordism was thus equated with *Unyonyaji* (exploitation, blood-sucking), and it was emphasised that the antidote to this was *Ujamaa* and *Uhuru* (independence, freedom) (Brennan 2012, 159). Tanzanian Indians and their role in society thus became a hindrance to the vision for the new, independent state's development, and nationalisations became a tool to wrest power from the strong and resourceful – and thus potentially dangerous – communities. For Tanzanian Indians, the reforms and public debate were frightening, and the dehumanisation that took place when they were referred to as 'parasites' and *wanyoniaji* ('suckers') (Brennan 2006), as well as Idi Amin's expulsion of Asians from Uganda in 1972, have been sources of great anxiety and fear in the Indian communities ever since.

But simultaneous with fear and anxiety was the feeling of deserving better, of having been neglected as 'good citizens'. Without exception, all my Tanzanian Indian interlocutors expressed satisfaction with, and pride in, the Indian communities' contributions to the country. 'They don't know how much we contributed,' they said, referring to the Africans and especially employees in public institutions such as the police, the municipality, the Tanzania Revenue Authority and the Immigration Department as well as politicians on different levels, who would 'harass' Tanzanian Indians by demanding bribes. By this, they meant that if the host community were aware of the contributions that the Indians had made in Tanzania, not least the hard work behind these contributions, the Indians would be honoured instead of harassed. After being sworn in in late 2015, President Magufuli decided that, instead of expensive celebrations on Independence Day, 9 December, all Tanzanians should spend the day cleaning the streets (DeFreese 2016), a practice resembling the Rwandan *Umuganda*, monthly communal work (Gundersen 2014).

As I was having breakfast one morning with Karan and Bhavana, Karan told me about Magufuli's proposal, which he had read about in the newspaper. His response was: 'If they knew how much we contributed, they would not ask us to clean the streets.' For Karan, the concept of compulsory communal work was an insult toward the Indian population in the country. How could the president demand that they, who had come as 'pioneers' and contributed extensively to the country's development, clean the streets? Karan kept his own plot tidy, and he made sure the street outside his shop was well maintained. He did not see any reason to engage in communal work. 'We have contributed enough,' he stated. In his view, Tanzanian Indians were anything but parasites.

Changing horizons

Identifying the 'horizon of expectation' as constituting the possibilities but also the limits of a human being's ability to see and grasp the world, Reinhardt Koselleck noted in his work on historicity that experience is 'present past, whose events have been incorporated and can be remembered. Within experience a rational reworking is included, together with unconscious modes of conduct which do not have to be present in awareness' (Koselleck 1979, 272). Expectation, on the other hand, is 'the future made present; it directs itself to the not-yet, to the nonexperienced, to that which is to be revealed. Hope and fear, wishes and desires, cares and rational analysis, receptive display and curiosity: all enter into expectation and constitute it' (Koselleck 1979, 272). The concepts we use to talk about events in the past 'provide the conditions by which our historical understanding becomes possible' (Pickering 2004, 274), and, hence, they frame what we know and what we expect.

Independence and the resulting reforms had become a temporal marker for the Tanzanian Indian communities of the division between 'then' and 'now' and thus a marker of a change of horizon. Younger writes that '[b]y the 1930s, the Asians living in East Africa realised that they were prospering and putting down roots. Unlike their parents, they intended to spend their life there and had no plans to go back to the dusty villages from which their parents had come' (Younger 2010, 215). 'Then' – the time before independence – was a time of prosperity and certainty. 'Now', after independence, was characterised by uncertainty, anxiety and disintegration. 'Then' was also a time when Indians settled permanently and built houses and established companies. 'Now', most Indians stayed in Tanzania knowing they would soon be leaving. The experiences that independence and nationalisations gave way to had radically changed their expectations for the future and thus also their way of living in the present. Many Tanzanian Indians invested in the UK and in the transnational religious communities while they lived their lives in Tanzania. My interlocutors called this practice of investing socially and economically in Tanzania and, simultaneously, abroad 'two feet' or 'having a foot in the door' (Pallesen 2017). Securing mobility by having multiple citizenships within each family, 'two feet' has made it possible for people to stay where it is most safe or comfortable. For many Indian families in Moshi, for example, 'two feet' has meant that the husband holding Tanzanian citizenship has continued running his shop or industry in Tanzania while the wife, with her British passport, has been able to keep the door to Europe open. Their children have inherited her British citizenship and have thus been able to go to the UK to study and work. The Indians' position in the margins has thus both been enforced by the surroundings and self-enforced by their communities as a way to secure themselves. And it is accompanied by a shallow and ambiguous way of belonging fuelled by anxiety just as much as self-sufficiency – a kind of belonging that has impermanence as a condition and is a critical strategy for creating fundamental social protection (Levitt et al. 2016).

While the future before independence looked prosperous and the horizon of expectation gave Tanzanian Indians the courage to invest their lives and resources in Tanzania, the kind of future they imagined and acted upon now was characterised by anxiety and, for some, almost hopelessness. As Manu told me in 2012, shortly before he and his wife Deepa moved to London:

> We're all a minority. Like now, in Tanzania, the Asian population is 0.02 per cent. So it is small . . . Even in work, we have to be careful. I mean, you can't be very criticising, with the government, you know, within the . . . The rules and all that . . . you can't always expect what you like to. Like the nationalisation thing, you know? The property was supposed to be nationalised on a sort of blanket basis, but most of the Africans, they got it back. But now, the Asian community, we have never been given back . . . Lifestyle was much better in East Africa, but the changes that were coming, you know there was a lot of harassment from the government in all three countries [Kenya, Uganda and Tanzania].

Deepa did not have much confidence in the surroundings either, and she was looking forward to settling into a new and, in her eyes, safer place. 'You have to be careful here,' she told me. 'Some people want to hurt you. And you never know what to expect from the authorities. Before the independence it was better, we felt safe then.'

Pre-independence, Indians formed the majority of town-dwellers in Moshi, and one could rely on 'law and order', an expression I often encountered during fieldwork. Bhavana recalled that era with a certain nostalgic smile in her eyes: 'At that time, there were only Indians living in Moshi. The double road was full of Indians, and only Indian shops. On Sundays, we used to go to the clock tower roundabout for picnics. Now they don't allow such things. And there are these young boys who will harass us if we sit there.' In contrast, 'now' was a time of uncertainty; the Tanzanian Indians did not enjoy the same privileges, and they had to share the town with African Tanzanians. When Bhavana was young, she and Karan lived with his parents and brothers, and their wives and children, in the same house where Bhavana and Karan now lived with their son and daughter-in-law. Walking around the garden surrounding the house, Bhavana showed me where the women used to sit on blankets with their children in the shadow of the mango tree. In December, the tree would produce an abundance of sweet mangoes. It was old now and not giving much fruit, Bhavana told me with regret in her voice. The past was, in the minds of many Indians, symbolised by fertility and accumulation: the communities were full of families with children, the businesses were expanding, the fortunes were growing – and even the mango trees gave high returns. The investments of the Indians grew, and their fruit ripened and could be harvested. Now, everything was different. Tanzania was not fertile ground anymore.

Valuing the past was a general tendency among Tanzanian Indians. From their standpoint, the expectations for the future were vague and unpredictable, and, in the absence of a tangible horizon, the past was pervasive. In a present where everything the Tanzanian Indians knew and trusted had crumbled, and where the horizon did not give rise to hopefulness, it seemed attractive to return to the past. Nostalgia seemed to permeate my interlocutors' expectations. Discussing nostalgia, Hutcheon writes that 'it is the past as imagined, as idealized through memory and desire. In this sense, however, nostalgia is less about the past than about the present' (Hutcheon and Valdés 1998, 3). The persistent longing for the past points toward the anxieties of the present. Nostalgia processed the painful realisation of the Tanzanian Indians that things had changed and that certain things were not forever. 'Nostalgia, in fact, may depend precisely on the *irrecoverable* nature of the past for its emotional impact and appeal. It is the very inaccessibility that likely accounts for a large part of nostalgia's power' (Hutcheon and Valdés 1998, 3).

The loss

One sunny morning in 1972, Karan and his family read in the local newspaper that the townhouse owned by Karan's mother, from which they were running a shop, was now national property and would be administered by the National Housing Corporation (NHC).

Many Indian families in Tanzania and Kenya decided to keep one or two family members based in the newly independent states to look after their nationalised properties and businesses (Oonk 2013, 218). This was also the case with several of my male interlocutors, including Manu and Karan. Some of them accepted the loss of the property; some refused to do so. Among the latter was Karan, who fought to get his mother's property back. Karan's mother lived on the first floor of the house and his brother ran a shop on the lower floor, which is why the house was nationalised in 1972.[2] Following nationalisation, Karan's brother moved into the house and paid rent to the NHC. By doing this, the family could maintain their status as 'former owners' of the property. Later, Bhavana's sister and her husband took over the apartment and Karan and Bhavana ran the shop. The sister and her husband then decided to move to the UK. When Karan and Bhavana, who continued to pay the rent for the apartment, realised their family would not be coming back from the UK, they moved in themselves. This was their only option if they wanted to keep the lease. When, in 2013, the NHC suddenly raised the monthly rent from TZS 900 (approximately USD 0.5) to TZS 500,000 (approximately USD 214), Karan took the corporation to court. He wanted to reclaim the ownership of his mother's house without being subjected to the NHC's escalating rents. He followed his lawyer's advice to stop paying rent while the trial was ongoing but, after six months without rent, representatives of the NHC prised open the outer metal door grille, kicked in the door and took everything from the apartment. Karan and Bhavana stood paralysed in the backyard as they watched their possessions being stacked on a big truck. 'Then I hired a new lawyer,' Karan said. 'I was afraid our first lawyer was collaborating with the NHC'.

'Karan paid the new lawyer lots and lots of money,' Bhavana told me one evening in 2016 while Karan was watching television and we were talking at the other end of the house. 'I told him to let go. We have lost so much money to this house. But he is stubborn. And he insists on paying back his brothers their share of their parents' company.' It had been three years since Karan and Bhavana were evicted from the apartment. After nine months, their furniture and possessions were returned to them and were now stored in different rooms in the house that Karan grew up in and where Karan and Bhavana had been living together with Karan's family since their marriage. They had obviously paid a significant amount of money to get their possessions back. Bhavana showed me cupboards, piles of mattresses, old stickers from the family's factory that had also been nationalised, chairs, tables, vases, china. The hallway was full of chairs, bureaus and dressers. Since everyone else from the family had left Tanzania, except Karan, Bhavana, their son and daughter-in-law, there was room enough for storage. But what was the future for all these things? Bhavana did not know. But Karan insisted on keeping them.

Even though Karan and Bhavana had been evicted from their apartment, they had continued to run their shop downstairs in Karan's mother's nationalised house. For Karan, this had been a way to continuously claim ownership. Some months after the return of their belongings, the couple had become accepted as ex-owners and now had the right to live in the house at a low rent. However, the African tenant who lived upstairs could not be evicted, so they had to wait until he left of his own will. 'You know, the problem is that he is working for Corruption Prevention,' Karan explained, pointing to the ceiling one day when we were in his shop. With a wry smile, he said quietly:

> He moved in the same day as the NHC removed our things from the apartment. They obviously had a tenant ready to take over. But after the trial, the NHC accepted that we are ex-owners and that we can stay here without paying rent. Now we are just waiting for him to move. But as he is working for Corruption Prevention, we cannot just pay him to move.

Until the tenant moved out, then, they would stay in their family house on the outskirts of town and simultaneously inhabit the nationalised house by opening their shop on the ground floor every day and filling it with the smell of home-cooked Gujarati food that Bhavana would bring at noon, along with flowers from their garden, pictures of Karan's late parents and the sound of Jain chanting that Bhavana would put on the CD player behind the desk. The claim was persistent, and the attempt to hold on to the house was palpable. Karan and Bhavana held on to the material remains of Karan's family's legacy and to the desire to be treated as lawful citizens in the country where they were born.

We feel nowhere

Many buildings in Moshi carry the names of their investors: Haria, Khambhaita, Patel, Sudhir. The names are inscribed in the concrete of the façades, but, on some buildings, the names have been changed or even removed. On one symmetrical, yellow building that houses a shop called 'Baby Junction' and features a hand-painted sign with the shop name and an elephant, a duck, and Mickey and Minnie Mouse over the door, there is a striking white oval plate in the middle of the façade. It is obvious that two words and a year have been removed; now the only trace left of the builder is three painted spots, which are a brighter shade of white than the background of the plate. On a large, pink two-storey building in the vicinity of the town centre, the name '*amed affer Dhanji*' was marked in large concrete letters. Between '*amed*' and '*affer*' was the logo of the NHC. After having passed this building numerous times without noticing that some of the letters were missing, one day, I met a man who told me he was a descendant of an influential Indian businessman named Muhamed Jaffer Dhanji. I then realised that the building carried certain legacies. It had been nationalised, and someone had removed 'Muh' and 'J' from the façade. The missing letters indicated that Mr Dhanji had lost his property and thus lost control of its appearance and, not least, his name on it.

At the same time, however, all the Indian buildings and all the Indian names on their façades were traces of the past; they were forms of persistence that continuously manifested the Indians' (former) power. The houses were decaying and disappearing, in the eyes of their former owners, but they were also places of becoming where African Tanzanian traders developed their businesses and where families lived their lives in concrete frames shaped by Indians. Thus, the concrete had permanent qualities; the houses are still there (Figure 6.2). But, for the Indians, the temporal break that nationalisation constituted marked a turning point at which a process of decay had begun and their permanent properties and belongings became impermanent. Thus, the buildings did not have any

6.2 Many nationalised houses are marked with the National Housing Corporation's logo. Moshi, Tanzania, 2016. Photo: Cecil Marie Schou Pallesen.

future-oriented qualities for the Indians; they did not figure as assets in their horizon of expectation. Rather, they continually dragged their former owners' attention back to the past and its lost potentials. The buildings were constant reminders that what seemed to be permanent turned out not to be, that belonging and belongings were concepts that offered no certainty to those with an Indian background living in Tanzania.

But, as Tanzanian Indians have been notorious for their success in private business and, responsible to a large degree, for the development of trade in the region (Heilman 1998, 380), the nationalisation of buildings containing rental businesses and shops also inflicted a serious wound to vital parts of the communities. 'Business is in our blood' was a common saying among the Tanzanian Indians, and, with African Tanzanians slowly but steadily entering the market and moving into former Indian houses with new and modern shops, the very visual and tangible development was painful for many Tanzanian Indians who felt they had lost their identity. One day in 2012, Deepa explained to me the complex feeling of not fully belonging, of being 'nowhere':

> Cecil: Would you call yourself Indian?
> Deepa: Yeah.
> Cecil: Have you been to India?
> Deepa: No, not yet.
> Cecil: There are a lot of people living here who feel that they are Indian, but India itself is very far away, also in their mind.
> Deepa: We are born here.
> Cecil: Yeah. So this is your home?
> Deepa: But we haven't seen India. Even we don't feel like Indians. So we sometimes feel nowhere. By birth, we are Tanzanian, but living here sometimes we feel we are outsiders, second-class citizens, not first-class. So sometimes we think we are nowhere. Even in London, it is not our hometown. It is the second. Even then it is like we don't belong . . . Even at the shop here in Moshi, sometimes they treat us like that.

Svetlana Boym writes: 'The fantasies of the past determined by the needs of the present have a direct impact on the realities of the future' (Boym 2011). The nostalgia and longing for a time before independence also drive a desire to be *someone, somewhere*. When Deepa said 'we feel nowhere', she also characterised the void left for many Tanzanian Indians following the marginalisation in society and disintegration of the communities that nationalisation had brought about. Without prospering businesses, without properties, without strong communities, who were they?

Injustice

Manu and Deepa left Moshi in 2013. In the run-up to their relocation to London, Manu struggled to win back ownership of his family's house to be able to sell it. The NHC logo, a huge sun rising behind a house, almost resembling an explosion, was painted on the front of Manu and Deepa's house. Marking a house that was taken away from its owners as part of a political project, the logo indicated that the building was a contested space and suggested both prosperity and despair. Manu's parents, whose photographs hung on the wall in the living room, claimed the family's ownership of the building from their place above the sofa, and Deepa and Manu were intent on fighting their quiet battle with the authorities until what they felt entitled to was returned to them. Manu told me:

> This house we live in has not been given back. I mean the whole building belongs . . . used to belong to my father. It was nationalised. So the part in which we live, we got a part-lease, that's sort of a joint lease with the government agency, which is managing all the government properties, which were nationalised. So, this part-lease, it's like . . . not a normal lease, where the government gives, you know, so this is your land, and this is this thing, you know . . . while we stay here, it's ours. If we leave, then the government takes over. Yeah. You can't sell it or something like that. First, this year, they have passed [a law] that now we can sell it but, again, it is not direct sale. And we have to go through the National Housing Corporation and get permission from them. So it is still, you know, there is this sort of discrimination like that, and we have to live with it. Yeah? These are the few things that made our children go away, they didn't want to get into this hazard. Because in Europe it's, like, what is law is law. You have to follow law properly, and you get your rights also . . . This nationalisation thing, you know, it affected us a lot. We couldn't build, we were never sure of our future. For those who stayed behind like us . . . we couldn't progress that much (September 2012).

HOLDING ON AND LETTING GO 95

The atmosphere in the Indian communities in Tanzania that Manu grew up in had changed dramatically during the 1960s and 70s. Manu and Deepa decided to try to regain control over their lives and future and sent their son to the UK to go to college. They bought a house in London and would follow their son some years later. However, they did not leave Moshi before they had succeeded in reclaiming part-ownership of Manu's parents' house. At the beginning of 2013, Manu finally accomplished his mission and was able to sell the part of the house where he and Deepa had been living. The shop at the other end of the building was still the NHC's property.

I returned to Moshi in 2015. Deepa and Manu's house was now inhabited by the African Tanzanian man who bought it. Apparently, not much had changed, except for the Chinese building that had been rising behind the backyard, now completed, and housing offices and a new supermarket. Prominent signs advertised vacant office spaces on the upper floors, and a big car park signalled expectations of a prosperous future. Manu and Deepa's house seemed tiny in comparison. In May 2016, however, when I went back for a short piece of follow-up fieldwork, I could not even recognise the house. Blue and red stripes covered the upper part of the building, and, in the middle, red and blue letters spelled out 'Modern Driving School'. The staff let me take a look around.

Manu and Deepa's heavy wooden chest of drawers was still standing to the right-hand side of the front door, where it had always been. This was where they would take the keys from when someone knocked on the door, and they would unlock the inner door and the padlocks on the outer door grille. Behind the house, Deepa's garden, which he used to look after so carefully and was full of plants, vegetables, flowers and herbs, was now a cemetery for three cars and a minibus, all with punctured tyres. No one had cut the grass or pruned the trees for months. The veranda was full of discarded furniture and carpets; and the ceiling, covered in large damp patches, was hanging down at one end, threatening to collapse. I took pictures and sent them to Manu on Facebook. He replied that he missed the house and that Karan could tell me much more about the fight to regain ownership. 'Try to imagine how we must have felt when the very house in which we lived was nationalised. Your lifetime's savings all gone with the stroke of a pen,' he wrote. Obviously, Manu had a love for Tanzania and his house. But, at the same time, it was clear from his reply that, just as much as the house was the place of a former 'home', it had also become a materialisation of feelings of injustice, loss and disappointment. The house was not only Manu's but also represented his parents' lifetime savings, and thus the lost house was a manifestation of the end of the family's legacy.

Losing the culture

In London, Manu and Deepa enjoyed life in the house where they lived with their son, daughter-in-law and granddaughter. But their history of being houseowners in Tanzania and victims of the nationalisation pursued them, and they lived with the feeling of having been treated unjustly in their former home country. At the same time, they had to accept that the future of the community, and the future of their son, daughter-in-law and granddaughter, would be dramatically different from the life they had been living and planning in Tanzania. It was simply not possible for them to uphold the level of cultural purity that had been the norm in Moshi. Despite the strength of the community network, the dispersal of people across borders and the influence from Western culture created permeability.

The continuous emigration of Tanzanian Indians signalled the end of close-knit communities as Manu and Deepa had known them since they were born. The fear of 'losing our culture' was often articulated among my interlocutors, and, in particular, moving to the UK or the US was expected to disturb the maintenance of 'culture'. In the West, the lifestyle was 'too busy'; women did not stay at home with their children, and the children would not learn to speak Gujarati, to cook Gujarati food, or to go to the temple or mosque as they did in Moshi. The next generation would not be as Indian as their parents and grandparents who grew up in East Africa:

> Inside the Jain temple, in the hall, the men are making cakes. They know exactly how to do it; they have obviously done it many times before. 'This type of cake we only make for this special occasion every year,' Manu tells me. I ask him if they use a recipe. He answers that they just know how to do it. They learned it from their parents. Two of the men are sitting around a huge copper bowl. Flour, sugar and other ingredients are already in the bowl and now two of the other men are pouring burning hot ghee into it. The sitting men put their fingers in the ingredients and mix them. They are screaming in pain. The other men look very satisfied and are laughing a bit. Obviously, the pain is part of the tradition. I ask the men if their children in the UK know how to make these cakes. 'No', they say.

'They are too busy, you know. They will buy it in the shops' (November 2012, fieldnotes).

India, on the other hand, was referred to as a place of purity and authenticity; but, at the same time, contemporary India was described as 'too modern' and 'too Western' and as a chaotic country with a lot of corruption. The idea of India was an imaginary of a place and a way of being rather than a concrete place of reference. Accordingly, India served as a backdrop against which the idea of the purity and superiority of the Indians endured and was legitimised. However, this 'India' was not contemporary India but an India that did not exist anymore, and which perhaps never existed: the majority of Indians arrived in East Africa in the late eighteenth or early nineteenth century, and, according to Hansen, '(t)he imagination of a unified Indian nation only gained popular momentum from the 1930s onward' (Hansen 2012, 200). Thus, East Africa was the only place where it was possible to uphold the right level of Indianness, through a traditional lifestyle and cultural purity.

Manu and Deepa had chosen to move to London despite the risk of losing the culture. When I visited them there in 2013, they were only rarely attending the local Jain temple. The place for community gatherings and worship that had been the centre of their everyday lives in Moshi was now not so central anymore; they had to drive 20 km through London to get there and would rather stay at home. And, whereas Deepa had always stayed at home and made sure the food was cooked in the right way and typically dressed in a sari, her daughter-in-law now went to work in her business suit and had dinner and drinks with her friends after work. Something had come to an end; something was lost. But Manu and Deepa seemed to have altered their expectations for the future and were slowly accepting the consequences. Karan and Bhavana, on the other hand, stayed in Moshi and were reluctant to give up their lifestyle. Even though they felt 'harassed', a concept widely used by Tanzanian Indians to characterise everything from small-scale bribery demands to theft, political marginalisation and nationalisation, it was important to them to stay and look after the temple and Karan's mother's house. Bhavana had even become preoccupied with reading religious texts and chanting in the temple. After many community members had left, she was in charge of the *poojas* (ceremonial worship ritual). Manu and Deepa were slowly letting go, while Bhavana and Karan insistently kept holding on. They felt they had lost enough.

Permeability

The loss of houses during nationalisation was not only a loss of property and resources but also a loss of concrete barriers around families and communities. The houses were slowly decaying while in the NHC's custody. Karan and Bhavana observed with anxiety how Karan's mother's nationalised house perished. They did not think the NHC looked after the house with the same care as they would have, and while they waited for the tenant upstairs to move out, the concrete crumbled away. Similarly, Manu and Deepa had been complaining about the state of their house and the NHC's lack of a will to do something about it.

Losing control of their houses also meant that the former owners had had to accept that other people moved in and used the premises. In general, the houses function as safe, protective spaces for women in the Tanzanian Indian communities, where 'Indianness' is kept alive through traditional cooking, language and religious activities. In these houses, purity is preserved; women are expected (to a much greater degree than men) to adhere to traditional values and not 'mix' with African Tanzanians, and the growing feeling of vulnerability has only enhanced the tendency of the Indians toward cultural and social isolation (Nagar 1998). According to Richa Nagar, the development of Tanzanian society since independence has given rise to a renewed focus on purity – concerning women's purity in particular:

> While communal purity previously implied both sexual and ritual purity, in the post-colonial period more emphasis came to be placed on Asian women's sexual purity and on the guarding of racial, religious, and caste-based frontiers against contamination by intercommunal sexual relationships . . . as the balance of power between Asian and African communities shifted in the post-colonial period, relationships between Asian women and African men became more threatening than ever to Asian men (Nagar 1998, 133).

Men's control over women's bodies, grounded in a culture of domesticity, has been a dominant power structure intended to avoid mixing (Pandurang 2009, 58). The house was thus a protective sphere that safeguarded women but also the families' honour and the communities' cohesion; hence, the loss of houses represented a more fundamental loss of cultural protection and control. The houses are in female spheres but, at the same time, they are men's domains (Figure 6.3). They are built and

6.3 The houses are female spheres but at the same time they are men's domains. Moshi, Tanzania, 2016. Photo: Cecil Marie Schou Pallesen.

administered by men, men run their businesses in the buildings, and it is the men for whom it is important to fight with the authorities to claim back ownership: a claim for justice and economic gain, but also a claim for specific places where purity and tradition are maintained.

Several times during fieldwork, I heard Tanzanian Indians express that African Tanzanians' 'blood is too mixed'. This was a way to describe and explain why it was inappropriate for Indians to mix with them. They were impure and would pollute the Indian communities. Correspondingly, many African Tanzanians ate meat and drank alcohol – Kilimanjaro Region is famous for its *nyama choma*, grilled meat – and most Tanzanian Indians did not drink alcohol, while Hindus and Jains were vegetarians. Thus, when African Tanzanians moved into the nationalised houses and inhabited them with their possessions, cooked meat in the kitchens, drank alcohol and made the house a part of themselves, the Indians' previously protective houses became polluted and lost their ability to protect. The houses did not form a secure barrier for the communities anymore, as they had become permeable.

Catherine Allerton writes that *permeability*, the ability of sounds, smells, smoke and people to travel through walls and roofing, is defining for Manggarai houses in Indonesia, and is a positive feature (Allerton 2013). The way in which my interlocutors talked about the decay of their houses resembled how they talked about the slow but steady disappearance of their communities in Tanzania and the decline of Indian influence in Tanzania in general: with anxiety and regret. These processes of decay and permeation are parallel and intersecting, and the impermanence of the concrete spurs a feeling of existential impermanence and anxiety about the future.

Seeing social structures and cosmology in the organisation and thinking of houses, as Lévi-Strauss (1983) and Bourdieu (1970) did, continues to be relevant. As Carsten and Hugh-Jones point out, '[i]f people construct houses and make them in their own image, so also do they use these houses and house images to construct themselves as individuals and groups' (Carsten and Hugh-Jones 1995, 3). The houses of both Karan and Manu had shifted from being female spheres protecting purity and Indianness to being centres of lengthy lawsuits run entirely by the men. The houses had changed from closed to open, from solid to permeable, from private to public; meanwhile, the communities had dispersed to several continents and the traditional lifestyle was threatened.

Among the Zafimaniry people in Madagascar, a house that is built by newlyweds is fragile at first and hardens over time as the couple inhabit it and continue building it. It ends up being an almost sacred source of blessings for descendants of the couple who built it (Bloch 1995). For the Tanzanian Indians, the process has two different directions. As in Madagascar, the house 'hardens' and increases in value over time as its builders in the past carry a certain legitimacy. But, at the same time, because the houses were acquired by the state and not taken care of very well, they have become soft and fragile. The quality of the house changes as the surroundings and the use of the house change, and, in the process, the people of the house change as well. An Indian man in Tanzania who loses the house built by his parents loses much more than a house: he loses a protective space for his wife and children, his status as a houseowner, his economic security and the heritage from his parents. The decay not only threatens to damage the buildings but also destabilises the former houseowners and the Indian communities in general. For the descendants of the Indians who settled and established homes and businesses, a massive change of horizon had materialised in the buildings, and every day they were reminded of their status as 'others' in Tanzania when watching the concrete transformations.

Holding on

Houses are continuously recreated as places, and people continuously reconfigure themselves and their position and opportunities in the community and society. Feelings of belonging are built on experiences of the past as well as expectations of potential futures, and, for Indians in Moshi, they interact with the continuous changes brought about by decay and emigration.

For both Manu and Karan, the nationalised houses were not just *their* properties but also their late parents' and their families' properties. Being in the house was also being with ancestors, their work and investment – the legacy of Indians in Tanzania. The houses were places full of meaning. But just as much as it was a legacy, it was also a source of anger, injustice and disappointment. Karan had a guilty conscience about not being able to care for the house as he would have done, had it not been taken away from the family. Being the last family member in Moshi, Karan felt obliged to look after the family's property, and he was unfailingly committed to not losing more. In his home, excess furniture and other possessions were stored and stacked, as if he expected a return to a time when they would be put to use again. For him as well as numerous other Indian men who stayed behind to look after their family's lost property, the houses helped them create some sense of their presence in Tanzania and maintain a focus on their right to be in the country where they had lived their whole life. The houses were meaningful attachments to a certain place and a certain nation. While the protracted and dramatic fight with the NHC was a source of frustration and worry in Karan's daily life, reminding him of the uncertainty and insecurity experienced by Tanzanian Indians, it also seemed to create meaning in his life in Moshi. The case was a statement of his claim for justice and appreciation as a citizen. Karan inhabited the house every day by opening up his shop and taking his place in it. He and Bhavana would make the house *lively* (Allerton 2013).

Inhabiting the house became a way to create meaning in their lives, just as claiming the concrete walls had become their – and especially Karan's – identity. Thus, they continued to honour the legacy of the family, and Karan hoped that, one day, he would be able to sell the house and achieve a reasonable price so that he could pay his brothers their respective shares. He was continuously trying to protect and maintain the family and its legacy despite the decay and permeability that both threatened their house and characterised the household scattered around the globe. The decay was shameful for Karan. It was shameful not to be able to continue the business empire. But, by fighting relentlessly with the authorities and reaffirming his claim to ownership, Karan sought to sustain a status and a self-image, and an image of his family and community, that, in fact, belonged to a long-gone past. The concrete walls were the material manifestation of a certain past, which many Tanzanian Indians, like Karan, had to hold onto to find a place to dwell. And simultaneously, they would all think of potential alternative futures: retirement in London with a freedom pass for public transport and soft carpets under their feet.

Conclusion

Independence and, in particular, the nationalisations that came with it constituted a radical turning point for Tanzanian Indians. These events mark a dividing line between two distinctive spaces of experience that each gave way to different horizons of expectation. Facing a new horizon, Tanzanian Indians lost their faith in a prosperous future in the country where they had grown up; and, fearing they would be let down by the state, they began to look for ways to secure themselves. Thus, since the nationalisations, many have practised what they call 'two feet' and have invested in Tanzania and abroad simultaneously. However, letting go of the nationalised buildings has been, and still is, difficult for many ex-owners, for whom the houses materialise their family's legacy and the Indians' contributions to the nation. But, as I have argued in this chapter, the houses also represent security, forming solid barriers around the families and communities; they protect the female spheres where traditions and 'culture' are being maintained. The fear of 'losing the culture' in this way coincides with the decay of the buildings, and thus a general moral and cultural decay. Through the stories of Karan and Bhavana, and Deepa and Manu, I have shown how both persistence and discontinuity influence the lives of those who left and those who stayed. Accepting that their traditional way of living and their role in society had come to an end, that what seemed permanent turned out to be changeable, was difficult and gave way to certain kinds of letting go and holding on. For a migrant group shaped by old trade systems, colonialism and post-colonial Africanism, the feeling of 'being nowhere', not being seen as belonging anywhere, seems to be pervasive.

Hannah Arendt introduced the notion of 'the right to have rights' (Arendt 1973). Her own experience, along with that of countless other stateless subjects in the years before, during and after World War II, showed how basic human rights are not so much based on a subject's membership of the human race, on humanity, as on membership of a political community – on citizenship. Building on this notion, Allison Kesby writes:

> In the present international system of states, it is imperative that each person has a 'place in the world' in the sense of a place of lawful residence and is not constantly shunted between states. At this moment, each one of us is situated at some point on the globe. Yet some of us will be, or be considered to be, 'in place' and others 'out of place'. We are not only located physically, but legally, because how our physical presence is characterized turns on our legal status (Kesby 2012, 13).

For the Tanzanian Indians who stayed behind when the majority left, the reclaiming of the nationalised houses has also been a way to assert a 'place in the world' and a persistent claim for the right to have rights. Throughout the experiences of disintegration and impermanence, the loss of property, material and moral decay, and the dispersal of families and communities, it has been, and still is, essential for them to be recognised for their and their ancestors' contributions to Tanzania and for what they had to let go.

Notes

1   It is important to note that the concept of 'middleman minorities' is problematic in its Eurocentric essence that does not take them seriously as people with their own agendas and strategies. Oonk argues that, for the Indians, the Europeans were the middlemen conveying a connection to European markets (Oonk 2013, 4).
2   Houses with a rental business or commercial property were part of a greater nationalisation scheme.

References

Allerton, Catherine. 2013. *Potent Landscapes: Place and mobility in Eastern Indonesia*. Honolulu: University of Hawai'i Press.
Arendt, Hannah. 1973 [1951]. *The Origins of Totalitarianism*. New York: Harcourt.
Bertz, Ned. 2015. *Diaspora and Nation in the Indian Ocean: Transnational histories of race and urban space in Tanzania*. Honolulu: University of Hawai'i Press.
Bloch, Maurice. 1995. 'The resurrection of the house amongst the Zafimaniry of Madagascar'. In *About the House: Lévi-Strauss and beyond*, edited by Janet Carsten and Stephen Hugh-Jones, 69–83. Cambridge: Cambridge University Press.
Bonacich, Edna. 1973. 'A theory of middleman minorities', *American Sociological Review* 38(5): 583–94.

Bourdieu, Pierre. 1970. 'The Berber house or the world reversed', *Social Science Information* 9(2): 151–70.

Boym, Svetlana. 2011. 'Nostalgia'. In *Atlas of Transformation*. http://monumenttotransformation.org/atlas-of-transformation/html/n/nostalgia/nostalgia-svetlana-boym.html (last accessed 27 October 2021).

Brennan, James R. 2006. 'Blood enemies: Exploitation and urban citizenship in the nationalist political thought of Tanzania, 1958–75', *The Journal of African History* 47(3): 389–413.

Brennan, James. 2012. *Taifa: Making nation and race in urban Tanzania*. Athens, OH: Ohio University Press.

Burton, Eric. 2013. '"... what tribe should we call him?" The Indian diaspora, the state and the nation in Tanzania since ca. 1850', *Stichproben–Wiener Zeitschrift für kritische Afrikastudien* 13(25): 1–28.

Carsten, Janet, and Stephen Hugh-Jones. 1995. *About the House: Lévi-Strauss and beyond*. Cambridge: Cambridge University Press.

DeFreese, Michelle. 2016. 'Is Magufuli the region's next Kagame?' *Huffington Post*, May. http://www.huffingtonpost.com/young-professionals-in-foreign-policy/is-magufuli-the-regions-n_b_9982846.html (last accessed 27 October 2021).

Fouéré, Marie-Aude. 2014. 'Julius Nyerere, ujamaa, and political morality in contemporary Tanzania', *African Studies Review* 57(1): 1–24.

Gregory, Robert. 1993. *South Asians in East Africa: An economic and social history, 1890–1980*. Oxford: Westview Press.

Gundersen, Ingvild 2014. 'Umuganda: A tool for reconciliation in Rwanda'. *TransConflict*. http://www.transconflict.com/2014/03/umuganda-tool-reconciliation-rwanda-263/ (last accessed 27 October 2021).

Hansen, Thomas Blom. 2012. *Melancholia of Freedom: Social life in an Indian township in South Africa*. Princeton, NJ: Princeton University Press.

Heilman, Bruce. 1998. 'Who are the indigenous Tanzanians? Competing conceptions of Tanzanian citizenship in the business community', *Africa Today* 45(3/4): 369–87.

Hutcheon, Linda, and Mario J. Valdés. 1998. 'Irony, nostalgia, and the postmodern: A dialogue', *Poligrafías* 3: 29–54.

Jones, Stephanie. 2007. 'Merchant-kings and everymen: Narratives of the South Asian diaspora of East Africa', *Journal of Eastern African Studies* 1(1): 16–33.

Kesby, Alison. 2012. *The Right to Have Rights: Citizenship, humanity, and international law*. Oxford: Oxford University Press.

Koselleck, Reinhart. 1979. *Futures Past: On the semantics of historical time*, translated by Keith Tribe. New York: Columbia University Press.

Kristiansen, Stein, and Anne Ryen. 2002. 'Enacting their business environments: Asian entrepreneurs in East Africa', *African and Asian Studies* 1(3): 166–86.

Lal, Brij V. 2004. *Bittersweet: An Indo-Fijian experience*. Canberra: Pandanus Books.

Lévi-Strauss, Claude. 1983. *The Way of the Masks*. London: Jonathan Cape.

Levitt, Peggy, Jocelyn Viterna, Armin Mueller and Charlotte Lloyd. 2016. 'Transnational social protection: Setting the agenda', *Oxford Development Studies* 45(1): 2–19.

Nagar, Richa. 1998. 'Communal discourses, marriage, and the politics of gendered social boundaries among South Asian immigrants in Tanzania', *Gender, Place & Culture: A Journal of Feminist Geography* 5(2): 117–39.

Oonk, Gijsbert. 2013. *Settled Strangers: Asian business elites in East Africa (1800–2000)*. New Delhi: Sage Publications.

Pallesen, Cecil Marie Schou. 2017. '"Two feet" as citizenship strategy: An anthropological perspective on instrumental approaches to citizenship among people of Indian origin in Tanzania', *Journal of the Indian Ocean Region* 13(3): 297–310.

Pandurang, Mala. 2009. 'Scrutinising the past: A review of socio-literary narratives of the East African Asian diasporic experience', *South Asian Diaspora* 1(1): 47–61.

Pickering, Michael. 2004. 'Experience as horizon: Koselleck, expectation and historical time', *Cultural Studies* 18(2–3): 271–89.

Tanzanian Affairs. 1997. 'CCM to win next time too?' Issue 58, September. https://www.tzaffairs.org/category/issue-number/issue-58/ (last accessed 20 October 2021).

Younger, Paul. 2010. *New Homelands: Hindu communities in Mauritius, Guyana, Trinidad, South Africa, Fiji, and East Africa*. New York: Oxford University Press.

Part 2
States of being and becoming

7
A Melanesian impermanence
Joe Nalo

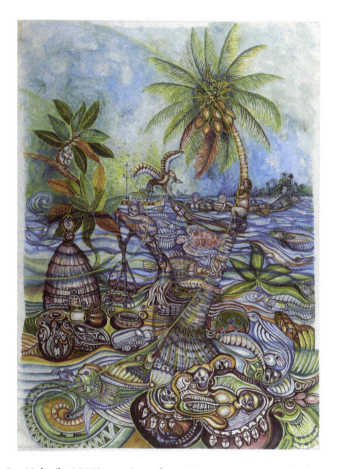

7.1 Joe Nalo (b. 1950), a painter from Manus, Papua New Guinea, who lives and works in Port Moresby, provides his vision of impermanence that includes the environment, plants, animals, humans, spirits, artefacts and technology.

8
'We are not an emblem': impermanence and materiality in Asmat lifeworlds

Anna-Karina Hermkens and Jaap Timmer

While people in contemporary European societies tend to prioritise notions of permanence in such domains as cultural heritage and development, in Melanesia,[1] notions of inevitable decay, loss, destruction and renewal prevail (Hermkens 2019). Among the Asmat people of West Papua, for example, lifecycle rituals and ritual cycles of headhunting were aimed at securing life force, *ji* or *ti* (van der Schoot 1969, 46) for constant renewal while *tes*, as an 'ethical mediation', similar to *mana* (Tomlinson and Tengan 2016, 20), was necessary to keep the cosmos in balance (Costa 2020, 64). As a meta-term pertaining to the Pacific region, *mana* is arguably most accurately defined by Valerio Valeri, as an 'invisible substance' that is 'the efficacy of a working "fellowship"', such as reciprocal relations with gods or ancestors (Valeri 1985, 99; see also Tomlinson and Tengan 2016). For Asmat, *mana* was gained through headhunting and, when successfully perpetuated through ritual cycles, would ensure society's and individual's *tes* ('bravery', 'success', 'power', 'charisma', 'prestige').[2] Carvings of deceased people that were used during the related ceremonies were completed once these objects were left to decay, or destroyed, to release and perpetuate the life force of the dead.

In this chapter, we focus on what happens when such cultural logics of impermanence are pushed toward what Asmat perceive as permanence. This permanence has been engendered through pacification implemented through missionisation, government policies, museums and art collectors. Asmat understanding of the term 'pacification' resembles its general definition as 'a process, in the course of which the state [and/or mission and art collectors] enforces its legitimate monopoly of power and brings wars between politically autonomous local groups to an end' (Helbling 2006, 128). Asmat people's reflections on, and conceptualisations of, pacification highlight both the colonial and postcolonial processes that have brought (and continue to bring) Asmat society 'under control', thereby creating an order of things experienced by Asmat as permanent or static. We will explore the perspectives of two Asmat men who reflect on the loss of *tes* and, concurrently, the importance of impermanence in relation to concerns about the future (and past) of their societies.

For Asmat, as for many other Melanesians, their cultural and social identity is entangled with 'things'. Prominent Melanesianists such as Roy Wagner (1991) and Marilyn Strathern (1988, 1999) have argued that things transacted as gifts constitute personhood and relationships. In other words, pearl shells and beads, but also pigs, human blood, semen and so on, are part of people's relational compositions. It is through the materiality and manipulation of these and other objects that persons and relationships are constituted, mediated and terminated (Hermkens 2019). Strathern claims that distinctions exist between persons but not so much between persons and things (Strathern 1999, 181). Her line of argument is that objects 'do not reify society or culture; they reify capacities contained in persons/relations' (Strathern 1999, 14). This constitutive relation between people and things is continuously reworked in the context of lifecycle rituals, such as initiation and mortuary rites, where the life-trajectory of humans is mediated through the manipulation of things (Hermkens 2013, 143; Bonnemère 2017). As noted by Annette Weiner, 'the work of reproduction', which is celebrated and constituted in lifecycle rituals, 'is enacted with a counter awareness of the force of decay, rotting, and death' (Weiner 1981, 7–8, in Herdt 1984, 202). And this awareness, and life and death themselves, are mediated through the creation and destruction of things, of objects.

James Leach (2015, 261–2) draws a distinction between two types of objects. On the one hand, he discerns things that can have the generative position of persons. These things, such as semen and blood, cannot be replaced as they are part of the constitution of persons and, hence, 'irreplaceable' (Leach 2015, 263). On the other hand, things may stand in place of something or someone absent. This especially occurs in death rituals, where the main person (the deceased) is absent, and the transformation of relationships can only occur through the mediation of objects (see also Silverman and Lipset 2016, 4, 7). Such objects are typically effective 'through eliciting memory or affect' (Leach 2015, 622). 'The conundrum of absence is solved by channelling the return of the dead primarily through things that stand for people' (Hermkens 2019, 422). These objects, which once belonged to the deceased, are irreplaceable things connected to them or depictions of them, and are often manipulated in particular ways, activating social processes of remembering and forgetting.

Prominent in Melanesian mortuary rituals is the tension between maintaining objects (and human remains) as keepsakes, heirlooms and relics and destroying these personal objects to avoid interference from the dead (Lohmann 2010). Among the most famous examples of the intimate connection between evincement and destruction are the elaborate woodcarvings of Asmat and Kamoro people in West Papua. The metres-high, intricately carved Asmat *bisj* poles (Figure 8.1) are specifically made for a ceremony called the *bisj mbu*, which serves as a tangible promise by the living to avenge the death of the people carved into the poles (Kuruwaip 1974). The *bisj* are a vessel for transporting souls to the realm of the dead. After the ceremony, the *bisj* are taken into the sago swamps

8.1 *Bisj* festival in the village of Biwar Laut on 24 September 2018. The public presentation of the *bisj* poles in front of the *jeuw* (meant to initiate revenge) was tuned to the visit of an organised tour of American tourists and some carvers were expecting tourists to purchase the poles. Photo: Jaap Timmer.

and allowed to rot, their life force transferring to, and sustaining, the sago palms' growth (Smidt 1993, 25).

For Asmat, these objects embody ancestors who, at set times, came into the cycle of life force that was transmitted through head-taking, sago production, societal fertility and male initiation. 'Viewed as objects of spiritual force, there was an emotionally cathectic identification with them by the living descendants who had commissioned their construction' (Schneebaum 1990, in Knauft 1993, 190). The objects trigger redress because of the life force of the ancestors who were present during the carving and remain in the carved object. Every act of war, every killing, destabilises cosmological balances; and, to restore those balances, the ceremonial cycle had to continue to generate life force for sustaining *tes*.

Securing the flow of life force enables ongoing restoration of the balance between poles of disorder and order, between decline and growth, between strength and weakness, between male and female, and so on. In that sense, Asmat cosmology embraces impermanence like the swing of a pendulum between degrees of entropy. Life force establishes order and thus constitutes humans and culture in a cyclical and evolving process of integration, which then comes apart in the dissipation and decay that accompanies the return to equilibrium. When the Catholic mission and the government abolished headhunting, this tethered the pendulum's oscillation. As a result, at present, some Asmat feel that their life has come to a standstill and has lost *tes*. The circle of revolving life force is broken but most see that the pendulum still wants to swing freely. On top of that, collecting activities and Church and government programmes to promote and conserve Asmat cultures and provide economic activities to local communities have transformed Asmat art and culture into what some label *lambang* (Ind., 'emblem'). By *lambang*, they mean 'trademark', in the sense that 'Asmat' has become an emblem that stands for headhunting, primitivism and primitive art.

This profound consequence of collecting, commercialising and conserving relates to two discussions in the fields of museum studies and anthropology: ephemerality and atemporality. The ethics surrounding care for ephemeral objects has been the topic of recent museum and heritage studies, opening up the possibility of embracing decay instead of pursuing the dominant conservation ethos (see Grünfeld, this volume). Relatively few studies have addressed the issues involved with curating mortuary objects – artefacts that were never meant to be displayed but destined to decay along with the human remains with which they were deposited. These studies highlight the dilemma between institutionalised 'care' and the concerns of local communities about the sacred and spiritual nature of these objects (McGowan and LaRoche 1996). Similar issues have been addressed in relation to the exhibition of religious objects, although the focus there has predominantly been on the three-way interaction between object, curator and visitor (see, for example, Paine 2000; Paine 2013; and Buggeln, Paine and Plate 2017). Questions surrounding the representation of indigenous communities in museums and collections have, fortunately, gained prominence in scholarly work. Most of this work has focused on ethics of display and the importance of researching and curating exhibitions in consultation with representatives of the cultures displayed (Karp and Lavine 1991; Krmpotich and Peers 2013; Carreau et al. 2018). However, the profound socio-cultural consequences of dominant Western curating practices for contemporary indigenous communities have been less acknowledged and highlighted.

The Asmat case illustrates how Christian, colonial and contemporary museum practices create powerful categories that evoke sentiments of being in a state of permanence. Asmat imagery is used by outsiders as a caricature, as a metonym for Papuan culture, as the trope of 'headhunters' and 'stone-age woodcarvers in our time' (Stanley 2002, 26). As observed by Nicholas Thomas, foreign collections often place indigenous practice 'in an obscure domain antecedent to the culturally formative actions of Europeans, whether the evaluations of members of the *avant-garde*, or the classificatory practices of museum employees' (2000, 277). This chapter highlights the complexities, existential dilemmas and anxieties that occur when inherently ephemeral objects come to stand for 'Asmat culture'. In the following sections, we will discuss the processes of pacification that have forced Asmat toward permanence, followed by fragments of interviews with Martinus Tijup and David Jimanipits, two Asmat men, who reflect on the cultural loss of impermanence in relation to woodcarvings and concerns around the future of their societies.

Erring pacification

Asmat is a society of some 75,000 people who dwell in the plains of southwestern Papua, which has received scant ethnographic attention (but see Eyde 1967; Sowada 1961; Van Amelsvoort 1964; Schneebaum 1976; Simpelaere 1983; Sudarman 1984; Voorhoeve 1986). From the early 1950s onward, Asmat were pacified and converted to Catholicism by Dutch and American missionaries (De Hontheim 2011). The first missionary to arrive in the Asmat region was Gerard Zegwaard of the Sacred Heart Order, in 1950. Following a few more short visits, Fr

Zegwaard established a mission post in Agats, near the settlement of Syuru, in 1952 (Boelaars 1997, 7–8). After the gradual expansion of the mission to more remote areas, the American Crosier fathers and brothers arrived in 1958 and continued the mission in the region from 1961 onward. One of the main projects of these missionaries was pacification. Fr Zegwaard, in one of his early 1950s notes on Asmat, recounts local catechist Pahok expecting praise from the missionary after he told him that he had managed to kill all Nafaripi people to avenge the killing of his father. Fr Zegwaard reflects, 'At that moment, I felt a deep gap between paganism and Christianity. How would I bridge that gap?' (Zegwaard, cited in Boelaars 1997, 11, our translation).

The gap between state and society has always been rather wide. In a detailed study of Dutch pacification policies in Netherlands New Guinea, former patrol officer Hein van der Schoot (1969) recounts numerous problems in the engagement of outsiders with Asmat since the establishment of the first post in 1953. The Dutch colonial government forbade warfare, cannibalism, large-scale rituals and wife-exchange. These decisions were made on the basis of prejudices stemming from moral standards that were far removed from how Asmat saw the reproduction of their society. Furthermore, the sheer volume of issues and the vastness of the area meant that effective responses to violent outbreaks and ceremonies were difficult to implement. Overall, the focus was on ending warfare, as the government, as well as the mission, saw it as the main impediment to socio-economic progress. But how such progress might be achieved among Asmat was not clear to anyone (Van der Schoot 1969, 227; Van der Schoot 1998, 300–1).

Following a period of ambiguous Dutch government approaches, the Indonesian administration took off from firmer premises from 1962 onward. Following independence, Indonesia built modernist policy out of an ideological commitment to state socialism and a valorisation of pre-colonial history and culture centred on Java (Hooker 1993). The periphery needed to renounce its backwardness to be aligned with the centre; and, supported by prejudices about Papuans, this propelled a unified effort to eradicate poverty and civilise Asmat through the imposition of state power in the form of the abolishment of traditional practices. Teams, including armed forces and representatives of the government, went from village to village, forcing people to wear modern clothes, stay in the villages, burn their carvings, destroy the longhouses, and stop ceremonies and other customary practices (Sowada 2002, 53–4; Pouwer 2010, 246).

The new administration afforded no opportunities for Asmat to connect with ancestors or *tes* for balancing the cosmos. Most Indonesian government officials at the time assumed that all Asmat ceremonies and rituals involved headhunting and cannibalism, and hence prohibited these. When, from the early 1970s onward, tourists returned to Asmat in large groups (de Hontheim 2005, 77), eager to see performances, carvings and carving practices, Asmat took advantage of this foreign interest. The government, realising they also benefited from this tourism, subsequently relaxed their measures a little. However, at times, ceremonies would still be forbidden, and up until the 1980s, military commanders and civil servants continued to regard most Asmat cultural practices as involving 'devils' (*setan*).

In the following sections, we present and discuss local reflections on this history of nearly seven decades of pacification, which surfaced during Jaap's conversations with a number of men during his research among Asmat in 2018. What came to the fore were the experiences of many, of trying to reconcile the Asmat past with Catholicism by fitting the ancestors somewhere in between and, from there, trying to engage with Indonesian development and progress. Others were dismissive of all things 'Asmat', apart from carvings, and appeared keen to be recognised by the state so that they could finally secure access to Indonesian modernity, education and healthcare. We focus here on Martinus and David, who both see that pacification has failed because key elements of Asmat life simply cannot be pacified – not by the Church and not by the government.

Asmat cannot be pacified

> Asmat cannot be pacified (*tidak bisa diamankan*), we still need to follow the ancestors and we will need to kill, we will always be on the move, because we need to restore *tes*. It is hard these days, but we can't escape it. The church, the government and 'the museum', 'they have made us into an emblem' (*mereka telah melambangkan kita*). But we are not an emblem. We are a people with needs and a culture that cannot be pacified. Our culture, our past needs to be valued higher (*harus dimahalkan*), it cannot be 'reduced' (*memurahkan*) (Martinus Tijup, Ewer, 20 September 2018).

Martinus' reflections on his world highlight two interconnected concerns. First, the urge to restore *tes* and continue the cycle of life and death, and

116   IMPERMANENCE

second, the widespread concern that Asmat people and culture are reduced, rendered smaller and insignificant. In highlighting the ongoing need for sustaining *tes*, Martinus advocates for restoring the prestige that is not embodied in the cheap emblem (*lambang*) that Asmat has become. By being reduced to an emblem, Asmat have become contained and permanent. Martinus' conception of *murah* ('worthless') – the root of *memurahkan*, 'to make something cheaper' as opposed to *mahal* ('valuable') in *dimahalkan*, 'to value higher' – needs to be read in that manner. Pacification, according to Martinus, refers to a process by which such foreign forces as Church, government and art collectors bring their terms of order, stability and permanence to bear on Asmat ways of being. Some of the men Jaap spoke with in the villages of Per and Ewer are also concerned about the loss of *tes* and fear that, if Asmat drift away even further from their ontology, they will be fully 'pacified' (*diamankan*). Too much pacification means loss of life force and *tes*, resulting in complete dystopia.

Significantly, Catholicism does not have the power to avert the decline of life force, and, as a result, Asmat are keen to bring traditional ways of maintaining *ces* back into their lives themselves. Some men mentioned the need for headhunting as a way to replenish life force and showed war paraphernalia stored on the rafters of their houses. Others addressed the importance of carvings for returning *tes*. However, Martinus sees the Asmat carvings that are bought by outsiders, as well as those made for decorating churches, as emblematised or even 'secularised' versions of previously 'religious' objects. From servicing original Asmat ways of being and constituting *tes*, they have become permanent (and hence, pacified) objects in public exhibitions, including at the Asmat Museum of Culture and Progress.

The Asmat Museum of Culture and Progress was established by the Catholic Church in the early 1970s in an attempt to preserve local woodcarving traditions. According to Martinus, however, the museum does not instigate moral regeneration as the mission had envisioned. Instead, it generates moral degeneration through its timeless aestheticisation of Asmat woodcarvings. For Martinus, the museum embodies the ills of 'pacification' because, through its exhibitions and curatorial practices, Asmat are being transformed into an emblem, thereby effectively annihilating 'Asmat impermanence'. Part of the museum's curatorial practices that constitute a key factor in the process of emblematising Asmat are the yearly carving contests and cultural shows that commenced in 1980. Following a selection process conducted by staff of the museum, carvers are invited to display and market their works at a showground in Agats (Stanley 2012, 143–69; Sowada 2002, 59–60; Biakai 2002, 67). By 1983, the Crosier Mission's newsletter reported that:

> . . . carvers are beginning to identify themselves as a special group with a support system concretised in the Asmat Museum of Culture and Progress and its staff. For instance, one of the carvers from Per recently invited both Mr Yufen Biakai and Mr Erick Sarkol (the two-member staff of the museum) to a spirit mask festival in Per. The carver insisted before fellow villagers that 'my men' have to witness this traditional feast. . . . We hope again that the annual cultural festival can be another important aspect in the conscientization process so important for these people now (Third Cultural Festival 1984).

The consciousness-raising alluded to here hints at the essence of the mission's goals in the region. In 1973, Alphonse Sowada, OSC, then Bishop of Agats, reported that, following years of fragmented efforts to Christianise Asmat, it was now time for the mission to focus on 'the whole man', 'to free themselves from inhibiting factors such as superstition' (Sowada 1973, 15). The main failure of the mission thus far was its lack of understanding and appreciation of Asmat ways of being in the world and failure to comprehend that baptism 'enslaved' them. 'This enslavement consisted essentially in the belief among the Asmat – especially the elders, that baptism afforded them the magic key by which they would be able to obtain cherished materials imported from the outside' (Sowada 1973, 10). To address these ostensibly inhibiting beliefs, the new integrated mission approach included (besides better schooling and cooperatives for economic development) appreciation for culture, in particular Asmat woodcarving. From his inaugural speech onward, Sowada had been convinced that collecting, documenting, preserving and studying Asmat art were important for the realisation and appreciation of Asmat culture (Stanley 2012, 113–16). While understanding that Asmat woodcarvings 'are essentially vital religious expressions of art', Sowada's support for continuing this tradition attempted to strike a balance between old meanings and some form of resocialisation of Asmat carvings (Sowada 1985, 11).

The mission's interest in Asmat art coincided with UN efforts to regenerate and sustain local artforms, or handicrafts, as a form of development aid. In the early 1970s, art collector Jacques Hoogerbrugge, in his role as project manager of the Fund of the United Nations for the

Development of West Irian (FUNDWI), which stimulated markets for Asmat crafts (Mbait 1973), deemed the conditions favourable to rebuild the prestige of the master woodcarvers and to support them in continuing the good quality of work. 'Comparison with former-day carving reveals that the present-day carvings (notwithstanding adaptations and minor changes) have succeeded in maintaining their Asmat identity' (Hoogerbrugge 1973, 29). When Hoogerbrugge left, the project lost momentum, but people continued to produce carvings for sale and for small local ceremonies (Schneebaum 1990, 27). Around the same time, the Catholic mission followed FUNDWI's advice regarding the importance of stimulating Asmat handicrafts. As the Indonesian government strongly opposed the revival of longhouses (Omberep 1973, 34) in which carving used to be taught and practised, the mission came up with the idea for an Asmat museum.

The Asmat Museum of Culture and Progress was founded in 1973 with generous support from the Catholic Church, assisted by numerous foundations and individuals such as Gunther and Ursula Konrad, Tobias Schneebaum and Nick Stanley. Schneebaum recounts the shock and awe of young Asmat during their first visit to the museum. All of a sudden, they were exposed to objects embodying ancestral powers, objects with which they were not meant to engage (Schneebaum, in Stanley 2012, 119). David Simni, an elder from Syuru, was stunned to see objects of 'his former life' when visiting the museum for the first time, and began to wonder why all those objects were brought together in the museum (Schneebaum, in Stanley 2012, 119). When Schneebaum explained to him that the museum was for all Asmat to appreciate the qualities of the past, Simni asked, 'but who sleeps here?' (Schneebaum, cited in Stanley 2012, 119). Simni's question refers to the intimate connection between woodcarvings and the longhouse (*jeuw*): the spiritual, cultural and political centre of the community. In the past, this is where men would sleep, ancestors dwelled, skulls hung from rafters and carvings were made. In most villages, the *jeuw* no longer fulfils all these functions and has often become simply a meeting place for men to welcome visitors and stage performances for tourists.

At the time of the opening of the museum, the role and meaning of carved objects were already changing rapidly and there was a gradual deconsecration of the carvings and growing ignorance of the objects' original contexts, among both Asmat and foreigners. The assessment of carvings by outsiders often betrayed the typical tendency to place Asmat carvings (and thus Asmat people) in particular temporal frameworks, basically as belonging to a past characterised by headhunting, cannibalism and overall primitiveness. Appreciation and condemnation of woodcarvings often follow this temporal classification: adding value to 'art' and museum pieces, while compelling Indonesian government officials to wield civilisation programs within the official nation-building policy. The government, as noted earlier, feared that carving might evoke headhunting and other 'primitive' behaviour, and, as a result, banned it for a time. However, increasing volumes of collectors and tourists, coupled with pressure from the Catholic Church, forged renewed interest and evoked ideas around preserving this cultural tradition (Stanley 2012, 112–42).

Significantly, the inspiration for the aforementioned programmatic plans for maintaining or rebuilding 'Asmat identity' derived more from mission and art collectors' ideas than from Asmat reflections on their situation. In fact, most of these foreign visions stand in stark contrast with how Asmat experience their carvings. As we will discuss in the next section, Asmat views reflect the tensions and inequalities between them and outsiders, which derive from – and continue to shape – Asmat interactions with art collectors and tourists, as well as with 'development' and 'mission', and with Catholicism in particular.

Carving Jesus

Commissioned by the Church to carve a statue of Jesus for the new church building in Ewer, David Jimanipits, school teacher and renowned carver, has retreated from much of society. In the sago grove (*dusun*) behind his house, under the shade of sago palms, he has cleared a spot to work on the statue, or corpus as he calls it.

During a conversation with Jaap about the making of the statue in September 2018, David remarks that the ethos of carving in Asmat has changed dramatically:

> Nowadays, we even have Islamisation. There's a growing amount of Asmat converting to Islam and more and more migrants from across the sea come here to make a living. This all distracts people from organising their own lives and managing their communities. The policies of the government around woodcarving are also not helpful as there are too many interests and too many voices, and since the American Crosier Brothers left, the Catholic Church has become the government's associate in this. At the same time, people continue to

struggle how to match (*memadukan*) Asmat stories about the origin of the world with Genesis. People are losing their roots (*akar*) and no longer know where they are going.

You see, Jaap, when I visited the Netherlands in 2013, I spent too much time in the Indonesian Embassy in The Hague. I had no time to visit the Tropenmuseum in Amsterdam where there is a canoe that I made and that was collected by Kooijman. I am not sure when Kooijman took it from here, it was in 1980s or in the 1990s. There is also a drum I made in the Metropolitan Museum of Art in New York and I have also visited a museum in Chicago where the collection is under the ground.

It is interesting to see that people in those countries store our culture while we forget about it. The *roh* ('spirit') and the *nyata* ('the tangible', 'the real') is in our own culture, but they [foreigners] love our culture more than we do. That's more evil than colonialism (*Itu lebih jahat daripada kejajahan*). They say that the Dutch colonised, that the Japanese colonised, but look at what is happening now. . . That there are so many Asmat carvings abroad does not help us. Foreigners come here for their own collections, for business, for art sales and what have you. Why do these people want to collect? Maybe because they see that our carvings are made by ancestor spirits?

Surely, they have power; they stun people. All these objects have spirits, some in those museums even more as they have the old strong spirits from the past. If you watch them for a while, like for three hours, you will see them move. They are not fixed or dead; they are alive. That goes to show that our culture is not a culture of preserving objects. But people now want us to make carvings for museums and churches.

Take this corpus, it is yet another story. I have tried hard to put a spirit in it! I was successful. I had to hide the workplace so no one was going to disturb me. Even the pastor cannot just come by and check on the progress. It needs to be a quiet place. If there [were] no spirit, the carving would have no meaning. If it has a spirit, the carving can give us strength, it can bless us. We call this spirit *teser* or mystery [or the sacred]. It is a mystery because it is outside our space, it has much stronger power (*daya*). It is with all my strength that I can get the *teser* in the corpus. It is from my inner self (*batin*) and not from my ancestors.

There is no connection with the ancestors. That is not allowed. They are guarding the process, that's all. Christian statues are not like Asmat statues. The ancestors give no guidance. I start from an illustration and the ancestors are just guardians. What I bring into the statue is the same as what people call 'God'; it is the Holy Spirit, like the strength of Jesus in our lives. It is that kind of spirit that makes it possible for me to make the corpus. So the power of God goes into the corpus through my *batin*. *Batin* cannot be translated into Asmat. You will sense the power once it is in the church. People will be stunned, they will be in fear, they will sense the power in the corpus (David Jimanipits, Ewer, 20 September 2018).

The key difference David discerns between Asmat carvings and Asmat Christian carvings concerns their respective dependence on ancestor spirits and the Christian mystery. In the case of Asmat carvings, the ancestors guide the maker or even, according to some, carve the statue, with the result that the final object is imbued with their power. Ancestral power lives on and keeps carvings alive, including in foreign collections and even when these objects start to emblematise 'Asmat culture'. In contrast, ancestors are merely guardians during the making of the statue of Jesus. In fact, the efficacy of the corpus depends not on the ancestors but upon David's piety, his Christian *batin* (inner self) and his relationship with the Holy Spirit to give it spiritual (Christian religious) power. Hence, the corpus is not an Asmat carving in the sense of an embodiment of

8.2 David Jimanipits and the corpus, as well as the Last Supper, that he is carving. Ewer village, 19 September 2018. Photo: Jaap Timmer.

ancestral spirits or, in past contexts, a medium for ancestors to intervene in the lives of the living and move on to the afterlife, or for people to avenge the ancestors. The corpus does not do that.

According to Catholic theology, the corpus is a spiritual object that only gains power after it has been blessed by a priest or bishop and has become part of the Church's inventory. It will then be a sacramental, a sacred sign. Unlike Asmat carvings, which are embodiments of the ancestors, sacramentals become sacred only through the Church's intercession and its blessing. Only then do they become a vehicle for God to work through. Moreover, while Asmat carvings require impermanence to sustain *mana* and *tes*, sacramentals like the crucifix require and evoke permanence to keep the faith in Christ alive. As David emphasised, 'it [the corpus] should not decay, no bugs are allowed to eat it'.

David's reflections on the Jesus statue, the Christian mystery and his *batin* in relation to ancestors in Asmat carvings contrast sharply with Nick Stanley's observations about a crucifix figure in the church of Kristus Amor in Sawa, northwest Asmat. Stanley suggests that this crucifix figure embodies the spirit of Christ in the same way as a *bisj* pole. This pole is arguably the most iconic Asmat ancestor figure for remembrance of the dead as well as a warning and initiation of vengeance (Van der Zee 2009, 42). Conflating salvation with vengeance, Stanley sees that 'so strong is the identification with the Christ figure carved by Yiwirjak that it has evoked "contagious" imitation' (Stanley 2017, 124). While we agree, as would David, that the Asmat Christian object also becomes an actor in a ritual enactment, the syncretism – let alone imitation – that Stanley observes is not recognised by any of our interlocutors. Instead, they emphasise that Christian statues are not imbued with life force and, hence, do not evoke redress, unlike *bisj* poles and all other objects classified as *ecopok* or *tereipok* (Costa 2020, 175–86).

In fact, the permanence of Christian statues positions them outside the category of Asmat carvings and locates them firmly inside Catholic logics and other frames of thought and action that originate elsewhere. This becomes especially clear when discussing the impact of Christian and Western doctrines of permanence on Asmat art. According to David, the Church and museums' ontology of permanence eradicate objects' life force and agency, reducing Asmat carvings and the Asmat peoples themselves to mere emblems:

> In the eyes of priests and also curators, the objects in their collections die. The moment they are obtained makes everything certain about them. They stop communicating with the object, they display it with

the meanings attached to [it] at the moment of collection. What they know about the object hardens and becomes definite. There then is where the Asmat emblem comes from and is nurtured. Our objects in the hands of outsiders stand for our primitiveness, our cannibalism, our headhunting, and all the rituals our ancestors engaged in (David Jimanipits, Ewer, 20 September 2018).

Martinus and David, who both critique the process and state of 'Asmat' permanence, point to the importance of ensuring greater Asmat agency over conscious self-formation through impermanence, a dawning ethics of a revolution, perhaps, in relation to original Asmat rituals as sources of *tes*.

Toward a new future's past

As stated by Nicholas Thomas in his introduction to the volume *Melanesia: Art and encounter*, 'art has loomed large in the lives of Melanesians for millennia' (Thomas 2013, xi). While material culture remains significant in local lives, Melanesian objects have also been abandoned, replaced by Western products, prohibited and destroyed, and systematically collected by colonial agents (Thomas 2013, xi). Entering European, Russian and North American collections, objects from the region have been 'admired, fetishized even, treated as specimens of one sort or another, classified and published, or put away in museum stores' and private collections (Thomas 2013, xi). This chapter has shown how not only objects but also indigenous people themselves have become 'emblems' due to foreign practices of 'pacification' and their collecting and museum displays.

The experience of Asmat having become an emblem is a critical reflection on the meaning attained by Asmat carvings in museums, private collections and tourist imagination. The Catholic Church and the long tradition of museum and art collecting, coupled with government policies, have contributed to this. The Church and state have caused an excessive reification of Asmat culture through the establishment of the Asmat Museum of Culture and Progress, the organisation of Asmat cultural shows, exhibitions of Asmat art in museums and galleries, and, in line with these efforts, attempts to ultimately tame unruly Asmat, by making them into either 'good Christians' or 'civilised citizens'.[3] In all these projects, Asmat have been pacified by the often-deliberate absence of any reference to the deep cultural meanings and context in which these objects have been made, both in the past and the present. References to headhunting are only made to promote 'Asmat culture' and its material representations abroad.

The permanence forced on Asmat woodcarvings has generated a complex paradox. While many in the region are quick to state that the mission and the government brought peace and that people are happy that most of the violent practices of the past have been left behind, according to Schneebaum, 'the majority continue to believe they are surrounded by spirits of all kinds, combining the old with what they understand of the new Catholic or Protestant faith' (Schneebaum 1990, 28).[4] However, many Asmat sense they cannot reconcile their emblematic identity, and its stubborn haunting of past headhunting and ancestor 'worship', with Catholic principles. This past is often drawn upon as an ironic commentary on the impossibility of pacifying the Asmat: to reconcile Asmat ideas around impermanence with Church and state doctrines. People challenge the Church's demand to make a break with their past and live in the present to prepare for redemption. Asmat insistence on the need for *tes* and the related impermanence of objects – their untameable nature, as it were – is not merely a counter-discourse but also alerts us to other futures inherent in the impermanence of Asmat objects.

Asmat reflections on their past are inherently connected to global processes of colonialism and imperialism and recent regional projects of revival. Colonialism has, to a large extent, directed 'the development of ethnographic museums and the growth of the collections', especially in Europe (ter Keurs 1999, 69). These museums, but also other institutions, have traditionally been used to evoke a sensibility of order, continuity and tradition, through a linear temporality and a sense of permanent materiality (see Introduction and Chapter 18 of this volume). Moreover, anthropological thinking about material culture has created a dichotomy, whereby the social and material have been viewed as distinct conceptual domains (Bell and Geismar 2009, 6). The result is that curatorial practices in ethnographic museums (which, until recently, were the domain of anthropologists) have also dominated conceptual approaches to ethnographic objects. These values of permanence and particular approaches toward materiality continue to inform contemporary anthropological thinking as well as curatorial and 'revival' practices. Recently, attempts have been made to reinvigorate the making and protection of 'customary' objects in the Melanesian region (see, for example, Akin 2014 and Hermkens 2019). Sometimes, this revival occurs with the assistance of institutions that, paradoxically, often had been established due to, or had benefited from, colonial expeditions. While these efforts to protect and preserve indigenous material culture seem to be directed to confound time through preserving objects that will outlast humans' physical selves, ephemeral objects confound time not through permanence but through renewal. These latter values clash with inherently Western values of care and conservation.

As this chapter has shown, cultural concerns for the ephemeral and metaphysical significance of artefacts can be antithetical to the museum approach, which subjects objects to particular forms of care. It cannot be assumed that the removal of an Asmat *bisj* pole by a collector or museum is analogous to its gradual decay in the sago swamps. As argued by Jeudy-Ballini in the context of Sulka dance masks, 'non-visibility . . . is not to be equated with a form of destruction' (2004, 111). For Asmat, the flow of *tes* is redirected outside the cycle of death and renewal, with Church and government 'care' imposing a form of permanence that results in cultural fragmentation and destabilisation of local ontologies. This illustrates how politics and ethics of care are effective top-down forms of governmentality (Puig de la Bellacasa 2017). Likewise, museum professionals have customarily viewed themselves as possessing ownership over the care, conservation and curatorial practice of indigenous material culture (McGowan and LaRoche 1996, 115), thereby controlling, denying or even oppressing indigenous subject positions. In particular, European museums have been criticised for working alongside 'a powerful White Western denial and disavowal of the implications of colonialism in museums' (Sandahl 2019, 75).

For museums to effectively decolonise, lingering Western sensibilities located within contemporary practices of conservation and curating ethnographic material need to be addressed. An Asmat 'museum of impermanence' might be one path to pursue the constitution of new ethical forms of subjectivity and the acceptance of inevitable decay and need for renewal, also for Western academics, societies and institutions. Such a museum would have to be conceptualised by Asmat as part of their search for possible pasts that suit their horizons of expectations (Koselleck 2004, 259–63). As this chapter has highlighted, some have embarked on this search by recognising Asmat objects in the hands of missionaries, museum curators and art collectors as inscribed with a past that has been violated. This is a reminder that these objects:

> are not what we have been socialized and trained to see: standalone artifacts whose inscribed content exists for experts to interpret. Rather, they constitute part of the material worlds out of which people's rights are made manifest (Azoulay 2019, 30).

It remains to be seen how Asmat are going to dislodge their emblematic past and generate a future that reimagines and embraces the impermanence and renewal of Asmat worlds.

Acknowledgements

We thank our Asmat interlocutors for sharing their knowledge and experiences, Bert Voorhoeve for his insightful reflections on the changing understandings of *tes* since he worked in the region in the early 1960s and in 1970, and the editors of this volume for their constructive feedback.

Notes

1. Melanesia, a concept of colonial origin, refers to lands and peoples in New Guinea, the Solomon Islands, Vanuatu and New Caledonia.
2. On the basis of recent fieldwork in the village of Atsj, Roberto Costa defines *ces* (the inland variety of *tes*) as 'a multifaceted force that captures potency, talent, bravery, pride, prestige and ethical prescriptions' (Costa 2020, 4).
3. Timmer (2011) observes a similar process for Tehit people in West Papua's Bird's Head.
4. Protestant missions from the Evangelical Alliance Mission (TEAM) have been active in the region since 1955 (de Hontheim 2011, 93–101).

References

Akin, David. 2014. 'Regenerating local arts at the Kwaio Cultural Centre'. In *The Things We Value: Culture and history in the Solomon Islands*, edited by Ben Burt and Lissant Bolton, 93–101. Canon Pyon, Herefordshire: Sean Kingston Publishing.

Azoulay, Ariella Aïsha. 2019. *Potential History: Unlearning imperialism*. London: Verso.

Bell, Joshua A., and Heidi Geismar. 2009. 'Materialising Oceania: New ethnographies of things in Melanesia and Polynesia', *The Australian Journal of Anthropology* 20(1): 3–27.

Biakai, Yufentius. 2002. 'The Asmat Museum: Why so important?' In *Asmat: Perception of life in art: The collection of the Asmat Museum of Culture and Progress*, edited by Ursula Konrad, Alphonse Sowada and Gunter Konrad, 65–8. Mönchengladbach: B. Kühlen.

Boelaars, Jan. 1997. *Met Papoea's Samen op Weg, Deel III: De Begeleiders*. Kampen: J.H. Kok.

Bonnemère, Pascale. 2017. 'The materiality of relational transformations: Propositions for renewed analyses of life-cycle rituals in Melanesia and Australia', *Anthropological Forum* 27(1): 3–17.

Buggeln, Gretchen, Crispin Paine and S. Brent Plate. 2017. *Religion in Museums: Global and interdisciplinary perspectives*. London: Bloomsbury.

Carreau, Lucie, Alison Clark, Alana Jelinek, Erna Lilje and Nicholas Thomas. 2018. *Pacific Presences: Oceanic art and European museums*. Leiden: Sidestone Press.

Costa, Roberto. 2020. 'Becoming Cescuipitsj: Prestige, woodcarving and a museum among the Asmat (West Papua, Indonesia)'. PhD thesis, Macquarie University.

de Hontheim, Astrid. 2005. 'De la collection missionnaire au commerce equitable', *Civilisations* 52(2): 75–104.

de Hontheim, Astrid. 2011. *Devil Chasers and Art Gatherers: Intercultural encounters with the Asmat*. Brussels: Éditions Modulaires Européennes & InterCommunications.

Eyde, David Bruener. 1967. 'Cultural correlates of warfare among the Asmat of South-West New Guinea'. PhD thesis, Yale University.

Helbling, Jürg. 2006. 'War and peace in societies without central power: Theories and perspectives'. In *Warfare and Society: Archaeological and social anthropological perspectives*, edited by Ton Otto, Henrik Thrane and Helle Vandkilde, 113–39. Aarhus: Aarhus University Press.

Herdt, Gilbert H. 1984. *Ritualized Homosexuality in Melanesia*. Berkeley: University of California Press.

Hermkens, Anna-Karina. 2013. *Engendering Objects. Dynamics of barkcloth and gender among the Maisin in Papua New Guinea*. Leiden: Sidestone Press.

Hermkens, Anna-Karina. 2019. 'Creation and destruction in Melanesian material culture'. In *The Melanesian World*, edited by Eric Hirsch and Will Rollason, 419–33. Abingdon, Oxon: Routledge.

Hoogerbrugge, Jacques. 1973. 'An evaluation of present-day Asmat woodcarving', *Irian, Bulletin of West Irian Development* 2 (1): 24–35.

Hooker, Virginia M., ed. 1993. *Culture and Society in New Order Indonesia*. Kuala Lumpur and New York: Oxford University Press.

Jeudy-Ballini, Monique. 2004. 'The lives of the mask: A few Sulka reasons for perplexity'. In *Shifting Images of Identity in the Pacific*, edited by Toon van Meijl and Jelle Miedema, 101–18. Leiden: KITLV Press.

Karp, Ivan, and Steven D. Lavine. 1991. *Exhibiting Cultures: The poetics and politics of museum display*. Washington, DC: Smithsonian Institute.

Knauft, Bruce M. 1993. *South Coast New Guinea Cultures: History, comparison, dialectic*. Cambridge: Cambridge University Press.

Koselleck, Reinhart. 2004. *Futures Past: On the semantics of historical time* (translated and with an introduction by Keith Tribe). New York: Columbia University Press.

Krmpotich, Cara, and Laura Peers. 2013. *This Is Our Life: Haida material heritage and changing museum practice*. Vancouver and Toronto: UBC Press.

Kuruwaip, Abraham. 1974. 'The Asmat bispole: Its background and meaning', *Irian, Bulletin of West Irian Development* 3(2): 32–87.

Leach, James. 2015. 'The death of a drum: Objects, persons, and changing social form on the Rai Coast of Papua New Guinea', *Journal of the Royal Anthropological Institute* 21: 620–40.

Lohmann, Roger Ivar. 2010. 'In the company of things left behind: Asabano mementos', *Anthropological Forum* 20(3): 291–303.

Mbait, Jeremias. 1973. 'The Asmat handicraft project', *Irian, Bulletin of West Irian Development*, Special Issue on Development in the Asmat 2 (1): 36–7.

McGowan, Gary S., and Cheryl J. LaRoche. 1996. 'The ethical dilemma facing conservation: Care and treatment of human skeletal remains and mortuary objects', *Journal of the American Institute for Conservation* 5(2): 109–21.

Omberep, Joseph, B. 1973. 'Penindjavan Asmat tahun 1963 dan Keadaan Sekarang Tahun', *Irian, Bulletin of West Irian Development* 2 (1): 19–23.

Paine, Crispin, ed. 2000. *Godly Things: Museums, objects and religion*. London: Leicester University Press.

Paine, Crispin. 2013. *Religious Objects in Museums: Private lives and public duties*. London: Bloomsbury.

Pouwer, Jan. 2010. *Gender, Ritual and Social Formation in West Papua: A configurational analysis comparing Kamoro and Asmat*. Leiden: KITLV Press.

Puig de la Bellacasa, María. 2017. *Matters of Care: Speculative ethics in more than human worlds*. Minneapolis, MN: University of Minnesota Press.

Sandahl, Jette. 2019. 'Curating across colonial divides'. In *Curatopia: Museums and the future of curatorship*, edited by Philipp Schorch and Conal McCarthy, 72–89. Manchester: Manchester University Press.

Schneebaum, Tobias. 1976. 'A museum as a focal point in acculturation: The Asmat Museum of Culture and Progress'. MA thesis, New York, Goddard College.

Schneebaum, Tobias. 1990. *Embodied Spirits: Ritual carvings of the Asmat, a traveling exhibition from the Gajdusek collection of the Peabody Museum of Salem and the Crosier Asmat Museum collection of Hastings, Nebraska*. Salem, MA: Peabody Museum of Salem.

Silverman, Eric K., and David Lipset, eds. 2016. 'Introduction: Mortuary ritual, modern social theory, and the historical moment in Pacific modernity'. In *Mortuary Dialogues: Death ritual and the reproduction of moral community in Pacific modernities*, edited by David Lipset and Eric Silverman, 1–22. New York: Berghahn.

Simpelaere, Paul. 1983. *Chez les Asmat: Papous de Nouvelle-Guinée Occidentale (Irian Jaya): Esquisses, parallèles, souvenirs*. Tielt: Lannoo.

Smidt, Dirk A.M. 1993. 'The Asmat: Life, death and the ancestors'. In *Asmat Art: Woodcarvings of Southwest New Guinea*, edited by Dirk A.M. Smidt, 16–25. Singapore: Periplus Editions and the Rijksmuseum voor Volkenkunde, Leiden, in association with C. Zwartenkot, Amsterdam.

Sowada, Alphonse A. 1961. 'Socio-economic survey of the Asmat peoples of Southwestern New Guinea'. MA thesis, Catholic University of America (Washington).

Sowada, Alphonse A. 1973. 'A mission's search for an integrated policy', *Irian, Bulletin of West Irian Development* 2 (1): 7–18.

Sowada, Alphonse A. 1985. 'Forward' [sic]. In *Asmat Images from the Collection of the Asmat Museum of Culture and Progress*, edited by Tobias Schneebaum, 7–11. Agats, Papua: Asmat Museum of Culture and Progress.

Sowada, Alphonse A. 2002. 'The decline, suppression and rejuvenation of Asmat culture and art: An historical approach'. In *Asmat: Perception of life in art: The collection of the Asmat Museum of Culture and Progress*, edited by Ursula Konrad, Alphonse Sowada and Gunter Konrad, 46–64. Mönchengladbach: B. Kühlen.

Stanley, Nick. 2002. 'Living with the ancestors in an international art world'. In *Asmat: Perception of life in art: The collection of the Asmat Museum of Culture and Progress*, edited by Ursula Konrad, Alphonse Sowada and Gunter Konrad, 23–32. Mönchengladbach: B. Kühlen.

Stanley, Nick. 2012. *The Making of Asmat Art: Indigenous art in a world perspective*. Canon Pyon, Herefordshire: Sean Kingston Publishing.

Stanley, Nick. 2017. 'Desire, imitation and ambiguity in Asmat sculpture'. In *The Inbetweenness of Things: Materializing mediation and movement between worlds*, edited by Paul Basu, 123–9. London: Bloomsbury Academic.

Strathern, Marilyn. 1988. *The Gender of the Gift: Problems with women and problems with society in Melanesia*. Berkeley, CA: University of California Press.

Strathern, Marilyn. 1999. *Property, Substance and Effect: Anthropological essays on persons and things*. London: Athlone Press.

Sudarman, Dea. 1984. *Asmat: Menyingkap Budaya Suku Pedalaman Irian Jaya*. Jakarta: Penerbit Sinar Harapan.

ter Keurs, Pieter. 1999. 'Things of the past? Museums and ethnographic objects', *Journal des Africanistes* 69(1): 67–80.

Third Cultural Festival. 1984. 'Third Cultural Festival, Agats, Irian Jaya, July, 1983', *Pacific Arts Newsletter* 18: 8.

Thomas, Nicholas. 2000. 'Epilogue'. In *Hunting the Gatherers: Ethnographic collectors, agents and agency in Melanesia, 1870s–1930s*, edited by Michael O'Hanlon and Robert L. Welsch, 273–8. New York and Oxford: Berghahn Books.

Thomas, Nicholas. 2013. 'Introduction'. In *Melanesia: Art and encounter*, edited by Lissant Bolton, Nicholas Thomas, Elizabeth Bonshek, Julie Adams and Ben Burt, xi–xix. London: British Museum Press.

Timmer, Jaap. 2011. 'Cloths of civilisation: *Kain Timur* in the Bird's Head of West Papua', *The Asia Pacific Journal of Anthropology* 12(4): 383–401.

Tomlinson, Matt, and Ty P. Kāwika Tengan, eds. 2016. *New Mana: Transformations of a classic concept in Pacific languages and cultures*. Acton, ACT: ANU Press.

Valeri, Valerio. 1985. *Kingship and Sacrifice: Ritual and society in ancient Hawaii*. Chicago, IL: University of Chicago Press.

van Amelsvoort, Vincent F.P.M. 1964. *Culture, Stone Age and Modern Medicine: The early introduction of integrated health in a non-literate society, a New Guinea case study in medical anthropology*. Assen: Van Gorcum.

van der Schoot, Hein A. 1969. *Het Mimika- en Asmatgebied (West-Irian) voor en na de Openlegging. Beleidsaspecten van een Overgangssituatie*. Tilburg: Gianotten.

van der Schoot, Hein A. 1998. 'De Asmat en de Pax Neerlandica'. In 'Papoea's, Paters en Politiek: Nederlands-Nieuw-Guinea 1945–1962', *Spiegel Historiael* 33(7/8): 297–302.

van der Zee, Pauline. 2009. *Art as Contact with the Ancestors: Visual arts of the Kamoro and Asmat of Western Papua*. Amsterdam: KIT Publishers.

Voorhoeve, Clemens L. 1986. '"We, people of one canoe – they, people of wood": Two Asmat origin myths'. *Irian: Bulletin of West Irian Development* 14: 79–125.

Wagner, Roy. 1991. 'The fractal person'. In *Big Men and Great Men: Personifications of power in Melanesia*, edited by Maurice Godelier and Marilyn Strathern, 159–73. Cambridge: Cambridge University Press.

Weiner, Annette, B. 1981. 'Transformations in gender constructs'. Paper delivered at the American Anthropological Association meeting, Los Angeles, December 1981.

9
The unmaking and remaking of cultural worlds: reinventing ritual on Baluan Island, Papua New Guinea

Ton Otto

One of the advantages of conducting long-term fieldwork in the same place is the chance of being surprised – again – by a society with which one has become very familiar. In April 2011, exactly 25 years after the start of my first fieldwork on Baluan Island, Papua New Guinea, I was invited by my long-term collaborator, friend and then clan-leader Sakumai to take part in a ritual I had neither seen nor heard about during the more than three years in total I had spent living on the island. He had assembled more pigs than I had ever seen before, and the purpose of the ritual was to confirm and celebrate his clan-leadership, a type of ceremony that, I had previously learned, had been abolished long ago as part of the transformations of the Paliau Movement (to which I will return).

For a quarter of a century, I had been studying social and cultural change on the island and I had been collecting memories of old people, most of whom had since passed away, about the key rituals that they experienced in their youth. I had also observed a revitalisation of interest in tradition and the reintroduction and refashioning of traditional rituals connected with birth, marriage and death since the late 1980s. But everyone had agreed that the old *lapan* (traditional leader or chief) feasts of the past had ceased for good. So why was Sakumai performing this ritual now, and how was he able to do it, as I had assumed that the knowledge associated with it had been almost completely lost?

The unexpected manifestation of the long-forgotten *yiwan kup* ritual, as it was called, will form the backdrop against which I will reflect on the anthropological concept of culture, and how it may or may not be useful to account for processes of change (gradual and radical), processes of loss and recreation, processes of rupture and continuity. In short, I wish to address the purchase of culture in the face of the question of impermanence that is the focus of this volume. Culture is, no doubt, one of the key concepts developed by the discipline of social and cultural anthropology, with a history dating back at least 150 years, since E. B. Tylor's famous definition: culture is 'that complex whole which includes knowledge, belief, art, morals, law, custom, and any other capabilities and habits acquired by man as a member of society' (1871, 1). Although, in Tylor's original conception,[1] culture was something that evolved and thus implied a temporality of progress, it was soon predominantly used to characterise and describe differences between human societies, which may or may not be assumed to be at different stages of development.[2] With a focus on contemporary, co-existing cultural differences, the predominant temporal connotation has been that of inertia: culture as something that keeps people in their present state by 'enculturating' them into pre-existing values, social categories, relations and practices.

Culture has thus been a key concept to describe and explain continuity and stasis rather than change and transformation. This applies both to its intellectual history of usage within the discipline of anthropology – including contemporary terminological alternatives such as 'ontology'[3] – and the appropriation of the term in popular debates and politics: culture is something that creates friction between groups because of the incompatibility and endurance of different customs. In short, the concept of culture generally promotes the status quo and engenders notions of permanence rather than impermanence. This is, of course, a huge generalisation that ignores numerous anthropological attempts at coming to grips with cultural change,[4] as well as the influence of cultural studies that promotes a more dynamic, oppositional and reactive understanding of culture. But rather than reassessing the relative merits of these alternative voices in anthropology, I will take a look outside of disciplinary boundaries to see whether there are some different models at hand that could usefully inform anthropological thinking about culture and impermanence.

In this chapter, then, I will explore whether recent theories deriving from phenomenology and cognitive biology that focus on processes of world-making can contribute to a fresh understanding of culture that is better equipped to analyse both continuity and change. In particular, the understanding of life as an autopoietic process based on the principle of 'changing to stay the same' (Margulis and Sagan 1995) appears promising with regard to identifying a different kind of temporality of the culture concept that is more in line with the notion of impermanence as addressed in this volume. Before elaborating on this theoretical claim, let me introduce the ethnographic setting.

The setting: cultural diversity on Baluan

When I set out to conduct my doctoral fieldwork on Baluan Island, then a little-studied place in Manus Province, I had been trained to find and describe traditional kinship and exchange patterns. But I also knew that Baluan had been the centre of the Paliau Movement in the 1940s and 1950s, which had abolished all major traditional ceremonies and rituals – key cultural events that involved many people and resources (Schwartz 1962). The movement's leader, Paliau Maloat from Baluan Island, had a vision of a new society in which the indigenous population would become autonomous once again and attain a standard of living equal to that of the white colonisers, while the traditional culture was to be abolished or adapted as it was considered an impediment to the attainment of progress and wealth (Otto 1992). The Christian missions, which had started their work on the island in the 1930s, had also rejected and opposed many aspects of traditional culture. However, when I arrived on the island in 1986, people were quite occupied with traditional exchanges around marriage and death, something they called *kastamwok* in Tok Pisin, which can be translated as 'the work of tradition'.

Soon, I realised that Baluan social life was not neatly organised around a coherent set of cultural principles and values but appeared, at first sight, to be quite diverse and dispersed. Nevertheless, I started to recognise certain fields that had some degree of coherence due to the interconnectedness of particular social institutions and concomitant social categories and practices engaged by the people. At the time, I identified three such fields as prevalent on Baluan: that of tradition (*kastam* in local Tok Pisin), that of organised religion (*lotu*), and one largely pertaining to state-controlled activities (*gavman*). Struggling to describe this kind of socio-cultural assemblage, I used the phrase 'institutional and semantic domains'. I also sometimes referred to 'societal spheres' (from Weber) and borrowed Bourdieu's (1977, 110) concept of 'universe of practice and discourse'.[5] In my doctoral dissertation (Otto 1991), I pursued a historical reconstruction of how this cultural diversity had come about as a result of exogenous and indigenous influences: colonisation, missionisation, the Paliau Movement, the movement for national independence with an emerging discourse about Papua New

Guinea Ways and a related but partly independent revitalisation of traditional practices in the villages. I discovered different temporalities and intensities of change. For example, conversion to Christianity and the Paliau Movement were instances of radical and comprehensive change (Otto 1992, 1998), leading to longer periods of the hegemonisation of a new set of cultural principles. But there were always also residual, albeit suppressed, spheres (Williams 1973), for example of traditional practices, and I could often identify forms of innovative opposition.

The emergence of the sphere of tradition (*kastam*) was a case of slow change stretching over several decades (Otto 2011). One of my key findings was that new domains were articulated in opposition to each other but that, in fact, many concepts, values and practices often cut across domains. In other words, these cultural spheres were not clearly bounded and impermeable entities but rather they appeared as porous conglomerates of different cultural materials with some form of semantic and practical interconnectedness and coherence.

My efforts to integrate a cultural approach with a historical one, including the different temporalities that this entailed for understanding the former, were, of course, influenced by anthropological debates of the time. In particular, I was seeking to position myself within a wider debate that developed in Melanesian anthropology in the early 1990s and that was articulated as the opposition between a New Melanesian Ethnography and a New Melanesian History (Josephides 1991; Foster 1995). Scholars who were linked with the New Melanesian Ethnography (Marilyn Strathern, Roy Wagner and Mark Mosko, among others) emphasised the alterity of different cultural systems, the interpretation of which was to be the key method of anthropology leading to a critical review of Western concepts of socio-cultural analysis. Although it was certainly not their intention to imply a stasis or fixity of cultural systems, the focus on difference rather than change nevertheless created a bias toward an atemporal type of analysis. In contrast, proponents of the New Melanesian History (Nicholas Thomas, James Carrier, Deborah Gewertz and Frederick Errington) stressed the shared colonial history of the Melanesian peoples and the different kinds of external visitors and settlers–occupiers, predominantly from European, Australian, American but also Asian countries. Rather than emphasising alterity, these scholars described how histories of interaction produced shared understandings, relations of inequality and articulations of difference.

Foster (1995) proposed that a New Melanesian Anthropology should be built on the integration of the two aforementioned perspectives of the New Melanesian Ethnography and the New Melanesian History.

His own book on social reproduction and history in the Tanga Islands is an attempt to achieve just that. In the book, Foster first provides a convincing rendering of the emergence of *kastam* as an indigenous categorisation of mortuary rites linked to the increasing commoditisation of Tanga society. He then offers a penetrating analysis of the categories and logics of mortuary rites as a cultural system. In a third and more comparative section, he points out how different cultural logics (or modes of social reproduction, as he calls them), facing similar historical circumstances, can create different historical outcomes in relation to the objectification of cultural domains. This point is well taken but, in my view (see Otto 1997), he does not take the final step toward the integration of historical and cultural perspectives – namely, to show how social reproduction through mortuary rites has a different significance and effect in a society characterised by a distinction between *kastam* and *bisnis* versus a society where there is no such distinction (for example, the Tanga Islands prior to the commoditisation process).

In my own work, I have focused more on the dynamics of cultural and social change (in line with the New Melanesian History), to the partial neglect of investigating how continuing cultural logics and materials are also part of the process of transformation. In this chapter, I will investigate how theories of world-making, autopoiesis and sympoiesis might help articulate the relation between culture as a conservative force and as a factor of change. Before elaborating on these newer theories, I will return to the scene of Sakumai's ritual, which affected my understanding of cultural change on Baluan Island.

The scene: *yiwan kup* ceremony, Baluan Island, 29 April 2011

Sakumai Yêp stands on the veranda of his house in Lipan village on Baluan Island (Figure 9.1). He holds a rope in his hand that is tied to six large (live) pigs laid out in a line on the yard in front of his house (*kulului*). They are placed in order of size, the largest closest to Sakumai. The pigs thus lined up and tied together are called *kup* in the Paluai language, the ethnic language of the community. At Sakumai's back, his eldest sòn and four paternal cross-cousins are standing upright, three of them holding his shoulder to give him support. Then he starts pulling on the rope, thus making the pigs scream. This action gives the ceremony its name: *yiwan kup* – to pull the pigs. On the other side of the rope, the main representatives of Sakumai's paternal grandmother's clan have taken

9.1 Sakumai Yêp is pulling the rope attached to the pigs while supported by his son and his patrilateral cross-cousins. Baluan Island, Papua New Guinea, 2011. Photo: Ton Otto.

place. They are called *pumbot* (after the root of the bamboo tree) because the woman who gave birth to his father originates from their clan; they are present to give their support to Sakumai's ritual.

Surrounding the scene of action, many people are observing the ceremony. I am among the public, moving about freely to take pictures. Dineke Schokkin, a PhD student in linguistics whom I am co-supervising, is making sound recordings. Sakumai pulls the rope again and the pigs scream once more. Now Sakumai calls out to his deceased father in a loud and strong voice:

> My Father, Yêp Ponaun.
> I am Sakumai Yêp.
> You are looking down on me.

> The female children of the Sauka, they are plentiful. [Sauka is the name of Sakumai's clan]
> The male children of the Sauka, they are plentiful.
> I am not able to keep them together. [literally, 'weave them together']

I was still small when you died and left me behind.
Who then will help me, who will give me strength
so that I can make a name for your place [or clan]?

But I did not forget you.
Father, you see me here with the rope of your *kup* in my hands.
Today I will pull your *kup*.
I will pull your *kup* with 10 pigs.[6]

Give me your strength and knowledge,
so that I can bring the *paralan* [the consanguineal relatives]
of your Sauka clan together.

Give strength and knowledge to my wife and children too.
Remove sickness from them, so that they may learn well in school
and may earn money and make the name of your Sauka big.

This is the end of my talk.

(Sakumai's speech, translation from Paluai)

The *yiwan kup* ritual was significant because it marked Sakumai's wish to take over the position of his deceased father, who had been an important traditional leader (*lapan*) of the Sauka clan, one of the largest clans on the island of Baluan. The pigs, termed *kup* only in the setting of the ceremony, represented the connections of the Sauka clan. After the pulling, they were formally given to important relatives and allies of the deceased leader, most of whom were dead too, whereas the meat was subsequently divided among their descendants.

Sakumai asked his father to give him wisdom (*mapian*) and strength (*porok*) so that he could keep the Sauka clan together. He used the word *awuy-an*, which means weaving the rim of a basket so that the interlaced coconut leaves stay together as one container. As the leader of the clan, it was Sakumai's task to keep the group together – both the male and the female descendants. By pulling the rope, he beseeched the spirit of his deceased father to transfer knowledge and strength to him so that he could perform his task as a leader. Standing behind him, the patrilineal descendants of the Sauka clan, in the person of Sakumai's eldest son, and the descendants of females of the clan, represented by four of his patrilateral cross-cousins, were embodying the patriclan of the Sauka brothers and their children as well as their *paralan* – the descendants of the sisters, who had married into other clans. On the other side of the line of pigs stood the leaders of the clan of his father's mother, the Muiou clan. Their support was essential for the transfer to be successful.

THE UNMAKING AND REMAKING OF CULTURAL WORLDS

9.2 Sakumai Yêp with the *kup* of six large pigs in front of him. Baluan Island, Papua New Guinea, 2011. Photo: Ton Otto.

9.3 Some of the crowd watching the *yiwan kup* ritual performed by Sakumai Yêp. Baluan Island, Papua New Guinea, 2011. Photo: Ton Otto.

The aim of the ceremony was to enable Sakumai to properly take up the position (*lopwan*) of his father, a position that he *de facto* had filled for quite some time. But he felt that he lacked legitimacy, both with regard to his deceased father, for whom he had yet to perform any mortuary rituals, and with regard to his living relatives. He explained in the ceremony (and later to me) that he was very young when his father died and that he had neither the knowledge nor the resources to perform the proper rituals.

What Sakumai accomplished by executing this traditional but extremely rare and almost forgotten ceremony was to establish his identity as a particular cultural agent, a self: a position from which to act and to have an effect on his social surroundings. Through the ritual, he identified and invoked the persons and relations that were important with regard to his position as a *lapan*, a traditional hereditary leader. He also created duration, a temporal extension for the identities he evoked, both backward in time and into the future. He called upon the strength and wisdom of his deceased father and presented pigs to his father's deceased relatives, represented by their living descendants. And he expressed the wish to pass on this strength to his children. In so doing, he recreated and enacted a cultural world with its own past and future, a world defined by specific social relations and obligations, a meaningful whole with himself at its centre. In short, the *yiwan kup* ritual can be seen as an act of world-making.

What surprised me most at the time was the neat coherence of the ritual, how it identified a particular, clearly defined social group with its boundaries, properties and exchanges with other similar groups. As we saw earlier in the chapter, Baluan social relations and social groupings generally did not appear as a neat coherent whole but rather provided a number of alternatives. For example, Sakumai could have claimed leadership and social agency by trying to become elected as a community leader, or he could have pursued a role as a religious leader or even as a specialist in traditional practices using his knowledge for commercial purposes, such as tourism. But, instead, he chose to recreate a ritual that was seen as purely *kastamwok*, the work of tradition.

Both his choice and his success in restaging an all-but-lost ritual are important aspects of cultural practice that prompt me to explore a new understanding of the temporalities of cultural continuity and change. Here, I have suggested the term 'world-making' to characterise what was happening in the ritual: the evocation of a coherent and meaningful whole carried out by the agents who are performing the ritual, both defining it and being defined *by* it. But note that this world also refers to and transgresses into other 'worlds': Sakumai asks his father to make his children successful in school so that they can earn money and make the name of the Sauka clan even greater. While building up the reputation of the clan is central to the world of traditional rituals such as the *yiwan kup*, going to school and earning money through business or government employment refer to other sets of cultural principles, mostly connected to different kinds of worlds. Before teasing out these entangled threads, I will offer some theoretical background to the concept of world-making which has now come into focus.

World-making and autopoiesis

In the previous section, I used the terms 'cultural world' and 'world-making' to describe and analyse the effects of a particular ritual. The use of the term 'world' or 'lifeworld' has a longer history in anthropology and has its roots in the phenomenological philosophy of Edmund Husserl, Martin Heidegger, Alfred Schutz and others (Desjarlais and Throop 2011). The aim of much phenomenologically inspired anthropology is to focus analytical attention on the experience and subjectivity of being in the world. While I share this interest in the subjectivity of human experience, my focus here is more on the creation of a subject, or agent, through cultural practice (such as the execution of a ritual) than on the details of the culturally mediated experience of the subject. Important for my purpose is the intricate connection between a particular human subject and 'their world'.[7]

To emphasise the processual aspect of this relationship, the term 'worlding' appears useful, which derives from literary critique and has been used, among others, by Gayatri Spivak (1990) and adopted by some schools of cultural studies.[8] Within anthropology, Donna Haraway (2007) and Anna Tsing (2010) have advantageously employed and developed the concept. The latter defines 'worlding' as 'the always experimental and partial . . . attribution of world-like characteristics to scenes of social encounter' (Tsing 2010, 48). More recently, Tsing has preferred the term 'world-making' to emphasise that this process involves both semiotic and material creation (Tsing 2015).[9] This is an important specification and, from my perspective, an essential further development of Geertz's semiotic understanding of cultural processes (see endnote 7).

To better understand the process of world-making as a matter of semiotic–material reproduction and survival, I suggest the use of the *autopoiesis* concept, which derives from cognitive biology. It was originally introduced by the Chilean neurobiologists Humberto Maturana and Francisco Varela to describe the self-maintaining chemical processes of living cells, but it was expanded by them and others to include all life including the human mind (Maturana and Varela 1987; Varela et al. 2016). In their inspiring book *What is Life?*, Margulis and Sagan write: 'Mind and body, perceiving and living, are equally self-referring, self-reflexive processes already present in the earliest bacteria. Mind, as well as body, stems from autopoiesis.' The essence of autopoiesis, they claim, is 'changing to stay the same' (Margulis and Sagan 1995, 31). Despite its apparent potential, the reception of this theoretical perspective in social theory has been slow and limited. Niklas Luhmann (1986) applied it to the reproduction of psychological and social systems, and the anthropologists Ivo Strecker and Stephen Tyler (2009, 25) used it to characterise cultures as 'interactive, autopoietic, self-organized configurations'. Christina Toren, drawing on her ethnographic work in Melanesia (Fiji), and João de Pina-Cabral have also argued for the potential of autopoiesis as a theoretical concept. Their view, that 'the understanding of human autopoiesis as always and inevitably a historical process' helps us to recognise, in particular, that 'we humans, considered collectively or as particular persons, really can – and really do – live the peopled world differently from one another and find our ideas of it by and large confirmed' (Toren and Pina-Cabral 2009, 12). Recently, the anthropological use of Maturana and Varela's theoretical insights – which, from the outset, assumed a continuity, rather than a break, between organic life and human culture – has received a significant boost through the work of Arturo Escobar (2018), de la Cadena and Blaser (2018), and others working with the concept of the pluriverse (the co-existence and interdependency of different worlds).

According to Maturana and Varela, the concept of autopoiesis refers to three fundamental processes necessary for the organisation of life: (1) the maintenance of a boundary of some kind that contains (2) a reaction network, which (3) produces and regenerates itself as well as the boundary. The philosopher Evan Thompson (2004, 2007), who is not only inspired by neurobiology but is also in dialogue with phenomenology and Buddhism, usefully identifies key processes of autopoiesis that appear centrally relevant for cultural analysis. Autopoiesis, he argues, entails the emergence of a self, an individual organism or agent. Simultaneously with the emergence of a self, a world emerges, a correlative domain of interaction specific to that self (see also von Uexküll's [1909] concept of *Umwelt*). The two together – self and world – equal sense-making. In other words, the organism's world is the sense it makes of the environment as a result of its actions within it. Translated to cultural theory, this biologically based perspective points to the intricate connection between selfhood and cultural world, between the practice and experience of being an agent and the continuous creation of reality through the process of living in, and interacting with, a changing environment.

To sum up: why do I prefer the concept of world-making to 'cultural domain' or 'sphere'; or 'lifeworld'; or 'ontology'? All these concepts refer to cultural diversity but world-making is a better theoretical tool because it focuses on the cultural practices involved in engendering worlds, which entail a continuous connection between agents reproducing and changing themselves and the cultural worlds they inhabit and create through their actions. How does world-making help us deal with the challenges posed by the concept of impermanence? On the one hand, it captures well the transience of cultural worlds as these have to be made and remade through continuous action. If actors no longer support a cultural world – or, in other words, if there cease to be selves that identify with a certain world – then that world ceases to exist. On the other hand, it helps to understand continuity as the autopoietic activity of self-identifying groups of people striving to persist in a changing environment. But this is not the whole story. The particular case study developed in this chapter concerning a lost and recreated ritual forces us to think about other factors that may sustain continuity across time, more or less independently from supporting agents.

To address this question, I will first elaborate on the kind of cultural material that Sakumai used in the performance of his ritual and that helped him invoke a cultural 'whole' or assemblage of people and their property – the Sauka clan – which contained certain identities, certain ways of establishing boundaries and certain ways of moving persons out of the group while at the same time maintaining exchange relationships with them.

The stuff of world-making

A central element of human world-making is – quite evidently – language (see Goodman 1978; Maturana and Varela 1987). A human world without some form of sign system is unthinkable, and languages, with their communicative complexities, are basic building-blocks of social institutions. Languages do change, and they also die out but, seen from a local and micro-social level, they provide a certain kind of inertia and thus resistance to change (see also Aikhenvald et al. 2021; Keesing 1979). This means that the cultural specifics of languages may continue to have an impact on practices of world-making, even in situations in which new institutions and alternative worldings are available and developing. In the following, I will argue that a substrate of knowledge concerning specific kin relations and personal characteristics, encapsulated in the Baluan language, provided a strong base for Sakumai's world-making, which entailed the re-launch and possibly recreation of a near-forgotten ritual that had not been practised for a very long time (probably more than 70 years).

Following local usage, also adopted by linguist Dineke Schokkin (2014), I will refer to the language spoken on Baluan as *Paluai*. Paluai is a fairly typical Oceanic[10] language in typological respects. Important for the present discussion is that nouns in Paluai can be divided into classes based on how they are used in possessive constructions. The term 'possessive' is used here in the sense of a grammatical construction that usually refers to a relation of close association characterised by an entity 'having', 'owning' or 'controlling' another entity. Formally, there are two types of possessive constructions in Paluai: direct and indirect (see Schokkin 2014; Schokkin and Otto 2017). With direct possession, a suffix is added directly to a nominal stem, whereas, in the case of indirect possession, a suffix is added to a possessive particle ('ta') following the noun. Semantically, the terms 'alienable' and 'inalienable' are often used to indicate two contrasting kinds of possessive relationship. Although there is probably not a one-to-one correspondence between 'inalienable' and the formal construction called 'directly possessed', there is at least an overwhelming overlap. Words that are typically found in the directly possessed form are terms for body parts and kin, indicating a very close and inalienable relationship. For example, 'my leg' (*kê-ng*) can never be 'your leg' (*kê-m*), but 'my pig' (*pou ta-ng*), which is always in an indirectly possessed form, can be transferred into 'your pig' (*pou ta-o*).

I will now discuss kinship relations and, thereafter, a number of key terms that refer to central qualities and properties of humans, seen as individuals and as groups. Interestingly, both types of words (kin terms and human qualities) are mostly found in the directly possessed form.

The *yiwan kup* ceremony carried out by Sakumai identified and confirmed the relevant traditional kin relations and group identities at play. One could say that, on Baluan, all traditional group identities derived from two key relations: that between a husband and wife (and thus the relationship between their respective families), and that between a brother and sister (and their descendants). The husband–wife relation can produce children and thus secure the continuation of the patrilineal descent group, which was (and partly is) the core property-owning entity in traditional Baluan society. The marriage between a man and a woman creates the category of the affines (in-laws), with the key or prototypical role allocated to the wife's brother, called *polam* (this is a reciprocal term – the sister's husband is also *polam*). While all relationships in the patriclan are expressed by nouns that take the directly possessed form (indicating inalienability), the key affinal relation is never expressed in this form (Schokkin and Otto 2017).

A similar structural feature of the Paluai language can be observed in the second set of traditional group identities to be discussed here, namely those deriving from the descendants of a brother–sister pair. These descendants are consanguineally related (indicated by directly possessed nouns) but, as a result of the dominant patrilineal descent logic, they become members of different property-owning social entities (clans). Correspondingly, their relationship is captured by another term, that of *pwai* (cross-cousin), which is in an indirectly possessed (alienable) form. While traditional Baluan cultural practices and kin-terms acknowledge the continuing links between cross-cousins based on common descent, they also provide for the gradual loosening of the rights on clan property of the cross-cousins originating from the sister who married out of the clan. This happened (and happens) through gift-giving during mortuary rites. The *yiwan kup* ritual performed by Sakumai and his family builds on this same logic.

IMPERMANENCE

The group that Sakumai aims to keep together as a distinct unit is the patriclan (*pusungop*) named Sauka. The members of a patriclan trace their descent back to one apical ancestor. The clan not only comprises human members but is also composed of certain characteristic qualities and material and immaterial properties. Significantly, the words with which such qualities and properties are expressed are also (almost always) put in the directly possessed – that is, inalienable – form.

The first term I wish to present is *arona*, which can be translated with 'way; procedure; nature; character; personality' and can refer to an attribute of both animate and inanimate entities. Interestingly, *arona* represents two senses at the same time: how an activity is *habitually* carried out, and how it *should* be carried out. Thus, the 'moral' or 'prescriptive' dimension is always intrinsic to the habitual, 'customary' dimension; the two cannot be regarded as separate from each other. When used to describe the qualities of a descent group like the Sauka, *arona* refers to the collective ways that are characteristic for this group, their collective 'character'. It is put in the directly possessed form *arona-n-ip Sauka*, which concretely refers to things like the clan's qualities in organising big and successful ceremonies, as well as their special skills as fishermen.

The second term that is often used in characterising a person or a group of persons is *mamarou*. In its narrow sense, *mamarou* means 'artefact'. This meaning has been metaphorically extended to also encompass the skills and knowledge necessary for making artefacts, as well as skills and knowledge in a more general sense. Further extending from there, it is also used to indicate the typical way of doing things, or the style, of a person or a group. In contrast to *arona*, it seems that *mamarou* can only modify a noun referring to human beings. In most instances, it is directly possessed, for example, *mamarou-n panu* ('the way of the village') or *mamarou-n-ep Paluai* ('the way of us Baluan people'). In connection to the Sauka clan, *mamarou-n-ip Sauka,* concretely refers to the clan's use of red cloth during their ceremonies and their production of beautifully carved ceremonial beds, as well as to other examples of their material style and production.

The third and possibly most frequently used term in the context of identifying and characterising a descent group is *nuruna*. The term appears quite often in its unpossessed or indirectly possessed (and shortened) form *nurun*. It then has a very general meaning, comparable to English 'things' or 'stuff', and seems to be able to refer to almost any object or abstract notion. In its directly possessed form, *nuruna* includes everything (either material or immaterial) typically associated with a certain person or clan. For a clan, this would be, for example, particular drumbeats, stories, styles of dressing, names and so on. It can be said that these are seen as 'belongings' or 'property' of that particular clan, for which it has the exclusive right of use, including the right to pass on use-right to members of other clans.

A central part of a clan's *nurunan* is its land (*ponat*), which often consists of many named parts that have different histories of usage and ownership rights. In the case of the Sauka, which is a clan with a strong reputation or name (*ngayan*), its *nurunan* also comprises a whole series of named objects and practices. This is considered important property that lesser clans envy and try to acquire as well, through marriage and exchange practices. The list of *Nurunanip Sauka* includes:

- title of their *lapan*: *Peu* ('shark')
- their canoe: *Sauka Kireng*
- the sail of their canoe: *Pale poralei*
- their ceremonial bed: *Pwat kiapung*
- a white cowrie shell used as decoration: *Naet ki se mwal* ('shell that surpasses the others')
- the lime used when chewing betelnut: *Kop Sapuran* or *Ki pong Paluai*
- their basket: *Sapuran*; *Kisaput* ('it will contain all things')
- their log drum: *Kolon konou* or *Lapan konou*
- their particular drum beat: *Pwase ki le kot*
- the name of their house: *Puli an lou* ('mountain of men'); *Wum lapan lou* ('house of the *lapan* of living people')
- their fishing net: *Kalon manuai* ('wing of the eagle')
- their spear: *Lemang*
- the knife (from shell) to cut the betelnut: *Yanul en se*
- the stone to make kava: *Yoi an kau / Narulapan* ('son of *lapan*')
- a particular ear decoration: *Ngapat*
- their red cloth (no special name; *tiap yamyaman*)

All their possessions (*nurunan*) and their actions contribute to the establishment of the Sauka's name (*ngayanip Sauka*), which is also used in a directly possessed form – that is, as inalienable property. In Sakumai's speech to his deceased father, the making of a name is a central aim of his leadership, in addition to bringing the people together. For this, he needs both strength (*porok*) and knowledge (*mapia*), which he requests from his father. *Porok* is not found in a directly possessed form and *mapia* is mostly found in the form *mapian*, which is grammatically in a third-person directly possessed form but without a noun that it modifies. An obvious conclusion would be that both *porok* and *mapia* are in a different category from the directly possessed concepts discussed here and that both can be moved from person to person. An interesting aspect of knowledge (*mapia*) is that it can be opened (*puk*) to others, a semantic construction that is also used with regard to money (*kokon*). This refers to a certain logic of keeping (within the family or by a single person) and giving (to acknowledge and maintain specific relationships).[11]

Sakumai's autopoietic world-making in the *yiwan kup* ritual built on the concepts that I have sketched in this section. Much specific knowledge about this and other rituals had been lost due to the conscious abolition of tradition by the Paliau Movement and as a consequence of the death of people who had observed such rituals in their youth. Yet basic concepts and structures necessary for the execution of these rituals survived in the Paluai language and thus remained in active linguistic use despite the emergence of other cultural worlds pertaining to the aforementioned *lotu* and *gavman*. What is the significance of this observation for understanding continuities and discontinuities of cultural worlds?

The temporalities and multiplexities of world-making

As mentioned in the introduction to this chapter, the *yiwan kup* ceremony had ostensibly been abolished and forgotten on Baluan, in contrast to many other traditional rituals that have seen a revival from the 1970s onward. Since the beginning of my fieldwork in 1986, I have witnessed many instances of *pailou*, the ceremonies immediately following death, and also *pukan kokon*, a mortuary ritual conducted several years later, and I have documented the emergence of a new mortuary ceremony called *cement* (Otto 2018). But I had heard about only two examples of performances that somehow resembled the *yiwan kup*, since they focused on the transfer of traditional authority and used pigs connected by a rope to the new leader, who would pull (*yiwan*) the rope.

These ceremonies happened quite some time before my first fieldwork and, according to my notes, were small-scale and conducted by leaders of less prominent clans. Sakumai was the leader of one of the largest clans on the island and he had slowly built up a wide-reaching reputation through his ability to initiate and lead traditional ceremonies, especially around marriage and death. I had known him from the time that he, as a young man, was much in doubt about his role as leader of the clan. He had been adopted by the last *lapan* of the Sauka, a hereditary

THE UNMAKING AND REMAKING OF CULTURAL WORLDS

leadership status normally transferred to the eldest son. Because his adoptive father did not have other male children, Sakumai should rightfully have been his successor. But his *lapan* father died while Sakumai was still young and therefore had not been able to pass on most of his cultural knowledge. Sakumai told me that, when the other clan members insisted that he take up the *lapan* position, he was reluctant at first. Once he had accepted, he tried to obtain much-needed cultural information from the elder clan-members but he was disappointed about how little his relatives knew or were willing to share. Therefore, he said, he had been forced to 'steal' his knowledge by observing other people's ceremonies as much as he could. The cultural knowledge that he finally gathered and used to perform the *yiwan kup* was the result of a continuous process of investigating, trialling, reconstructing, combining and inventing.

The chain of knowledge transfer, necessary for the continued performance of the ritual, was not only broken by the early death of his adoptive father. It was also, and to a high degree, disturbed by the cultural changes that had taken place on the island and in which his father had wholeheartedly participated. This included conversion to Christianity in the 1930s, leading to the repression of ancestor worship and the rejection of the active invocation of ancestral support, which is one of the key elements of the *yiwan kup* ceremony. An even more comprehensive cultural change was instigated by the indigenous Paliau Movement, which succeeded in discarding all major traditional rituals and, in particular, the grand feasts surrounding the death of a clan leader and the transfer of his authority to a new leader. These large-scale celebrations were seen as wasteful and hindering economic and political progress. The Paliau Movement resulted in the loss of much traditional cultural knowledge, which had become not only irrelevant for daily practice but also illegitimate according to the aims and values of the 'new way' of the Movement (Otto 1992). Finally, the colonial government introduced many new institutions such as cooperatives, schools and elected local councils, none of which fitted in with traditional cultural knowledge and practices. Despite these massive influences for change and the concomitant destruction of traditional knowledge, surprisingly much of it survived (often among just a few individuals). It then reemerged in situations where it became possible and advantageous for certain people to (re)assert a different kind of agency by evoking and rebuilding a world based on traditional concepts and practices. And here they were helped by the different temporalities of the 'stuff' that I discussed in the previous section, such as the concepts and grammar of kin relations and the material and immaterial properties of kin groups.

IMPERMANENCE

I argue that the whole idiom and logic of kin relations and clan groupings, although neglected and even suppressed in alternative world-makings, was still present in the local Paluai language. In that way, it formed a substrate of knowledge that Sakumai and others, tapping into the potential of traditional worlds, could build upon. The inertia of linguistic forms (concepts and grammar) became a resource for their world-making. Additionally, the old social units and relations (patriclans, affines and cross-cousins) were still closely connected to different forms of property and their transfer, most importantly land, despite consistent attempts by the colonial government to individualise land tenure. This tendency to hold on to traditional property practices had been enforced by post-independence legislation, acknowledging traditional ways of reckoning land rights to be defended before local land magistrates. Therefore, the recollection of ceremonial exchanges conducted in the past became an important asset once again, when it could be used to contest and defend claims to land property in court.

The historicity connected to past and present exchanges, now often recorded in private notebooks, has become an important aspect of the cultural world that Sakumai invoked and recreated in his *yiwan kup* ritual. With it, he also created an enduring claim to his clan property that he can use in future conflicts and challenges. Finally, the different properties belonging to the clan, in the form of named objects and practices – the *nurunanip Sauka* – constitute additional tokens of support for memory and practice to conceive of an entity that has an enduring existence and right of being. Thus, all these elements refer to, and conjure up, a kind of cultural world that ceased to exist for many decades (roughly from the 1940s to the 1980s) but that nevertheless can be claimed to have a demonstrable continuity with the past. However, the existence of this world in the present configuration of alternative and competing worlds dramatically changes the parameters of its functioning as a viable form of social reproduction.

The contemporary world of *yiwan kup* cannot stand or develop by itself. This applies equally to other traditional practices that involve mechanisms of traditional social reproduction, as discussed by Foster (1995) and the New Melanesian Ethnographers. As was already clear from Sakumai's invocation of his deceased father to help his children succeed in school and secure paid jobs, this traditional world existed in symbiosis with the worlds of modern schooling, business and the state – just like these other worlds co-existed with, and partially depended on, land-owning units (for example, those created by traditional practices of inheritance and exchange). Sakumai's *yiwan kup* world can be described

THE UNMAKING AND REMAKING OF CULTURAL WORLDS

as an autopoietic cultural whole, as I have argued in this chapter, but this whole only manifested itself fully at the moment of the ritual. In daily practice, Sakumai had to negotiate school fees, market prices of copra, cocoa and fish, political elections and so on. But the world of *yiwan kup* occupied much of his mind and he invested much time and effort in maintaining his *lapan* status and the relationships with relevant kin-groups by taking the lead in numerous other traditional exchange ceremonies. In this way, he not only kept up his reputation as a widely respected traditional leader but he also put himself in a position in which he could call on his relatives for support with activities that were not strictly traditional. In other words, his position as a traditional leader provided him with access to resources that extended beyond the confines of the world of tradition.

Thus, the world of *yiwan kup* is only 'whole' at certain instances – in particular, at the time of the execution of the ritual itself – and its existence is more diffuse and even contested in other contexts, such as those of organised religion or the state. Its boundaries may be more or less articulated in these other contexts, especially if there is competition over similar resources. This happened, for example, when another aspirant leader organised a large cultural festival on the island to stimulate the performance of traditional dances and attract tourists. As the events of the festival unfolded, traditional practices such as the *yiwan kup* were distinguished from those of the festival by calling the former *kastam* and the latter *kalsa*, thus demarcating a boundary between 'real tradition' and 'tradition in a Western sense', which aims to generate international attention and draw in tourist money (Otto 2015).

Since the different cultural worlds on Baluan exist in symbiosis and develop both through mutual dependency and strenuous competition with each other, I suggest that the term *sympoiesis* (Haraway 2016) may be an apt characterisation of how their autopoietic processes are impacted by – and even driven by – their co-existence. In Haraway's understanding, sympoiesis is not necessarily based on peaceful collaboration but can also be the result of struggle, amalgamation, domination and repression. While autopoiesis may refer to the world-making and ordering practice of human beings, sympoiesis connotes the complex fields of symbiosis in which the autopoietic practices happen and influence each other. In Haraway's words, 'Sympoiesis enfolds autopoiesis and generatively unfurls and extends it' (Haraway 2016, 58).

Conclusion

My story of the almost-lost ritual of *yiwan kup* touches on a number of issues that are relevant from the perspective of the impermanence of cultural forms. First, the abolishment of the ritual was part of a conscious effort by the Paliau Movement to create another cultural world at a specific colonial historical conjuncture, to regain a sense of agency for the indigenous population. This new cultural world included many innovations taken from other worlds, such as Christian missions and colonial administrative institutions, and rejected many of the cultural institutions of the old indigenous world. In this chapter, I have shown that this cultural erasure, though successful for several decades, has failed to prevent the reemergence of a specialised and spectacular type of ritual linked to the abolished rituals of leadership transition from the past.

Second, analysing the process of world-making, I argue that substantial information about the old rituals had been lost due to the interruption of the chains of knowledge-transfer through the new practices of the Paliau Movement and the death of key knowledgeable persons. However, a considerable amount of contextual knowledge persisted in the concepts and structures of the local language and in the continued practices of kin relations. This knowledge constituted the basic material used in the reconstruction and reinvention of the ritual. The crucial factor of its reemergence was the activity of one individual, Sakumai Yêp, with his network of kin, who, in the autopoietic process of the *yiwan kup* ritual, gave meaning and content to his agency as the leader of his kin-group and its traditional properties.

Third, the decision and actions of Sakumai and his family were not an isolated factor but have to be seen in the postcolonial context in which different cultural worlds co-exist and are in a kind of symbiotic relation with each other, which implies both competition and interdependency. Therefore, the significance and effect of the ritual in the present day are very different from those of similar rituals in the past. This complex process of loss, change and (re)creation may be aptly captured by the concept of sympoiesis that Haraway has suggested as a necessary corollary of autopoiesis. Seeing cultural worlds as driven by the simultaneous processes of autopoiesis and sympoiesis thus provides a way to tackle questions of both cultural change and (unexpected) cultural continuity – in short, questions that address the impermanence of cultural worlds.

Acknowledgements

As always, I wish to express my deep appreciation and gratitude for how the people of Baluan have tolerated me, engaged with me and made me feel welcome during our long-term collaboration extending over 35 years. Concerning the present chapter, I am particularly indebted to Sakumai Yêp and the other members of my Sauka family. For highly constructive critique and comments on earlier versions of this chapter, I am grateful to Alexandra Aikhenvald, Peter Bakker, Dineke Schokkin, Iwona Janicka, Anna-Karina Hermkens and my two co-editors Haidy Geismar and Cameron Warner. Finally, I wish to thank the participants in the Language and Culture Research Centre at James Cook University for their lively discussion of my presentation of material from this chapter during a seminar held on 4 March 2020.

Notes

1. In Tylor's conception, culture (used in the singular) was synonymous with the notion of civilisation, but this was different from its subsequent use, emphasising differences between cultures (in the plural) rather than the development of human culture in different stages.
2. The concept of culture has been particularly important for the American tradition of cultural anthropology, starting with Boas and continuing through Geertz to the present (see Otto and Bubandt 2010). Johannes Fabian (1983) argues that the culture concept, despite its focus on contemporary differences, has often maintained a connotation of differences in stages of development, thus implicitly adding a temporary dimension to the cultural differences between people that live at the same time. He calls this the denial of coevalness.
3. See, for example, Holbraad and Pedersen 2017.
4. See, for example, Wolf 1982, Keesing 1992 and Sahlins 2004.
5. Later Barth (1993) proposed the concept of 'tradition of knowledge', which I find useful because it also refers to different spheres within the same society and because, in his usage, it links a body of knowledge with social organisation, communication and social action.
6. Sakumai had gathered ten pigs in all, but he had already used four of them in the two ceremonies he had performed prior to the *yiwan kup*.
7. This connection has already been pointed to and articulated by the semiotic approach to culture of Clifford Geertz (1973, 1980).
8. See, for example, Wilson and Connery (2007). The idea that a world is always 'worlding' goes back to Heidegger (see Ingold 2010).
9. In a footnote, Tsing (2015, 292) points to overlap with, but also difference from, the concept of 'ontology'. Ontology refers to philosophies of being, cosmologies, while world-making focuses on practical activities. All living beings make worlds, and world-making projects overlap. Whereas ontology is occupied with differences and is mostly used to segregate perspectives, 'thinking through world-making allows layering and historically consequential friction' (Tsing 2015, 292).
10. Oceanic languages constitute a subset of the larger family of Austronesian languages.
11. The development of this interesting logic awaits another article; but see Weiner (1992) on the paradox of keeping while giving.

References

Aikhenvald, Alexandra Y., R.M.W. Dixon and Nerida Jarkey, eds. 2021. *The Integration of Language and Society: A cross-linguistic typology*. Oxford: Oxford University Press.

Barth, Fredrik. 1993. *Balinese Worlds*. Chicago, IL: University of Chicago Press.

Bourdieu, Pierre. 1977. *Outline of a Theory of Practice*. Cambridge: Cambridge University Press.

de la Cadena, Marisol, and Mario Blaser, eds. 2018. *A World of Many Worlds*. Durham, NC, and London: Duke University Press.

Desjarlais, Robert, and C. Jason Throop. 2011. 'Phenomenological approaches in anthropology', *Annual Review of Anthropology* 40: 87–102.

Escobar, Arturo. 2018. *Designs for the Pluriverse: Radical interdependence, autonomy, and the making of worlds*. Durham, NC, and London: Duke University Press.

Fabian, Johannes. 1983. *Time and the Other: How anthropology makes its object*. New York: Columbia University Press.

Foster, Robert J. 1995. *Social Reproduction and History in Melanesia: Mortuary ritual, gift exchange, and custom in the Tanga Islands*. Cambridge: Cambridge University Press.

Geertz, Clifford. 1973. *The Interpretation of Cultures*. New York: Basic Books.

Geertz, Clifford. 1980. *Negara: The theatre state in nineteenth-century Bali*. Princeton, NJ: Princeton University Press.

Goodman, Nelson. 1978. *Ways of Worldmaking*. Indianapolis, IN: Hackett.

Haraway, Donna J. 2007. *When Species Meet*. Minneapolis, MN: University of Minnesota Press.

Haraway, Donna J. 2016. *Staying with the Trouble: Making kin in the Chthulucene*. Durham, NC, and London: Duke University Press.

Holbraad, Martin, and Morten Axel Pedersen. 2017. *The Ontological Turn: An anthropological exposition*. Cambridge: Cambridge University Press.

Ingold, Tim. 2010. 'Drawing together'. In *Experiments in Holism*, edited by Ton Otto and Nils Bubandt, 299–313. Oxford: Wiley-Blackwell.

Josephides, Lisette. 1991. 'Metaphors, metathemes, and the construction of sociality: A critique of the new Melanesian ethnography', *Journal of the Royal Anthropological Institute–MAN* 26(1): 145–61.

Keesing, Roger M. 1979. 'Linguistic knowledge and cultural knowledge: Some doubts and speculations', *American Anthropologist* 81(1): 14–36.

Keesing, Roger M. 1992. *Custom and Confrontation: Kwaio struggle for cultural autonomy*. Chicago, IL: University of Chicago Press.

Luhmann, Niklas. 1986. 'The autopoiesis of social systems'. In *Sociocybernetic Paradoxes*, edited by Felix Geyer and Johannes van der Zouwen, 172–92. London: Sage.

Margulis, Lynn, and Dorion Sagan. 1995. *What is Life?* Berkeley, CA: University of California Press.

Maturana, Humberto, and Francisco Varela. 1987. *The Tree of Knowledge: The biological roots of human understanding*. Berkeley, CA: Shambhala.

Otto, Ton. 1991. 'The politics of tradition in Baluan: Social change and the construction of the past in a Manus society'. PhD thesis, Australian National University.

Otto, Ton. 1992. 'The Paliau movement in Manus and the objectification of tradition', *History and Anthropology* 5: 427–54.

Otto, Ton. 1997. 'Review of *Social Reproduction and History in Melanesia*, by Robert J. Foster', *The Contemporary Pacific* 9(2): 529–32.

Otto, Ton. 1998. 'Local narratives of a great transformation: Conversion to Christianity in Manus, Papua New Guinea', *FOLK: Journal of the Danish Ethnographic Society* 40: 71–97.

Otto, Ton. 2011. 'Inventing traditions and remembering the past in Manus'. In *Changing Contexts, Shifting Meanings: Transformations of cultural traditions in Oceania*, edited by Elfriede Hermann, 157–73. Honolulu: University of Hawai'i Press.

Otto, Ton. 2015. 'Transformations of cultural heritage in Melanesia: From Kastam to Kalsa', *International Journal of Heritage Studies* 21(2): 117–32.

Otto, Ton. 2018. '*My culture, I perform it, I can change it*: Film, audience and cultural critique', *Visual Anthropology* 31(4–5) 318–35.

Otto, Ton, and Nils Bubandt. 2010. 'Beyond cultural wholes? Introduction to Part II'. In *Experiments in Holism: Theory and practice in contemporary anthropology*, edited by Ton Otto and Nils Bubandt, 89–101. Oxford: Wiley-Blackwell.

Sahlins, Marshall. 2004. *Apologies to Thucydides: Understanding history as culture and vice versa*. Chicago, IL, and London: University of Chicago Press.

Schokkin, Gerda. 2014. 'A grammar of Paluai, the language of Baluan Island, Papua New Guinea'. PhD thesis, James Cook University.

Schokkin, Dineke, and Ton Otto. 2017. 'Relatives and relations in Paluai', *Oceanic Linguistics* 56(1): 226–46.

Schwartz, Theodore. 1962. 'The Paliau movement in the Admiralty Islands, 1946–1954', *Anthropological Papers of the American Museum of Natural History* 49: 207–421.

Spivak, Gayatri. 1990. *The Post-Colonial Critic*. New York: Routledge.

Strecker, Ivo, and Stephen Tyler, eds. 2009. *Culture and Rhetoric*. New York and Oxford: Berghahn.

Thompson, Evan. 2004. 'Life and mind: From autopoiesis to neurophenomenology. A tribute to Francisco Varela', *Phenomenology and the Cognitive Sciences* 3: 381–98.

Thompson, Evan. 2007. *Mind in Life: Biology, phenomenology, and the sciences of mind*. Cambridge, MA: Harvard University Press.

Toren, Christina, and João de Pina-Cabral. 2009. 'Introduction: What is happening to epistemology?' *Social Analysis* 53(2): 1–18.

Tsing, Anna Lowenhaupt. 2010. 'Worlding the matsutake diaspora: Or, can actor-network theory experiment with holism?' In *Experiments in Holism: Theory and practice in contemporary anthropology*, edited by Ton Otto and Nils Bubandt, 47–66. Malden, MA, and Oxford: Wiley-Blackwell.

Tsing, Anna Lowenhaupt. 2015. *The Mushroom at the End of the World: On the possibility of life in capitalist ruins*. Princeton, NJ, and Oxford: Princeton University Press.

Tylor, Edward B. 1871. *Primitive Culture, Volume 1*. London: John Murray.

Varela, Francisco, Evan Thompson and Eleanor Rosch. 2016. *The Embodied Mind: Cognitive science and human experience* (revised edition). Cambridge, MA: MIT Press.

von Uexküll, Jakob. 1909. *Umwelt und Innenwelt der Tiere*. Berlin: J. Springer.

Weiner, Annette B. 1992. *Inalienable Possessions: The paradox of keeping-while-giving*. Berkeley, CA: University of California Press.

Williams, Raymond. 1973. 'Base and superstructure in Marxist cultural theory', *New Left Review* 1(82): 3–16.

Wilson, Rob, and Christopher Leigh Connery, eds. 2007. *The Worlding Project: Doing cultural studies in the era of globalization*. Santa Cruz, CA: New Pacific Press.

Wolf, Eric R. 1982. *Europe and the People without History*. Berkeley, CA: University of California Press.

10
'Do what you think about': fashionable responses to the end of Tibet

Cameron David Warner

Reflecting on 20 years of visiting Tibetan friends in India, Nepal and China, when I catch up with someone, they often end up pessimistically contemplating the changes they see around themselves. The Dalai Lama is ageing. Young people are not learning Tibetan well enough. Tibetans in Nepal and India are leaving Asia. The Chinese government is resettling nomads in squalid, economically and socially deprived villages. The glaciers are melting and poachers are murdering wild animals. Tibetan society is becoming amoral and materialistic. These lamentations are not just the product of North American and European media but circulate quietly among Tibetans in the People's Republic of China (PRC), who often have no access to information outside of their own economic and social sphere. Some are perennial concerns, others more recent (Thurston 2015). Some are generational, others are not (Adams 2007). To quote one representative example from a 2016 post on the very popular WeChat channel, Tibet Sheep (lung tshang dpal yon), about language use on signboards in Tibetan areas of the PRC:

> Tibet is like a huge bag stuffed with many crucial things or a solitary flower wrapped with poisonous thorns. Particularly in this twenty-first century when changes are taking place in pronounced ways, the fate of our people is becoming like the setting sun. Consequently, I want to touch on some of the dark critical issues on our path (High Peaks Pure Earth 2020).

The ubiquity and long history of the doom-and-gloom narratives have spurred a cottage industry of research that attempts to capture the complexity on the ground, often under difficult circumstances (Bauer and Gyal 2015; Liu 2015; Gaerrang [Kabzung] 2015; Dak Lhagyal 2019; Roche 2019). My interest here is in those who intentionally eschew these discourses but do not espouse a naïve optimism – Tibetans who, as my friend said to me, '[a]void the hope and sorrow trap'. But how, as researchers, do we get purchase on something as elusive and mercurial as perceptions and experiences of cultural change? How do we tease apart globalised and politicised discourses from ontological Buddhist notions and localised interpretations, such as our (perhaps ill-founded) expectations that Buddhists in Tibet would naturally be accepting of impermanence? Travelling through Tibetan communities in Sichuan and Qinghai in the spring of 2018, I started paying closer attention to an alternative discourse on the process of cultural change. A representative snippet from my fieldnotes reveals the following:

> Change is inevitable. That is what the lamas mean when they say 'impermanence'. But you know, sometimes some things never seem to change. However, if you look closer, there is usually change there too. So many people complain now about the changes to Tibetan society. So many people are nostalgic for the old ways. Don't get me wrong, some of the changes are not good. But we Tibetans need to save the best things about our culture and just let some things go. So many times we are told, 'if this happens, that will be the end of Tibet'. 'Like what?', I asked. 'You know. Like forgetting our language or religion. Like the nomads being moved into settlements. But you have to look closer . . . Tibetan culture has always been changing. We Tibetans are so narrow-minded, so superstitious. Tibetan culture is more than just Buddhism, and it should be more in the future too.' 'Like what?', I asked again. 'Whatever we want it to be . . .'

This statement, and others like it, came in response to my showing Tibetan fashion designers and musicians pictures of Tibetan clothing and jewellery from 1950–1, a period immediately preceding widescale iconoclasm, and asking them to reflect on contemporary trends in Tibetan popular culture. Why have some patterns, colours, shapes, sounds and expressions in Tibetan clothing and music either persisted over centuries or only slowly changed, while others seemed to appear and disappear with incredible speed? Why do some come and go and others just disappear? What made an item of clothing or a song quintessentially 'Tibetan' in 1950 and in 2018?

I focus here on an admittedly small and select group of Tibetans who knowingly act within this discursive field, choosing to respond to the impermanence of Tibetan society and culture with creativity rather than accept the fatalistic nihilism of their compatriots that, at times, seems on the brink of engulfing them. Their responses exhibit subtle pivots between striving for preservation and embracing change's liberative potential. I draw on the idea of impermanence as articulated in Buddhist discourses that surround Tibetans in order to make a deliberately decolonial move intended to open the canon to a wider diversity of intellectual inspiration. In that sense, impermanence is working here on two interrelated levels: occasionally as an emic concept between Tibetans and myself and as a *sui generis* critical theory of change that I argue is applicable in a wide variety of non-Buddhist contexts. The way impermanence lurks in the toolkit of Tibetan fashion designers is comparable to Arturo Escobar's recent use of Buddhist notions of interdependence as one pillar of his manifesto for the future of design (Escobar 2018) because of the interlocking nature of interdependence and impermanence in doctrines of Mahāyāna Buddhism, such as those found in Tibet.

For some Tibetans who work as musicians and fashion designers – on the cusp between heritage preservation and popular innovation – the changes happening in Tibet and to Tibetans worldwide are an opportunity to develop new and profound connections to their cultural and material inheritance for themselves, their generation, and non-Tibetan audiences inside and outside of the PRC. My portrait of Tibetan designers is crafted to deliberately challenge the Eurocentric concern for cultural authenticity and its power, cultural appropriation and orientalism. Tibetan designers are not passive victims of global processes if we choose to see them as they see themselves.[1] (And if the fans[2] of these brands recognise the authenticity and agency of these designers, so should we.) In short, I draw our attention to how Tibetan designers create continuity of their culture through designing how it will change. They preserve Tibetan culture by continually remaking music and fashion in the world around them.

My approach to this material derives from a multi-year collaborative project to study the practice of ethnographic collection and museum exhibitions as collaborative forms of participant observation and data collection that speak to the intersections of social and material values.[3]

Artefact collection and ethnographic exhibition as research method

The value of ethnographic artefacts and the practice of collection itself, one of the roots of anthropology as a scientific endeavour, has reemerged as a basis for European museums to collaborate with sister-institutions in the Global South and investigate their own history (Johnsen 2020). My interest in the Tibetan fashion designers at the heart of this study came about indirectly, via a collection of Tibetan artefacts in Denmark. The early history of anthropology in Denmark is inseparable from the collection of artefacts, the rise of the ethnographic museum and the design of ethnographic exhibitions. This is especially evident in Denmark's interest in Mongolia and Tibet. As part of the Third Danish Expedition to Central Asia, HRH Prince Peter of Greece and Denmark, who studied anthropology with Bronislaw Malinowski at the London School of Economics, amassed a large collection of biological samples, anthropomorphic measurements and ethnographic artefacts from Tibetan migrants to Kalimpong during two extended stays between 1950 and 1957.

In recent years, renewed academic interest in materiality and value, together with the reassessment of the role of ethnographic museums in contemporary society, has brought attention back to earlier researchers and their data, including Prince Peter and his collection (Brox and Zeitzen 2017). These academic concerns have also dovetailed with para-academic conversations about the value of ethnographic artefacts globally and the question of repatriation, especially in relation to incidents of theft or colonial manipulation and oppression. However, Prince Peter's collection differs from other collections of Tibetan artefacts (Harris 2012) in that he meticulously documented his acquisitions in reports to the National Museum of Denmark, which detail how Tibetans approached him to sell their possessions, for which he paid handsomely. Rather than labour surreptitiously like many in his day, he collected biological samples at the local police station and kept in frequent contact with India's postcolonial government. To my knowledge, no one from the Tibetan community has ever suggested his collection ought to be repatriated. The value of his collection to my research lies, therefore, in a different set of questions about the practice of ethnographic collection and display itself. What are the social and material values of Prince Peter's collection to contemporary Danes and Tibetans? What does a case like this tell us about the relationship of social values to material value? And how have value regimes changed over time?

To push these emergent paradigms further, in 2016, I began a project to study Prince Peter's work, conduct a 'research and ethnographic collection' expedition of my own and curate a series of museum exhibitions as a form of participant observation and experimental research design. My subproject was part of a collaborative project entitled 'Precious Relics: Materiality and Value in the Practice of Ethnographic Collection', developed together with colleagues from Aarhus University, the Moesgaard Museum, the National Museum of Denmark, the Library of Tibetan Works and Archives, Patan Museum, Lumbini Buddhist University, and scholars in Papua New Guinea. We set out to collect new artefacts for the purpose of designing four museum exhibitions: one among each of the collaborative populations, and an integrated exhibition at Moesgaard Museum in Denmark. For further information on one of these exhibits, see Chapter 18 on 'Museum of Impermanence' in this volume. Eventually, my efforts to build a new collection for display in India and Denmark led me away from trying to understand the value of Prince Peter's collection today and toward Tibetan perceptions of how their culture has changed from 1950 to 2018, and especially the perils and promises of impermanence for Tibet's creative class.

A focus on fashion

The items from Prince Peter's collection that stood out to me as a researcher were the same ones that seemed to stand out the most to him, too: articles of clothing previously worn by particular members of the Dalai Lama's government, well-known Tibetan aristocrats and their families.[4] For Prince Peter, these items represented a way of life eliminated from existence by the invasion of Tibet by the People's Liberation Army in 1949–51 – objects that Tibetan aristocrats were willing to sell in Kalimpong but would never have sold while in Tibet months earlier. For me, the frayed cuffs, the oil stained into the brims of the hats, the gem missing from an earring – these are all traces left behind by particular men and women whom we know. We have photos of them in this regalia, details of their roles in society, and know the stories of their often-tragic lives. These are not impersonal objects collected to prove a mid-century anthropological theory. These were the possessions of privileged people who held special offices and left their imprint on both material artefacts and the course of history. These artefacts represent the decline of those privileged worlds.[5]

In the Tibet collection at the National Museum, there survives a series of uncatalogued letters between Prince Peter and employees of the National Museum documenting his collection practices, the expenses involved and other anthropological research. On 23 January and again on 9 March 1951, Prince Peter wrote letters to Kaj Birket-Smith at the National Museum of Denmark requesting funds to purchase a number of unique historical artefacts offered for sale by 'George' Dundul Namgyal Tsarong (1920–2011), the son of Tsarong Dazang Dramdul (1888–1959), one of the wealthiest and most politically powerful men in Tibet prior to 1950. In particular, while in the company of the Dalai Lama at Yatung,[6] George Tsarong sent a letter to Prince Peter stating that he knew of the latter's interest in 'Tibetan curio' and that many of his friends had been looking for someone who wanted to buy their property, such as cups, carpets, ready-made dresses and ceremonial robes, thangka paintings and so on. Prince Peter asked Birket-Smith, 'What should I do? Is the museum interested in these items? . . . They are the direct result of the Chinese conquest of Tibet, and one can see these are not from a common salesperson, but offered by a member of the Lhasa aristocracy.' The items presented by George Tsarong formed the basis of my interest in Prince Peter's collection. I showed pictures of these items when in the field and had planned to display them at our exhibition at Moesgaard Museum:

188.[7] The *zhathul* (*zhwa thul*) meditation shawl of the Fifth Reting Rinpoché Thubten Jamphel Yeshe Gyaltsen (1911–1947). George Tsarong sold the *zhathul* to Prince Peter for INR 1,500 (c. USD 326 or DKK 2,253) in 1952.[8]

189. The *dhingwa* (*gding ba*) of the Fifth Reting Rinpoché, sold to Prince Peter by 'George' Dundul Namgyal Tsarong for INR 800 in 1952.

252, 253, 251. Pema Dolkar's amulet case (*ga'u*), neckband and coral headdress (*mi tig spa phrug*). Pema Dolkar was one of the wives of Tsarong Dazang Dramdul. The amulet case is of a design still popular in Tibet today and resembles the *zemaramgo* (*gze ma ra mgo*) flower. It contains an interior space for the amulet, a special prayer for protection written on paper wrapped tightly in cloth. Worn around the neck, women's amulet cases are often adorned with jewels, but this particular example is decorated with a number of particularly fine *dzi*, red coral, topaz, turquoise, pearls, rubies,

160   IMPERMANENCE

sapphires and diamonds. In a letter dated 9 March 1951, Prince Peter reported that he had bought the amulet case and neckband for INR 6,300 (*c.* USD 1,369). The last piece of Pema Dolkar's jewellery in the collection of the National Museum is her pearl-and-coral headdress. In the 9 March letter, Prince Peter valued the item at INR 2,985 (*c.* USD 649).

242. The Minister's (*zhabs pad*) robes of Tsarong Dzasa, Namgang Dazang Damdul (1888–1959). George Tsarong sold his father's ceremonial robes to Prince Peter for INR 6,000 (*c.* USD 1,304) in 1952.

In the National Museum, the extremely high regard for Prince Peter's collection and the sense of its precious value demonstrate themselves through the difficulty of working with these artefacts. To obtain access as a researcher, one must make arrangements with the museum many months (up to a year) in advance. Even after booking a time and date to view the items in person, the museum requires a statement from one's local police department, a private research room, a white laboratory coat, shoe coverings and gloves, the services of the museum's in-house photographer, and chaperoning of the researcher by a member of the Ethnographic Department. When the objects are returned to the depository, they are first placed in a giant freezer to kill any pests that might have found their way in. Under these carefully controlled conditions, I was fortunate to spend a day and a half examining these items before embarking on my own expedition to collect new artefacts in Kathmandu, Nepal, Dharamsala, India and two cities in the PRC close to the Tibetan plateau – Chengdu and Xining – in the spring of 2018.

Fieldsite impermanence

After numerous trips to Dharamsala and Kathmandu, I began the PRC portion of my fieldwork in the Tibetan neighbourhood of Chengdu, called Wuhouci (Wǔhóu Qū), in Sichuan Province and the surrounding area. Everywhere I looked in Wuhouci, impermanence, in terms of both the promise and pitfalls of change, confronted and enticed me. Nowadays, many Lhasa Tibetans spend the winter months or at least Tibetan New Year in second homes in Chengdu. So, I began visiting countless Tibetan shops while meeting up with old friends and making new contacts. Immediately, it became apparent from the items on sale that redesigning 'Western' or perhaps 'globalised' commodities had become even more

10.1a. and 10.1b.   *Trukcha* on blankets (left) and *trukcha* on items at Munsel's store in Chengdu (right), 2018. Photo: Cameron David Warner.

popular than I had remembered from previous trips. For example, I saw baseball hats, shoes, handbags, wallets and belts transformed into a stereotypically Tibetan style through the addition of small details. Certainly, these trends were not brand new in 2018 (McGuckin 1997) but their pervasiveness surprised me. For example, it struck me how varied and ubiquitous were items such as a backpack with a small patch of Tibetan fabric, called *trukcha* in Amdo, being marketed to Tibetan shoppers (Figure 10.1).

One particular brand, Munsel (*mun sel*) (Illuminating the Darkness), features an incredible variety of contemporary streetwear items all adorned with *trukcha* in the form of a strip of the same tightly packed weft-faced cloth featuring a cotton warp and a woollen weft, woven in a twill pattern of diagonal parallel ribs. Art historians have identified this fabric pattern in mural paintings over 800 years old.[9] The Munsel brand thus hinted at the simultaneous conservatism and progressivism of contemporary Tibetan fashion, a dynamic that Nyema Droma clarified for me.

Nyema Droma, or Nyedron as her friends know her, emerged onto Tibet's art scene as Tibet's first female photographer. Her photography often features young Lhasa Tibetans in both urban and rural settings wearing clothes and jewellery similar to those seen in Prince Peter's collection, or juxtaposed with icons of modernity and globalisation such as a Coca-Cola bottle.

When I first met Nyedron, in Chengdu, I discovered that her artistic photography is a natural extension of her fashion design, sold under the label Hima Ālaya (a play on Sanskritic syllables that means something like 'to dwell in the Himalayas'). As I showed her my photographs of

10.2 Nyedron recommended this particular photograph for the Moesgaard exhibition because the young woman also wears this silk necklace while performing *nangma*, professional singing and dancing at bars. The shape calls to mind Pema Dolkar's amulet case. Nyedron viewed this as symbolic of cultural loss over time. The outer form still exists in a diminished way, while the inner significance has been lost entirely. Photo: Nyema Droma, 2018, from the Precious Relics Project Collection.

Prince Peter's collection and asked about her photographs and background, she explained that, after growing up in Lhasa, she studied Fashion Styling and Photography at the University of the Arts in London. Nyedron's fashion design practice necessitated her photographic practice as she did not know of any fashion photographers working in Lhasa.

The emerging field of Tibetan fashion

Serendipitous encounters often lead to the most fruitful analytical insights, a phenomenon Tibetans might term 'auspicious connections coming together'. A number of connections came together for me while meeting with Nyedron that first time, which could all be conceived under an umbrella of Tibetan *design*: different periods of Tibetan fashion, photography, music, rural vs. urban life, and increasing wealth and consumerism. For example, Nyedron criticised Munsel's tendency to sew *trukcha* onto common urban items as 'not really Tibetan design'. In contrast, Nyedron described Hima Ālaya's aesthetic as going well beyond Munsel's 'shortcut' approach.

Nyedron sees Hima Ālaya's designs as embodying a Tibetan perspective in terms of materials, their sources, colours, shapes, functions and ideal consumers. She designs the entire experience. She does not try to make a pre-existing object appeal to Tibetan buyers. Hima Ālaya's brand manifesto, found on their social media channels and printed catalogues in multiple languages, recapitulates the design ethos she expressed to me:

> Hima Ālaya is a lifestyle brand originating from Tibetan culture in the sacred city of Lhasa. We strive to create a platform for artistic expression of a distinctive street sensibility grounded in traditional Tibetan culture. The label works with independent designers to create a minimalist design with unique Tibetan stylistic elements drawing from our creative visual design core. Striking iconic patterns from Tibetan Buddhist mountain culture are integrated with modern fabrics to create compelling new versions of streetwear for youth. Hima Ālaya thus aims to fashion creative spaces through clothes, events, photography, and videography to reimagine traditional Tibetan culture in new spaces that are intrinsically modern and hip.

While Hima Ālaya-branded streetwear is aimed at 'youth', this is not necessarily Tibetan youth. Nyedron sees 'traditional' Tibetan 'mountain culture' as a resource for Hima Ālaya's Tibetan designers to utilise in their artistic expression and innovation on streetwear, unlike Munsel's attempt to make streetwear appealing to Tibetans through the occasional addition of stereotypically Tibetan design elements. One example of Hima Ālaya's design is a turquoise women's spring jacket (Figure 10.3). It is styled to be

10.3 A women's jacket from Hima Ālaya with a design based on a Tibetan *chuba*, as displayed in the 'Museum of Impermanence' exhibition, 2019. Photo: Sarah Schorr.

reminiscent of a sheepskin *chuba* (*phyu pa*), a long sheepskin coat made of thick Tibetan wool popular among nomads for its warmth. Hima Ālaya's jacket is made entirely of plant-derived materials, is much shorter and lighter than a traditional *chuba*, and is dyed turquoise to resemble the precious stones with which Tibetans – nomad women in particular – enjoy adorning their hair. The cut of the fabric and the placement of the clasps above the right shoulder and under the right arm are unmistakably recognisable to a Tibetan eye; but, at the opening of the 'Museum of Impermanence' exhibition, a group of Danish woman approached me and complimented the jacket, commenting that it did not have 'an ethnic look'.

Hima Ālaya blends Nyedron's interests in fashion, fine art photography and her cultural background into a seamless globally oriented entrepreneurship. She is not alone in this endeavour. Near the end of our interview, Nyedron said to me, 'If you really want to see Tibetan fashion, you should visit Anu Ranglug's store in Xining. They are friends of mine. I can put you in touch with them.' To which I replied, 'Are you kidding me? You know Anu? They make clothes? You could introduce me?'

'Do what you think about'

On 19 May 2017, the Tibetan hip hop group Anu Ranglug (*a nu ring lugs*) released a new song, 'Fly (*phur*)'. Featured in the 2017 Miss Tibet Pageant in India, within a few weeks of its release, Voice of America Tibet noted the popularity of the song, reflected in the many videos Tibetans had made of themselves praising it. And, by the end of the summer, Anu were clearly Tibet's biggest act ever. Sonically, lyrically and visually, 'Fly' soared high above the contemporary Tibetan pop music preceding it. Two aspects of 'Fly' made it stand out: the lyrics[10] and the clothes. The lyrics to 'Fly' invite Tibetans to:

> Break free from the chains of fate
> If you yearn for liberty . . .
>
> Fly
> If you want to search for your true soul
> Fly
> If you want to search for your highest dreams . . .
>
> If you don't fly, your life will be over
> If you don't fly, your hopes will be wasted . . .
>
> Extending your wings of freedom
> Carry those wondrous dreams
> Transcending the ocean of existence
> Fly to the realm of happiness . . .[11]

In 'Fly', Anu have transformed the image of the failed struggle for Tibetan political freedom into a call for a more existential orientation toward personal liberation from one's own karma, self-doubt and lethargy. Playing on the language of Buddhist soteriology, it reminds listeners to use their own self-power to escape the suffering of cyclic existence ('transcending the ocean of existence') and achieve rebirth in a heavenly realm ('fly to the realm of happiness'). Due to its positive, uplifting message and soundscape, 'Fly' went on to become a massive, unprecedented hit with millions of views on video-sharing websites in China and on YouTube.

The optimism of 'Fly' contrasts sharply with the critical, ironic and melancholic tone of Anu's previous songs, 'Leaving Home', 'ANUism' and

'Joke'. 'ANUism' speaks to the challenge young Tibetans face when assimilating to Chinese society in growing urban environments:

> Unhappily I am roaming over foreign lands since I have no power
> Though my eyes are wet, I am faking a smile on my face
> Whatever . . .

'Joke' criticised hypocrisy, greed and inauthenticity – themes found in centuries of Lhasa street songs and recent popular political commentary (Wangchuk 2018).[12] For Anu, however, they are particularly indicative of contemporary Tibetan life, especially urban life:

> Mother installs her son on a throne creating a label
> Father strolls around the marketplace holding a rosary
> Mother buys meat from the bazaar chanting mantras
> Uncle Tashi gets high on barley beer talking about loyalty
> Aunt Lhamo runs away with her phone shunning the world
> A religious rite from Uncle costs 200 Yuan
> It's all a game
> It's better to sing with good intentions than
> Recite mantras with a bad mind
> The essence of Buddhism is being kind-hearted
> With a good heart, one will have an obstacle-free path . . .

Anu sing of a series of paradoxes that define how older Tibetans appear to the new generation – in particular, professing religion in public but acting in nonvirtuous ways in private. Despite the popularity of their music, Anu's innovation lies not in pointing out the contradictions and paradoxes of hypocrisy, greed and inauthenticity within their lyrics but in how they have designed Tibetan political commentary into the clothing they wear and sell under various labels. Therefore, following Nyedron's advice, I decided to fly to Xining the next day and rushed straight to Anu's store, '1376', to meet them and perhaps purchase their clothing for the upcoming exhibitions.

Preservation through reconfiguration

In the spring of 2018, 1376 inhabited a section inside of the large Jinhe Bookstore in Haihu Wanda Plaza shopping mall in the new western half of Xining. Western Xining comprises a relatively new assortment of high-rise hotels, luxury apartments and shopping malls with expensive boutiques selling top Chinese brands. Jinhe Bookstore takes up the entire basement level of one mall. In addition to selling a large array of books, including an impressive collection of Tibetan books from the minority publishing houses, it has many sections selling ethnic art, handicrafts and, at that time, 1376.

When I arrived at 1376, Payag and Gonpa, the singer-songwriters who founded Anu, were waiting for me. We spoke, but only briefly. There had been some confusion and they had been waiting a long time. They introduced me to Payag's younger brother, Monster. Monster dances in some of the music videos from Anu and SCARK!D (formerly Uncle Buddhist). He is silly, crazy, fun. We talked about all the clothes in the store, the stories behind some of the designs, and the different labels they had developed – Anu, Black Lotus and, finally, 1376. Among my other routines in Xining, I would circle around to 1376 each day to check in with Monster. Sometimes, I would arrive toward closing time so we could go out for a late bowl of noodles. And we often texted over WeChat very late into the night. But, most importantly, we talked about the idea of showing 1376 clothes in India and Denmark. What would Tibetans in India and Danes want to see? What would they understand about the ideas behind the clothes? We agreed Tibetans in India would enjoy seeing the clothes in the 'Fly' video. Monster told me how Anu had made the first items themselves by hand, and speculated that Tibetans in India were probably unaware Anu designed clothes, let alone had their own store. (His assumptions proved correct.) As for how Danes might react, Monster had never discussed Anu's clothes with a foreigner before. The idea of Europeans seeing their designs intrigued him, and he emphasised that we needed to communicate the ethos of 1376.

When expressed in Tibetan, 1376 is not 13-76 or 1,376. It is one-three-seven-six (*gcig gsum bdun drug*). But when the numerals are said quickly in that order, they sound very similar to '*ci gsam don 'grub*', which means literally 'whatever you think about, that goal can be achieved' or 'whatever you wish, may it be fulfilled'. Anu have variously translated 1376 as 'do what you want', 'do what you think about' or even 'do what you desire'. 1376 served as the material manifestation of the band's ethos. The band's full name, Anu Ranglug, would translate as the Philosophy of Youth, Youthism or ANUism. Therefore, 1376 served as a further articulation of 'the doctrine of Anu'.

Anu articulated part of the 1376 'do what you think about' ethos in a song called '1376 Rap of Tibet Cypher' (High Peaks Pure Earth 2018). Here, we see Anu working with other emerging rappers, such as TMJ and

Dekyi Tsering, to elaborate on the concept of 1376 and explain that, in essence, they seek to comment on generational change.[13] They want to highlight that true love between the older and younger generations comes when they notice each other's creativity. At the same time, the band pursues a consistent theme of criticising drunks, people with too much pride, the ignorant and the jealous. Anu begin this song with a plea to fellow Tibetans to achieve authenticity, defined as a continuity between inner and outer qualities, such as aligning one's private ethics with one's public behaviour (Handler 1986; Clifford 1988). Examples of inauthenticity include friends who are really enemies and – reminiscent of Nyedron's photograph of the fake amulet case (Figure 10.2) – people who have 'a beautiful exterior empty inside'. Anu's collaborators alternate between positive and critical messages. TMJ, for example, praises the creativity and cooperation of the new and older generations of Tibetans. Dekyi Tsering plays on the Buddhist image of the hungry ghost (Skt. *preta,* Tib. *yi dwags*), a being whose avarice is so immense that it has a bloated stomach and swollen face, to criticise the current direction of generational change. Another collaborator, Tashi (Eric) Phuntsok, tempers that image with a reminder of the Dalai Lama's vision that, ideally, Tibet could be an environmental utopia, akin to being in a heavenly realm of happiness and wisdom that could be a source of peace for the world.

The conflicting images of Tibetan society as either rife with hypocrisy and corruption or else a source of inestimable value through intergenerational cooperation pervade both Anu's music and also their fashion. In Anu's videos during this period, but especially 'Fly' and '1376 Rap of Tibet Cypher', the band and their friends model clothing from their various labels, which I found for sale at the 1376 store. Items include a black shirt that Payag wore in the 'Fly' video, where the bottom resembles a Tibetan horse blanket. The most popular item with visitors in both the exhibition at the Library of Tibetan Works and Archives and at Moesgaard proved to be a black hoodie with the logos 1376 and *'ci gsam don 'grub'* written on the sleeves. The zip continues all the way to the top of the hood so that, when zipped up, the hood covers one's face, in Anu's interpretation of a traditional Tibetan opera mask (Figure 10.4).

This hoodie and its special adornments are featured in the '1376 Rap of Tibet Cypher' video at the point where Tashi (Eric) Phuntsok sonically breaks through the rap with Tibetan opera, a potentially politically charged move (Ahameda 2006; Fitzgerald 2014), praising Tibet's landscape, history and association with aspirations for peace. Together, the songs and the clothes simultaneously embrace change,

10.4 The opera mask hoodie featured in the '1376' rap of Tibet Cypher's video, purchased from the 1376 store (left) together with Rewa's formal *chuba* (right) in the 'Museum of Impermanence' exhibition, 2019. Photo: Sarah Schorr.

preserve positive aspects of the past and reject perpetual threats to Tibetan society. This gentle and often humorous social commentary continued through t-shirts featuring imagery such as the Mona Lisa wearing Tibetan women's jewellery,[14] the Statue of Liberty made to hold a Buddhist rosary, and, especially, a series of shirts making fun of Tibetan *'tiggas'*,[15] defined by Anu as rural Tibetans who paradoxically flaunt both their Buddhist piety and their wealth through adorning themselves in comically huge precious stones such as coral, amber and turquoise. Promoted via social media, especially WeChat and Sina Weibo, during an incredibly creative period, 1376 released new shirts, jackets, sweatshirts and baseball hats every other week in 2018.

Tibetan social entrepreneurship through music and fashion

Celebrities, whether they be musicians, reality TV stars or athletes, participate in the cross-promotion of various consumer streams. This is just as true of Tibetan celebrities. While Anu design their own clothes, other Tibetan musicians are associated with, or promote, particular brands. For example, Dukar Yak (*gdugs dkar yag*) promotes Lamdo (*lam 'gro*). SCARK!D (whose personal name is *klu sgrub rgya mtsho*) promoted 1376 and City Tibetan, and, with Anu, continues to promote Sarduba (*gsar gtod pa*). Most notably, one of the most important and successful brands in Tibet, Rewa (*re ba*), meaning hope, works in close collaboration with Dekyi Tsering (*bde skyid tshe ring*) and Tibet's most popular singer, Sherten (*sher bstan*)(Warner 2013). Popular throughout Tibetan areas of China, the Rewa brand, like Hima Ālaya and 1376, sees itself as more than just a clothing brand. Rewa's WeChat channel regularly posts poems written by Tibet's best poets, new songs from emerging singers and short essays on inspirational global figures; and it grants scholarships to promising young students.

Indicative of the social entrepreneurship trend popular among Tibetan-owned businesses (Craig and Glover 2009; Liu 2015), Rewa goes so far as to sponsor an annual award banquet honouring two Tibetans who have worked to preserve Tibetan culture in their lives. Where Hima Ālaya sees itself as drawing on traditional Tibetan culture to create unique products for a global audience, Rewa echoes the main themes present in Sherten's music: in the face of daunting odds, Tibetans have reasons to be hopeful for the future – as long as they support social unity and recognise Tibetan Buddhist heritage as a rich resource of wisdom and peace for the world. This ethos is expressed in Rewa's official manifesto, often repeated on their WeChat channel:

> 'Rewa' in Tibetan means 'hope'. Hope is the centre and value of life. If hope is absent, life is simply aimless and unsuccessful. Therefore, the brand 'Rewa' attempts to deliver a philosophical message of hope. Rewa's products symbolise a call to world peace and an effort to awaken the wisdom of mankind. Every person will be moved when they see the Tibetan antelope on the logo. Thus, we should make note of this calling and rise to the occasion of a bright future. Although Rewa products cannot stand for all hopes, the unique features of Rewa products usher us through a door of hope by combining tradition and modernisation.

Rewa's ethos very carefully employs bivalent terms, which communicate a message of national pride to Tibetans who might 'hope', for example, for the return of the Dalai Lama or greater political autonomy, but without running afoul of Chinese communist censorship. 'Combining tradition and modernisation' becomes like a tightrope act materially manifested in their clothing. For example, Rewa sells both urbanwear, such as padded down jackets and tracksuits, and formal *chubas* made of fine fabrics appropriate for special occasions such as weddings, funerals or Tibetan New Year (Figure 10.4). Rewa's *chubas*, expensive compared to other *chubas* and made of high-quality materials, and cut as long, luxurious robes, have more in common with the robes George Tsarong sold to Prince Peter than the sheepskin nomad coats that inspired the turquoise coat from Hima Ālaya. Rewa tends to take a common streetwear item, such as a padded jacket, and add the shape and fastenings that appear stereotypically Tibetan, plus an extra design element such as the *trukcha* pattern. The overall effect of the design is more conservative and subdued than 1376's style.[16] It is also the only popular brand in Tibet focused on menswear. All of the other brands make mens- and womenswear, except for 1376, whose clothing is deliberately gender-neutral.

One of the foci of the Tibetan social entrepreneurship movement is stewardship of the environment (Liu 2015). The roots of this ethos can be traced back to the Dalai Lama's proposals in the 1980s to make the Tibetan plateau a demilitarised, politically autonomous environmental zone similar to a national park. While businesses and artists in Tibet cannot make direct reference to him or his ideas, the popularity of his vision continues in the work of many environmental groups and activists. Rewa's logo features the *chiru* (*gstod*, *Pantholops hodgsonii* or Tibetan antelope), which has been a symbol of self-sacrifice on behalf of the environment and animals ever since the hit film 'Kekexili: Mountains Patrol' (2006) dramatised local efforts to stop poachers from killing the *chiru*. While Anu play with the idea of cultural preservation and openly criticise Buddhist inauthenticity, Rewa makes a direct appeal to the Buddhist virtue of self-sacrifice on behalf of the collective, which includes other-than-human beings and Tibetan heritage.

Designing with impermanence in mind

Buddhists are often concerned with the experience of 'compounded phenomena' – that is, all things are made of other things. A flower is sun, water and earth. A mobile phone is a compound of glass, metal and plastic. Of course, this is obvious to us. Regarding impermanence, a Buddhist teacher of mine, Khenpo Pema Wangdak, explained that 'suffering arises when we grasp onto things in the false belief they will never change.' We falsely expect that compounds will stay together, that even relationships and mental states will not return to the elements comprised in them. We learn that one cause of suffering is our attachment and desire for stability. Impermanence is persistent and pervasive but only intermittently experienced. Like the imperceptible shift of tectonic plates that leads to catastrophic earthquakes, it is microscopic quietude that leads to macroscopic erasure. However, when Khenpo Pema continued, he said, 'When I was young, impermanence saddened me. It was depressing to think of impermanence. But not now. Impermanence is wonderful to me because it means everything is always changing. And change is a good thing. Change can be liberating.'

Despite a panoply of apocalyptic discourses prevalent among Tibetans for decades, there exists today a constellation of Tibetans strewn across the Tibetan diaspora who do not view changes to Tibetan culture and society as necessarily unidirectional. Interconnected through friendship, patronage and competition, some of the leading participants in Tibet's creative zeitgeist, for the most part, embrace impermanence. They know their compatriots are often nostalgic, lamenting what Tibet is losing. But, unlike their compatriots, they do not feel sorrow or at least try not to be despondent. They strive instead for impermanence to mean possibility and perhaps a degree of agency through activating their customers to think consciously on the connections between how they choose to spend their money, Buddhist virtues and national identity.

Part of my interest in developing impermanence into an anthropological concept is an expression of resistance to the tendency to limit non-Abrahamic terms to a subsidiary or supportive role in relation to pre-existing European philosophical concerns or social science discourses. In the Buddhist articulation of impermanence, it is not simply change. Impermanence is the stress, anxiety, unsatisfactoriness, the suffering produced through change, and especially the knowledge that the pain of it is nearly inescapable, regardless of the litany of our experiences of it or the degree of our self-awareness. But it also encompasses the opposite: the sense of freedom that a song like 'Fly' conveys so well: the experience of liberation, the nimble, parkour-like nature of dancing on the surface of changes themselves.

In comparison, the anthropology of becoming, for example, emphasises the plasticity and possibility of ethnographic subjects, their bodies, materiality and the worlds they inhabit. This plasticity has a Latourian feel to it. Humans and nonhumans interact simultaneously in multiple systems 'with varying degrees of agentive capacity' (Biehl and Locke 2017, 5–6). Plasticity and possibility converge with impermanence in the sense that plasticity points toward an unstable nature and the malleability of all social fields and subjectivities. When experienced over time and space, Biehl and Locke point to 'an aggregating capacity and the operative fields in and through which institutions and social processes combine and collapse' (2017, 6), which is strikingly similar to the metaphysical language of early Buddhism and the need for teachings on impermanence.

Every identifiable entity comprises what the Buddha termed the 'five aggregates' (Skt. *skandha*, Tib. *phung po lnga*): form, sensations, perceptions, mental activity and consciousness. In early Buddhism, the teaching of the five aggregates served to deconstruct the notion of an independent, self-originating and stable self. Later, Mahāyāna Buddhism famously labelled the five aggregates empty (Skt. *śūnyatā*, Tib. *stong pa nyid*). Emptiness here means that, ultimately, there are no building-blocks for phenomena, whether we are discussing the physical world, experience of it, institutions, social processes or structures. Nor do the building-blocks we might have thought existed have any essence of their own. The flower is not actually composed of earth, water and sunlight if those things can be broken down further. And my perception of the flower and cognition about it also have no independent, self-originating, stable essence. Therefore, one of the means to counter the suffering experienced from impermanence is to focus on how the object in question is not independent of other factors, did not arise of its own accord and does not contain some stable essence. But is it enough to say that we can lessen suffering by accepting these three factors? Can we go a step further and find positivity in relational dependence, co-origination, instability?

Impermanence puts nondualist relationality into practice.[17] There is currently a bevy of theories on how to escape the trap of Cartesian duality, ranging from proposals based on philosophers such as Spinoza, Whitehead, Dewey and James, to the pluriversal cosmopolitics of the anthropology of indigenous Latin America (de la Cadena and Blaser 2018), to the feminist physics of Karen Barad and Rosi Braidotti.[18] But it is Arturo Escobar who explicitly brought those discourses together with his knowledge of Buddhist notions of interdependence/co-origination deriving from his work with Francisco Varela (Escobar 2018).

Escobar sets out to articulate an ontology of design for the twenty-first century that will first acknowledge design's participation in the making of the worst abuses and excesses of human life, and then take advantage of its liberative potential. Design ought to be based on a relational ontology in which 'nothing preexists the relations that constitute it' (Escobar 2018, 101) and 'can thus become an open invitation for us all to become mindful and effective weavers of the mesh of life' (Escobar 2018, 215). In this ontology, worlds come into being through one's immersion in them, through a coincidence of being–doing–knowing. What it means to be a Tibetan person, living in Tibet and making Tibetan clothing or music, happens coincidentally (not without causal connection, but *with* correspondence). *To make in a world is to world-make.*

Nondualist perspectives in the humanities and social sciences have arisen as politically expedient responses to climate change, due to the need to critique the nature–culture dichotomy of the modern West; but, on their own, nondualism and interdependence are politically insufficient. Nondualist ontologies that recognise the crucial role of interdependence are a description of an ideal to attain but are not a prescription for a way forward. Escobar's ontology of design points to the need for a thorough critique of the current fetish for sustainability. The practice of design, at best, begins from the acknowledgement that the world is never finished, complete or stable, but lies instead in the perpetual unfinishing of things, where endings become beginnings and the old becomes the new (Ingold 2015, 120–3). Sustainability ought not to be about the preservation of form but of life itself (Ingold 2019). This is where impermanence can play a key role because it points to both the impossibility of preserving forms (because of inevitable ends) and also the creative potential unleashed as endings become beginnings.

For some of the Tibetans I interviewed for this project, there is a possibility inherent in instability (that is, entropy) (DeSilvey 2017). I would argue that, in the case of the Prince Peter Collection of Tibetan artefacts, the Danish National Museum invests far too much energy in maintaining a steady state.[19] In the case of intangible Tibetan heritage, instability (impermanence) preserves. Nyedron and 1376 reinterpret a style of clothing rather than preserve an actual *item* of clothing. Though Hima Ālaya roots its design in 'traditional culture', its aesthetic actually pushes authenticity in new directions. The dichotomous frame of tradition versus modernity, explored so often in the study of Tibet, presents a false choice to creative Tibetans outside and inside the PRC (Whalen-Bridge 2011; Diehl 2002; Kolås 2003).[20] Therefore, rather than investing a massive amount of work in preserving a steady state, what we might call one configuration, the goal ought to be multiple configurations. Impermanence should not be fought in order to preserve. *Impermanence should be encouraged in order to preserve.* For example, redesigning a sheepskin jacket in plant-based materials or quoting from Tibet's shamanic national epic in the middle of a televised pop competition introduces audiences to sources and styles of culture outside of their ken, and provides support to others in related cultural domains. Many young Tibetans, for instance, attended the exhibition in Dharamsala having heard Anu's music, but like me, being unaware of 1376 and other brands. They found the originality of the mixture of old and new styles inspiring. Some older Tibetans said seeing the clothing caused them to change their opinion of Tibetan hip hop. Before the exhibition, they thought hip hop attacked Tibetan culture. Afterward, they said, 'I did not know they were so aware of the challenges our culture faces. Or that they cared so much about preserving [the diversity] of so many regions.' Therefore, I have chosen to highlight instances where Tibetans are not just preserving intangible heritage in the sense of trying to capture what it once was, but where they are deliberately liberating the precious relics of their heritage 'into other systems of significance' (DeSilvey 2017, 17).

Through the lens of Tibetan fashion, we have seen three contexts through which to glimpse Tibetan agency as a subtle and nuanced, localised state of being: 1) through the strategic sale of their material patrimony at a time of political and social upheaval, 2) through their active participation in globalised popular culture (hip hop) and global commodity capitalism that is mass-produced but also reimagined within the PRC, and 3) within the context of Tibetan identity politics and emic tensions between perceptions of tradition and modernity. Whereas anthropology has documented many instances of global commodity capitalism dominating, homogenising and erasing expressions of local culture, I deliberately paint a picture here that focuses on Tibetan agency rather than oppression.

As a coda to the meditations on impermanence and agency, I should add that the subject of my research is, itself, impermanent. As our exhibition was opening, Anu's popularity in China skyrocketed. They appeared on 'Sing China!', a major reality-TV singing competition.[21] And their song 'GAGA' reached number one on the China Billboard pop charts. As soon as our exhibition opened, many people started asking if they could buy the clothes in the exhibition. I regretted both not acquiring some for the museum store and not acquiring more examples for my collection, so I wrote to Monster to buy more. However, he explained he would not be able to send me any clothes and that Anu had decided to cease operating the 1376 brand and destroy all of the clothes left. They wanted to start something new that would appeal to a wider audience than ever before, or, as he put it, 'Go in a really big way'. A few months later, Anu launched their newest fashion label, Sarduba (*gsar gtod pa*), and a new anthemic song manifesto to go with it. Sarduba literally means 'the act of creating'.

Notes

1   Cf. attempts to change the narrative around youth and East Africa from that of AIDS and soldiers to that of entrepreneurship and creativity (Schneidermann 2020).

2   Just as Daniel Miller pointed out how consumers are not necessarily individualistic and materialistic (Miller 2012), the term 'consumer' itself does not capture well the person who buys the clothing described in this chapter.

3   Support and funding for this project derive from Aarhus University and the Danish Council for Independent Research grant # 4180-00326B, Precious Relics: Materiality and Value in the Practice of Ethnographic Collection (2015–2021). Thank you to all of the authors of this volume, but especially Haidy Geismar, Ton Otto and Carole McGranahan, and to the presenters and attendees of the Tibetan Ethnographic Theory panel of the 15th Seminar of the International Association of Tibetan Studies, for their helpful comments.

4   For more information on Tibetan clothing and textiles, see Brown et al. 2018 and Corrigan 2017.

5   Prince Peter also collected more proletarian items, such as the complete costumes of Tibetan nomads. But his letters to the National Museum give the impression that those items were commissioned by the National Museum as fitting comparisons to artefacts already present in their Mongolian collection. Deductively, they served to support racial theories of Tibetans exhibiting physical 'Mongoloid' features, whereas Prince Peter appears to be the one to initiate and encourage the National Museum's interest in the aristocratic items.

6   Out of fear of the People's Liberation Army advancing on Lhasa, the Dalai Lama and his court fled to Yatung (Ch. Yadong), a Tibetan valley that borders both Sikkim and Bhutan, arriving on 2 January 1951.

7   These numbers correspond to the acquisition register of the National Museum. Where the Tibetan words for the items and their descriptions differ from descriptions at the Museum and other published accounts, this is due to my own fieldwork for this project. Other accounts include too many errors for me to detail in this chapter.

8   All the values are set to their equivalents in 1952.

9   Amy Heller, personal communication.

10 All of the quoted lyrics are originally in Tibetan. Unless indicated otherwise, the translations to English are my own.

11 English translation by High Peaks, Pure Earth. https://highpeakspureearth.com/music-video-fly-by-anu/.

12 https://case.edu/affil/tibet/moreTibetInfo/street_songs_collection.

13 Generational change has been a theme of Tibetan pop music since at least the mid-2000s, when bands like Yudrug Tsendep (*gyu 'brug tshan sdeb*) released songs such as '*Phama (pha ma)*' ('Our Parents'). https://www.youtube.com/watch?v=9PjALHvSATc (last accessed 27 October 2021). A direct antecedent to '1376' and 'ANUism', 'New Generation (*mi rabs bsang ba)*' was a rap song from Yudrug that unabashedly proclaimed it cool to be a young Tibetan because of their confidence, pride and playfulness (High Peaks Pure Earth 2010; Lama Jabb 2018).

14 The Lhasa-based painter Langdun Dedron completed a series of Tibetan Mona Lisa paintings, at least one of which was exhibited in Singapore in 2012.

15 The Tibetan adaptation of *nigga* to *tigga* predates Anu and has a potential semantic range and history too complex for me to fully account for here.

16 In the spring of 2020, Rewa launched a new label, Nyima Lhasa (*nyi ma lha sa*) (Sun Lhasa) featuring less conservative unisex t-shirts and hooded sweatshirts with the 'NL' logo and a cartoonish half-yak/half-man figure similar to Hima Ālaya's cartoon yeti mascot.

17 Escobar (2018, 244) comes close to acknowledging this point, but his focus on interdependence and nonduality relational ontologies prevents him from seeing its value to his argument.

18 For a longer exposition on the lexicon of change and how it relates to impermanence, see the Introduction to this volume.

19 For more information on this particular issue, see 'Museum of Impermanence' by Ulrik Johnsen, Ton Otto and Cameron Warner in this volume.

20 There are so many publications on Tibetan culture and modernity that I have only included a small, representative sample.

21 https://www.youtube.com/watch?v=qOHFwDiHvZU&list=PLAE50F9C016DF872D&index=40&t=0s (last accessed 27 October 2021).

References

Adams, Vincanne. 2007. 'Saving Tibet? An inquiry into modernity, lies, truths, and beliefs', *Medical Anthropology* 24(1): 71–110.

Ahameda, Saiyada Jamila. 2006. 'Tibetan folk opera: Lhamo in contemporary cultural politics', *Asian Theatre Journal* 23(1): 149–78.

Bauer, Kenneth, and Huatse Gyal. 2015. 'Introduction', *Nomadic Peoples* 19(2) (Special issue: Resettlement among Tibetan nomads in China): 157–63.

Biehl, João, and Peter Locke, eds. 2017. *Unfinished: The anthropology of becoming*. Durham, NC: Duke University Press.

Brown, Anne Jennings, Nyima Stewart, Zara Fleming and Thubten Kelsang. 2018. *The Fabric of Tibet: Regional dress from the roof of the world*. London: Tibet Relief Fund.

Brox, Trine, and Miriam Koktvedgaard Zeitzen. 2017. 'Prince Peter's seven years in Kalimpong: Collecting in a contact zone'. In *Transcultural Encounters in the Himalayan Borderlands: Kalimpong as a 'contact zone'*, edited by Markus Viehbeck, 245–72. Heidelberg: Heidelberg University Publishing.

Clifford, James. 1988. 'Identity in Mashpee'. In *The Predicament of Culture: Twentieth-century ethnography, literature, and art*, 277–346. Cambridge, MA: Harvard University Press.

Corrigan, Gina. 2017. *Tibetan Dresses in Amdo & Kham*. London: Hali Publications.

Craig, Sienna R., and Denise M. Glover. 2009. 'Conservation, cultivation, and commodification of medicinal plants in the Greater Himalayan-Tibetan Plateau', *Asian Medicine* 5(2): 291–42.

Dak Lhagyal. 2019. '"Linguistic authority" in state–society interaction: Cultural politics of Tibetan education in China', *Discourse: Studies in the cultural politics of education* 42(3): 353–67. https://doi.org/10.1080/01596306.2019.1648239.

de la Cadena, Marisol, and Mario Blaser, eds. 2018. *A World of Many Worlds*. Durham, NC: Duke University Press.

DeSilvey, Caitlin. 2017. *Curated Decay: Heritage beyond saving*. Minneapolis, MN: University of Minnesota Press.

Diehl, Keila. 2002. *Echoes from Dharamsala: Music in the life of a Tibetan refugee community*. Berkeley, CA: University of California Press.

Escobar, Arturo. 2018. *Designs for the Pluriverse: Radical interdependence, autonomy, and the making of worlds*. Durham, NC: Duke University Press.

Fitzgerald, Kati. 2014. 'Tibetan opera in and outside the Tibet Autonomous Region', *Asian Theatre Journal* 31(1): 270–78.

Gaerrang (Kabzung). 2015. 'Development as entangled knot: The case of the slaughter renunciation movement in Tibet, China', *The Journal of Asian Studies* 74(4): 927–51.

Handler, Richard. 1986. 'Authenticity', *Anthropology Today* 2(1): 2–4.

Harris, Clare. 2012. *The Museum on the Roof of the World: Art, politics, and the representation of Tibet*. Chicago, IL: University of Chicago Press.

High Peaks Pure Earth. 2010. '"New Generation" – hip hop music video from Amdo'. https://highpeakspureearth.com/new-generation-hip-hop-music-video-from-amdo/ (last accessed 30 October 2021).

High Peaks Pure Earth. 2018. 'Music video: "1376" by ANU featuring TMJ, Dekyi Tsering, Tashi Phuntsok, Uncle Buddhist and Young13DBaby'. https://highpeakspureearth.com/music-video-1376-by-anu-featuring-tmj-dekyi-tsering-tashi-phuntsok-uncle-buddhist-and-young13dbaby/ (last accessed 30 October 2021).

High Peaks Pure Earth. 2020. 'The standard of Tibetan language on signboards indicates the decline of our basic rights'. https://highpeakspureearth.com/the-standard-of-tibetan-language-on-signboards-indicates-the-decline-of-our-basic-rights/ (last accessed 30 October 2021).

Ingold, Tim. 2015. *The Life of Lines*. Abingdon: Routledge.

Ingold, Tim. 2019. 'Art and anthropology for a sustainable world', *Journal of the Royal Anthropological Institute* 25(4): 659–75.

Jabb, Lama. 2018. 'Acting and speaking through modern Tibetan poetry'. In *Tibetan Subjectivities on the Global Stage: Negotiating dispossession*, edited by Shelly Bhoil and Enrique Galvan-Alvarez, 95–107. Lanham, MD: Lexington Books.

Johnsen, Ulrik Høj. 2020. 'In the trails of the Goddess: The value of museum collections'. PhD thesis, Department of Anthropology, Aarhus University.

Kolås, Åshild. 2003. 'Modernising Tibet: Contemporary discourses and practices of "modernity"', *Inner Asia* 5(1): 17–37.

Liu, Jianqiang. 2015. *Tibetan Environmentalists in China: The King of Dzi* (translated by Ian Rowen, Cyrus K. Hui and Emily Ting Yeh). Lanham, MD: Lexington Books.

McGuckin, Eric. 1997. 'Tibetan carpets: From folk art to global commodity', *Journal of Material Culture* 2(3): 291–310. https://doi.org/10.1177/135918359700200302.

Miller, Daniel. 2012. *Consumption and Its Consequences*. Cambridge: Polity.

Roche, Gerald. 2019. 'Articulating language oppression: Colonialism, coloniality and the erasure of Tibet's minority languages', *Patterns of Prejudice* 53(5): 487–514.

Schneidermann, Nanna. 2020. 'Ugandan music stars between political agency, patronage, and market relations: Cultural brokerage in times of elections', *Nordic Journal of African Studies* 29(4): 1–19.

Thurston, Timothy O'Connor. 2015. 'Laughter on the grassland: A diachronic study of Amdo Tibetan comedy and the public intellectual in Western China'. PhD thesis, East Asian Languages and Literatures, Ohio State University.

Wangchuk, Tsering. 2018. 'Verses of praise and denigration: Finding poetic creativity in the Tibetan election in exile', *HIMALAYA: the Journal of the Association of Nepal and Himalayan Studies* 38(1): 177–88.

Warner, Cameron David. 2013. 'Hope and sorrow: Uncivil religion, Tibetan music videos, and YouTube', *Ethnos: Journal of Anthropology* 78(4): 543–68. https://doi.org/10.1080/00141844.2012.724433.

Whalen-Bridge, John. 2011. 'Multiple modernities and the Tibetan diaspora', *South Asian Diaspora* 3(1): 103–15.

Part 3
Structures and practices of care

11
Negotiating impermanence: care and the medical imaginary among people with cancer

Henry Llewellyn

Life-threatening diseases induce specific demands of care. Yet how these demands are considered and responded to differs considerably between medical constituencies. Divergent visions of cancer care exist between the biomedical subspecialties of oncology and palliative care, two principal medical arenas through which care is enacted for people with advanced cancer in the United Kingdom and most countries with well-resourced healthcare systems. These subspecialties differ notably in telos, philosophy, practice, technique and the tools through which care is achieved (Kaasa et al. 2018). While oncology generally seeks to prolong life via biotechnical means, palliative care privileges symptom relief and comfort in dying. Often considered in temporal relation to patients' disease progression, both subspecialties are embedded in highly structured systems that govern the basic terms through which each can access patients and authorise and enact care. While striving for integrated care, these systems can embed disciplinary hierarchies and ambiguous social and technical arrangements. The on-the-ground experiences of clinicians from multiple subspecialties, patients and families who are caught in the crosshairs of contrary narratives and practice bespeak the ontological and moral ambiguity surrounding how to understand and manage bodies in deterioration and lives toward death.

Central to my discussion is the issue of recognition, which, following Petryna's (2016) reading of Aristotle, I understand as a critical discovery existing incrementally along 'a spectrum between seeing and blindness' (Petryna 2013, S69). As Joan Tronto (1993) has argued in her feminist ethics of care, recognition and care are intrinsically related through the moral task of attentiveness. She speaks of the recognition of a need for care as well as the recognition of agency and responsibility to act in the caring process. A focus on recognition helps unpick the divergences between oncological and palliative visions of care, both in terms of the demands they 'see' and also the responses they inspire. It helps surface the historically contingent, socially stratified, relational, ambiguous and power-riven dynamics through which calls for care might be obscured and neglected (Tronto 1993).

In this chapter, I am interested not simply in the recognition of needs and responsibility but also recognition of the broader existential and ontological state of affairs regarding the perceived status of disease – whether it is 'reversible' or 'irreversible' according to the terms of biomedical intervention. As my interlocutors explained to me, this is critical to how oncology and palliative care gain their respective positions and authorities with regard to patient access and *when* each of their projects makes sense as an appropriate care modality – ultimately, whether death is positioned as 'the enemy' or a 'normal' part of life. It is recognition of the grounds of human agency in intervening in the course of disease and thus a fundamental terrain for the expression of care.

Here, I explore this notion of recognition and the dynamics through which it emerges in the care of people with life-threatening cancer. I follow how the demands of care are variously constructed and obscured around patients, and how these divergent visions of care shape the affective concerns and existential dilemmas of patients and families. I discuss these concerns with particular reference to human impermanence, which I foreground as a deeply contested but foundational and mobilising concept for the projects of oncology and palliative medicine.

I present these dynamics through three ethnographic cases, all from the National Health Service in England, that are drawn from an examination of care for people with brain cancer, a disease with extremely low odds of survival and for which there is little effective treatment. My fieldsite is a specialist brain tumour unit in a hospital I call the Warner where I undertook 18 months of ethnographic fieldwork (2014–16, with preliminary fieldwork in 2012). There, I set out to examine how people with brain cancer navigated care under conditions of overwhelming change – bodily, technical and institutional (Llewellyn and Higgs 2021; Llewellyn et al. 2018a; Llewellyn et al. 2018b). Staffed by surgeons, oncologists, neurologists, nurses and supportive and palliative care professionals, the Warner serves a large urban population and draws

184   IMPERMANENCE

referrals nationally. It is an elite institution with significant resources dedicated to research and clinical practice.

In the first case, I show how a medical imaginary in oncology constructs death as a partly soluble problem and, in turn, informs an imperative to provide aggressive treatment for people with a brain tumour. Here, I detail the sense of urgency that accompanies diagnosis, disclosure and treatment and the hopes that bind patients, clinicians and capital together in an affective embrace of biotechnology (DelVecchio Good 2001). I also show how an understanding of futility in treatment is concealed in idioms of 'radical treatment', a description that implies treatment with the intent of cure, yet which is often shown to be inappropriate in the case of brain cancer, where only 12 per cent of patients survive beyond five years and most die with one year (Cancer Research UK 2020).

In the second case, I introduce palliative care as an alternative care model that privileges not the extension of life through biotechnical means but the preparation for death and relief of symptoms. I describe how efforts to integrate palliative care have struggled amid enduring professional hierarchies and referral structures that prioritise mainstream oncological approaches and limit the potential for patients to access palliative care. I recount the words of clinicians espousing a palliative model that emphasise the critical work of recognising irreversible disease in reorienting approaches to care.

My final case explores how patients experience oncology's imperative to treat. I recount the last months of life for a patient I call Rebecca who had been diagnosed with an aggressive brain tumour just over a year before I met her. During these brief months, the good news of a positive brain scan was followed by a sudden deterioration and the recognition of tumour growth, which resulted in further treatment until weeks before Rebecca died. In recounting the contingency and ambivalence of care, I show why the recognition of irreversible disease required for achieving meaningful palliative intervention and the release from aggressive treatment was so challenging. I present Rebecca's case as a chronology of events using minimally edited fieldnotes and interviews with Rebecca and her husband Sam, to stay close to events as they happened and evoke the uncertainties, feelings of imminent but unknowable death, and the hopes that characterise what Jain calls 'living in prognosis' (Jain 2013). Focusing solely on their perspectives, I show care as they encountered it, the uncertainties they faced and the emotional and moral turmoil that accompanied the lack of preparation for the end of Rebecca's life.

Radical intentions

Oncology is emblematic of medical progress. It has made meaningful impacts on interventions in the course of disease, demonstrating a progressive understanding of cancer and a highly sophisticated treatment infrastructure. Cancer draws huge investment, dwarfing that of other diseases. In the UK in 2012, for example, cancer drew almost two-thirds of all medical research spending among four common conditions (cancer, coronary heart disease, dementia, stroke) from government and charitable organisations (Luengo-Fernandez et al. 2015). While its successes are by no means distributed evenly – by cancer type, geography or society – they are often celebrated among biomedicine's major achievements.

Moving through arenas of research, policy, advocacy and direct care, I documented the organisational cultures of neuro-oncology, the branch of oncology that manages brain tumours in the UK and most well-resourced healthcare systems. In my observations of information disclosure, treatment planning in weekly multidisciplinary team meetings, and decision-making in consultations between clinicians and patients, I became attuned to oncology's powerful imaginary of hope and its structuring effects on care. I observed how this imaginary was shared and enkindled among clinicians, patients, the wider public, the media, and an active and growing advocacy movement in brain tumours.

Care pathways at the Warner followed familiar patterns of intervention. A typical treatment plan, following the suspicion of an aggressive brain tumour prompted by clinical symptoms or radiological scan, would be surgery to remove the tumour or reduce its size, and radiotherapy and chemotherapy to prevent cancer cells from growing and reproducing. Treatment would appear early in patients' journeys and often seemed to distract from more detailed conversations about prognosis and the likely course of the disease if left untouched. As with other suspected cancers in the UK, access to cancer specialists for people suspected of having brain cancer is mandated in the 'two-week wait' – a two-week fast-track service from suspicion to appointment, which initiates an urgency to care and to make decisions. There are good reasons: brain tumours can grow fast, and even small amounts of growth can have devastating consequences for patients. This urgency continues and, after meeting with a specialist, patients might be admitted for surgery within days. Diagnosis is therefore inherently entangled with treatment. This happens further in the sequencing of tests, disclosure and intervention, as the diagnostic event often happens *after* surgery to remove or shrink the tumour, unless a biopsy has been performed in advance. Sometimes, targeted chemotherapy is given during this surgery by placing chemotherapy wafers directly in the brain.

Beyond the logic of urgency and the practicalities of ordering events, I often heard diagnosis and treatment coupled in clinicians' desires to maintain hope. I observed, for example, how clinicians would break bad news and pivot quickly toward planning treatment. Mr Muldoon, one of the most experienced neurosurgeons at the Warner, described to me his approach to diagnosis and breaking bad news:

> I walk through, talk through, what we jointly, patient and I, already know, rehash it and bring us with a, not a blaze of trumpets, but 'ta-rah', and 'so now here we are and this is the information'. The last act, as it were, is to feed into 'and where we go is' – I don't have the ability to look someone in the face and say, 'By the way, the news I've got for you is that this is cancer.' I can't do that. I have to dig my own foundation every time.*

Other clinicians also described a process of phased disclosure and how they narrated the revelation of disease alongside hope, in reference to the efficacy of biotechnology and the imperative to intervene. This brings to mind Foucault's observation that, while medicine 'ceaselessly reminds man of the limit that he bears within him, it also speaks to him of that technical world that is the armed' (Foucault 1973, 198). Foucault's observations are similarly taken up by anthropologist Bryon Good in his descriptions of medicine's soteriological vision – a vision that figures suffering as something to be transcended and for salvation to be achieved (1994). Medicine itself, Good writes, 'is a search for significance . . . and a complex technological imagination of immortality' (Good 1994, 60).

Clinical trials also featured strongly in the aspirations of both the patients and clinicians I met (Llewellyn 2021). While access to trials remains extremely limited for people with a brain tumour, patients invested in their possibilities, engaging considerable effort compiling research findings, contacting experts and asking their doctors for the scoop on the future promises of care. Calls for greater access to trials are increasingly made by advocates with attempts to embed the experimental as a universally available treatment option. Huge investment, in the UK and more widely, has recently been made in clinical-research cancer platforms that aim to re-envision patient access to experimental treatments and offer greater opportunities for them to share the rewards of high science. These new styles of care propel conceptions of trials as forms of care rather than simply experiments (Keating and Cambrosio 2012). They adhere to the logic of mastery over disease, further embedding discourses that 'proselytize [cancer's] transcendence through hope and individual will' (Banerjee 2019, 582).

Yet there is a paradox. While it is certainly the case that care was driven by this imperative to treat, clinicians were also aware of its futility. I was struck by repeated descriptions of 'radical treatment' in conversations between clinicians and its mentioning in large clinical team meetings and occasionally in the headers of letters to patients. 'Radical' in the context of medicine, I was told, means treatment 'with intent to cure'.* It opposes 'palliative'. However, in the case of brain tumours, these terms assume different meanings. Most brain tumours, regardless of grade, are incurable. 'Radical just means higher doses and longer courses of treatment,' one oncologist told me. 'Really all the patients we see are palliative.'* The difference between radical and palliative in this context is that radical treatments maximise the impact on the tumour and delay its progression; palliative describes a treatment schedule that is shorter and for older patients and those less functionally able.

The use of the word 'radical', I was told by one nurse, was further proof of 'a death-denying environment' in oncology, something scholars have documented extensively (DelVecchio Good et al. 1990). 'The average prognosis for the majority of [glioblastoma] patients is 14 months,'* the nurse told me:

> The fact that [oncologists] call the treatment radical [is ridiculous] – it's not radical treatment. For the vast majority of patients, it's palliative, they are not going to survive this. But it's still termed radical treatment. And oncologists say, 'Well, because that's our goal.' But it's the goal for, like, 5 per cent. We know for the vast majority, we're not going to cure them, so I find it incredible . . . cancer centres are such death-denying environments . . . You would think, of all environments, as opposed to a respiratory, or cardiac, that oncology would be more acknowledging and maybe more open about it; but it's not!*

As these examples show, oncology's imaginary achieves a complex semiotics of hope in the intersubjective encounters between clinicians and patients, through idioms of radical treatment, and where care is driven by a rendering of death as soluble by biotechnical means. In the following case, I examine palliative visions of care and how they are situated vis-à-vis oncology.

'Recognising when it's irreversible'

Palliative care emerged in the UK through the hospice movement in the mid-twentieth century in reaction to a construal of medicine's overtreatment and hospital regulation that disrupted intimate ties to the dying (Abel 2013). In contrast to oncology, it is characterised as 'patient (host) directed' rather than 'tumour directed' (Kaasa et al. 2018). In other words, it is less interventionist, tending toward the withdrawal of technology, with the aim of preparing for death rather than attempting to master it. It thus manifests an alternative soteriological vision in which human impermanence is centred in approaches to care and suffering transcended not through the deferral of death but through the mitigation of 'total pain' – physical, psychological, social and spiritual. In the UK, palliative care remains mostly community-based. While direct care might be provided by NHS employees (for example, the case of specialist palliative care nurses), the state also contracts care out to private companies; and charities provide significant resources including community nursing. Hospice care is available but limited, and many choose to die at home.

Research and activism increasingly advocate for earlier and more integrated access to palliative care for patients with advanced cancer, including brain tumours; however, how such integration should be realised is contested (Kaasa et al. 2018). The logics driving these calls emphasise that palliative care's expertise in symptom management should be available throughout the disease course and that earlier access to palliative care leads to better end-of-life preparation. These calls thus attempt to disembed palliative care from its historic and singular association with the end of life, toward a broader conception of symptom control alongside end-of-life care. Policy has been equivocal. In the context of brain tumours, regional guidelines across the UK recommend that palliative care specialists be included in multidisciplinary teams with consideration of palliative care needs and referral at multiple specific times throughout the disease (London Cancer Brain and Spine Pathway Board 2014). However, these recommendations stop short of mandating palliative involvement for brain tumour patients, meaning that access is not given by default. Recent national guidelines on brain tumour care compound this ambivalence by explicitly citing a lack of evidence on the relative benefits of earlier versus later palliative care and making a sole recommendation that palliative care be considered for people with high-grade glioma when prognosis is poor (NICE Guideline 2018).

Dr Marcus, a palliative care physician I interviewed during fieldwork, was an advocate for early access to palliative care. He managed a team of community-based practitioners and worked closely with allied healthcare professionals, including psychologists, physiotherapists and speech and language therapists at the Warner. As a member of the multidisciplinary team, he would attend weekly meetings to discuss patients' diagnoses, care and treatment plans. He was busy, yet told me his input with patients was comparatively marginal. He recounted disagreements and misunderstandings with other members of the team about his approach to care as well as the common perceptions of being 'on the losing side in the battle against cancer'. A critical feature of his work was negotiating access to patients in the first place, and this starkly illustrates the power relations among subspecialties in the clinic: managerial structures at the Warner dictate that palliative care is only involved with patients via referral; and, in most cases, these referrals would be for planning discharge from hospital, which Dr Marcus said typically 'doesn't really need palliative care'.

Dr Marcus and his team were not the only route to palliative care access and referral at the Warner. In fact, those coming through the service would typically access palliative care through the community. Again, access depends on referral; yet I would learn that referral was no guarantee of meaningful engagement with palliative care.

Several brain tumour specialists I interviewed in 2012 told me that community palliative care teams had only recently started taking referrals for people with a brain tumour because the disease was so unpredictable and rapid, and, historically, end-of-life care needs were under-recognised. While these specialists described a changing landscape for palliative care in brain tumours, with greater recognition of the complex needs of patients and families, challenges endured. The predicament they outlined was one of timing. Even if they made referrals to community palliative care teams for local support, these teams would often not accept patients who, being relatively well, were not yet eligible for specialist palliative care. 'They fall through the gaps in the net,'* one nurse told me:

> Some [patients] are not eligible for palliative care because they are not that bad yet, but we've got nothing more to offer them so they know that they're facing disease progression at some point where they will decline. But, irrespective of that, there's never going to be

IMPERMANENCE

any treatment for them and they fall through the net a lot – because palliative care wouldn't pick them up.*

This certainly accorded with my later observations as I saw patients referred to community teams with the outcome of deferring palliative involvement. Put simply, these early referrals did not seem commensurate with patients' situations because, at this point in their disease, they were relatively well. For most patients who accessed palliative care, contact with community teams would be remade (or made anew) much later in their disease, when it had progressed significantly; and, as I show later, this significantly compromises the support teams are able to give.

In a subsequent interview, Dr Marcus told me that this unfortunate timing of palliative involvement was due to 'a lack of understanding' across the board, where death and dying are figured as the 'worst outcome possible'. In a description redolent of the accounts of others I spoke with, who were sympathetic to a palliative model of care, he explained:

> It's a clash of cultures to do with what are we trying to achieve . . . a biomedical model versus a much more biopsychosocial model. And most people in medicine feel themselves to be trying to prolong life where death is the enemy. It's almost clichéd this stuff but there's a truth to it. Whereas, if death isn't the enemy, if it's normal and the circumstances in which it's normal is when it is irreversible, then recognising when it's irreversible is the trick. And if you are not used to thinking in those terms then you'll never recognise that it's irreversible – you'll try and try and try.*

Such recognition, I argue, is an important feature of care not simply in the acknowledgement of the demands of care and the assumptions of responsibility, as in Tronto's ethics of care, but also regarding the broader state of affairs with a patient's condition and the commensurability of care with the situation as it is understood – that is, whether disease is amenable or not to interventions of radical or life-prolonging treatment. As this case shows, calls for better integration of oncology and palliative care struggle amid organisational structures that privilege mainstream oncological approaches and those that are more clinically measurable. Even when referrals to community palliative care are made, they do not necessarily follow with meaningful commitments to palliative intervention because patients are not recognised to be at a point of need. As Dr Marcus tells us, this question of recognition is further concealed in models of care centred around prolonging life, where 'death is the enemy'.*

The following case shows how these dynamics of recognition play out in real time by focusing on the experiences of patients and families caught between conflicting care narratives. It shows the contingent, provisional nature of recognition and care and the challenges that come when the recognition of irreversible disease, in the sense given by Dr Marcus, comes too late.

Rebecca

I met Rebecca and her husband, Sam, when Rebecca was in her late forties. She died a year later, almost four years after being diagnosed with a glioblastoma. Rebecca lived well beyond the expected prognosis for glioblastoma but, in other ways, her trajectory was typical. She underwent three major operations at the Warner, radiotherapy, and chemotherapy in the first year following diagnosis. When we met, Rebecca was just beginning a second chemotherapy course. Here, I recount the last seven months of her life, beginning the day she received good news from the doctors about her scan.[1]

17 September

Fieldnotes from clinic – It's good news about the scan, Rebecca is told by Mr Fitzroy (the surgeon). She looks tired and underwhelmed by the news. She wants to see the scan and Fitzroy explains: 'Here's where you had surgery.' Fitzroy points towards a dark circle on the right of the image on his computer – there's no white, which would indicate cancerous tissue. He loads another scan, 'For comparison, this is your scan last November with some tissue picking up contrast here.'[2] He runs his finger along the white lines around the circle. 'This is when we thought we'd give you some more treatment. And this is another scan done midway through your treatment.' He runs his finger along a thinner white line around the tumour. 'And here is now.' He pulls up the latest scan again. It seems convincing evidence that the tumour suppressed.

Rebecca is pleased but surprised because she's been having headaches and what she thinks are seizures. 'Well there's no sign of anything untoward,' Fitzroy says, 'Headaches come and go and there's often little explanation.' When prompted, Rebecca describes her latest seizure and difficulty speaking. She says her GP thinks it's migraine. Fitzroy refers her to the neurologist.

Returning to the scan, Sam asks has it shrunk or is it just not visible? 'It's not visible on the scan,' Fitzroy says, 'that doesn't mean that it's not there but it's not on the scan'.* Sam says they've been erring on the negative side because of 'all the symptoms'.*

Sam is jubilant after the consultation, Rebecca more reserved. 'It's strange', she says, 'when I feel like this and with the headaches. It's good. But I am so tired.'*

13 October

Interview with Rebecca and Sam at home – Exhausted, Rebecca now frequently loses track of her thoughts. When I ask about September's consultation Rebecca tells me about the letter they received from the doctors the following week. She was hoping for something more effusive: 'It just says "she had good response" and that's it.'* Sam is more conciliatory: 'There isn't much more they could add. You could flower it up but the core of it is that the scan shows that the tumour isn't there, that's all they could say.'*

Overall, she and Sam have mixed feelings but Rebecca is more circumspect. When Sam says, 'It's really good news. We're going in the right direction!'* Rebecca counters: 'It can spread very quickly. That's why I'm always conscious about it, why I get worried. Last time I was well after six months and then suddenly I'm not. Imagine that timespan: it's very short. That's why sometimes I get worried or scared.'*

18 November

Telephone conversation with Sam – I was due to see Rebecca at home today but Sam cancelled. Rebecca had some sort of paralysis and fell. She went by ambulance to Whitefield (the local hospital) – returning home last night. Sam's waiting to hear from the Warner.

24 November

Telephone conversation with Sam – Sam says things aren't good. The doctors at the Warner think it's migraine and have changed Rebecca's medication. But Rebecca had more attacks, possibly seizures: 'They seem to be getting less severe but more frequent.'* She's now lost movement in her hand.

Sam's struggling to make sense of things: 'I don't know what to do. I don't think the doctors know what to do. I thought they'd want to see her so they could see how severe it is. But they seem reluctant.'* A scan Rebecca had at Whitefield 'looked alright'.*

25 November

Interview with Rebecca and Sam at home – Sam answers the door and immediately explains it's been difficult since returning from Whitefield. He thinks Rebecca should have stayed in. In the sitting room, Rebecca is slouched in a large chair, covered in blankets, a woolly hat pulled over her head.

Rebecca had another attack last night, milder than before. Several times she says she's ready to give up and speaks even more slowly. Sam fills in more than usual though she sometimes corrects him and they disagree on some details – who they talk to, what they said, when they said it. They agree on 'feeling lost',* 'waiting for answers'.* The clinicians at the Warner, Whitefield and Rebecca's GP are coordinating things but it's uncertain who's taking the lead at the Warner:

Sam: It would be good if they saw her – her state – from what she was before to what she is now; just to see her walk, talk, watch her hold something – even to hold something she has to concentrate to do it. Her dates have gone wrong and now even her spelling – it wasn't like this a month ago.

Rebecca: No – I've had more of these issues haven't I –

Sam: With each attack she loses a little bit more. For her it's very frustrating. She just about managed to shower this morning and I helped her dress –

Rebecca: This morning was bad – it's horrible – I try to sleep – I can't do much (she laughs). Yesterday was okay – I could do my puzzle. But the last few days I wasn't able to do anything . . . last night something wasn't right. My hand starts jerking – and I can't do anything. I said to myself, 'You know what f-f-f-f-f-forget about it – go back to sleep.' Because there's nothing I can do. I should have w-w-w-w-woken you up but I didn't. I couldn't move. And I am hoping that everything is okay.*

Not knowing is difficult. But nobody, including the doctors, knows what the attacks are and Rebecca and Sam struggle in this void. 'If they could find out, pinpoint what it is and say, for example, this is definitely migraine then it would help massively,'* Sam says.

It's especially hard given the dissonance between how Rebecca is and the scan results in September:

Sam: When we had the news about the scan that everything was looking good –

Rebecca: I never said that –

Sam: And then from that day it actually seems to just go downwards –

Rebecca: I never thought 'this is good.' Because I never believed it –

Sam: She's very sceptical –

Rebecca: Because it can't be. Because the tumour is so – it's so difficult. How can the tumour have gone away?

Sam: The only thing they said was it's not visible on the scan. And she was unconvinced by that – because leading up to that she'd had seizures and we were expecting a bad scan. But to say that it's a clear scan, well, I was shocked . . . What is it? What can it be? Stroke? Migraine? Why isn't she recovering from the attacks? . . . I spoke to Suze (the nurse) and she thinks get another scan. But that was overruled by the doctors, I think. They seem to think just change the medication and see how that goes.*

We speak nearly two hours. Once, Rebecca stands very slowly to walk to the window, with Sam standing close by in case she falls. A distance of about seven metres but it takes minutes for her to shuffle inches at a time, her feet barely lifted. She insists on standing to say goodbye.

7 December

MRI scan at the Warner – Urgent scan is done.

10 December

Fieldnotes from clinic – Today there is resolution to the past weeks' uncertainty with news of tumour progression. Rebecca consents to third course chemotherapy. Her condition is worse than when I last saw her two weeks ago; she arrives to clinic in a wheelchair and wrapped in black winter wear, having taken hospital transport. 'Four weeks ago we took the tube,' Sam says. 'It just shows you how quick.'*

As we wait, Sam tenderly takes Rebecca's hand in his and rests them together on the arm of his chair. He tells me that Macmillan (a cancer charity) have been very good and an occupational therapist has visited: 'We now have handrails around the house and we're mainly upstairs.'* Suze arrives soon to escort us to the clinic room.

Fitzroy tells Rebecca and Sam about the progression, his words clear and unambiguous. More surgery isn't a good option but Dr Anton (the oncologist) explains chemotherapy options. Rebecca stares blankly, her eyes wetting. Gripping her hand, Sam asks if treatment would allow Rebecca to regain function and he's told it depends how she responds to therapy. Rebecca asks how long she would live without treatment, her speech laboured. 'We never know,' Fitzroy says slowly, 'but given it changed a lot over three months – you might find you are sleeping an awful lot more as the tumour starts to take effect.'

After the consultation, Rebecca tells me: 'I've reached the end of my run . . . it's time to go.'* She'll start to think of the things she wants to do; she wants to go to New York and see family. Sam repeats, 'It's a game changer.'* They move between the sadness, the surprise – 'they thought it was migraine!'* – the rapidity – 'three months!'* – and the absence of cure – 'there's nothing!'* Rebecca's resolve to treat is solid: 'I will try the treatment, if that's what they say. What's the point in not?'*

18 December

Fieldnotes from clinic – Rebecca's first chemo appointment since the bad news last week runs longer than usual with another lengthy discussion about treatment benefits. 'We know there's not much time no matter,' Sam says. 'The big thing is whether the chemo would help with Rebecca's symptoms.'* Anton and Suze listen patiently as Sam explains how Rebecca is 'progressively getting weaker'.*

Rebecca listens, then says: 'For me, it's to see through my daughters.'*

Sam fills in: 'Her ultimate goal is to see them through their first year of uni.'*

About the chemo: Anton says, 'We don't know if it will have a good response, or a quick response, and it has to be weighed against the possible side effects. But you coped well last time.'* Anton thinks Rebecca should try the chemo: 'You'll always wonder if you hadn't. I've known you a long time and think that's probably what you're feeling.'*

In the last minutes of the consultation Suze asks about palliative care and 'making the home safe'.* Sam says they've thought about making a bedroom for Rebecca on the ground floor to avoid the stairs.

'I haven't given up hope,' Rebecca tells me after the consultation, 'It's nice to have Anton's guidance.'* She thinks she's sympathetic and feels Anton knows her.

23 December

Interview with Rebecca and Sam at home – Rebecca and Sam have started talking about the future and making plans. The uncertainty is different now. They have an explanation for the attacks and a plan. Sam says:

It's a relief to know what it is . . . We couldn't figure out why she'd been taking all this medication and it's just not working, she's still getting ill. And then when we had that scan and it showed the tumour was back, then you think 'oh yeah, well that's the reason why: it's nothing to do with migraine.'*

Whether the plan will work and what will happen remains unknown. Rebecca has told friends to come and see her now, 'because I don't know what will happen tomorrow or the next day'.* Seeing Anton and Suze last week has reinforced their commitment to treatment; Sam says, 'it's something for Rebecca to cling onto.'* Rebecca agrees but sometimes sways:

'Sometimes I think I want more, I want another day, I want to see the girls at least go through the first year of uni and I haven't had my bucket list (laughs) – there's a lot of things I want to do. So in one way I'm quite determined to go through another half a year of chemo. And there are days that you say, "Sod it! I've had enough."'*

They're planning a holiday. Sam also tells me they've arranged to meet with the bank about finances and with a Macmillan coordinator, to talk palliative care and things like Power of Attorney and funerals. 'Unsavoury things',* he calls them.

15 January

Fieldnotes from clinic – Rebecca looks so much better today. Her speech is more fluid and she's able to get around more using her walker.

For the first time, Sam asks about trials: 'I'm sure you've already thought about it.'* Anton says they have and smiles. Sam takes the cue and asks why they can't operate. This time Anton responds more fully and explains that they hope to reverse the disease with chemo, which the surgery wouldn't do in Rebecca's case. The risks are high and surgery might make things worse. In cases like Rebecca's, she says, 'you only really remove part of the tumour. And often it grows back to fill the space, unless it's an anticancer treatment and this is the advantage with chemo. And it looks like it's working.'*

12 February

Field notes from clinic – Rebecca has improved again and she's more animated: 'I've been doing my puzzles, and reading and doing some writing,'* she says, 'for my girls'* – for when they're older – things she might not be able to tell them later. She's reclaiming some of the things she lost, Sam says. Anton is visibly moved and positive. She says they were worried about her and about trying treatment, 'But it seems to have been the right decision.'*

27 February

Telephone conversation with Sam: 'Rebecca's in hospital,' he says, his voice flat. She was having more seizures so he called the ambulance. They've boosted her steroids (to improve her symptoms; steroids help reduce swelling in the brain) and they're in touch with the Warner deciding what to do. The choices are either to send her to the Warner or keep her at Whitefield with input from the Warner doctors. 'We're in a difficult situation and she's losing a bit of herself after every seizure,'* he tells me. 'Next week they're making a plan. It's basically down to the neurologist and what he wants to do.'* Sam asks me to call on Monday: 'Right now we don't know what's going on.'*

29 February

Telephone conversation with Sam: 'Things aren't good,' Sam says. 'You almost can't have a conversation with her now.'* The team at Whitefield are trying to get her to another ward – 'I need to contact Suze to see if we can get her over to the Warner – they haven't seen her – they've just increased her medication.'*

1 March

Fieldnotes from Whitefield – The ward is huge with many beds, several hidden by curtains. 'It's the first day she's started to pick up,'* Sam says. Rebecca turns to me, her skin shiny and taut (a side effect of steroids).

Sam says she was admitted eight days ago. The Warner are directing things. They're waiting for Rebecca to get well enough to go home, 'but at the moment she can't even sit up'. He's in touch with Macmillan: 'They've got a place a bit like a hospice and it's just across the road. It's called the Mary Centre.' It's easy for him to get to and they do 24-hour care, 'which is more than I can do at home – I need to sleep too and I don't know anyone who can give me a night off.' He thinks it's good if Rebecca could go there while he sorts things out at home. Suze told him to make sure that a care package is properly in place before she's discharged – he's hoping to get carers coming four times a day. His phone rings and he answers.

I ask Rebecca how the food is. She screws up her face and shakes her head. I hear Sam on the phone arranging visits, coordinating their daughters and friends. He later explains their friends from Sweden just flew in: 'On Sunday I didn't know what was happening, so I called everyone and said, "You better come and see her."'*

1 April

Telephone conversation with Sam – Rebecca is now in the Mary Centre. She's been there a week. She's awake but things 'aren't brilliant'.* 'She had a big seizure on Friday,' Sam explains. 'It took a lot to get her out of it but we finally did. We're trying to get her to Coombs House (a local care home). She's been accepted but the commissioning group is quibbling over costs.'*

5 April

Telephone conversation with Sam – Rebecca is still at the Mary Centre. Sam explains: 'I think they've decided on a way to go. They've decided to stop the steroids completely – 8mg to zero – and I think it's going to be quite catastrophic. We'll see – it's all been done in consultation with Rebecca.'* I ask, why now? 'Well – she's not getting better. She's slowly losing everything and even her dignity. She's not in a good place so this will speed things up, to put it bluntly. She can think and talk but she can't communicate that well. She's basically locked in – that's the only way I can put it. I wasn't aware they were going to drop [the steroids] so fast – I think it will take her into a kind of – ' He trails off, and then: 'It's, in a way, trying to control things . . . it's just so sudden – there's no pain and they're prepared for any that would come – they've got mechanisms for that.'*

6 April

Fieldnotes from the Mary Centre – Sam is at reception looking under-slept, his eyes glistening in the harsh fluorescence of the light above him.

'They've dropped Rebecca's steroids right down in one go and it seems to be having an effect already,' he says, 'Yesterday I was talking to her and today she won't wake up. Actually, she was awake a little in the morning; she ate a banana – part of it – but now I can't wake her. So this is it – this is how it is. You can never really prepare yourself for it. She was aware of what it would do. It was just so frustrating for her. Watching her struggle to say something – exhausting herself – she was just so tired. And she was so frustrated with me for not getting it.'

He talks about their life together until we're interrupted by a phone call from the care commission. He tells the person on the phone that Rebecca 'would have loved to have died at home',* but that the care they sent wasn't adequate, that they didn't have the experience: 'My wife is a very complex case – they didn't know how to deal with her – and they couldn't have used the medications she needs.' He tells the person on the phone that things have suddenly changed: 'My wife is very seriously ill now. This is why I was saying arrangements had to be made fast.' When he's off the phone he says it has been hard and frustrating trying to coordinate things.

He says the care home is very nice and close to the house, but they were quibbling over costs. He says Rebecca wanted to die at home. He says they wanted to get Macmillan nurses at home. He's not really in touch with the Warner now: 'I think they are more focused on treatment.'*

There is a lament in Sam's words and a bitter sadness that things have come to this: 'You can never prepare yourself for this,'* he says again.

When I see Rebecca, she's asleep. 'She knew you were coming,' Sam says. 'I asked her and she said it was fine.' I stand by Rebecca's head, facing her. 'Henry's here,' Sam says. She doesn't register but sleeps silently. 'Henry's come to see you,' he repeats, standing at her feet, leaning against the wall. We stand in silence looking at her small movements as she breathes. Bed covers are pulled up to her shoulder; a white dotted gown up to her neck. She looks peaceful.

. . .

Rebecca died at the Mary Centre the following week. It was four months since the scan had signalled progression and eight weeks after her last chemotherapy appointment. It was only seven months since the positive news from her scan in mid-September.

Conclusion

Caring for people with life-threatening diseases is complicated by diverging visions about the demands of care and how to respond. In cancer, oncology and palliative care often remain committed to different ends despite long-held ambitions for better integration. Mainstream oncology's mandate to prolong life is embedded in powerful imaginaries that promote cancer's transcendence through hope, determination and the efficacy of treatment. This imaginary is fostered through intersubjective encounters of clinical consultations and care pathways that suggest an optimistic future. Patients receive and collaborate in this embrace of biotechnology and its promises to prolong life through so-called radical treatments. Plenty submit to bioscientific grail-quests for a cure in clinical trials, mostly with their aspirations unrealised. For many, these quests and collaborations foreclose meaningful engagements with other care trajectories, notably palliative care, that seek less interventionist modalities and orient care toward comfort in dying, dignity and reconciliation. At stake is the preparation for death and the moral approbation of those who care.

My clinical interlocutors referred to the critical issue of recognising irreversible disease in orienting their work away from life-prolonging treatment, a form of recognition I have marked as ontological in its association with the fundamental nature of disease and its relation to human agency. Here, I refer to recognition of the basic terrain for the expression of care entangled with the recognitions of care need and respective responsibilities (Tronto 1993). Yet, as this chapter shows, constructions of situations – as terrains of possibility – differ vastly; they are highly contingent and socially wrought.

Rebecca's and Sam's experiences illustrate the ambiguities encountered by patients and families as they confront these multiple visions of care. They show how recognition emerges incrementally and ambiguously in the progressive ordering of new moments, missed opportunities, misattributions of symptoms, in patients' decisions not to call doctors, in doctors' decisions to scan or not scan, and in the other myriad ways in which patients and clinicians interpret and weigh information. They show how hopes, doubt, sadness, determination and resignation commingle in attempts to plan, and how plans rise and fall amid broader institutional orders, economic rationalities and, ultimately, the effects of treatment and surging disease. While Rebecca added to her 'bucket list' and hoped to see her daughters through their first year of university, she would also say that she would not live to complete her treatment. While Sam called people to come and visit Rebecca and thought about how to broach the 'unsavoury details' of preparing a future without her, he supported Rebecca in relentlessly pursuing treatment. When I saw him two months after Rebecca died, he told me the treatment was futile but it gave Rebecca hope. He lamented her not being able to die at home, as they had wished, and told me it was a tragedy that she could not say goodbye in the way she had wanted to.

Although this study has focused on the logistics of care, my intention has not been to evaluate the provision of cancer care. Rather, it has been to show one important – and challenging – manifestation of a fundamental ambivalence around human impermanence in Western biomedicine. The respective soteriological visions of oncology and palliative care embody and promote notably different orientations and practices around impermanence and whether to resist or embrace it. The experiences of people with a brain tumour, who find themselves in the position of confronting their impermanence directly in the face of progressive disease and through these visions, reveal – to use Lisa Stevenson's memorable phrase – some of the 'ambivalence of our desires and the messiness of our attempts to care' (Stevenson 2014, 3). They show how forms of care, despite best intentions, can lead to undesirable consequences by foreclosing the possibilities of other care trajectories that might be more commensurate with patients' situations (Stevenson 2014; Tronto 1993).

Acknowledgements

I am deeply grateful to Rebecca and Sam, and the many other patients and families I have met who so generously allowed me into their lives, and to the many clinicians who patiently fielded my questions and showed me their work. For inspiration, insights and edits, I am grateful first to the editors of this this volume – Haidy, Cameron and Ton – and the other participants at the Inevitable Ends symposium. Finally, I thank UCL and Macmillan Cancer Support for funding my work.

Notes

1 Dates have been changed to avoid revealing the identities of Rebecca and Sam and others mentioned; intervals between events are similar.
2 'Contrast' refers to the dye used to mark tumour tissues on scans.

* As with many ethnographies, I place quotations around all speech. An asterisk denotes that I am sure I have recorded someone's words verbatim, either in field notes or on a voice recorder.

References

Abel, Emily. 2013. *The Inevitable Hour: A history of caring for dying patients in America*. Baltimore, MD: Johns Hopkins University Press.

Banerjee, Dwaipayan. 2019. 'Cancer and conjugality in contemporary Delhi: Mediating life between violence and care', *Medical Anthropology Quarterly* 33(4): 579–94.

Cancer Research UK. 2020. 'Brain, other CNS and intracranial tumours statistics'. http://www.cancerresearchuk.org/health-professional/cancer-statistics/statistics-by-cancer-type/brain-other-cns-and-intracranial-tumours (last accessed 29 October 2021).

DelVecchio Good, Mary-Jo. 2001. 'The biotechnical embrace', *Culture, Medicine and Psychiatry* 25(4): 395–410.

DelVecchio Good, Mary-Jo, Byron Good, Cynthia Schaffer and Stuart Lind. 1990. 'American oncology and the discourse on hope', *Culture, Medicine and Psychiatry* 14: 59–79.

Foucault, Michel. 1973. *The Birth of the Clinic: An archaeology of medical perception*. London: Routledge.

Good, Byron. 1994. *Medicine, Rationality, and Experience: An anthropological perspective*. Cambridge: Cambridge University Press.

Jain, S. Lochlann. 2013. *Malignant: How cancer becomes us*. London: University of California Press.

Kaasa, Stein, Jon Loge, Matti Aapro, Tit Albreht, Rebecca Anderson, Eduardo Bruera, Cinzia Brunelli, et al. 2018. 'Integration of oncology and palliative care: A *Lancet Oncology* commission', *The Lancet Oncology* 19(11): e588–653.

Keating, Peter, and Alberto Cambrosio. 2012. *Cancer on Trial: Oncology as a new style of practice*. Chicago, IL: University of Chicago Press.

Llewellyn, Henry. 2021. 'Emerging tissue economies: Personalised immunotherapies and therapeutic value in cancer', *Medical Anthropology*. DOI: 10.1080/01459740.2021.1902322.

Llewellyn, Henry, and Paul Higgs. 2021. 'Living suspended: Anticipation and resistance in brain cancer'. In *Immobility and Medicine: Exploring stillness and the in-between*, edited by Cecilia Vindrola-Padros, Bruno Vindrola-Padros and Kyle Lee Crossett, 251–72. London: Palgrave Macmillan.

Llewellyn, Henry, Paul Higgs, Elizabeth Sampson, Louise Jones and Lewis Thorne. 2018a. 'Topographies of "Care Pathways" and "Healthscapes": Reconsidering the multiple journeys of people with a brain tumour', *Sociology of Health & Illness* 40(3): 410–25.

Llewellyn, Henry, Jane Neerkin, Lewis Thorne, Elena Wilson, Louise Jones, Elizabeth Sampson, Emma Townsley and Joseph Low. 2018b. 'Social and structural conditions for the avoidance of advance care planning in neuro-oncology: A qualitative study', *BMJ Open* 8: e019057.

London Cancer Brain and Spine Pathway Board. 2014. 'Neuro-oncology guidelines'. http://www.londoncancer.org/media/84343/london-cancer-neuro-oncology-radiotherapy-guidelines-2013-final-v1-0.pdf (last accessed 29 October 2021).

Luengo-Fernandez, Ramon, Jose Leal and Alastair Gray. 2015. 'UK research spend in 2008 and 2012: Comparing stroke, cancer, coronary heart disease and dementia', *BMJ Open* 5(4): 1–7.

NICE Guideline. 2018. 'Brain tumours (primary) and brain metastases: Management options for people with newly diagnosed grade IV glioma (glioblastoma)'. NICE Guideline No. 99. http://www.nice.org.uk/guidance/ng99.

Petryna, Adriana. 2013. 'The right of recovery', *Current Anthropology* 54(7): S67–76.

Stevenson, Lisa. 2014. *Life Beside Itself: Imagining care in the Canadian Arctic*. London: University of California Press.

Tronto, Joan. 1993. *Moral Boundaries: A political argument for an ethic of care*. London: Routledge.

12
Caring for the social (in museums)

Haidy Geismar

Despite the commonplace assumption that museums are primarily defined by their collections of objects, it has become overwhelmingly clear that knowledge, stories and values are just as integral to museum collections as material things are. Today, museum practitioners working with collections management are increasingly raising questions about who is to collect, and conserve, the skills and knowledge that underpin the artefacts that museums acquire.[1] In this chapter, I draw on my background in museum anthropology to explore how these questions are emerging within the art museum. In both contemporary art and ethnographic collections (and, of course, in many other institutional contexts), practitioners are exploring the challenge of how to collect, preserve and conserve that which is generally defined as immaterial, contingent and impermanent.

Here, I explore some contemporary conversations about impermanence in reference to two London-based museum projects: 'Finding Photography', a project at Tate Gallery to explore the networks of skill that underpin contemporary art photography, and 'Encounters on the Shop Floor', a project led by the V&A Research Institute (VARI), which explores embodied knowledge through a wide range of skilled practices. As discourses of conservation and collections management shift from the protection and preservation of material forms to the inclusion of more social understandings of care, I ask what it means to care, in the museum, for social networks and relationships as well as objects. The question that underpins this chapter is: when we ask how museums can care for and maintain sociality over the long term, are we thinking about museums as social communities or are we thinking of social relations as objects? Can museums develop new practices and interventions to care for people, or will doing so inevitably just produce new kinds of objects? I argue that the notion of care, in fact, holds these two questions and concepts together, in a similar fashion to the movement between ideas of permanence and impermanence being explored in other chapters in this volume. Can concepts of care and skill provide blueprints for museums to manage the precarity, obsolescence and impermanence that inflect the techniques and technologies used to make many of their collections, as well as support the discourses of preservation that underpin traditional definitions of heritage and conservation?

Impermanence in museums

Traditional academic narratives have explored how museums create and disseminate knowledge of the world through the collection, storage, preservation, conservation and display of things, forming national identities and educating and disciplining citizens. Museums have also played a vital role in debates about inclusion and exclusion, imperialism and colonialism, history, heritage and culture (for example, Bennett et al. 2016; Karp and Lavine 1991; Karp et al. 1992, 2006). While museums participate in these broader fields of inquiries through so-called 'object lessons', they are, themselves, meta-object lessons – forms of inquiry into the nature of objects (Geismar 2018). Practices of collection, conservation, curation, display and representation do not simply act on objects; they help to construct the categories, such as property, ownership, interpretation, value and meaning, that define things as collections. For instance, Elizabeth Edwards has described how photographs in museums have shifted over time from being 'non-collections' to being recognised as documentation, as supplementary and archival material and, finally, as historical artefacts, ethnographic collections and fine art (Edwards 2019). Each shift resulted in changes not only to how photographs are displayed, cared-for and valued but also to the ontological status and value of photography in the museum (see Edwards and Morton 2015). In this way, museums might be understood as 'objectification machines' (Domínguez Rubio 2014, 620) that work to substantiate, legitimate and preserve things *as* objects. Drawing on fieldwork at the Museum of Modern Art in New York, Domínguez Rubio describes the processes of 'containment and maintenance' of environments and materials to preserve what, in the Western art museum, is an 'extremely narrow "regime of objecthood"' (2016, 68; 69).

There is, however, a paradox here: museology and museum practice have not only been integral to a broader renewal of interest in the object world and materiality but are also a vital part of a turn away from the narrow understandings of the material usually associated with museum collections, toward a more expansive perspective on objects that focuses on their inherent immateriality as well as material fluidity. Recent debates within the International Council of Museums (ICOM) over proposed changes to the globally accepted definition of a museum highlight how global understandings of museums are shifting from collections of objects toward being recognised more prominently as social and political spaces.[2] In advance of their annual meeting to discuss the proposed change to the definition in Tokyo in September 2019, ICOM initiated an open call to 'members and other interested parties' to submit definitions of their own to a central website.[3] Many of the submissions, as well as the proposed new definition, moved away from the language of objects and collections to a socially focused language of collaboration, participation and inclusion. Surveying the proposals (unattributed but for the national affiliation of authors), few refer specifically to objects or collections. Instead, museums are described as affective spaces (Greece: 'The factory of our dreams'), committed to notions of the public sphere, social justice and identity construction (Colombia: 'The Museum is a Cultural Horizon where human life forms converge with nature and the universe'). The majority of the submissions used the terms 'heritage' or 'asset' rather than 'collection' and located objects at the service of the framing of ideas about identity, humanity and citizenship rather than as ends in and of themselves.

Even though the new definition was rejected at the time, and remains controversial pending further debate, it is clear that museums today are widely understood as spaces in which historic 'regimes of objecthood' are being challenged as much as upheld (see Harrison et al. 2020). It is also increasingly recognised, especially within conservation and collections management, that objects themselves are not fixed and immutable but are continually changing their material form, as well as shifting in terms of meaning and value (Wharton 2012; Clavir 2002; Sully 2007; Grünfeld, this volume). In a meditation on museological impermanence, *Curated Decay* (2017), Caitlin De Silvey explores a number of different sites and institutional frames that are experimenting with the idea of leaving heritage objects and sites to 'decay', rather than fixing, repairing or conserving them to prior states of being. To 'curate' decay is to acknowledge the fragility and continual erosion and transformation of the material world as a worthy visitor experience. It also signals how museums and heritage sites must regularly evaluate what is worth preserving in an economic landscape of limited funds within a political economy of, in DeSilvey's terms, 'post-preservation' (2017, Chapter 1). The notion of 'curating decay' therefore links the acknowledgment of material transformation as being fundamental to all heritage objects, to the emergence of an aesthetic interest in decay and decline and to regimes of value in which only some, not all, things may be preserved. In the case of Mullion Cove in Cornwall, the National Trust has made the decision to leave the harbour to erode, rather than invest in its rebuilding each time it is damaged by rising tides (DeSilvey 2017, Chapter 3). As much as these decisions reflect an evolution of concepts of preservation and conservation, and a form of renewed attention to the imperatives of the material world, they also reflect cost–benefit analyses and the decision-making of heritage regimes under conditions of austerity, reflecting an economy as well as a philosophy of care.

This notion of institutional care jostles with conceptions of care that have emerged outside of institutional frames, where care has become a powerful lens through which to expose existing power relations and inequalities (see McAtackney, this volume). For instance, in many ethnographic collections, the mapping of cultural values onto the permanence or impermanence of artefacts, and the discussions about care that follow, are increasingly bound up in fraught discussions about colonial history and repatriation in which the remit of museums to define the conditions of care for collections is challenged by community groups, source communities and other stakeholders. In a notable example, the G'psgolox totem pole, which was collected from the Kitamaat Village in Haisla territory (British Columbia) in 1929 under contested circumstances and eventually gifted to the Ethnographic Museum in Stockholm, was the subject of a lengthy repatriation claim that surfaced competing definitions of care and visions for the future of the pole as a permanent museum object. When contemporary Haisla descendants realised the pole was in Sweden, they initiated a repatriation request. The subsequent negotiation over many years (1991–2006) could be seen as an exemplar of opposing philosophies of impermanence and preservation: the Haisla community requested the return of the pole and emphasised that their aim was to both connect to Indigenous customs of care and to effect a form of restorative justice and cultural healing that would only be achieved if the pole were returned to its place of origin and left to decay into the earth. They generously offered to carve a replacement pole for the museum in exchange for the original. Initially, the Stockholm Ethnographic Museum agreed to the repatriation on the condition that the pole be returned to be cared for in a museum setting, which, at the time, was far beyond the means of the community (see Jessiman 2011 for an overview of the lengthy negotiation).

The case can be framed as surfacing two competing views of the object world, with the museum emphasising the importance of preserving a material artefact for display and community stakeholders highlighting the need to preserve ancestral spirit, connections to place and material lifecycles. But this dichotomy is also, by definition, a conversation about colonial histories, inequality and power in museums and over collections. Eventually, after the debate garnered global attention through Gil Cardinal's film 'Totem: The Return of the G'psgolox Pole' (2003), the pole was returned to the community, who had managed to raise sufficient funds to house it in a museum-like setting. In 2012, the community decided to move the pole back to the Kitlope Valley and leave it to return to the earth (Björklund 2018). Here, discussions of permanence and impermanence link cultural and cosmological framings of the material world and object biographies to broader issues of the politics of recognition, sovereignty over collections, colonialism and ongoing inequalities over access to land and cultural and political self-determination.

In this chapter, the debates that have arisen around ethnographic collections form the backdrop to an exploration of the emerging conversation about care in other museum contexts and pick up on the notion of care as something unsettled and filled with ambivalence (Cook and Trundle 2020). What responsibility do museums have to collect or preserve the knowledge about making that is embodied in people? How can museums care for the social networks and experiences that define these kinds of work into the future, beyond the life of an artist or even an artwork? In ethnographic collections, these kinds of questions are also, by definition, questions about cultural protocols, alternative forms of knowledge and cultural expression, and alternative ownership and rights regimes (see Geismar 2013; Morphy 2021). The legacies of colonialism and ongoing sovereignty claims are also always present and underpin the focus of conservation as 'the care of what has been transmitted through the generations and the guarantee to transmit this to future generations' (Wijesuriya 2007, 67; see also Sully 2007).

In the rest of this chapter, I explore how these issues are arising within two projects that grapple more explicitly with how to bring precisely that which is *not* recognised as residing in object form into museums: the recognition, collection and preservation of the skills embodied within people that are vital to both the making and care of collections. In the case of contemporary photographic technologies, the knowledge-base is not conventionally a part of the portfolio of skills held by museum conservators and it requires collections managers to look outside of the museum toward wider networks of practice. Both of the projects I discuss here question the ethics of care and the social responsibilities of collecting institutions and both explore how museums might engage with social configurations understood to be fundamentally precarious and impermanent. It is also true that the social is increasingly instrumentalised within museums: participation and collaboration are now commonly defined as measurable outputs of museum work (see Jackson 2011, 10) and intangibles such as 'artist's intentions' or 'source communities' may become new objects of collection, frozen in time and space.

The subject positions of museological impermanence

Much of the literature in museum studies and museum anthropology is implicitly presented from one of two institutional vantage points. The first, and by far the most common, we might understand as the subject position of the visitor (or visitor-scholar), who explores the meanings of objects as they are choreographed into exhibitions. This perspective has been influentially developed in the writing of such critical museum visitors as James Clifford (for example, 1988; 1997; 2013), Sally Price (1989) and Tony Bennett (1995). More recently, this approach has been further extended into studies that focus on the museum's visitor experience, from a generic public to specific stakeholder groups (for example, Simon 2010; Janes and Sandell 2019). A second subject position might be best summarised as 'curatorial' – accounts that present the work of museums from the other side – focusing on the institutional processes and practices that produce knowledge. Such accounts are exemplified by a growing ethnography of museums (for instance, Macdonald 2002; Shannon 2014). In both of these positions, collections provide fixed points within this fluid sociality, gathering people, meanings and values around them.

Here, I posit that it might be productive to explore a third kind of museum subject position (one of a potential multitude), a different perspective on the relation between the material and the social that highlights concepts and practices of maintenance and care. Conservators have traditionally assumed the role of the silent technicians charged with keeping objects in museums stable, using both artistic and scientific techniques. Historically, their labour has been, for the most part, invisible to the public, concerned with stabilising objects before they enter into the museum's social spaces. It is only recently that conservation itself has been recognised as a social activity (see, for example, Wharton 2012). Conservators are also, traditionally, the practitioners that quietly explore the interface between the social and the material *before* the object emerges into the processes of signification within exhibitions.[4] They are also frequently gatekeepers behind the scenes who manage the possibility of engagement with both curators and communities, often deciding what is and what is not possible in terms of using the object, whether for research, display, or engagement (see Clavir 2002). The conservator's role is therefore not merely to stabilise material form but also to authorise 'care' for collections and manage the physical interactions that we have with them.

Definitions of 'collections care' powerfully circumscribe the kinds of relations that can be had with collections. In the present day, conservators work with a range of different methods drawing on technical art history or material science, and increasingly with social research methodologies that enable them to understand cultural values and protocols, artists' intentions and networks that produce objects and authorise the conditions of care (for example, Wharton 2015). The remit of collections care requires reflexive practice as well as knowledge of not only the material structure of collections and the atmospheric structure of the institution but also of the conceptual scaffolding that supports the objects and enables them to continue to exist in the museum in ways that sustain the intentions of their makers. Shifting our analytic focus into the subject position of the conservator might help us to bridge some of the tensions between the material and the social, the fixed and the malleable, the permanent and the impermanent that exist within other interpretive frameworks we tend to use to understand museum collections. Rather than understanding objects as fixed points around which, and within, meaning and social action are articulated, the theory and practice of conservation can enable us to add a number of other questions. How is the social contained within the material? What institutional forms and practices can mobilise and conserve the social? How is impermanence managed through processes of care? In the following discussion, I explore how these questions emerge in two museum-based research projects.

'Finding Photography'

'Finding Photography' is an ongoing collaboration between me and Pip Laurenson, Head of Collections Care Research at Tate. The project is closely aligned with a larger project entitled 'Reshaping the Collectible: When Artworks Live in the Museum', also led by Laurenson.[5] 'Finding Photography' brings anthropology and museum conservation into conversation with one another to explore the networks of materials, technologies and skills that underpin contemporary fine art photography, drawing on both ethnographic and conservation research methodologies. Photography is an interesting case study to think through concepts of impermanence as it is particularly enmeshed within ongoing technical processes of obsolescence and is also seen – through fading, crackling, discolouration and other material responses to light – to be a fragile and impermanent medium. The fast-changing world of commercial photographic processing and printing is often perceived to have moved away from the recognisable skills and crafts of photography (for instance, in the darkroom) to a largely black-boxed series of automated tasks that can be delivered within software and hardware, from digital cameras to printers. Knowledge of these processes is not part of traditional museum conservation, and photographic conservators often have a background in paper conservation, which can leave large gaps in their knowledge when working with digital technologies. 'Finding Photography' explores how photographic craft is developed, recognised and maintained in a commercial industrial setting where practitioners have to work around the reality of materials and machines becoming obsolete and extend their skillsets from one form to another in short periods of time.[6]

From the vantage point of Tate collections-care researchers, the project has a practical ambition: to inform conservation decision-making around contemporary art photography by enabling conservators to better understand artist networks and techniques connected to these processes. However, the project also opens up larger questions about the responsibility of museums to understand, and potentially support, broader social networks underpinning art, especially those that are vulnerable to rapidly changing socio-economic and material circumstances. This mirrors some of the concerns arising around other heritage collections in which critics may ask why museums are interested in preserving objects while not actively intervening in the decline of making communities or social worlds vulnerable or at risk from war, climate change or other crises that impact the continuity of practice and the intergenerational transmission of knowledge and tradition.

'Finding Photography' started with a single artwork in Tate's collections, *Corridors* (1994) by Catherine Yass.[7] Working with the artist and her networks, we sought to unpack the skills and connections that underpin this work (a colour transparency light box) in an environment of rapid technological change. We used the archaeological method of *chaîne opératoire* (see Coupaye 2009; and Sellet 2016 for an overview of the history and application of the methodology) to reconstruct the technical processes that Yass followed during the making of *Corridors*, tracking the changes she made to her practice as the materials and processes she was working with became obsolete. We also undertook a short stint of observational fieldwork and interviewed some of the commercial printers that formed a part of Catherine's networks, in particular at Bayeaux in Fitzrovia. Our project developed an awareness of how much craft and artistry underpin the industrial processes of photography, and of the work that goes into stabilising images across an ever-changing range of materials and processes. We started to challenge some of the narratives of impermanence that were concerning conservators evaluating reprinting as a conservation strategy for photographic prints when the substrates, chemicals and machines that had produced them were no longer available. Working with Yass and her network exposed how powerful narratives and practices of resilience, flexibility, translation and persistence worked alongside those of obsolescence and precarity (Geismar and Laurenson 2019):

> Unless the government moves the retirement goalposts, I've got about 10 years. It's my mission to keep them going for at least that long. It might not happen. We're very close to being priced out of [these] premises and moving the kit would possibly be financially prohibitive. Again, it's costs. Rent in London is stupid. All the landlords are greedy (J, photo technician and consultant, Metro Imaging, interview 2 February 2018).

When we asked printers what the most important skills of their job were, all of them talked about how social skills are fundamental to their successful craft. One vital skill is to manage the relationship with the artist within the constraints of both time and materials – knowing when to hold firm and stop making test prints, or to create limits or boundaries about the time that an image is taking to make. At Bayeaux, clients can pay an extra amount to have more dedicated time with one of the skilled

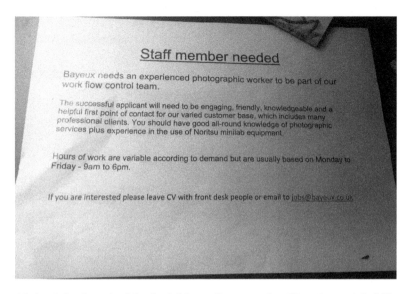

12.1 Job advertised in the lobby at Bayeaux detailing the social skills needed for the position. Photo: Haidy Geismar.

technicians, measured in half-hour increments. In turn, technicians need to establish a balance between being responsive to the demands and vision of the artist and managing the constraints of cost, space and labour. It is through the entanglement of this social negotiation and constraint, mediated by the experienced eye of the printer, as well as that of the artist, that the 'finished' image emerges.

Trying to capture the network on which Yass depended for her practice also demonstrated the powerful ways in which the contemporary art world structures these relationships. Despite working intensively on the images, photo technicians must also work hard to situate their work as technical support, disavowing discourses of either art or craft. They are careful to discuss their work using terms like 'support' and 'problem-solving', avoiding words like 'creative' and downplaying notions of skill that might link them to a more craft-oriented discourse. This mirrors an emerging lexicon focused on technical expertise across studios that support artists' work. In a recent volume celebrating Mike Smith Studio in London, which has underpinned the practice of a generation of contemporary artists in the UK, Germano Celant describes the work of the studio as embodying all 'technical functions, those deriving from knowledge as much as from discussions and intuitive modifications . . . an interface where all the data are accumulated to arrive at the definitive result . . . This is a specific knowledge based on the "technique of transforming", so is very flexible and open to solutions in the course of production' (Celant 2003, 15). Here, studio workers are technical enablers, flexible and responsive to the creative energies of the artist, rather than creative practitioners, or artisans, in their own right.

Encounters on the shop floor

In 2016, 'Finding Photography' was invited to become part of another research project run from the Victoria and Albert Museum (V&A). Led by Marta Ajmar, Deputy Director of VARI, and Roger Kneebone, Professor of Surgical Education at Imperial College, 'Encounters on the Shop Floor' explored the nature of embodied knowledge across a range of different making practices, in dialogue with academics and museum professionals.[8] The project brought together a diverse set of scholars and practitioners to work collaboratively to understand the significance of embodied knowledge in the transmission of ideas through processes of making.[9] The project team was interested in how insights from within skilled craft practices could make, inform or be transferred into other practices (for example, between pottery and guitar-playing or embroidery and surgery). By making connections across making practices, the project aimed to develop a language for talking about the relation between making and knowing, and to construct an argument for taking embodied know-how seriously, especially at a time when art and design subjects are being cut from school curricula, and digital skills are perceived to be more central to learning at all levels than other crafts (Durham Commission 2019; Kneebone 2020).

The project took a number of forms alongside academic conferences and meetings, including several making and doing sessions in which participants reflected on their own practice by teaching others to do what they do. Sessions were also held with educators exploring pedagogies focused around embodied learning, and thinking about how this project might intervene in the contemporary landscape of teaching design and technology within the UK National Curriculum and placing learning-by-making more centrally within higher education. The group of disparate practitioners split into smaller 'design clusters' and worked collaboratively to explore a more specialised question across different practices and forms of making and doing. Pip Laurenson, Catherine Yass and I joined through 'Finding Photography', continuing our work with Yass and her worlds of photographic processing. In an example of another cluster, potter Julian Stair and classical guitarist Pétur Jónasson explored the

CARING FOR THE SOCIAL (IN MUSEUMS)   215

nature of touch across their practices, comparing body–hand interactions and creating a typology of touch and pressure that drew connections between making music and pots. Using film to simultaneously record images of the role that touch plays in their practice, and their reflections on this, Stair and Jónasson are developing a lexicon or typology of touch. This work is feeding into the V&A's work aimed at addressing the loss of embodied knowledge of making from the school curriculum, and the group has already been invited to present about the future of design and technology in education to the All Parliamentary Design and Innovation Group in the House of Commons.[10]

Skill and loss

> The traditional industry is limping along. I described 2004 as when the digital apocalypse happened. A lab like Metro went from well over 200 employees to around 20 in 2008 (J, photo technician and consultant, Metro Imaging, interview 2 August 2018).

An important starting point for the 'Encounters' project is the belief, shared by many of the practitioner-participants, that embodied skills are being lost to rapid changes led by an economy focused on knowledge and information, rather than on production and making. This, in turn, was perceived by project members as devaluing hand-work in favour of 'cognitive labour'. Project members described chemistry students arriving at university without ever having handled lab pipettes, or humanities students who struggle to write with a pen or pencil. The perception of hand-work or skilled practice was that it was perpetually being superseded, especially by digital technologies and shortcuts that were described by many of the project members as disembodied, distancing the hand from processes of making and shifting embodied skills into pre-programmed operations of both hardware and software.

In this context, we found that the knowledge-base we had been developing in 'Finding Photography' raised a number of provocative questions about how understandings of skill and knowledge interconnected with ideas about materiality and impermanence. While the advent of digital technology had certainly dramatically altered the photography printing industry, we found that many of the embodied skills gained through traditional, non-digital printing in the darkroom were still present within commercial and industrial photographic

12.2 Analogue and digital practices at Bayeaux. Photo: Haidy Geismar.

printing. While skilled practitioners imagined themselves not as craftsmen or creatives but as 'technicians' or workers who support and facilitate the work of the artist, they also described a number of ways in which they were translating skills from the darkroom into the world of digital or machine-based processing.

> It's just a matter of getting used to the machine but that's why you're a technician, that's part of it, being the technician part isn't it? (B, CPL, Edenbridge, interview 23 August 2017).

The transfer of human skill into machines has been conventionally framed through the politics of alienation and capitalism, in which workers are distanced from their own labour (and therefore from their own agency and creativity) through processes of industrialisation (see, for example, Gibson 2019). We found that the story in the world of photographic processing was more complex. Photographic processing is clearly imagined as both commercial and craft-like, industrial and artisanal at the same time, with people identifying strongly with the machines – the cameras, printers and enlargers – that they worked with:

> We had 30 printers there and they were all skilled people. We did, there were printers that only went up to about 30 x 20 inches and the biggest room was 30-foot-wide so you were printing one piece of paper 30-foot x 6-foot print. I've used that, I've been in every room. I've done every room in that place . . . So we used to have an army of girls on the various mezzanines. They used to get every printer . . . and they'd spot all the white dots out, basically, with a little artist's brush, you know, tiny little small ones and they had these dyes which they could mix up together . . . That's what my wife used to do. That's where she started off, that's where we met, in there (B, CPL, talking about commercial hand printing, interview 23 August 2017).

Understandings of skill in the world of commercial photography are framed by the skilled ability to enable machines to successfully translate the vision of the photographer into final form, working across a range of technical and material environments, understood as constantly in flux. This social work was supported by a do-it-yourself ecology in which skills migrated across platforms, machines were cajoled into use long after their supposed obsolescence, and complex networks of reciprocal labour developed both within and between studios. That is, jobs were often being undertaken by many different hands, sometimes without the client being aware of how many people were working collaboratively to produce a finished work. In this way, past practice is always incorporated into new media, and precarity is not simply a form of erasure but may also enable some kinds of persistence and resilience. We were working with people who often effaced their own labour, who did not articulate their work in terms of a skilled practice – in part, because it was necessary to do so to support the creative practice of their clients. One should certainly read these different approaches in terms of how labour is structured by class hierarchies of value, especially in the art world. However, we are also interested in how they might inform and, indeed, open up the art museum's understandings of social care.

Infrastructures of care

Earlier, I proposed that the subject position of the conservator is an important place from which to ask questions about how the museum can collect and care for the impermanent and intangible. While the etymology of 'curate' comes from the Latin *cura* or care, today caring is a term that is institutionalised in museums more in relation to 'collections care' – the domain of conservation as well as collections management. Caring not only signifies practices of consideration and concern but also implicitly speaks to techniques and technologies of maintenance, preservation and repair (Mattern 2018). In turn, care in museums is also a technique of applying institutional authority to ensure that the web of value that the museum produces is made material and, as such, may be seen as an important form of power over collections.

Social theories of care have emerged out of the intersection of feminist thinking and science and technology studies, exemplified by the work of Susan Leigh Star (for example, 1990), Donna Haraway (2016), and Maria Puig de la Bellacasa (2017). Feminist theories of care emphasise how care-taking practices are often invisible or go unrecognised (Tronto 2015). Within social theory, care has emerged as a way to look within and between the nodes and connections visualised on the flat plane of the network, to manifest invisible and marginal labour and position care as a form of world-making through maintenance, making visible the infrastructures of support that enable networks, or objects, to emerge into the world. There is therefore a tension between top-down forms of care (care as control, care as a form of visibility) and theories of care that foreground the invisible and the powerless.

Discourses of maintenance and repair also puncture the material completeness or processes of artistic creativity that have traditionally underpinned our understanding and interpretation of art and other forms of material culture, 'trained as we have been in technology and the social sciences by the primacy of production and design' (Jackson 2014, 225) and exhibition as processes that define objects (see Bennett et al. 2016). As Jackson argues, the language of care works on two planes: both speaking to the ongoing work of maintenance but also opening up our understanding of how our relations to things may be structured through moral and ethical frameworks (Jackson 2014, 232; Drazin 2021, 244).

This conceptualisation of care emerged within 'Finding Photography' and also 'Encounters on the Shop Floor', which both started with the intention to make visible the relationships of knowledge and expertise that supported material practices of making. I want to end here by considering the implications of these conversations about skill, labour and expertise for practices of care in the museum, to return to the lessons learned in the ethnographic museum and to draw on both to start to theorise the role of impermanence as an important component of caring for social relations in museums. Both of these projects are de facto explorations of impermanence that enquire into the importance of social networks and embodied experiences within the context of a broader narrative of precarity and obsolescence. 'Finding Photography' directly engaged with the rapid (often inbuilt) obsolescence of commercial photographic technologies, which are only amplified within the realm of digital media. Understanding photography in terms of networks of materials and skills links the museum collection to broader social worlds of apprenticeship and training, global supply chains and material infrastructures, and the politics of gentrification in central London that has put additional pressures on the working lives of photo-technicians in Soho, Fitzrovia and Clerkenwell. 'Encounters on the Shop Floor' took as its starting point a similar perception of precarity and obsolescence, again perceived to be built into the information and digital economy, which is understood to devalue manual skill and craft in favour of a more conceptual focus on design. Here, manual skill (in the project parlance, 'the hand of the maker') is perceived to be under threat and in need of protection and preservation to constitute the next generation of skilled makers and practitioners.

The idea that museums are spaces that conserve the social in the form of collectible objects is a foundational part of the history of the ethnographic collection and it is instructive to look at how museum anthropology has, in acknowledging this, provided some useful resources for other kinds of collections. In the nineteenth century, anthropology was, in part, born out of museums through a drive to preserve the material remnants of what were perceived to be disappearing worlds: cultures under threat from the ravages of colonially borne disease, the hard-nosed intolerances of missionaries and the radical transformations brought in through the imperialisms of capitalist modernity. In large part, the perception of cultural fragility or impermanence and the nostalgia for a more authentic past practice (tradition) drove the invention of the ethnographic collection, accompanied by a research process that came to be described as 'salvage anthropology' (Gruber 1970). Today, museum practitioners increasingly recognise that objects alone cannot activate knowledge, and preservation and collecting initiatives are extended into the social worlds. This is most prominently embodied within UNESCO's 2003 Convention for

Safeguarding of the Intangible Cultural Heritage, which has shaped a politics of recognition (and practices of collection) for the immaterial, attempting to maintain an immaterial form of permanence (see Hafstein 2018). This is also reflected in contemporary debates that frame repatriation as a form of ethical relating (Sarr and Savoy 2018) and by the emergence of categories such as guardianship as new forms of institutional responsibility that foreground care-taking over terms relating to the ownership of collections (see Geismar 2008; Marstine 2011).

The discourse of the new museology (see, for example, Vergo 1989) that underpins many of these shifts in museum practice is often characterised as shifting away from objects and toward people, but this can, in fact, be misleading. Many museums still remain objectification machines, drawing on historic 'object logics' (of ownership, preservation and display) as templates for practice. And this tendency toward objectification has been a primary critique of collecting, from salvage anthropology to intangible cultural heritage. 'Finding Photography' and 'Encounters on the Shop Floor' raise questions about how to care for the social worlds that surround, and are intimately entangled within, these object worlds. Both projects implicitly ask institutions to reflect on their responsibility for bringing social worlds of skill inside the museum and recognise how the question of impermanence, in fact, becomes a question of care and ethical responsibility. In turn, both projects have unearthed the persistence and resilience of material knowledge (and social networks) as they adapt to, and accommodate, material, economic and political transformation.

'Finding Photography', however, also draws attention to the longer history of institutional responses to broader social change in which museums may be seen to be paradoxically both reactionary or nostalgic storehouses of precarious traditions, as well as the very laboratories that help produce cultural practices or processes of design and making. Both of these projects expose anxieties around authenticity and containment that are generated by the museum in its role as a collecting machine. In the case of digital technologies, they are often viewed as fundamentally ungraspable, black-boxed, ephemeral – defined by built-in obsolescence that seems to refuse the key tenets of the museum as an objectification machine (complicating definitions of the object, challenging intellectual property and ownership, and so on; see Domínguez Rubio and Wharton 2020).

Simultaneously, these same technologies are also underpinning the new forms of collecting and archiving that museums are currently embracing, including aspirational projects to bring the museum online as the form and aesthetic through which people increasingly understand participation and inclusion (Simon 2010). Even within the celebratory hype surrounding the digital in museums, these projects present a more cynical view in which digital materiality and practice are understood to be perpetually erasing past materialities and practices, as a hyper-capitalist mode of production that is continually overwriting itself (see Geismar 2018 for a more sustained discussion of perceptions and understandings of digital technology in museums; see also Cameron 2021).[11] The questions raised in this simultaneous embrace and refusal of the digital echo some of the paradoxes this volume is exploring in relation to impermanence. Can immateriality and impermanence be brought into museums without creating new institutional structures and objects to be preserved into the future? And what might museum conservation and care look like without objects?

The practices of care may be seen to bring the concept of impermanence into the conceptual frames through which museum workers understand their collections, challenging the capacity of museum technologies of collection, conservation and display to grapple with precarity and immateriality. Both of the projects I have described raise questions about the ethics and responsibilities of collecting institutions to collect and conserve the social forms of knowledge that lie within skilled practitioners. As Pip Laurenson commented on an early draft of this chapter: 'I think making visible the social networks supporting these works is different from claims of collecting or conserving. I am interested in quieter claims about the significance of simply noticing and paying attention to these networks' (personal communication, June 2019). What new practices, and indeed objects, might this quieter form of attention produce?

Acknowledgements

Thank you to Pip Laurenson and Marta Ajmar for inviting me to participate in their research projects and for lively conversations about these issues stretching back many years. Thanks also to Marta, Pip, Cameron and Ton for critical feedback and input on this chapter.

Notes

1   See, for instance, the grant awarded to the British Museum from the Arcadia Foundation, focused on endangered material knowledge. https://www.britishmuseum.org/our-work/departments/africa-oceania-and-americas/endangered-material-knowledge-programme (last accessed 30 October 2021).

2   The current definition, dating to 2007, defined a museum as 'a non-profit, permanent institution in the service of society and its development, open to the public, which acquires, conserves, researches, communicates and exhibits the tangible and intangible heritage of humanity and its environment for the purposes of education, study and enjoyment'. In 2018, ICOM proposed the following new definition:

> Museums are democratising, inclusive and polyphonic spaces for critical dialogue about the pasts and the futures. Acknowledging and addressing the conflicts and challenges of the present, they hold artefacts and specimens in trust for society, safeguard diverse memories for future generations and guarantee equal rights and equal access to heritage for all people.
> Museums are not for profit. They are participatory and transparent, and work in active partnership with and for diverse communities to collect, preserve, research, interpret, exhibit, and enhance understandings of the world, aiming to contribute to human dignity and social justice, global equality and planetary wellbeing.

Source: https://icom.museum/en/news/icom-announces-the-alternative-museum-definition-that-will-be-subject-to-a-vote/ (last accessed 29 October 2021).

3   https://web.archive.org/web/20191111121220/https://icom.museum/en/news/the-museum-definition-the-backbone-of-icom/ (last accessed 29 October 2021).

4   Some institutions, for instance the Getty Institute in Los Angeles, the Whitney Museum and the Metropolitan Museum of Art in New York, have started to display the work of conservators in museum galleries. This, however, is by no means commonplace across the world of museums and tends to focus on conservators as technological masters rather than social agents within museum processes of interpretation and meaning-making for collections. See, for instance, this presentation of conservation within the Acropolis Museum in Athens, Greece: https://www.theacropolismuseum.gr/en/multimedia/conserving-karyatids-laser-technology (last accessed 20 October 2021).

5   Funded by the Andrew W. Mellon Foundation:". . . Reshaping the Collectible: When Artworks Live in the Museum", builds on Tate's pioneering research and expertise in this area of conservation; responding to Tate's bold acquisitions policy. It will contribute to theory and practice in collection care, curation and museum management, and will focus on recent and contemporary artworks which challenge the structures of the museum with a particular focus on time-based media, performative, live and digital art.' https://www.tate.org.uk/about-us/projects/reshaping-the-collectible (last accessed 30 October 2021).

6   See https://www.youtube.com/watch?v=O479TjbmMo4&t=75s for a short video about the project produced by Tate (last accessed 29 October 2021).

7   http://www.tate.org.uk/art/artworks/yass-corridors-t07069 (last accessed 29 October 2021).

8   The project is a flagship of the V&A Research Institute (VARI), a five-year programme of projects and partnerships supported by the Andrew W. Mellon Foundation. Working within VARI, 'Encounters on the Shop Floor' is a collaboration between V&A, Imperial College London, UCL, the Royal College of Music, Tate, the Art Workers' Guild and a group of artists, makers and performers. '"Encounters on the Shop Floor" is a . . .collaboration between museum professionals, medical practitioners, scientists, educationalists, anthropologists, historians and art historians, performers, artists and designers to explore and develop apt ways of articulating and championing the significance and value of the knowledge created through making, sometimes called "embodied" or "tacit". Encounters aims to create and showcase new models for the inclusion of learning through making in education.' Source: https://www.vam.ac.uk/research/projects/vari-encounters-on-the-shop-floor. The Principal Investigator is Dr Marta Ajmar (VARI) and the Co-I is Prof. Roger Kneebone, Imperial College London.

9   Some images from the project can be found here: https://www.vam.ac.uk/blog/news/encounters-of-a-museum-kind (last accessed 29 October 2021).

10   https://www.policyconnect.org.uk/apdig/news/make-and-create-design-and-innovation-practice-based-research (last accessed 29 October 2021).

11   Exemplified by claims about the participatory museum, which inscribes the visitor as consumer, for example: 'Rather than delivering the same content to everyone, a participatory institution collects and shares diverse, personalised, and changing content co-produced with visitors' (Simon 2010, 'Preface'). http://www.participatorymuseum.org/preface/ (last accessed 29 October 2021).

References

Bennett, Tony. 1995. *The Birth of the Museum: History, theory, politics*. London and New York: Routledge.

Bennett, Tony, Fiona Cameron, Nélia Dias, Ben Dibley, Rodney Harrison, Ira Jacknis and Conal McCarthy. 2016. *Collecting, Ordering, Governing*. Durham, NC: Duke University Press.

Björklund, Anders. 2018. 'The case of Chief G'psgolox's totem pole: "Rescuing, Keeping and Returning"', *Baltic Worlds* 1: 72–6.

Cameron, Fiona. 2021. *The Future of Digital Data, Heritage and Curation in a More-than-Human World*. Abingdon and New York: Routledge.

Celant, Germano. 2003. 'Art and project'. In *Making Art Work: Mike Smith Studio*, edited by Patsy Craig, 12–16. London: Trolley.

Clavir, Miriam. 2002. *Preserving What Is Valued: Museums, conservation, and first nations*. Vancouver, BC: UBC Press.

Clifford, James. 1988. *The Predicament of Culture : Twentieth-century ethnography, literature, and art*. Cambridge, MA: Harvard University Press.

Clifford, James. 1997. *Routes: Travel and translation in the late twentieth century*. Cambridge, MA: Harvard University Press.

Clifford, James. 2013. *Returns*. Cambridge, MA: Harvard University Press.

Coupaye, Ludovic. 2009. 'Ways of enchanting: Chaînes opératoires and yam cultivation in Nyamikum village, Maprik, Papua New Guinea', *Journal of Material Culture* 14(4): 433–58. https://doi.org/10.1177/1359183509345945.

Cook, Joanna, and Catherine Trundle. 2020. 'Unsettled care: Temporality, subjectivity, and the uneasy ethics of care', *Anthropology and Humanism* 45(2): 178–83. https://doi.org/10.1111/anhu.12308.

DeSilvey, Caitlin. 2017. *Curated Decay: Heritage beyond saving*. Minneapolis, MN: University of Minnesota Press.

Domínguez Rubio, Fernando. 2014. 'Preserving the unpreservable: Docile and unruly objects at MoMA', *Theory and Society* 43(6): 617–45. https://doi.org/10.1007/s11186-014-9233-4.

Domínguez Rubio, Fernando. 2016. 'On the discrepancy between objects and things: An ecological approach', *Journal of Material Culture* 21(1): 59–86. https://doi.org/10.1177/1359183515624128.

Domínguez Rubio, Fernando, and Glenn Wharton. 2020. 'The work of art in the age of digital fragility', *Public Culture* 32(1): 215–45. https://doi.org/10.1215/08992363-7816365.

Drazin, Adam. 2021. *Design Anthropology in Context: An introduction to design materiality and collaborative thinking*. London and New York: Routledge/Taylor & Francis.

Durham Commission. 2019. *Durham Commission on Creativity and Education*. https://www.dur.ac.uk/resources/creativitycommission/DurhamReport.pdf.

Edwards, Elizabeth. 2019. 'Thoughts on the "non-collections" of the archival ecosystem'. In *Photo-Objects: On the materiality of photographs and photo archives in the humanities and sciences*, edited by Julia Bärnighausen, Costanza Caraffa, Stefanie Klamm, Franka Schneider and Petra Wodtke, 67–82. Berlin: Max-Planck-Gesellschaft zur Förderung der Wissenschaften.

Edwards, Elizabeth, and Christopher A. Morton, eds. 2015. *Photographs, Museums, Collections: Between art and information*. London: Bloomsbury Academic.

Geismar, Haidy. 2008. 'Cultural property, museums, and the Pacific: Reframing the debates', *International Journal of Cultural Property* 15(2): 109. https://doi.org/10.1017/S0940739108080089.

Geismar, Haidy. 2013. 'Defining the digital', *Museum Anthropology Review* 7(1–2): 254–63.

Geismar, Haidy. 2018. *Museum Object Lessons for the Digital Age*. London: UCL Press.

Geismar, Haidy, and Pip Laurenson. 2019. 'Finding photography: Dialogues between anthropology and conservation'. In *Photo-Objects: On the materiality of photographs and photo archives in the humanities and sciences*, edited by Julia Bärnighausen, Costanza Caraffa, Stefanie Klamm, Franka Schneider and Petra Wodtke, 177–98. Berlin: Max-Planck-Gesellschaft zur Förderung der Wissenschaften.

Gibson, Miriam. 2019. 'Crafting communities of practice: The relationship between making and learning', *International Journal of Technology and Design Education* 29(1): 25–35. https://doi.org/10.1007/s10798-017-9430-3.

Gruber, Jacob W. 1970. 'Ethnographic salvage and the shaping of anthropology', *American Anthropologist* 72(6): 1289–99. https://doi.org/10.1525/aa.1970.72.6.02a00040.

Hafstein, Valdimar Tryggvi. 2018. *Making Intangible Heritage: El Condor Pasa and other stories from UNESCO*. Bloomington, IN: Indiana University Press.

Haraway, Donna Jeanne. 2016. *Staying with the Trouble: Making kin in the Chthulucene*. Durham, NC, and London: Duke University Press.

Harrison, Rodney, Caitlin DeSilvey, Cornelius Holtorf, Sharon Macdonald, Nadia Bartolini, Esther Breithoff, Harald Fredheim et al. 2020. *Heritage Futures: Comparative approaches to natural and cultural heritage*. London: UCL Press.

Jackson, Shannon. 2011. 'Working publics', *Performance Research* 16(2): 8–13. https://doi.org/10.1080/13528165.2011.578722.

Jackson, Steven J. 2014. 'Rethinking repair'. In *Media Technologies*, edited by Tarleton Gillespie, Pablo J. Boczkowski and Kirsten A. Foot, 221–40. Cambridge, MA: MIT Press. https://doi.org/10.7551/mitpress/9780262525374.003.0011.

Janes, Robert R., and Richard Sandell, eds. 2019. *Museum Activism*. Abingdon and New York: Routledge.

Jessiman, Stacey R. 2011. 'The repatriation of the G'psgolox totem pole: A study of its context, process, and outcome', *International Journal of Cultural Property* 18(3): 365–91. https://doi.org/10.1017/S0940739111000270.

Karp, Ivan, and Steven D. Lavine. 1991. *Exhibiting Cultures: The poetics and politics of museum display*. Washington, DC: Smithsonian Institution Press.

Karp, Ivan, Corinne A. Kratz, Lynn Szwaja and Tomas Ybarra-Frausto. 2006. *Museum Frictions: Public cultures/global transformations*. Durham, NC: Duke University Press.

Karp, Ivan, Christine Mullen Kreamer and Steven Levine, eds. 1992. *Museums and Communities: The politics of public culture*. Washington, DC: Smithsonian Books.

Kneebone, Roger. 2020. *Expert: Understanding the path to mastery*. London: Viking.

Macdonald, Sharon. 2002. *Behind the Scenes at the Science Museum*. Oxford and New York: Berg.

Marstine, Janet, ed. 2011. *The Routledge Companion to Museum Ethics: Redefining ethics for the twenty-first century museum*. Abingdon and New York: Routledge.

Mattern, Shannon. 2018. 'Maintenance and care', *Places Journal*, November. https://doi.org/10.22269/181120.

Morphy, Howard. 2021. *Museums, Infinity and the Culture of Protocols: Ethnographic collections and source communities*. London and New York: Routledge

Price, Sally. 1989. *Primitive Art in Civilized Places*. Chicago, IL: University of Chicago Press.

Puig de la Bellacasa, María. 2017. *Matters of Care: Speculative ethics in more than human worlds*. Minneapolis, MN: University of Minnesota Press.

Sarr, Felwine, and Bénédicte Savoy. 2018. 'Rapport sur la restitution du patrimoine culturel africain. Vers une nouvelle éthique relationnelle [The restitution of African cultural heritage: Towards a new relational ethics]'. www.restitutionreport2018.com (last accessed 31 October 2021).

Sellet, Frédéric. 1993. 'Chaine operatoire: The concept and its applications', *Lithic Technology* 18(1–2): 106–12. https://doi.org/10.1080/01977261.1993.11720900.

Shannon, Jennifer A. 2014. *Our Lives: Collaboration, native voice, and the making of the National Museum of the American Indian*. Santa Fe, NM: SAR Press.

Simon, Nina. 2010. *The Participatory Museum*. Santa Cruz: Museum 2.0.

Star, Susan Leigh. 1990. 'Power, technology and the phenomenology of conventions: On being allergic to onions', *The Sociological Review* 38: 26–56. http://journals.sagepub.com/doi/10.1111/j.1467-954X.1990.tb03347.x.

Sully, Dean, ed. 2007. *Decolonizing Conservation: Caring for Maori meeting houses outside New Zealand*. Walnut Creek, CA: Routledge.

Tronto, Joan C. 2015. *Who Cares? How to reshape a democtratic politics*. Ithaca, NY: Cornell University Press.

Vergo, Peter. 1989. *The New Museology*. London: Reaktion Books.

Wharton, Glenn. 2012. *The Painted King: Art, activism, and authenticity in Hawai'i*. Honolulu: University of Hawai'i Press.

Wharton, Glenn. 2015. 'Artist intention and the conservation of contemporary art', *Objects Specialty Group Postprints* 22: 1–12.

Wijesuriya, Gamini. 2007. 'Conserving living Taonga: The concept of continuity'. In *Decolonizing Conservation: Caring for Maori meeting houses outside New Zealand*, edited by Dean Sully, 59–71. London: Taylor & Francis.

13
Transitional sites and 'material memory': impermanence and Ireland's derelict Magdalene Laundries

Laura McAtackney

> I'd make sure it was gone . . . Burn the bloody thing down
> (Anon, O'Donnell et al. 2020, 44).

Magdalene Laundries were gendered institutions that operated from at least the eighteenth century until the late twentieth century in a variety of societal contexts and forms. They were administered primarily by religious bodies and there were major fluctuations in how they were perceived and used by the occupants. Initially, they were created as 'asylums for "fallen" women' (Smith 2007, xiv), with an explicitly Christian ethos, utilising the manual labour of socially marginalised women and girls in laundry and associated activities in exchange for refuge. They were neither exclusively Irish nor Catholic, but James M. Smith has argued that the Irish Catholic experience took on a particularly punitive character after the formation of the Irish state in the early 1920s (Smith 2007, xv). This was due to the explicitly Catholic and middle-class identity projected by the Irish state, which saw itself in opposition to what was perceived as the negative presence of the Protestant British state, to the east, and the retained British statelet of Northern Ireland, to the north (White 2010). Moving from ideological to practical terms, the fledgling Irish state relied heavily on the Catholic Church, not solely in its self-conception but also because the Church provided institutional social services for the state, from schools to hospitals and from mental institutions to orphanages. Together, they aggressively pursued a policy of institutionalisation of those deemed to exist outside the moral ideals of the combined Church and state. In this context, Magdalene Laundries flourished and were used to incarcerate at least 10,000 women and girls (JFMR n.d., a–b) considered guilty of shame-ridden 'feminine transgressions' (Fischer 2016).

The last active Magdalene Laundry in Ireland permanently closed its doors from the bustle of Sean MacDermott Street, in inner-city Dublin, in 1996. This was an unusually late date for the closure of a Magdalene Laundry globally, but not in Ireland. While the ten Magdalene Laundries active in Australia, a frequent comparative, had all but closed by the mid-1970s (only St Magdalen's, Tempe, New South Wales, endured until the 1980s), in the Republic of Ireland, a third were still active after 1990 (the other two were High Park and Donnybrook, both in Dublin). The relative longevity of these institutions (albeit with dwindling numbers since at least the 1970s [McAleese 2013]), combined with recent government public inquiries that have revealed the scale of abuse of inmates in residential institutions across the social care sector in Ireland (Ryan 2009; McAleese 2013; Commission of Investigation into Mother and Baby Homes 2021), has had a significant impact on the Irish national psyche. The recognition of the systemic and structural abuses perpetuated by the Catholic Church, facilitated by the Irish state, has created a significant shift in Irish identity to the extent that the nation is now considered by religious scholars as 'post-Catholic' (McAuliffe 2017). The increasingly secularised state has belatedly introduced new social and moral codes – such as marriage equality (2016) and the introduction of access to abortion (2018) (Andersson 2018; Mullally 2018) – and is attempting to deal with state-complicit past wrongs.

This recent societal reckoning has had a number of repercussions in terms of how we deal with the legacies of the aforementioned institutions moving forward. The McAleese Report (2013) was the result of the public inquiry set up to investigate the role of the state in facilitating the abuses that occurred in Magdalene Laundries. While the inquiry was welcomed, it has been criticised for deliberately limiting the scope of the investigation due to the circumstances of its creation: the determination by the UN Committee Against Torture (UNCAT 2011) that the Irish state was complicit in the running of these particular institutions. Despite the limited remit, the McAleese Report provided damning evidence of the role of the Irish state in facilitating the operation of Magdalene Laundries but it did not systematically investigate what exactly happened inside them. This partial focus meant the four religious orders that ran these institutions have not been sanctioned by the state for their activities and have kept their archives closed to wider investigation. They have also refused to contribute financially to the government redress scheme for survivors (Ó'Fátharta 2017). As time moves on from these shocking disclosures, it has been argued that wider society is exhibiting features of 'denial and minimisation' (McAlinden, 2013, 192). Specifically relating to Magdalene Laundries, counternarratives are appearing that are restating the Orders' traditional insistence that their role was primarily one of protection and care (including Prunty 2017). In this context, there remains potential for roll-back on societal reckonings and so the McAleese recommendation for a form of memorialisation to remember the survivors' experiences is being viewed as increasingly important by the women and activists concerned (see Open Heart City 2020).

Archaeology and the Magdalene Laundries

At the request of the activist group Justice for Magdalenes Research (JFMR), I took on archaeological consultations as part of evolving transitional justice measures (O'Donnell, O'Rourke and Smith 2020) relating to the remaining laundries. The traditional archaeological role in such a process is based on the legal obligation, on the part of the developer of any site in Ireland, to mitigate the impacts of construction on the 'environment' (archaeology is included in this definition in the Irish context). This means that archaeology has a heightened role to play in determining how the extant sites from Ireland's original post-independence Magdalene Laundry network survive into the future. As of 2020, this role could only fully relate to three of the ten original Magdalene Laundries as the rest had been either demolished or significantly redeveloped.

While archaeology is generally used during the planning process as a tool to predict where subterranean archaeological material may exist and to facilitate design to avoid it or removal (through excavation) that mitigates damage through preservation by record, it can be used in more creative ways. Magdalene Laundries would not usually be considered 'archaeology' in the Irish planning process. The structures and contents are not usually subterraneous, they are not ancient enough and, generally, they are too unexceptional to be mitigated due to any inherent value placed on their material remains. However, it has been notable that, in the post-McAleese Report era, some council planning departments have been reluctant to allow the redevelopment of Magdalene Laundries without extensive archaeological work being conducted. For the Magdalene Laundry at Donnybrook, a planning application in 2016 was rejected due to 'the potential for burials to be uncovered' (Kelly 2017). This decision was undoubtedly influenced by recent public scandals surrounding the discovery of unconsecrated, unmarked and unidentifiable mass graves at both the former Magdalene Laundry of High Park in Dublin in 1993 (Humphreys 2003) and, more infamously, the Bon Secour Mother and Baby Home at Tuam in Co. Galway (Barry 2017). However, legislation has not changed to systematically deal with the social relevance of these sites, so decisions are not uniform. But the implicit premise of any archaeological work in a development context in Ireland is the understanding that the remaining material remains will be removed, demolished or greatly altered and recontextualised. Engaging with this work means being prepared to work with materials that are in transition and on the cusp of great change.

As a contemporary archaeologist, my engagement with the questions of how society remembers, in general, and how Irish society will remember Magdalene Laundries, in particular, is entwined with how we understand and deal with material remains in the present. Following the French archaeologist Laurent Olivier, my archaeological sensibility is based on the acceptance that the past is not retrievable as it was experienced but that we can work with what remains of the past, which is 'constantly accumulating and breaking down' (2011, 4), in the evolving present. This position accepts that all archaeology is essentially contemporary, in flux, and is constantly being made and remade (McAtackney 2020a). This view of archaeology continues to receive some pushback from the prevailing conception of the discipline as being essentially about the retrieval of 'old things', of its Greek etymology, but the distinction is important in this particular context. Focusing on Magdalene Laundries through a contemporary, rather than historical, archaeological approach requires us to grapple with the realities of material change, transformation, entanglement and, by necessity, impermanence right now.

Working with the 'material memory' (Olivier 2011) of Magdalene Laundries as potential elements of government-mandated memorialisation also requires an archaeological refocus away from simply mitigating the impact of development. In doing so it accepts that what remains of Magdalene Laundries may have to change to facilitate a memorial function and that this change is not necessarily negative. Material loss will be inevitable but conceiving of this loss as a function of impermanence allows for the former laundries to be part of a process of positive change. Such a perspective can allow for some demolition, alongside the addition of new elements and meanings, to ensure that these sites will not simply become fossilised reliquaries but can be living, meaningful memorials in the present and future.

Of course, there remains a tension between theory and practice in this process. While we may wish to retain some of the material structures of former institutions as *aide-mémoires* – while allowing for new and future uses – there is potential for destruction to be facilitated without the associated retention. Currently, the three extant Magdalene Laundries are materially under threat, and at least two will almost certainly be redeveloped into housing complexes. Two of the three laundries – Donnybrook in Dublin and Sunday's Wells in Cork – are in private ownership and are currently proceeding through planning procedures that will almost certainly facilitate significant demolitions of the standing remains with little of the original sites being retained in the process. We can anticipate this fate simply because no public body, to date, has shown any interest in purchasing the sites for memorialisation or other purposes. The remaining laundry – on Sean MacDermott Street – is owned by Dublin City Council but this circumstance does not guarantee its retention. Since the site was transferred to the Council in the 1990s, significant elements have already been demolished, including after a fire in 2006, and there was an attempt to sell it to a budget hotel chain in 2018. The site was only retained after a high-profile grassroots campaign including politicians, activists and survivors (Gannon 2018) ensured elected representatives voted to block the sale (O'Shea 2018). While it is still not guaranteed to be retained, it has become the focus of activist attempts to secure at least one of the original Magdalene Laundry sites as part of the memorialisation process.

At this time, one cannot avoid the interpretation that there is no real political will within the Irish establishment to retain these sites. Previous attempts at more local forms of memorialisation of these laundries in Ireland have focused on erecting discrete statues in spatially relevant locations. Of course, their material claims of permanence can be contradicted by removal or relocation when they become inconvenient (as was the case in Galway with the 'Final Journey' statue [Smith 2010]). No buildings have been retained to act as a memorial so far. Rather, there is a long and established trajectory in Ireland of derelicting and then demolishing difficult sites (McAtackney 2014) because they are unnerving and uncomfortable presences. I argue that their enduring materiality, even if ruinous and derelict, has the potential to communicate a past that is tangibly close. They could play a significant role in communicating the realities of that closeness and act as a material reminder of how the state facilitated the treatment of marginalised women. Following Olsen and

Pétursdóttir's observations – on the unsettling nature of active, modern ruins – these laundries are not quiet follies, prosaically persisting or imperceptibly disintegrating (2014). They are caught in the limbo of being 'in-between and not belonging' (Olsen and Pétursdóttir 2014, 7) and it is in this state of active dereliction – when they are materially vulnerable, disintegrating and increasingly under threat – that they are simultaneously most demanding of our attention. It is while they are actively ruinous that public anxiety regarding the need to make decisions about their future – including their role in government-mandated memorialisation – is most notable.

Material remains

In the recent past, archaeological work has been conducted at two of the three remaining Magdalene Laundry sites: Sean MacDermott Street and Donnybrook, both in Dublin. They provide useful comparatives as to the very different material conditions, and survivals, of these institutions. The site at Donnybrook is situated in an upper-middle-class suburb of South Dublin. Its material remains take the form of a relatively complete industrial laundry with no associated domestic or religious buildings; the latter were retained by the order of nuns who still occupy the large adjacent site. The industrial laundry was sold as a going concern in 1992 and it only ceased to function sometime between 2006 and 2013 (the official closing date reported in the McAleese Report was 2006 [2013, 27] but, on accessing the site, calendars and letters dating up to 2013 were in situ [McAtackney 2018]).

Donnybrook is owned by a developer who plans to demolish most of the site, keeping only the original mid-nineteenth-century building as part of a series of private-owned luxury apartments. Amazingly, there is a vibrant market for these kinds of redevelopment that retain parts of social welfare institutions in Ireland. As recently as 2019, the developers of a former orphanage in Dún Laoghaire, which had closed in 1977, received criticism for marketing the structure as 'The Orphanage, a luxury co-living residence' for a €1,500 monthly rental (Quinlan 2019). A similar fate awaits Donnybrook as there is little chance that it will be retained as a memorial, even without planning permission, as it would require many millions to acquire it and, as already noted, this has not been forthcoming from the public purse. My focus on working with the site as an archaeologist was in the full knowledge that this work was to facilitate the redevelopment of the structure that would ensure it is largely demolished and its contents discarded. I was requested by the developers to consult primarily on the contents – to advise on a strategy for recording, retaining and possibly recontextualising them.

Internally, Donnybrook contains the material world one would expect from a recently operational laundry: large industrial machines, significant numbers of trolleys, folding-and-sorting tables and an office space complete with label machines and plastic dry-cleaning bags (McAtackney 2020b). On closer inspection, however, the material world of Donnybrook also reflects a time when it was a Magdalene rather than just an industrial laundry. Many of the industrial machines greatly pre-date the 1992 sale of the site, including machines with date stamps from the 1930s, and almost all the infrastructure appears to be original to its use as a Magdalene Laundry. More unexpectedly, religious paraphernalia were scattered throughout the structures, from statues on plinths to rosary beads and Catholic mass cards (memorialising the dead) abandoned on the upstairs floor (McAtackney 2020b, 235–9). It is a site that speaks of a lengthy operational period, with a reticence to replace original contents, followed by a swift abandonment. A recent architecture report described Donnybrook as 'a building which was simply locked and abandoned . . . Although there is debris, dirt and bird droppings throughout, the previous history of the building is fully legible (MESH 2018, 10).

In contrast, the structures associated with Sean MacDermott Street are simultaneously more complete but also more selective representations of the operational Magdalene Laundry. Similar to Donnybrook, the current state reflects both deliberate and unforeseen changes over a period of inoperation and eventual abandonment that have had different material consequences. The Sean MacDermott Street site contains the structures and partial contents of the material world one would associate with a recently operational church, convent and women's domestic living quarters. The industrial laundry structures and contents are almost completely absent from the current site, excepting their footprint that is relatively complete in the large vacant spaces where the industrial buildings were situated before their demolition in 2006. This includes part of the external perimeter wall of the site, which still retains fans and barred windows that would have allowed the hot air, but not the forced workforce, to escape. There is evidence of previous large, static machines requiring bolting to the floor, tiling from toilet facilities and long ridged floors that denote drying areas. These footprints are potentially important as they represent an almost complete floor plan and, as such, 'present absence' (Buchli and Lucas 2001) of the pre-demolished structure.

Alongside historic plans from the site, they make it relatively easy to reconstruct at least the ground level of the industrial laundry (a task that is currently being undertaken in digital form by an architecture PhD student at Queen's University Belfast, Chris Hamill. See http://atlasoflostrooms.com/). In one sense, the industrial laundry footprint at Sean MacDermott Street defies the material impermanence of the site. It also potentially allows for the proposed memorial site to be a palimpsest evoking what was there but no longer survives, what is extant and what will be added in the future.

The fact that the standing structures at Sean MacDermott Street are largely religious and domestic buildings has material implications. In contrast to Donnybrook, the site includes the high-status contents of a nineteenth-century Italianate church with its many decorative features, including white marble high altars, stained glass windows, decorative brass railings and large religious statues, all in situ (National Inventory of Architectural Heritage 2014). Although deconsecrated, the church is almost completely intact and only recently starting to show signs of dereliction, including peeling paint on one wall and evidence of pigeon intrusions behind the altar. Within the convent, the rooms on the ground and upper floors are in greater disarray. There are significant assemblages of furniture in the domestic areas but they are not arranged as they would have been when the site was occupied. A small number of rooms remain intact but most are either empty or include large assemblages of furniture from many periods piled together. The latter rooms include the large reception room where the nuns would have received guests on the ground floor of the church, and one or two bedrooms per landing on the upper floors of the convent.

This disarray of the site may be of relatively recent vintage. There is evidence of significant changes and additions made to the site over a decade after it closed, including as part of experimental theatre productions in 2011. This suspicion was confirmed by the locating of set plans in an upper room of the convent in September 2020 that revealed some areas had been repainted (dark red walls were added to the upper-floor hallway of the convent), substantial religious artefacts were moved (a life-sized crucifix also placed on the upper-floor hallway) and scatter cushions were introduced. Some of these alterations may have been part of a site-specific, immersive theatre production, 'Laundry', performed by the ANU Productions theatre company in 2011 (ANU n.d.), but others pre-dated it (personal communication, Brenda Malone 2021). While traditional archaeological approaches would view these changes as later intrusions, my conception of them was as evidence of the changing uses of the site. As such, they represented its material impermanence. They were part of the site's biography and were authentic representations of what had happened there in the post-operational recent past of the Magdalene Laundry. We therefore conceived these additions as part of the package we had to work with rather than as an intrusion to remove or ignore.

The convent attic contained an assemblage of dated furniture and empty luggage cases in 2018. At the time, these were noted as particularly compelling objects as they appeared to have been the discarded belongings of those who entered Sean MacDermott Street (and presumably never left). By my next visit in September 2020, the attic was not accessible. There were sizeable holes in the roof that were allowing pigeons to nest in the attic and water infiltration had damaged the ceilings and walls, making access unsafe. The material remnants of this structure were deteriorating rapidly; its impermanence writ large on the sloping ceilings and peeling paint. The women's dormitories were in a similarly neglected state with the upper floors inaccessible due to fallen ceilings; trees could be seen growing through broken windows

In 2018, we were not permitted to enter the women's dormitories due to health and safety concerns, but in September 2020 we were led through the corridor by our guide, and the ground floor was found to be largely intact. At the far end of this corridor a small domestic laundry, which had previously been unknown to us, was located. While there is little evidence of personal mementoes remaining in the dormitories – or elsewhere on the Sean MacDermott Street site – clearly, the women's dormitories are the most materially meaningful part of the site due to these structures (and some contents) being the only tangible links to the women and their lives there. The remaining structures on the site are associated with the Catholic Church and their personnel – church and convent – and, as such, they act to communicate its functions and power. It is essential for any potential memorialisation project at Sean MacDermott Street to focus on the spaces and things that were most connected to the women who were forced to inhabit the site.

The differential survivals of these two sites provide both a quandary and a potential opportunity to consider how their material natures – and vulnerabilities – can be understood and negotiated together. This will not be a straightforward process: the spectre of impermanence haunts all movements forward as we attempt to negotiate what can and should be retained as the 'material memory' of the Magdalene Laundries while allowing other facets of their current material worlds to be demolished or disappeared. As of October 2020, the probability of site retention was

13.1 Remnants of the laundry room attached to the women's dormitories at Sean MacDermott Street, September 2020. Photo: Laura McAtackney.

firmly focused on Sean MacDermott Street, whereas the possibility of contents-salvaging has relied on the National Museum of Ireland at Donnybrook. Brenda Malone, the Military curator from the National Museum of Ireland, has been working through this process to retrieve a collection of materials that reflects the material world of Donnybrook while also potentially plugging gaps in what remains at Sean MacDermott Street. The potential of meaningfully combining material elements from both these sites will be an ongoing and delicately negotiated process. Little can be definitively said on how this process will unfold, but some initial thoughts can be presented. Most important is to think about how the transition of these materials is mediated through survivors. Survivors have been central in determining what happens by feeding into the processes of transformation at both sites. This chapter will conclude by presenting some initial findings from a recording exercise that used experimental site-responsive work with survivors as part of the creative archaeological recording of Donnybrook.

Site-specific survivor testimonies at Donnybrook

The temporal proximity of operational Magdalene Laundries allows for a significant number of survivors to be present and active witnesses, advocates and participants in the memorialisation process. It was their voices demanding recognition and reparations that have been constant since the last laundry closed in 1996, so it is fitting that they should be central to how archaeologists work with these sites. In 2014, it was estimated that at least 600 survivors of Ireland's Magdalene Laundries were still alive (BBC *Newsnight* 2014) and many of them have provided details of their difficult experiences as evidence to both UN committees (UNCAT 2011) and the McAleese Inquiry (2013). Naturally, the welfare of survivors was the initial focus for reparative actions. Now, the need for memorialisation has become more of a priority as the material remains rapidly deteriorate. The surviving material worlds of Magdalene Laundries hold a number of potential roles in this process but they are not neutral spaces. For some activists, they represent potential sites of conscience that could ensure the memory of abuse is retained by Irish society (Open Heart City 2020), but they can also be viewed as a malign and haunting presence for many who were forced to live and work in them. At the recent 'Dublin Honours Magdalenes' Listening Exercise, which took place in June 2018, survivors were specifically asked: 'How – in what ways – should we remember what happened in the Magdalene Laundries?' A range of answers was offered, with 'Burn the bloody thing down' being a common refrain (O'Donnell et al. 2020). But there was a strong insistence that remembering and educating was integral for society to move forward and this included a recognition that demolition was not the only answer. As one woman reflected, 'still wouldn't take away your memories, though, would it?' (O'Donnell et al. 2020, 44).

Donnybrook's relatively long period of post-operational use, private ownership and suburban location have all worked against its being seriously considered for retention as a memorial site. But the appeals and objections of local residents and a small number of survivors were enough to stall its progress through the planning process. The rejection of the planning proposal was also related to the lack of engagement with the social significance of the site by previous archaeologists, who were pressed to think more broadly and creatively about how to work with the material world of this site in ways that capture its more intangible, social histories. Alongside the archaeology contractors who scanned for disturbances in the ground, looking for potential burials, or who carefully recorded a wide range of industrial, religious and social contents (ABH 2019), I tried to push the boundaries of what archaeologists could do as part of the planning process by working with survivors. Rather than be guided by the 'proper' way to do archaeology, I decided to reformulate an archaeological methodology I had previously used working with ex-prisoners at the derelict Long Kesh/Maze prison site in Northern Ireland (2014). The aim, then and now, was to allow for the human relationship with the material site to bring us closer to understanding previous connections to it. I posited two proposals: (1) to conduct site-responsive oral testimonies with survivors in the now-derelict laundry and (2) to work with the National Museum of Ireland to facilitate a new collection of artefacts that would become part of the national collection and potentially loaned to a future memorial site at Sean MacDermott Street.

Over the summer of 2018, two oral testimonies were conducted with survivors from Donnybrook. That only two were involved was the result of the decision to approach women with whom JFMR had ongoing contact and who they knew had spent time at the site and were previously open to discussing their experiences. There was no open call or advertising of this process, due to the need to retain confidentiality, with deference to the wishes of the developers, and due to previous experiences that JFMR had had with public calls that resulted in problematic contacts. With two participants and a short time-scale, this exercise was conceived as an experimental addition to the usual outputs of an archaeological, developer-funded mitigation exercise. The aim was to enable survivors to add their narratives to the recording exercise so that their thoughts were incorporated into archaeological reports. Of secondary importance was the hope that the testimonies would have practical implications as narratives that would provide insights into how various elements of the extant material world had worked together as an operational site. It was felt these testimonies might assist with the selection process for the National Museum of Ireland and they could be used as part of their eventual interpretation in the memorial or museum context (the option to donate their testimonies to the National Museum was included in the consent forms).

What I did not expect was quite how much the contemporary materiality of the site – and especially its tangible impermanence – would shape and determine the survivors' responses to it. The site's active dereliction and ruination made it an uncanny space to encounter, and this was exacerbated by their initial introduction to the site. We entered the laundry via the reception area (which did not exist when the two women had been present at the site) and passed through to what had been the large sorting area, which was also added after their time incarcerated at Donnybrook. These areas would not have been known to the women, and the fact they were now devoid of previous furniture, filled with dirt and debris – including graffitied walls and floors punctuated with large holes – made them a shocking entry point.

Archaeological interventions in the sorting area since the failed planning application had added to its aesthetic of disturbance. Trenches had been excavated and their contents were hastily deposited in the general vicinity rather than being backfilled. They had been necessary to examine anomalies in the geophysical survey data that may have indicated unmarked graves, although none were uncovered through this method (IAC 2018). One can only imagine that the archaeologists expected the site to be redeveloped soon, so there was no need to backfill the trenches. Prior to the introduction to the site, the survivors had been shown photos of its current state to prepare them before the visit, but this did not lessen their shock. The oral recording from the first survivor picks up her audible and involuntary intake of breath at the derelict and disturbed state of the room.

Such an entry to the site clearly disorientated the survivors to the extent that, for both women, the site-responsive intention of the oral testimonies quickly derailed as they silently tried to make sense of the material disruption in front of them. To enable some form of reconnection to the site they had known, and facilitate some audible responses, I deviated from my intention to allow the women to be solely directed by their responses and movements. Rather than invite them to find their own way through the site, I proceeded to guide them to some of the oldest and most complete areas to allow them to refamiliarise themselves with the site. These were the places that communicated the laundry function of the buildings, where the large industrial laundry machines still remained. The industrial remains included large modern washing and drying machines, older commercial calendaring machines used to dry sheets, and a range of pressing machines. Some of these machines had been in this space for a very long time, including two pressing machines placed under an ornate plinth complete with a Sacred Heart statue pragmatically sharing its platform with an electric fan.

The manufacturers' metal labels were studded to the bases and indicated the machines' origins in the Clydebank factories of D. & J. Tullis

13.2 A scene from the laundry room at Donnybrook, June 2018. A large plinth featuring a statue of the Sacred Heart of Jesus sits beside a small fan located directly above two industrial laundry pressing machines. A large crucifix hangs over the doorway. Photo: Laura McAtackney.

Ltd from 1937 and 1951, respectively. Due to the spatial arrangement of this assemblage – the sheer weight of the presses bolted to the floors and ornate plinth set into the wall – I expect they had not moved since they were originally put in place.

Reacquaintance with the laundry machines brought back memories to the women of where they had worked and how the machines and associated infrastructure had functioned. Brief discussions about how one would actually operate the machines were often used – by me and them – as a way to reset the conversations or insert some form of control back into the site-responsive engagement when it became difficult to verbalise reactions. These interludes were most effectively used by one of the survivors who had a more empowering and longstanding connection to the laundries than most. Part of the biography she had imparted to me at the start of the oral testimony was that, soon after she escaped the laundries, she left Ireland for a job at an industrial laundry in the South of England. She met her husband through this role and they went on to successfully own and run their own network of private laundries. Her husband accompanied her to the site-responsive visit and, while he was primarily occupied by one of my colleagues, he frequently came to find his wife to point out machines similar to models they had once owned that dotted the site.

The range of religious paraphernalia that remained on-site was as extensive as it was unexpected to me. On first entering the building, one was met with a picture of Pope John Paul II nailed above the time-card holders (the latter being from the post-Magdalene operations of the laundry). Large crucifixes remained over doorways; and plinths, which had once supported religious statues, were strategically located throughout all the work rooms excepting the laundry room itself. On my first visit to the site, the large Sacred Heart statue (mentioned earlier) was in situ, but two other statues lay broken on the floor. Small medals, crosses and mass cards were found throughout the site. One had to keep reminding oneself that the site had not been a Magdalene Laundry for nearly 30 years by this time, but the two survivors commented only infrequently on this abundance of religious paraphernalia that remained in situ. While it would not have been unusual in Ireland, some decades ago, to see a religious calendar or a small icon in an industrial workplace, it would not have been commonplace to see such a scale and array of religious items in a secular setting. It was shocking to everyone who entered the site but was unremarked upon by the survivors. This oversight seemed unusual to me, at first, but it became clear, when the survivors were specifically asked about these objects, that they were not shocking to them. They had been so closely tied to their experiences of the operational Magdalene Laundries that they were not viewed as an exception worthy of highlighting or discussing. Rather, they acted as a constant, almost reassuring presence – a backdrop to this greatly changed material environment.

Both of the survivors, in their site-responsive oral testimonies, explicitly commented on the materially changed and precarious nature of the laundry at Donnybrook and what this meant to them. The second survivor did this throughout her testimony, as she voiced her concerns about how little she could remember of the site due to how changed it was from her previous experiences many decades before. Both of the survivors also spent some time reflecting on what would eventually become of the laundry. Like the activists, their focus was not on this site as being part of the promised memorialisation process (rather, they assumed this would happen elsewhere), and both commented on the retention plans for Sean MacDermott Street. They seemed to be keenly aware that their part in this process – of providing site-responsive oral testimonies – was tied to facilitating Donnybrook's transformation into something else. They had already assumed that this site was in the process of transitioning away from being the laundry of their memories and they were eager for it to have a different future. The first survivor commented, 'Yeah, it would be better if it was being used. I hope they do it quickly. I hope they do it so that I could see that it has been done. It would be nice before I go to see it all done and settled, especially now I have seen what High Park [the other Magdalene Laundry in Dublin, which was demolished and converted into housing in the 1990s] has been doing and it is lovely to see what they have done. So I was happy about that.'

What was hard to ignore as we conducted the site-responsive testimonies, a couple of months apart, was that this materially rich site had not been inactive in between our visits. The sporadic additions of graffiti, sprayed across one large wall in the sorting room but especially in the heavily vandalised back office, were being added to. As well as presenting some conundrums in terms of interpretation, they acted as a clear indication of ongoing illicit entry to the site. It became evident people were accessing the site for different reasons and, with those incursions, changing it. The sheer thrill of gaining access to a derelict Magdalene Laundry cannot be dismissed (especially when one searches for the various uploaded videos added to crowdsourcing sites such as YouTube), yet one cannot discount some form of performative social justice function (the word 'abuse' prominent in graffiti; vandalism almost completely confined to the inner administrative space). However, objects were also being removed from the site. More specifically, three classes of objects were disappearing from the site at an alarming rate: metal from grates and large industrial machines (undoubtedly to sell for scrap), all the original sinks (even one that was partially broken), and also more Magdalene Laundry-specific objects. The latter group of disappearances included the more obvious religious paraphernalia, including the religious statues (the last remaining Sacred Heart of Jesus statue disappeared between June and August 2018), small religious artefacts that had continued to reside on plinths, and a makeshift bell from the sorting room.

There were probably many other removed objects that we did not notice but the ongoing nature of these removals generated anxiety – professionally but also personally. Were these objects being collected by macabre trophy hunters, to be retained or sold onward, or were they removed with the opposite intention, to save them? It was clear from various media reports and letters pages that speculated on what was happening with the site that a generalised anxiety surrounded the question of what the redevelopment of this 'material memory' could mean. There was a feeling that material disappearance – of site, structures and contents – would enable the continuation of the Irish tradition of obscuring problematic histories, or what Guy Beiner, referring to another facet of Irish history, has called 'forgetful remembrance' (Beiner 2018).

Conclusion

At its most basic level, this chapter is a partial tale of two derelict institutions on the cusp of fundamental, material change. Their dereliction subsumes the fact that, in many ways, they are the same – Magdalene Laundries – but that, in more ways, they are different. These differences are not simply reducible to what survives of their material worlds but extend to how those survivals reflect different past realities, how they are understood by survivors, and how they will (probably) result in very different futures. Working with these material worlds in flux was central to understanding how impermanence can take many forms and elicit many responses. The site on Sean MacDermott Street, in inner-city Dublin, is the focus of activists' practices of care. Superficially, it appears to be destined for at least partial survival but, in reality, what remains at the site will need to be recontextualised, added to and mediated. Donnybrook, in the middle-class South Dublin suburbs, almost certainly faces a very different future. In private hands and moving through the planning process, the structure is intended to be redeveloped into private housing in the near future. Its extant material world reflects both its industrial life and religious institutional origins, but its increasing vulnerability is also prompting strong responses from survivors and the wider community, some of which are now captured as part of the archaeological record for the site.

Archaeologists are inherently drawn to the material. Traditionally, we view materials as a means of accessing the human experiences of the deep past. In recent years, a counter-position has emerged, a post-human 'defence of things' that calls for us to engage with materials on their own terms (Olsen 2003). Our obsession with materials – be they as human indices or in their own right – has seen us critiqued for assigning ourselves the role of material defender (Domanska 2006). Fundamentally, archaeological practices of care tend to focus on recording and maintaining material worlds. This is a difficult mindset to change, especially when confronted with the differential material vulnerability of the sites at Donnybrook and Sean MacDermott Street: we want to retain them and protect them, even when it is not desired by those who were forced to survive them or those who own them. As this project is ongoing, conclusions cannot be definitively stated. But, for me, it continues to be an enlightening process in embracing the impermanence of materials and considering how to incorporate change.

References

Andersson, Jasmine. 2018. 'Opinion: LGBT+ people have the power to repeal the 8th amendment'. *Pink News*, 24 May. https://www.pinknews.co.uk/2018/05/24/opinion-lgbt-people-have-the-power-to-repeal-the-8th-amendment/ (last accessed 23 October 2021).

ANU. 'Laundry'. http://anuproductions.ie/work/laundry/ (last accessed 22 October 2021).

Archaeology and Built Heritage (ABH). 2019. *Survey and Inventory of Industrial Plant and Other Items Associated with the Former Sisters of Charity Magdalene Laundry, Donnybrook, Dublin 4.* RP Ref 8713. 8 March. (Unpublished)

Barry, Dan. 2017. 'The lost children of Tuam'. *New York Times*, 28 October. https://www.nytimes.com/interactive/2017/10/28/world/europe/tuam-ireland-babies-children.html (last accessed 20 October 2021).

BBC *Newsnight*. 2014. 25 September. https://www.youtube.com/watch?v=uuEw1--wMKI (last accessed 20 October 2021).

Beiner, Guy. 2018. *Forgetful Remembrance: Social forgetting and vernacular historiography of a rebellion in Ulster*. Oxford: Oxford University Press.

Buchli, Victor and Gavin Lucas. 2001. *Archaeologies of the Recent Past*. London: Routledge.

Commission of Investigation into Mother and Baby Homes. *Final Report*. Dublin: Department of Children, Equality, Disability, Integration and Youth. 2021. https://tinyurl.com/nmaepbpw (last accessed 26 October 2021).

Domanska, Ewa. 2006. 'The material presence of the past', *History and Theory* 45: 337–48.

Fischer, Clara. 2016. 'Gender, nation, and the politics of shame: Magdalen laundries and the institutionalisation of feminine transgression in modern Ireland', *Signs: Journal of Women in Culture and Society* 41(4): 821–43.

Gannon, Gary. 2018. Online petition: 'Stop the sale of the Sean McDermott Street Magdalene Laundry site'. https://my.uplift.ie/petitions/act-now-to-remember-the-magdalene-laundry-survivors (last accessed 30 October 2021).

Humphreys, Joe. 2003. 'Magdalen plot had remains of 155 women'. *Irish Times*, 21 August. https://www.irishtimes.com/news/magdalen-plot-had-remains-of-155-women-1.370279 (last accessed 30 October 2021).

IAC (Irish Archaeological Consultancy Limited). 2018. *Archaeological Assessment at the Crescent, Donnybrook, Dublin 4* (unpublished report, May).

JFMR (Justice for Magdalenes Research). n.d. a. 'About the Magdalene Laundries'. http://jfmresearch.com/home/preserving-magdalene-history/about-the-magdalene-laundries/ (last accessed 20 October 2021).

JFMR (Justice for Magdalenes Research). n.d. b. 'High Park'. http://jfmresearch.com/home/preserving-magdalene-history/high-park/ (last accessed 20 October 2021).

Kelly, Olivia. 2017. 'Donnybrook Magdalene laundry demolition proposal scrapped'. *Irish Times*, 8 April. https://www.irishtimes.com/culture/heritage/donnybrook-magdalene-laundry-demolition-proposal-scrapped-1.3041047 (last accessed 20 October 2021).

McAleese, Martin. 2013. *Report of the Inter-Departmental Committee to Establish the Facts of State Involvement with the Magdalen Laundries* ('McAleese Report'). Dublin: Department of Justice and Equality. http://www.justice.ie/en/JELR/Pages/MagdalenRpt2013 (last accessed 29 October 2021).

McAlinden, Anne-Marie. 2013. 'An inconvenient truth: Barriers to truth recovery in the aftermath of institutional child abuse in Ireland', *Legal Studies* 33(2): 189–214.

McAtackney, Laura. 2014. *An Archaeology of the Troubles: The dark heritage of Long Kesh/Maze Prison*. Oxford: Oxford University Press.

McAtackney, Laura. 2018. Monitoring Report. Former Donnybrook Magdalene Laundry, Dublin 4. 20 July 2018. (Commissioned by Hardwicke Developers. Submitted August 2018. Unpublished.)

McAtackney, Laura. 2020a. 'Contemporary archaeology'. In *The Routledge Handbook of Global Historical Archaeology*, edited by Charles Orser Jr, Andrés Zarankin, Pedro Paulo A. Funari, Susan Lawrence and James Symonds, 215–31. Abingdon and New York: Routledge.

McAtackney, Laura. 2020b. 'Materials and memory: Archaeology and heritage as tools of transitional justice at a former Magdalen laundry', *Éire-Ireland* 55(1&2): 221–44.

McAuliffe, Pádraig. 2017. 'Comprehending Ireland's post-Catholic redress practice as a form of transitional justice', *Oxford Journal of Law and Religion* 6(3): 451–73.

MESH Architects. 2018. *Preliminary Historic Structure Report* (Unpublished).

Mullally, Una. 2018. 'Referendum shows us there is no Middle Ireland, just Ireland'. *Irish Times*, 28 May. https://www.irishtimes.com/opinion/una-mullally-referendum-shows-us-there-is-no-middle-ireland-just-ireland-1.3509905 (last accessed 28 October 2021).

National Inventory of Architectural Heritage. 2014. Entry for Monastery of Our Lady of Charity, Sean MacDermott Street, Dublin 1, Dublin City. https://www.buildingsofireland.ie/buildings-search/building/50060466/monastery-of-our-lady-of-charity-sean-macdermott-street-dublin-1-dublin-city (last accessed 20 October 2021).

O'Donnell, Katherine, and Claire McGettrick with James M. Smith, Maeve O'Rourke and Clare Moriarty. 2020. *Dublin Honours Magdalenes Listening Exercise Report: Volume 1, report on key findings*. Dublin: Justice for Magdalenes Research.

O'Donnell, Katherine, Maeve O'Rourke and James M. Smith. 2020. 'Editors' Introduction: Toward transitional justice in Ireland? Addressing legacies of harm', *Éire-Ireland* 55(1&2): 9–16.

Ó'Fátharta, Conall. 2017. 'Religious orders rebutted appeal for clerical abuse redress payout'. *Irish Examiner*, 14 March. https://www.irishexaminer.com/news/arid-20445186.html (last accessed 20 October 2021).

Olivier, Laurent. 2011. *The Dark Abyss of Time: Archaeology and memory*. New York: AltaMira Press.

Olsen, Bjørnar. 2003. 'Material culture after text: Re-membering things', *Norwegian Archaeological Review* 36(2): 87–104.

Olsen, Bjørnar and Thora Pétursdóttir. 2014. *Ruin Memories: Materialities, aesthetics and the archaeology of the recent past*. London: Routledge.

O'Shea, Cormac. 2018. 'Dublin City Council vote overwhelmingly to block sale of Magdalene Laundry site'. *Dublin Live*, 13 September. https://www.dublinlive.ie/news/dublin-news/dublin-city-council-vote-overwhelmingly-15149866 (last accessed 20 October 2021).

Open Heart City. 2020. 'Sean McDermott Street'. http://openheartcitydublin.ie/ (last accessed 20 October 2021).

Prunty, Jacinta. 2017. *The Monasteries, Magdalen Asylums and Reformatory Schools of Our Lady of Charity in Ireland, 1853–1973*. Dublin: Columba Press.

Quinlan, Ronald. 2019. 'Former orphanage reinvented as co-living space – called The Orphanage'. *Irish Times*, 3 July. https://www.irishtimes.com/life-and-style/homes-and-property/former-orphanage-reinvented-as-co-living-space-called-the-orphanage-1.3944610 (last accessed 20 October 2021).

Ryan, Seán. 2009. *Report of the Commission to Inquire into Child Abuse*. http://www.childabusecommission.ie/rpt/ (last accessed 20 October 2021).

Smith, James M. 2007. *Ireland's Magdalen Laundries and the Nation's Architecture of Containment*. Manchester: Manchester University Press.

Smith, James M. 2010. 'Don't let Magdalene statue go the way of Padraic O Conaire, warns Boston Professor'. *Galway Advertiser*, 5 August. https://www.advertiser.ie/Galway/article/29360/dont-let-magdalene-statue-go-the-way-of-padraic-o-conaire-warns-boston-professor (last accessed 20 October 2021).

UNCAT. 2011. 'Concluding observation of the committee against torture. Forty-sixth session'. 9 May–3 June 2011. https://digitallibrary.un.org/record/706554?ln=en (last accessed 24 November 2021).

White, Timothy. 2010. 'The impact of British colonialism on Irish Catholicism and national identity: Repression, reemergence, and divergence', *Études Irlandaises* 35(1): 21–37.

14
Photos and artist statement

Alison Lowry

I have always been interested in textiles, especially clothing. Fabric preserves the essence of its maker; traces of the wearer become entwined with the warp and weft, allowing physical objects to become containers for memory.

My interest in fabric and embroidery started with some family heirlooms. A christening robe that has been in my family for over a hundred years inspired a major body of work. Through this work, I examined my family links and ties to the past. I examined how delicate life is, and how the states of birth and death can be similar in their fragility and vulnerability. As this body of work developed, I realised that these 'little dresses' could be interpreted in a variety of ways by the viewer, allowing me to explore many other issues using clothing as a metaphor.

Recent work, such as the exhibition '(A)dressing Our Hidden Truths', has focused on how art can help narrate past events and offer a safe space from which to engage with our history as a nation. Ireland is only just starting to come to terms with its past wide-scale institutionalisation of women and children, in religious-run mother and baby homes, industrial schools and Magdalene Laundries. Across these sites, hidden in plain sight, women and children were imprisoned, abused and stripped of identity.

In the work, 'Instead of the fragrance there will be stench; instead of a sash, a rope; instead of well-dressed hair, baldness; instead of fine clothing, sackcloth; instead of beauty, branding (Isaiah 3:24)', a pair of imposing glass scissors swing from strings of rosary beads over a mound of human hair (Figure 14.1). I aim to engage the viewer with the seductive beauty of the cast glass scissors while, on second glance, the work reveals a benevolent threat. Headphones beside the work enable the viewer to listen to the late Catherine Whelan, a Magdalene Laundry survivor, talk about the punishment of being held down by the nuns and orderlies and having her hair hacked off. It's incredibly powerful to be able to marry the objects with testimony like this.

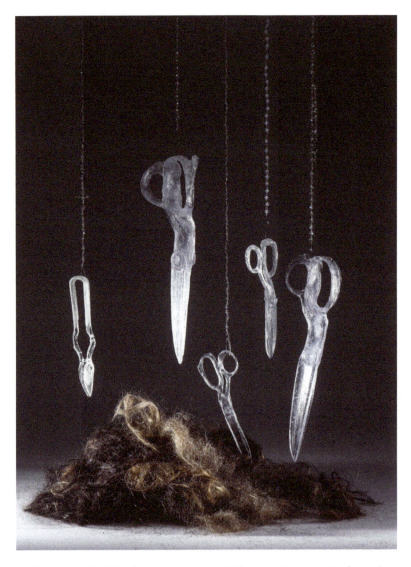

14.1 'Instead of the fragrance there will be stench; instead of a sash, a rope; instead of well-dressed hair, baldness; instead of fine clothing, sackcloth; instead of beauty, branding' (Isaiah 3:24) (cast glass, found objects, human hair, 2019). Photo: Alison Lowry.

14.2 'The Cardigan' (a cast glass children's cardigan inspired by the poetry of Connie Roberts, 2019). Photo: Alison Lowry.

'The Cardigan' is a work based on a poem by poet Connie Roberts, herself a survivor of Ireland's industrial school system (Figure 14.2). Connie and her 14 siblings were 'sentenced' to years in various industrial schools by the state, as a 'refuge' from her father, a violent alcoholic. Years later, and after her mother's death, her father presented her with this argyle cardigan – a small artefact from her lost childhood – and Connie reimagines in her poem her mother stitching and re-stitching while lamenting her lost children. In the exhibition, visitors can listen to Connie read the poem beside the artwork. The words of the poem are cast into the cardigan and weave their way through the glass, much like the knitted wool itself.

Glass, for me, is the perfect medium to encapsulate memory. Glass offers endless sculptural possibilities and, as a material itself, is full of contradictions – fragile/strong, molten/solid, everyday/extraordinary – a mirror of life itself.

Part 4
Curating impermanence

15

'Neurosis of the sterile egg' – permanence and paradox: museum strategies for the representation of Gustav Metzger's auto-destructive art

Pip Laurenson and Lucy Bayley

Examples of art practice that primarily produce impermanent artistic outputs are represented in museum collections in a myriad of ways including photographs, video, film, 35 mm slides or installations of objects. Take, for example, Mona Hatoum's 'Performance Still' (Figure 15.1).[1] This is a work that stands in for a complex set of practices centred around an hour-long performance called 'Roadworks' and its documentation that took place between 18 May and 8 June 1985. Hatoum was one of ten artists who were invited by the Brixton Art Gallery to present work outside of the gallery to document these performances and display the documentation in the gallery (Perrot 2016). This image was born out of this event.

Ana Mendieta's 'Untitled (Blood and Feathers #2)' exists within Tate's collection as an installation (titled 'Blood + Feathers', 1974) that comprises film and slides documenting a performance from 1974 in which Mendieta stands alongside a creek and pours blood down her chest, stomach and legs and then rolls in feathers that cover her body.[2] The film ends with Mendieta standing before the camera with her arms bent. This performance, evoking the rituals of the African Cuban religion Santeria, places the artist's body at the centre, and was subsequently repeated in Antwerp and Belgrade. Although it is not known who shot the film or took the slides, we do know that a group of fellow students from the intermedia arts course at the University of Iowa watched the

15.1 Mona Hatoum, 'Performance Still', 1985–95, Tate. © Mona Hatoum.

performance and presumably helped with the filming and the taking of photographs. That who made the documentation is unknown highlights the fact that it is the performance, and not the act of the making of the film and the slides, where the artwork is seen to reside.

Other artists have used installations that include objects as well as other media to act as a reference point to a past performance. One of the most dramatic of these is Marina Abramović's 'Rhythm O' (Figure 15.2).[3] This work exists as an installation in Tate's collection. It is made up of replica objects from the performance and is accompanied by slide documentation. In the original performance, the artist presented 72 objects on a long table with a white tablecloth; and, for the six-hour duration of the performance, she invited the audience to use them on her 'as desired'.[4] The objects range from the benign (for example, flowers, honey, bread and a coat) to those that presented a real threat to the artist, such as a gun, razor blades and a pocket-knife.[5]

The representation of these performances with the use of film, video, photography and objects allows these forms of practice to be included within the art historical narrative presented within the galleries of the museum. These performances were not intended to be repeated – a point underscored by the risk to the artist's life presented by the performance of 'Rhythm O' and the intimate relationship between the performances by Ana Mendieta and Mona Hatoum and their respective

15.2 Marina Abramovic, 'Rhythm 0', 1974. Installation view Tate Modern. Photograph: Sculpture Conservation Tate © Marina Abramovic.

identities. Nor were they intended, however, to be impermanent but to live on through their documentation; and, in some instances, the documentation and additional elements have been transformed from something ephemeral into art objects in their own right. Increasingly, performances are designed to be repeated as live events following a score or instructions that enable them to be performed by people other than the artist over time, rendering them collectible and providing an opportunity to insert them into broader art historical narratives, removing them from their previously fleeting ontologies (Bishop 2012; Laurenson and van Saaze 2014; Calonje 2015; Wood 2018; Giannachi and Westerman 2018).[6]

Conscious of this broader museological and curatorial context, this chapter examines strategies for transforming the impermanent into stable material form through one work, 'Recreation of First Public Demonstration of Auto-Destructive Art', by Gustav Metzger (1926–2017; Figure 15.3).[7] At first glance, this might be seen as a clear-cut result of an impulse among those who work within the museum and its logic to render static and stable something that was previously ephemeral. However, to the contrary, we argue that the contradictions embodied through this work and its representation in the museum unsettle any straightforward account of the respective intentions and roles of both the artist and the museum in this transformation. This is a work that was recreated for an exhibition in 2004, and whose recreation as a static display was instigated by entangled desires – both those voiced within the culture of the museum

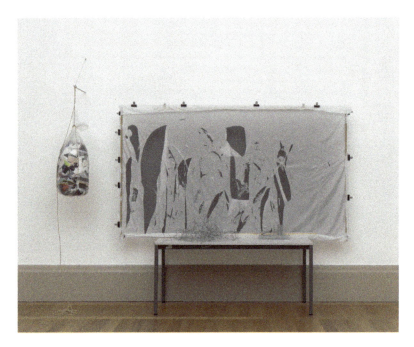

15.3 Gustav Metzger, 'Recreation of First Public Demonstration of Auto-Destructive Art', 1960, remade 2004, 2015. © Gustav Metzger, Photograph © Tate.

and those of the artist. It serves to encapsulate two paradoxes: first, the transformation of auto-destructive art, from a theory and practice designed to result only in that which is impermanent, into a work held by a permanent museum collection; and second, as a record of the engagement between the museum and an artist who both desired to be represented within the museum *and* campaigned for its destruction. In this chapter, we explore the underlying logic and drivers underpinning this recreation. Our aim is not so much to present a problem to be solved but, rather, to use this work as a lens through which to make visible some of the dilemmas at play more generally in museums when it comes to the display and conservation of works not originally intended to be permanent.

'Recreation of First Public Demonstration of Auto-Destructive Art' was accessioned into Tate's collection in 2006 as a work by Gustav Metzger with the following account of its dates: '1960, remade 2004, 2015'. The components that make up this display reference a lecture/demonstration on auto-destructive art at the Temple Gallery in London on 22 June 1960. For this event, Metzger showed and performed a number of processes that he identified as auto-destructive (Wilson 2008, 11). These included 'Model for Auto-Destructive Art Monument' (1960, 1997), an object formed of office staples stuck onto the back-plate of an old radio to represent three towers, one leaning,[8] and a pile of wire 'reinforcing armatures used in bricklaying' that had been found by Metzger in skips and were arranged randomly on the table next to the model (Wilson 2015).[9] Also present at the Temple Gallery demonstration was a transparent rubbish bag filled with scraps of fabric and paper that had been taken by Metzger from the streets outside textile shops on Regent Street. In the lead-up to the demonstration, Metzger had been experimenting in his studio in Kings Lynn with a new technique of painting with hydrochloric acid on synthetic nylon, and, at Temple Gallery, he provided the first public demonstration of this technique as an example of auto-destructive art.[10]

In this demonstration, Metzger stood behind a pane of glass (also found on the street), with the audience in front watching as he painted acid onto the nylon fabric.

Metzger's auto-destructive art was a 'public art for industrial societies' (Metzger 1960) that was intended to be an 'instrument for transforming peoples' thoughts and feelings, not only about art but about how people could 'use art to change . . . themselves and society' (Metzger 2015, 3). Metzger outlined his intentions for auto-destructive art in five manifestos (written between 1959 and 1964), and, from these, we gather that it was a 're-enact[ment]' (Metzger 2015) of societies' obsessions with destruction, found in the expansion of nuclear weapons, in war, forms of extinction and mass pollution. It also had clear art historical roots in Russian Revolutionary art (1910–20) and a persistent thematic of destruction that could be found in the movements of Cubism, Futurism and Dadaism (Metzger 2015, 1). With these roots, auto-destructive art (and, later, auto-creative art)[11] was a theory and a practice that could be performed and demonstrated, as well as manifest in materials and processes. Metzger's acid action painting on nylon is just one instance of auto-destructive art. And, in 'Recreation of First Public Demonstration of Auto-Destructive Art', we find Metzger's auto-destructive art recomposed, by Tate and Metzger, into a 'tableau' (Wilson 2015).

Curatorial strategy

The work was first recreated for the Tate Britain exhibition 'Art & the 60s: This Was Tomorrow' (2004), curated by Chris Stephens and Katharine

Stout, with reference to photographic documentation from the Temple Gallery exhibition. The exhibition was intended to explore developments in content and form in British art between 1956 and 1967, placing these shifts in the context of the 'myths and reality of "The Sixties" and of "Swinging London"'.[12] Given that Metzger was a central player in the London art scene during this period, the curators wrote to the artist proposing they show his work in relation to a presentation of archive material of an infamous art event in the 1960s, the 'Destruction in Art' Symposium. It was Metzger who had initiated and, among others, organised this symposium (9–11 September 1966), bringing together artists, poets and scientists to discuss the theme of destruction in art.[13] Following an initial invitation from Tate curators, it was agreed that, alongside an archival display about the symposium and the film 'Auto-Destructive Art: The Activities of G. Metzger' by Harold Liversidge, Metzger would recreate his acid painting from the Temple Gallery in 1960 at Tate Britain, and that the results would form an 'Auto-Destructive Art' installation to be included in the exhibition. This would be shown along with 'A Model for an Auto-Destructive Monument' 'on a (found) table' and 'a clear plastic bag filled with found rubbish'.[14] The demonstration took place in the loading bay at Tate Britain (26 May 2004, at 2pm) and was attended by a few members of staff.[15]

Working with various Tate staff members, including the art installation team (specifically, Terry Warren, Andy Shiel and Liam Tebbs, and conservation scientist Dr Joyce Townsend, who advised on the treatment of the fabric with hydrochloric acid), the artist recreated the installation that was subsequently presented to Tate in 2006. As part of accessioning the work into Tate's collection, the sculpture conservation team carefully documented the material elements of 'Recreation of First Public Demonstration of Auto-Destructive Art' and requested that Metzger complete a questionnaire to clarify the material details of the work. This included recording the artist's desire for the work to remain in its current condition and allowing for elements to be replaced or remade if necessary. In 2015–16, Andrew Wilson (who joined Tate in 2006) curated a display of Metzger's work at Tate Britain. In preparation for the display and in conversation with the artist, changes were made to it: the bag that had previously been placed on the floor would now hang from the wall, creating a more accurate depiction of the arrangement of objects and materials from Temple Gallery in 1960.[16]

This display acts as a placeholder representing a series of historical events by an artist who proclaimed in his second manifesto that auto-destructive art is 'Not interested in ruins' (Metzger 1960). As such, this display represents a curatorial strategy where material elements are taken to stand in for something that would otherwise defy objecthood – events that were initially intended as a protest against the creation of stable and autonomous art objects, against the art market, capitalism and the museum. As curator Wilson observes:

> This object is a demonstration; an event. Auto-destructive art exchanged an art of objects made up of mass, volume and area, for an art of time; an art that was in flux; an art of immediacy; an art of cumulative and diminishing moments. This reconstructed work is an object, a collection of objects, that show time arrested (Wilson 2015).

Composing the remains of a performance (one that was, itself, recreated) into an object can be understood within the context of strategies for revisiting performances from the 1960s and 1970s that surface within curatorial practice from the late 1990s. A perfect example is the exhibition, curated by artist Paul Schimmel, entitled 'Out of Actions: Between Performance and the Object' at the Los Angeles Museum of Contemporary Art (1998). This exhibition 'had at its center the conviction that performance, actions, Happenings, events and activities associated with the act of creation had an enormous impact on the object that emerged from them' (Schimmel 1998, 17). The exhibition included both re-staged performances, documentation and installations representing past performances. 'A Short History of Performance', curated by Iwona Blazwick at Whitechapel Gallery, 2002, saw the representation of live works by artists from the 1960s and 1970s.[17] A few years later, 'Marina Abramović: Seven Easy Pieces' (2005) took place at the Guggenheim New York, an exhibition in which the artist re-enacted 'seminal performance works by her peers'.[18] Each of these exhibitions, and others, brought to audiences seminal artistic performances from the 1960s and 1970s. In the process, they created greater curatorial freedom around these practices and histories, leading the way for a rise in the acquisition of performance by museums from the turn of the twentieth century.[19] Also relevant here is the growing trend in curatorial practice of recreating 'pioneering' exhibitions, mostly from a similar period (1960s and 70s).[20] Synchronous to this curatorial interest in revisiting and reconstructing performances and exhibitions, Metzger's work had also begun to be reconsidered through exhibitions in Germany and the UK. As we will see here, these involved both restaging events and remaking models, some of which would then be ready for acquisition.

15.4 Gustav Metzger at his first lecture demonstration at the Temple Gallery, possibly by John Cox, for Ida Kar, 2¼ inch square film negative, June 1960, Purchased, 1999, Photographs Collection, NPG x199033 © National Portrait Gallery.

15.5 Gustav Metzger practising for a public demonstration of auto-destructive art using acid on nylon, possibly by John Cox, for Ida Kar, 2¼ inch square film negative, 1960, Purchased 1999, Photographs Collection, NPG x134796 © National Portrait Gallery.

Contradictions: Metzger and the museum

The museum has been described by the sociologist Fernando Domínguez Rubio as a tool to transform evolving things into stable art objects. In his paper 'On the discrepancy between objects and things: An ecological approach', Domínguez Rubio considers the role of the museum in preventing the collapse of art objects – preventing the loss of their status as art objects through, among other factors, processes of deterioration (Domínguez Rubio 2016). In that paper, Domínguez Rubio also identifies one of the defining properties of the art system as the inviolable bond between artist intention and material form. However, Domínguez Rubio's account of the artwork-maintaining machine does not quite fit with 'Recreation of First Public Demonstration of Auto-Destructive Art' – or, at least, if it does, it is a machine that has been repurposed for a different end, perhaps hacked. Instead of collecting an artwork that is slowly auto-destructing, as all material things are, to keep the bond between intent and material form, in this case, the machine has taken something transitory[21] and slotted it into the museum. In so doing, it transforms it into a materially stable and static object or 'a collection of objects, that show time arrested' (Wilson 2015). In both cases, however, the museum's intent is one of stabilising.

In auto-destructive art, Metzger actively worked against the production of stable, autonomous art objects; and these recreations (2004 and 2015) therefore arguably represent not a manifestation of auto-destructive art but a proclamation of its absence. Metzger's manifestos and actions, his choice of industrial materials and found objects and his interest in collaborating with individuals outside of art (such as scientists, architects and engineers) were all 'way[s] to repudiate the notion of art's autonomy and reinstate its social function' (Fisher 2017, 11). These materials, actions and processes clearly proclaimed the intent of auto-destructive art as an attack on capitalism, the capitalist art market, and systems of war and warmongering by denying the production of art objects.[22] To this end, Metzger was clear that, at the end of any demonstration of auto-destructive art, the objects should be destroyed, stating: 'When the disintegrative process is complete the work is to be removed from the site and scrapped' (Metzger 1959).

Later on, Metzger's rejection of institutional and capitalist systems and structures, including museums, led to his call for artists to withdraw from the art world entirely to bring about institutional collapse and redistribute money away from institutions and into the hands of artists

(Metzger 1974). But, even at this point, there were signs of the edges of a contradiction beginning to emerge. As part of the International Coalition for the Liquidation of Art, Metzger, alongside others,[23] protested on the steps of museums, including Tate and the Royal Academy, 'lobbying for an end to the museum as the arbiter of aesthetic judgement and moral power' (Taylor 1999, 230). But he could also be found inside the very galleries he protested against, attending openings and talks, or voicing the art historical roots of his work in his lectures and writing. In 1965, for example, he located auto-destructive art in the destructive impulses of Dada, the Futurists, Cubists and Surrealists,[24] many of which grew out of (and benefited from) the art market. This is an example of how, despite – or alongside – the desire to create institutional change, Metzger simultaneously made efforts to place his work, including auto-destructive art, within a modernist legacy of the avant-garde.

In reflecting on Metzger's relationship with the market, the curator Andrew Wilson noted that collections in contemporary art museums often mirror the workings of the market, whereby an object's capacity to be traded relies on its status as museum-ready.[25] But the complicity between the museum and the market is sophisticated, and we should also recognise how the market similarly reflects the strategies of the museum.[26]

Metzger's work undermines the normal sequence of things, as, after 1959, his ideological position rejected the market; and his works, such as his lecture demonstrations, failed to produce objects. In fact, as noted in the earlier quote, Metzger went out of his way to ensure that relics of these performances were *not* left behind to be commoditised. However, his position shifted in the 1990s when he began to revisit his events and proposals from the 1950s and 1960s, in some instances involving the production of autonomous objects. In 1996, for the exhibition 'Made New' (curated by Andrew Wilson) at City Racing, Metzger reconstructed his 'Cardboards' from 1959, not as an 'exact replica' but as a concept; eight boxes found in the street were shown 'filled with compressed boxes' (Breitwieser 2005).[27] In 1998, he repeated his 1961 'Acid Nylon Painting' from the South Bank, London, in 'Out of Actions: Between Performance and the Object, 1949–1979', at the Los Angeles Museum of Contemporary Art.[28] In 'Speed: Visions of an Accelerated Age' at the Whitechapel Art Gallery, (London, 1998, curated by Jeremy Millar and Suzanne Cotter), the reconstruction of 'Drop of the Hot Plate' (1968) was included.[29] This object reappeared in Metzger's solo exhibition at Modern Art Oxford (curated by Astrid Bowron and Kerry Brougher) in 1998, along with a remade 'Mica and Air Cube' from 1968 and a reconstruction of his 'Liquid Crystal Environments'. Soon after the 2004 Tate exhibition, a number of these reconstructions (and others) were included in the retrospective 'Gustav Metzger: History, History' at the Generali Foundation in 2005.[30] Some of the reconstructed works ended up in collections, including at Tate and the Generali Foundation.[31] In the development of this practice of providing documentation of an event, recreating earlier works or recreating an event in a new form, it is unclear when these displays started to take on the form of a physical object that could be kept for the future.[32]

The revisiting of Metzger's work coincided with a series of exhibitions focusing on ephemeral, performative practices within which curators were seeking ways to bring these works and experiences from the past into the proximity of contemporary audiences, either by restaging a performance, displaying documentation or working with an artist to create a physical object through which to represent something that had once been a performance. In some instances, the objects created out of something initially live have found their way into collections, Marina Abramović's 'Rhythm 0' (1974) being one such example. This is a practice that demonstrates an imperative coming from museum curators to create, contain and preserve, and also to find a place in the museum for these practices and histories. For museum curators, bringing works into a collection is an important legacy. For curators who specialise in more ephemeral artforms, this might require particular creativity, for example in imagining how to bring a palpable sense of the live event into a static display. Museum collecting has traditionally been driven by a desire to fill gaps in the narrative of art history and grow the canon.[33]

Central to the paradoxical nature of auto-destructive art and Metzger's position of wanting to both operate within institutions and attack them is his work against erasure and forgetting. Metzger was born to Polish Jewish parents in Nuremberg on 10 April 1926; his family was murdered by the Nazis, with Gustav and his brother owing their survival to being put on a *Kindertransport* train to Britain in 1939 as part of the Refugee Children's Movement. Metzger's obsession with documentation as proof of his existence and artistic ideas is evident in 'Recreation of First Public Demonstration of Auto-Destructive Art', which precisely followed the documentation of the Temple Gallery display in the making of the work in 2004 and subsequent adjustments in 2015. 'Recreation' carries both these impulses to stand witness to these systems of war, destruction and extinction, and to persist inside a memory institution with which he had a deep, if contested, connection. In his writings and manifestos, Metzger was at pains to place his work within an art historical context. The room devoted to his work within the context of the chronological rehang of Tate Britain in 2015, and his inclusion within Tate's collection, achieved this even more explicitly than his inclusion within exhibitions.

Many artists working at the fringes of what might be considered 'collectible' creatively find ways to render their work 'museum-ready'.[34] Think, for example, of the 'delegated performance'[35] or the didactic or archival display, or installation versions of performances. In other cases, documentation enters the archive.[36] Tate has, on several occasions, worked closely with artists to establish the form in which artworks that do not conform to static material objects might enter the collection. As such, the museum is at risk of reversing the relationship with the market, so that the market would not declare something museum-ready but rather the museum would actively create the possibility of practices that otherwise would not have been considered collectible being 'market-ready'. This possibility haunts actions that may be driven by a museological desire to ensure that these practices are represented in the histories of art.

The ethics of these decisions are therefore the frequent subject of discussions within the museum. Compare, for example, the creation of 'Recreation of First Public Demonstration of Auto-Destructive Art' to a discussion that was had at Tate about Tony Conrad's 'Ten Years Alive on the Infinite Plain' (1972). This is a sound and film work that was performed on numerous occasions by Tony Conrad, musicians and a projectionist. After Conrad's death, his part was replaced by a recording, and the work entered Tate's collection in 2020 as a performance that can be reperformed.[37] Initially, Conrad's gallery proposed that, alongside the performance, an additional and distinct work entitled 'Elements of Ten Years Alive on the Infinite Plain' also enter the collection. This was a way for the work to be present within a gallery display and, therefore, part of an art historical narrative when it was not being performed. It was also perhaps driven by a concern about trading in something as ephemeral as a performance. Here was similar logic, in some ways, to 'Recreation of First Public Demonstration of Auto-Destructive Art', except, in this case, the artwork also persisted as a live performance that could be reperformed. After a wide-ranging discussion between curators, conservators, registrars and researchers, it was decided that 'Elements of Ten Years Alive on the Infinite Plain' was essentially a didactic display and that Tate could put such a display together at any time. For such a display to exist, it did not need to be considered an artwork. It was therefore agreed by the curators and through the acquisition committees at Tate that it would not be acquired and, as such, it did not enter Tate's collection alongside the performance. Is 'Recreation of First Public Demonstration of Auto-Destructive Art' also closer to a didactic display than a work of art?

262   IMPERMANENCE

The display points to tensions among practices in the museum, between the commitment to tell the histories of art and its purpose as a treasure-house designed for the protection and connoisseurship of precious objects. This dichotomy has a long trajectory and is captured by Paul DiMaggio in the two models of the art museum proposed by Gilman (1918) and Dana (1917) (DiMaggio 1991, 267). For those for whom the museum is about the collection, conservation and connoisseurship, 'Recreation of First Public Demonstration of Auto-Destructive Art' has less legitimacy than for those for whom the museum is primarily about education, interpretation and learning. Does this recreation successfully arrest time? Does it allow these objects to stand in for something once intended to be transitory? Does it successfully communicate the concept of auto-destructive art? '. . . every gap is matter'.[38]

The curatorial strategy of 'Recreation' is a device that enables the afterlives of projects to be recreated as stable objects when the event may have only existed for a few weeks or months, or just an evening. It can be a means of filling the gaps in collections for works that have got lost along the way, from artists who, at the time, were working in objection to, or at the fringes of, the commercial art world, with no representation, where things took place in bookshop windows, at musical performances or in festivals. This desire to fill a gap is common among Western museums and can be understood as an attempt to create the illusion of complete representation by 'cutting objects out of specific contexts (whether cultural, historic, or intersubjective) and making them "stand for" abstract wholes' (Clifford 1988, 220). But, in the creation of a placeholder, it's possible that further gaps become exposed: in this case, perhaps, as Clifford has argued, 'social labour' becomes erased by the ability of the museum to 'override specific histories of the object's production and appropriation' (Clifford 1988, 220).

The recreation of this work demonstrates a curatorial desire to represent Metzger's practice in the round, including in the narrative his political actions captured in photographs, video, memory, newspaper clippings (one of Metzger's favourite media) and now as a selection of sculptural objects. But, despite careful reconstruction – drawing precisely on documentation, evoking notions of accuracy by those who worked alongside Metzger, to realise this display – Metzger himself is strangely absent in what is experienced in the gallery and communicated online. His activism, his voice and the agency envisioned for art in society are missing. Another important dimension of Metzger's work was the role of cross-disciplinary collaboration. How much is this mediated for audiences by Tate?

In this wonky process where the maintenance machine has been re-wired to make a stable museum object out of something intended to self-destruct, has this process unwittingly erased the artist and his intent? Perhaps in the extremity of this demonstration of the museum as object-making machine, we see this more starkly than we would in other circumstances. The care shown (in discussion with Metzger) has served to flatten, clean up, dehumanise, depoliticise and institutionalise. The messiness, the humanity and the politics of these desperate, urgent acts of destruction have gone. We see these gaps not just in the display but in the conservation files, which carefully narrate the present materiality of the recreation but perhaps miss a reflection on when and why the decisions were made to affect this transformation.

When we read the conservation questionnaire for the work filled out by Metzger, we wanted someone to ask: 'Why did you want to fix auto-destructive art as a stable art object? And why now?' Over and above the questions *not* asked is the sense that the documentation does not fully serve the work and convey not only its intent but also something of its politics and the artist's practice. The records made were the result of working closely with Metzger and his assistant on the reconstruction for the display. Metzger, while his health was failing, was still present. Looking back after his death, perhaps unsurprisingly, we feel his absence. Despite limited resources, conservators are excellent record-keepers; however, the sense that curators hold knowledge of artist intent precludes these records from being more holistic and from allowing for a potential gap in our understanding in the future. This is compounded by the traditional alignment between conservation and those who see the primary mission of the museum as being to act as the keepers of precious objects rather than to focus on the telling of narratives. In the research project 'Reshaping the Collectible: When Artworks Live in the Museum',[39] we are asking the question, first raised by the curator Rudolf Frieling, of whether we are collecting objects or practices. The asking of this question reflects a trend within contemporary art conservation to recognise that artworks have biographies (van de Vall et al. 2011) and have lives before they enter the museum and are bound up with the development of an artist's work over a lifetime, situated within a political and social context and history. In this case, the artwork references a performance that was tightly bound to a particular moment in the life of the artist and the political context in which he found himself. For 'Recreation of First Public Demonstration of Auto-Destructive Art', if we tried to convey the artist's practice, would this allow us to feel and convey his presence more strongly? As with exhibitions and displays of other charismatic artists, such as Joseph Beuys, this display serves to highlight the artist's absence, but this is not solely a problem associated with charisma. It is also a problem of the political and the struggle that political works have, which is to both be *of* a moment and *transcend* that moment.

Conclusion

Certain decisions are informative as we navigate the ethics of our practice: for example, how we present this recreation, why it is accessioned and why it is not a didactic display. In thinking about museum audiences, this raises questions around what is not made transparent about the curatorial and conservation strategies, the latter of which intriguingly often merge with Metzger's own obsession with matter, materiality and documentation.

In a lecture presented to the Architectural Association in 1965, published as a transcript in that same year, Metzger stated:

> There are examples in nature where animals go on laying and looking after eggs that never hatch. The artist today has this problem in an extremely complex form. Artists are very sensitive to the vulnerability of their work to annihilation. Artists are also acutely aware of social reality, see little point in producing art in this situation, but go on doing so. This leads to numerous complications in their lives and art. We might call this the neurosis of the sterile egg. The artist in the field of auto-destructive art has to some extent escaped this particular conflict (Metzger 2015, 21).

Has this collection of objects become like the sterile egg, cosseted by the museum but denied its agency and vitality? The work exposes the central paradox in Metzger's life and work between wanting to both attack and be inside the institution. The object does communicate the instabilities and paradoxes that are inherent in the work.[40] Looking at 'Recreation of First Public Demonstration of Auto-Destructive Art', we see great gashes in the nylon (as though ripped, rather than painted), precarious objects, ready to collapse, a bag of collected rubbish hanging from a pole. Viewing this alongside the title, we might have a sense of destruction, but this is destruction that only exists as remains or potentiality, not as something to be directly experienced. If it did not exist, would the work of Metzger still maintain its currency in the narratives of art history at Tate? Is there something these objects perform that the narrative accounts do not? And in what other forms might these lecture demonstrations persist in cultural memory?

What if we didn't assume that a gap in a collection should necessarily be filled but instead saw this gap as productive, in and of itself? Curator Gilly Karjevksy has described gaps or the spaces in between as matter, through which 'new terminology peeks through the cracks, when lost terms are found again, or are being renegotiated' (Karjevksy 2019, 451). If we apply this idea to the gap of ephemeral works from collections, we might think of another way to allow this gap to be productive. There is something about this imperfect and paradoxical representation of auto-destructive art that demonstrates the museum's potential to recreate its narratives and realities. Metzger's gesture could be read as one of hope in the museum as a democratic memory-institution rather than simply the home of an art world elite. The difference between living inside and outside a public institution may lie in the capacity of 'Recreation of First Public Demonstration of Auto-Destructive Art' to represent the artwork's social function in acting as a placeholder to represent a history of protest and refusal and the troubling paradoxes that underpin the conflicting realities of the contemporary art museum to anyone curious enough to enter the building.

Acknowledgements

We are grateful to the following individuals who have contributed to this chapter by providing reflections on their experience of either working with Metzger directly or curating and conserving his work in Tate's collection.

Andrew Wilson, Senior Curator, Tate Britain, knew Metzger from the early 1980s until the artist's death. Wilson's writing on Metzger has been drawn on extensively in this chapter; a conversation was also held between Wilson and the authors in August 2020 to reflect on the ideas. Wilson also kindly provided a review of this chapter.

At the time of writing, Valentina Ravaglia (Curator, Displays and International Art, Tate Modern) was in the process of planning a display of 'Recreation of First Public Demonstration of Auto-Destructive Art' at Tate Modern, December 2020. A conversation was held between Ravaglia and the authors in August 2020 around her plans for the display, which fed into our reflections.

As co-curator of the exhibition *Art and the 60s: This was Tomorrow* at Tate, Katharine Stout was involved in the 'Recreation of First Public

Demonstration of Auto-Destructive Art' in 2004, and a conversation was held with the authors in August 2020, recalling her experience of working closely with Metzger. Liam Tebbs, Art Installation Manager, Tate Britain, installed 'Recreation of First Public Demonstration of Auto-Destructive Art' at Tate Britain in 2004. He was also involved in the 2015 installation. Gates Sofer, Sculpture Conservator, Tate, prepared 'Recreation of First Public Demonstration of Auto-Destructive Art' for display at Tate Britain in 2015. We are grateful to Liam and Gates for sharing their knowledge and experience.

Notes

1   Mona Hatoum's 'Performance Still, 1985–95'. Tate Accession Number P80087. https://www. tate.org.uk/research/publications/performance-at-tate/perspectives/mona-hatoum and https://www.tate.org.uk/art/artworks/hatoum-performance-still-p80087 (last accessed 29 October 2021).
2   Ana Mendieta, 'Blood + Feathers', 1974, Tate Accession Number T12916. https://www.tate. org.uk/art/artworks/mendieta-blood-feathers-t12916 (last accessed 29 October 2021).
3   Marina Abramović, 'Rhythm 0', 1974, Tate Accession Number T12916. https://www.tate.org. uk/art/artworks/abramovic-rhythm-0-t14875 (last accessed 29 October 2021).
4   Marina Abramović, quoted in the Summary Text for the work on Tate's website written by Tate curator Catherine Wood (https://www.tate.org.uk/art/artworks/abramovic-rhythm -0-t14875).
5   The perishable foodstuffs are replaced regularly during the display of the work.
6   The artist Tino Sehgal is interesting in this context in that he does not allow the documentation of his performance artworks, denying the possibility of objects standing in for the live work and distancing himself from this history (Laurenson and van Saaze 2014, Finbow 2016). This relates to a political stance to move away from the unsustainable transformation of material into the transformation of acts. Clare Bishop quotes an artist's statement by Sehgal published as part of the group show 'I Promise it's Political' at the Museum Ludwig, Cologne, in 2002, as follows: 'I consider communism and capitalism as two versions of the same model of economy, which only differ in their ideas about distribution. This model would be: the transformation of material or – to use another word – the transformation of "nature" into supply goods in order to decrease supply shortage and to diminish the threats of nature, both of course in order to enhance the quality of life. Both the appearance of excess supply in western societies in the 20th century, as well as of mankind's endangering of the specific disposition of "nature" in which human life seems possible, question the hegemony of this mode of production, in which the objecthood of visual art is profoundly inclined' (Bishop 2005).
7   Gustav Metzger, 'Recreation of First Public Demonstration of Auto-Destructive Art', 1960, remade 2004, 2015. Tate Accession Number T12156. https://www.tate.org.uk/art/artworks/ metzger-recreation-of-first-public-demonstration-of-auto-destructive-art-t12156 (last accessed 29 October 2021).
8   'Model for Auto-Destructive Art Monument' relied on a principle and technique 'suggested by Mr E. Ll. Evans, who worked in the corrosion of metals research group at the National Chemical Laboratory' (Metzger 2015, 19). The original, made in 1960, did not survive. The version at Tate was made by Metzger in 1997 for 'Gustav Metzger', Kunstraum München, Munich, then subsequently shown at Modern Art Oxford in 1998. It was then included at Tate Britain in 'Recreation of First Public Demonstration of Auto-Destructive Art' in 2004.
9   It is worth noting that Metzger worked as a junk dealer in Kings Lynn, Norfolk, in 1956.
10 The first successful painting with nylon was captured by John Cox in Metzger's studio in Kings Lynn in 1960. Following the Temple Gallery, there were demonstrations of acid action painting on 3 July 1961 on the South Bank, London, where he painted onto three sheets of nylon, black,

'NEUROSIS OF THE STERILE EGG'   267

red and white, in October 1962 at the Institute of Contemporary Arts, London, and then in February 1963 at the Bartlett Society. The demonstration of acid painting on the South Bank was repeated in the summer of 1963 and filmed by Harold Liversidge. In October 1965, Metzger performed a lecture/demonstration of acid painting on nylon at 'The Chemical Revolution in Art' at the Engineering School, University of Cambridge. For further background, see Wilson 2015; Fisher 2017.

11 Auto-creative art is referenced in Metzger's third manifesto, dated 23 June 1961, where it was described as 'art of change, growth, movement' (Metzger 1961). Fisher writes: 'Auto-creative art, unburdened by the weight of political critique, allowed Metzger to pursue a broader spectrum of aesthetic experiences, defining a new role for the artist in relation to the work of art (further removed from the act or gesture itself), and a new form of art. "The immediate aim" he wrote, "is the creation, with the aid of computers, of works of art whose movements are programmed and can include 'self-regulation'" (Metzger 1961)' (Fisher 2017, 8).

12 Letter dated 30 July 2003 from Katharine Stout to Gustav Metzger, inviting the artist to participate in the exhibition 'Art and the Sixties'. Tate Archives, EX 121.3, 'Artist Correspondence – Art & the 60s' (30 June–26 September 2004). See also Stout and Stephens 2004.

13 For more on the 'Destruction in Art' Symposium, see Stiles 1987, 22–31; Stiles 2005, 41–66.

14 'EX 121.3 Artist Correspondence – Art & the 60s (30 June–26 September 2004)', Tate Archive.

15 'EX 121.3 Artist Correspondence – Art & the 60s (30 June–26 September 2004)', Tate Archive.

16 While on display at Tate in 2004, the bag of materials was accidentally thrown away by a cleaner and was replaced with a new bag by Metzger. By the time Tate came to redisplay the work in 2015, new photographs of the Temple Gallery demonstration in 1960 had come to light and a new bag was brought to Tate from Metzger and his assistants. A new method of display was also decided on, so that it would be closer to the 1960 demonstration. Jones 2004; BBC News 2004.

17 Over six days, live works by Carolee Schneemann, Stuart Brisley, Bernsteins, the Kipper Kids, Hermann Nitsch, Bruce McLean and Jannis Kounellis were re-presented in the Whitechapel Gallery. See Withers 2002.

18 Abramović re-enacted: Bruce Nauman, 'Body Pressure', 1974; Vito Acconci, 'Seedbed', 1972: VALIE EXPORT, 'Action Pants: Genital Panic', 1969; Gina Pane, 'The Conditioning, First Action of Self-Portrait(s)', 1973; and Joseph Beuys, 'How to Explain Pictures to a Dead Hare', 1965. Abramović also re-enacted her own works 'Lips of Thomas', 1975 (Galerie Krinzinger, Innsbruck) and 'Entering the Other Side', 2005. http://pastexhibitions.guggenheim.org/abramovic/ (last accessed 29 October 2021).

19 The first live work to enter Tate's collection was Tino Sehgal's 'This is Propaganda' (2002), acquired through Gallery Jan Mot, which had to be learned through 'body to body transmission' rather than through instructions or documentation. This work was followed into Tate's collection in 2008 by a performance by David Lamelas, 'Time 1970', which was purchased from the same gallery but via the Frieze Art Fair, beginning a trend for live performance art to be represented within the commercial art world. Lamelas' 'Time' is a simple instruction piece that involves a group of participants standing side-by-side along a line marked on the floor. Once the performance begins, the person at one end of the line tells the time to the person next to them and this process continues until the other end of the line is reached, when the performance ends with the last person announcing the time in the language of their choice (Hodge 2015). These works were the first live performances to be collected by a museum.

20 Examples include: 'Live in Your Head: When Attitudes Become Form' (1968), re-staged at the Prada Foundation, Venice Biennale, 2013; Richard Hamilton, 'an Exhibit' (1957) and 'Man, Machine and Motion' (1955), re-staged at Institute of Contemporary Arts, 2014; Stephen Willats, 'Visual Automatics and Visual Transmitters' (originally shown at the Museum of Modern Art, Oxford, in 1968), re-staged at the exhibition 'Control. Stephen Willats. Work 1962–69', Raven Row, 2014; Les Immatériaux, Centre Pompidou 1985, re-staged, Kunstverein Dusseldorf, 2014.

21 For a discussion of ephemerality and permanence in relation to performance and theatre, see Schneider 2011, 94–6.

22 Peyton-Jones 2009, 25.

23 The International Coalition for the Liquidation of Art comprised Stuart Brisley, John Plant, Gustav Metzger and Sigi Krauss.

24 Metzger wrote that the artists in these movements understood the physicists' desire to 'smash to try to annihilate matter because it is the only way to understand its secrets' (2015, 7).

25 Conversation with the authors (19 August 2020).

26 It is notable that Metzger's Estate and Foundation were taken on by Hauser & Wirth Gallery. The lead image for the July 2020 announcement is of an auto-destructive art demonstration on the South Bank in 1961. https://www.hauserwirth.com/news/29227-announcing-representation-gustav-metzger (last accessed 30 October 2021). This is despite Metzger's stating the following in his Architectural Association lecture of 1965: 'Auto-destructive art is an assault on the dealers' system. It undermines this system in numerous ways. I laid so much emphasis on the public nature of the auto-destructive art not only because I believed that was the correct position, but in order to direct the movement away from the dealers' system' (Metzger 2015, 10).

27 'Made New: Barry Flanagan, Tim Mapston, Gustav Metzger, Alfred Jarry', curated by Andrew Wilson, took place between 25 October and 17 November 1996. City Racing archives are held by Tate.

28 The exhibition subsequently toured to Vienna, Barcelona and Tokyo.

29 'Drop of the Hot Plate' was first shown in1968 in 'Extremes Touch: Material/Transforming Art', as one of a series of experiments performed in a new filtration laboratory in the Chemical Engineering Department of University College, Swansea, as part of the 1968 Swansea Arts Festival, Wales.

30 'Untitled', 1959–60, aluminium wire, reconstructed 2005, Generali Foundation; 'Auto-Destructive Monument', 1960, staples, steel, varnished, reconstructed 2005, Generali Foundation; 'Acid Nylon Painting', 1960, produced 2004, Tate Britain; 'Liquid Crystal Environment', 1965–6, installation, produced 1998, Museum of Modern Art, Oxford; 'Drop on the Hot Plate', 1968, installation, reconstructed 2005, Generali Foundation; Mica and Air Cube, 1968, reconstructed 2005, Generali Foundation; 'Mobbile', 1970, reconstructed 2005, Generali Foundation; 'Projects Unrealised I', 1971, reconstructed 1998, Museum of Modern Art Oxford; 'Projects Unrealised I (Monument to Bloody Sunday)', 1972, reconstructed 1998, Museum of Modern Art, Oxford. See Breitwieser 2005, 'Exhibition Checklist', 304–7.

31 'Liquid Crystal Environment', 1965 (remade 2005), for example, was restaged for 'Summer of Love: Art of the Psychedelic Era' at Tate Liverpool, and acquired by Tate the following year. https://www.tate.org.uk/art/artworks/metzger-liquid-crystal-environment-t12160 (last accessed 29 October 2021).

32 This is a point raised by Andrew Wilson in an email exchange with the authors.

33 Charles Esche (2020) has challenged this approach to collecting by proposing a 'degrowth' agenda, whereby, instead of expanding the canon, museums seek to overwrite and change it.

34 Conversation between Andrew Wilson and the authors (19 August 2020).

35 'Delegated performance' is a term developed by Claire Bishop, which she defined as 'the act of hiring non-professionals or specialists in other fields to undertake the job of being present and performing at a particular time and a particular place on behalf of the artist, and following his/her instructions' (Bishop 2012, 219).

36 See, for example, the artworks mentioned in the introduction to this chapter.

37 https://www.tate.org.uk/about-us/projects/reshaping-the-collectible (last accessed 30 October 2021).

38 '. . . every gap is matter, is substance in itself, which occupies space in between. Gaps in understanding are formed through the emergence of (or the search for) a language at a time when the old one is not completely dead yet, when new terminology peeks through the cracks, when lost terms are found again, or are being renegotiated. Such gaps become space of production to experiment with new material, new becomings, which open up new possibilities' (Karjevsky 2019, 451).

39 'Reshaping the Collectible: When Artworks Live in the Museum' (2018–21) is a three-year museum-wide research project at Tate, funded by the Andrew W. Mellon Foundation. https://www.tate.org.uk/research/reshaping-the-collectible (last accessed 21 October 2021).

40 Metzger argues for keeping contradictions intact and present. In a similar vein to the writer Ariella Aïsha Azoulay, Metzger resists Hegel's idea of *Aufhebung* and the notion of a single cohesive perspective (Azoulay 2019, 178).

References

Azoulay, Ariella Aisha. 2019. *Potential History: Unlearning imperialism*. London and New York: Verso.

BBC News. 2004. 'Cleaner bins rubbish bag artwork', 27 August. http://news.bbc.co.uk/1/hi/entertainment/arts_and_culture/3604278.stm (last accessed 30 October 2021).

Bishop, Claire. 2005. 'No pictures, please: The art of Tino Sehgal'. *ArtForum International*, 2005. https://www.artforum.com/print/200505/no-pictures-please-the-art-of-tino-sehgal-8831 (last accessed 24 November 2021).

Breitwieser, Sabine, ed. 2005. *Gustav Metzger: History history*. Ostfildern-Ruit: Hatje Cantz.

Calonje, Teresa, ed. 2015. *Live Forever: Collecting live art*. Cologne: Walther König.

Clifford, James. 1988. 'On collecting art and culture'. In *The Predicament of Culture: Twentieth-century ethnography, literature, and art*, edited by James Clifford, 215–52. Cambridge, MA, and London: Harvard University Press.

DiMaggio, Paul. 1991. 'Constructing an organizational field as a professional project: The case of U.S. art museums'. In Walter W Powell and Paul J DiMaggio, eds, *The New Institutionalism in Organizational Analysis*, 267–93. Chicago and London: University of Chicago Press.

Domínguez Rubio, Fernando. 2016. 'On the discrepancy between objects and things: An ecological approach', *Journal of Material Culture* 21(1): 59–86.

Esche, Charles. 2020. Lecture presented at a virtual event, 'Institutions Must Go?', hosted by the Research Centre for Material Culture, Amsterdam, 22 October. https://www.materialculture.nl/en/events/institutions-must-go (last accessed 20 October 2021).

Finbow, Acatia. 2016. 'Tino Sehgal, This Is Propaganda 2002/2006' in *Performance at Tate: Into the space of art*. Tate Research Publication. https://www.tate.org.uk/research/publications/performance-at-tate/perspectives/tino-sehgal (last accessed 29 October 2021).

Fisher, Elizabeth. 2017. 'Iconoclasm and interdisciplinarity', *Interdisciplinary Science Reviews* 42: 4–29.

Giannachi, Gabriella and Jonah Westerman, eds. 2018. *Histories of Performance Documentation: Museum, artistic and scholarly practices*. London and New York: Routledge.

Hodge, David. 2015. '"Time", David Lamelas, 1970'. Tate. https://www.tate.org.uk/art/artworks/lamelas-time-p79205 (last accessed 29 October 2021).

Jones, Sam. 2004. 'How auto-destructive art work got destroyed too soon'. *Guardian*, 27 August. https://tinyurl.com/rje9a2en (last accessed 30 October 2021).

Karjevsky, Gilly. 2019. 'Gaping'. A reader published for *(Un-)Learning Place*, 9–13 January, Haus der Kulturen der Welt (HKW), Berlin, 451.

Laurenson, Pip, and Vivian van Saaze. 2014. 'Collecting performance-based art: New challenges and shifting perspectives'. In *Performativity in the Gallery: Staging interactive encounters,* edited by Outi Remes, Laura MacCulloch and Marika Leino, 27–41. Oxford: Peter Lang. https://www.academia.edu/20762297/Collecting_Performance_Based_Art_New_Challenges_and_Shifting_Perspectives (last accessed 30 October 2021).

Metzger, Gustav. 1959. 'Auto-destructive Art: First Manifesto', 4 November 1959, reprinted in *Gustav Metzger: History history*, edited by Sabine Breitwieser. Ostfildern-Ruit: Hatje Cantz, 2005.

Metzger, Gustav. 1960. 'Second Manifesto for Auto-destructive Art', 10 March 1960, reprinted in *Gustav Metzger: History history*, edited by Sabine Breitwieser. Ostfildern-Ruit: Hatje Cantz, 2005.

Metzger, Gustav. 1961. 'Auto-Destructive Art, Machine Art, Auto-Creative Art'. Third manifesto. London, 23 June 1961.

Metzger, Gustav. 1962. 'Manifesto World'. Fourth manifesto. London, 7 October 1962.

Metzger, Gustav. 1964. 'On Random Activity in Material/Transforming Works of Art'. Fifth manifesto. London, July 30, 1964. In *Signals* (news bulletin of the Centre for Advanced Creative Study) 1(2), September 1964, 14.

Metzger, Gustav. 1974. 'Artist Statement'. In *Art into Society: Society into art: Seven German artists*. London: Institute of Contemporary Arts.

Metzger, Gustav. 2015. 'Auto-destructive art: Typescript of a lecture given at the Architectural Association, 24 February 1965'. Third edition. London: Bedford Press, 19.

Perrot, Capucine. 2016. 'Mona Hatoum, Performance Still 1985–95'. In *Performance at Tate: Into the space of art*. Tate Research Online Publication. https://www.tate.org.uk/research/

publications/performance-at-tate/perspectives/mona-hatoum (last accessed 25 October 2021).

Peyton-Jones, Julia. 2009. *Gustav Metzger: Decades 1959–2009*. London: Serpentine Gallery/Koenig Books.

Schimmel, Paul (ed.). 1998. *Out of Actions: Between performance and the object, 1949–1979*. Los Angeles: Museum of Contemporary Art/New York: Thames & Hudson.

Schneider, Rebecca. 2011. *Performing Remains: Art and war in times of theatrical reenactment*. London and New York: Routledge.

Stiles, Kristine. 1987. 'Synopsis of the Destruction in Art Symposium and its theoretical significance', *The Act* 1: 22–31. https://monoskop.org/images/c/c9/Stiles_Kristine_1987_Synopsis_of_the_Destruction_in_Art_Symposium_and_Its_Theoretical_Significance.pdf (last accessed 30 October 2021).

Stiles, Kristine. 2005. 'The story of the Destruction in Art Symposium and the "DIAS Affect"'. In *Gustav Metzger: History history,* edited by Sabine Breitwieser, 41–66. Ostfildern-Ruit: Hatje Cantz.

Stout, Katharine, and Chris Stephens. 2004. *Art & the 60's: This Was Tomorrow*. London: Tate Publishing.

Taylor, Brandon. 1999. *Art for the Nation: Exhibitions and the London public, 1747–2001*. Manchester: Manchester University Press.

van de Vall, Renée, Hanna Hölling, Tatja Scholte and Sanneke Stigter. 2011. 'Reflections on a biographical approach to contemporary art conservation'. In ICOM-CC: 16th Triennial Conference, Lisbon, 19–23 September 2011: Preprints [Cd-Rom]. Almada: Critério. https://dare.uva.nl/search?identifier=d2340d58-6edb-49e9-baa8-c87ee11804e9 (last accessed 1 November 2021).

Wilson, Andrew. 2008. 'Gustav Metzger's auto-destructive/auto-creative art: An art of manifesto, 1959–1969', *Third Text* 22(2): 177–94.

Wilson, Andrew. 2015. Presentation on Gustav Metzger, 'Recreation of First Public Demonstration of Auto-Destructive Art', in the session 'Migrating meaning: Contextual claims and the work itself', 20 November 2015, for the conference 'Media in Transition', Tate Modern, 18–20 November.

Withers, Rachel. 2002. 'Review of "A Short History of Performance: Part One", Whitechapel Art Gallery 15–21 April 2002', *ArtForum*. https://chisenhale.co.uk/artists/files/2010/06/ArtForum.pdf (last accessed 1 November 2021).

Wood, Catherine. 2018. *Performance in Contemporary Art*. London: Tate Publishing.

16
Culturing impermanence at the museum: the metabolic collection

Martin Grünfeld

The lost wig: a questioning into the life of collections

In May 1940, a wig was donated to Copenhagen's Medical Museion.[1] It was the colour of strawberries and had belonged to a patient diagnosed with paranoia. The patient had cut four holes through which she poured water to ease her headaches. Today, all that is left of the wig is the register page, which briefly tells us the story of the item. In the margins of the register, it is noted that the wig was deaccessioned because it was ridden with maggots. Its material erasure, however, is not merely marked by the deaccessioning note but also a later note in a different handwriting exclaiming 'Æv!!' – a Danish expression for something unfortunate. Without the object, the story has lost its material referent and remains a thing of the past. Besides the brief description of its colour and condition, we can only imagine what it looked like and how it felt to touch.

But why should we care about the wig today? Because it evokes an immediate feeling of loss. The historical erasure of the wig immediately provokes a response similar to the 'Æv!!', perhaps followed by the question: but couldn't it have been saved if we had taken better care of it? Today, the story of the wig is not merely a story of a patient in pain but also a story of conservation practices and loss. It marks something that we try to keep out of our collections and the states of being we want our objects to be in. The wig had entered the life cycle of gradual deterioration and breakdown, eventually becoming a nutritive habitat for the maggots.

It had established an unholy relation to the living, something that is strictly forbidden for museum objects. As Susan Pearce (1999, 24) explains, museum objects are removed from their original contexts and become dead in their living time to gain immortality – an immortality that depends on the museum as a preservative site for objects. The museum is an institution constantly striving for permanence and suppressing the forces of time, while ideally freezing historical snapshots.

For me, however, the strawberry-coloured wig provokes a different response, one that is not concerned with whether the wig could or should have been saved but, rather, could we have done something more with it if we had been less hostile toward the cycle of life? The absence of the wig challenges us to rethink not only what we can do with museum objects but also whether the museum must always attempt to suppress life-processes and strive for permanence. As Jennie Morgan and Sharon Macdonald have recently shown, de-growth practices are already at play in museums: for example, re-evaluating collections as naturalistic entities with a finite lifespan and re-using objects in ways that enrich their afterlife (Morgan and Macdonald 2018, 6–7). These are practices that resonate with my aim here to rethink museum objects as parts of an all-encompassing ecological cycle, and to consider whether the 'end' of these objects could be turned into a site for becoming and multiplication: perhaps an experimental-ontological site that, similar to *experimental preservation*, interrogates ways of preserving objects that reach beyond institutional modes of practice and increase the risk of failure (Otero-Pailos 2016, 11). Such practices challenge the alleged immortality of museum objects. In contrast to Pearce's metaphorical description of objects entering the museum as a transformation from 'life' to 'death', I want to think of the life of museum objects literally.

In this chapter, I explore the life of objects in collections within and outside the museum and consider what a truly metabolic collection might look like. I begin by focusing on preservation practices at the Medical Museion as a time-suspending caring that attempts to save things from the forces of time (*conserved permanence*). Within the museum, conservation seeks to suspend life-processes in the collections. But, is the role of the museum always to attempt to suspend life-processes and aim for permanence? Here, my aim is to explore the possibilities for hosting life at the museum and culturing impermanence. Methodologically, I explore objects, collections and practices that function as driving forces in my conceptual unfolding of the idea of culturing impermanence. First, I discuss fly stock centres to carve out a contrast between caring as *conserving* and as *culturing*. Second, I turn to Thomas Feuerstein's bioart as an opening to think about objects beyond the ideal of permanence. Through engaging with his work 'One and No Chair', I will develop the concept of *cultured impermanence* as a transgressive notion that pushes our thinking beyond questions of identity and authenticity toward difference and entropy. My conceptual unfolding leads to a proposal for a truly metabolic collection as an ontological-experimental site ('The Living Room'), where we no longer attempt to hinder metabolic processes but nurture them and enable things to proliferate into multiple modes of existence.

Towards a metabolic analytic[2]

Why enquire into the *metabolic* instead of using the more familiar concept of *life*? Because by bringing the *metabolic* into view, I wish to defamiliarise the way we think about the life of museum objects and what it means for a collection to be alive. Yet *metabolic* is such an unusual term outside the life sciences that it may end up obscuring my exploration, so let me begin by specifying what I mean by *metabolic* and how it becomes an analytic that guides my questioning into life-processes, (im)permanence and practices of care in collections.

 Metabolic is the adjectival form of *metabolism*, derived from the Greek *metabole*, which means change. Broadly speaking, the term designates the exchange of matter, as the German expression *Stoffwechsel*, introduced in 1815 by chemist G. C. L. Sigwart, neatly captures (Bing 1971, 179). Yet *metabolism* has not enjoyed a stable life as a concept since its first appearance in English physiology textbooks in around 1878 (Bing 1971, 174–75). According to Hannah Landecker, today, metabolism designates 'the interface between inside and outside, the space of conversion of one to another, of matter to energy, of substrate to waste, of synthesis and break down. A process-thing, it is always in time' (Landecker 2013, 193). Metabolism marks a chiastic exchange between inside and outside; we are part of the environment and the environment is metabolically inscribed in us (see Grünfeld 2020a for more on this). This sense of intertwinement resonates with the late Maurice Merleau-Ponty's description of the 'flesh of the world' as an adhesive weaving together (Merleau-Ponty 1968, chapter 4). Metabolism is thus always *relational* (an in-between inside and outside) and *temporal* (dynamically exchanging, converting and breaking down), in processes that develop across scales from cells, organs and individuals to communities and ecologies. It is everywhere and nowhere, as Landecker fittingly describes it.

Today, metabolism is one of the most widely agreed criteria for being alive (Dupré and O'Malley 2009, 12). In the 1960s, Hans Jonas already argued that metabolism is not some peripheral activity but all-pervasive within the living system (Jonas 2001, 76, n. 13). Jonas' focus on metabolism is a reaction to a post-dualistic materialism in which life is contracted from nature and separated as a distinct specialty (Jonas 2001, 19). This materialism embodies what Jonas calls *an ontology of death* 'whose model entity is pure matter, stripped of all features of life' (Jonas 2001, 9). For Jonas, metabolism becomes a key concept with which to think about organisms as different from dead matter because they are continuously the results of their own metabolising activities – they persist as the same organisms by not remaining the same matter (Jonas 2001, 75–6). This resonates with Humberto Maturana and Francisco Varela's understanding of living systems as *autopoietic*. Similar to Jonas' description of the living system, they argue that it is through interactions and transformations that living systems continuously regenerate and constitute their unity (Maturana and Varela 1980, 78–9). In contrast to living organisms, for Jonas, inorganic entities are characterised by having enduring matter and fixed identities, with no metabolising activities to transform them into something else (Jonas 2001, 80).

However, while it may seem impossible to think about inorganic matter as anything other than dead, we must remember that, once, everything was thought to be intertwined with life. This is also pointed out by Jonas in his brief history of how we went from an *ontology of life* to an *ontology of death*: 'Bare matter, that is, truly inanimate, "dead" matter, was yet to be discovered – as indeed its concept, so familiar to us, is anything but obvious' (Jonas 2001, 7). Yet his philosophy of metabolism seems to stay within the boundaries of the very ontology of death he criticises by carving out a specialised subsection of matter for living organisms. This is where the metabolic analytic I am developing here departs from Jonas' philosophy. The metabolic analytic is an attempt to establish a viewpoint that is sensitive toward the circulation, exchange and conversion of matter across the organic/inorganic divide. But, to apply a metabolic analytic does not entail a return to *hylozoism*. While inanimate matter is not metabolising materially in the same way as an eating and digesting organism, over time, its materiality does transform – *intra-acting* with, for example, microbial presences (such as bacteria and fungi), the environment and our practices of use and care. I use the notion of 'intra-acting' following Karen Barad to mark their ontological inseparability (see Barad 2007, 128). The broadening of the metabolic analytic across the organic/inorganic divide finds support in the biological sense of the adjective *metabolic*, which is not delimited to living organisms but extends to things affected by metabolism – for example, the strawberry-coloured wig acting as a nutritive habitat for the maggots. To this, we might also add factors that affect metabolism, for example streetlights interrupting the circadian rhythms of city dwellers (birds, rats, humans and so on). Thus, the metabolic analytic implies a weakening of the borders between organic/inorganic, active/passive and living/bare matter, and points toward a vitality intrinsic to materiality akin to Jane Bennett's conception of *vibrant matter* as 'an active, earthy, not-quite-human capaciousness' (Bennett 2010, 3). Even a museum collection consisting solely of 'dead' inorganic matter is nonetheless part of the exchange of matter from this perspective.

The breadth of the metabolic analytic potentially poses a problem because it may render it unfocused and ill-suited as an analytic. Without wishing to sound too much like the Newspeak of *1984*, however, I feel that this weakness accentuates the strength of the metabolic analytic. Within academia, we usually seek to limit the problem under scrutiny, but this inevitably also delimits the arguments we can unfold, the degrees of mess we can deal with and the questions we can pose (Grünfeld 2020b, 109–10). Within such reductive tendencies, multiplicity, difference and the bigger perspectives are often lost. Such dimensions are crucial when we wish to deal with collections across temporal regimes, varieties of materials and ecologies. This is precisely what constitutes the potency of the metabolic analytic: it is a perspective that opens up the possibility of thinking within a set of dynamic tensions, such as inside/outside, continuity/rupture, build up/break down, energy/waste, growth/de-growth, life/death, without abolishing them. This is an analytic capable of unravelling a temporal interface between 'thing' and 'environment' that enables us to explore the dynamics between permanence and impermanence always already at work in collections (and everywhere else).

The life of objects in collections: conserved permanence

In the spring of 2019, I conducted four interviews with conservators working with the collections at the Medical Museion, a combined museum and research unit, where I work as a researcher jointly affiliated with the Center for Basic Metabolic Research.[3] The interviews revolved around questions about museum objects and the tools the conservators found most significant for their work: jars, liquids, gloves, boxes. Objects that are invisible for museum visitors yet are crucial in this area. Objects that not only tell us about the practices of care at the museum but also provide glimpses into the ideals behind those practices. In this section, I analyse the time-suspending practices of preservation and show how the conservators are navigating a tension between reality and ideal in their striving to maintain objects in a state of *conserved permanence*. In this state, the concept of life splits into two – a cultural-metaphorical sense that must be preserved and a metabolic-literal sense that must be suppressed, yet always keeps crawling back into the picture. Within these tensions, the conservators care for objects to save them for the future and maintain them in a permanent state of identity and authenticity.

Suspending time: the box as a time-capsule

Let us begin with something simple: a box for storing objects. Yet 'a box isn't just a box', as Amalie emphasised in our conversation, but 'perhaps the most significant thing' at the museum (interview with A. Suurballe Schjøtt-Wieth and M. Ploug Risom, 4 April 2019). To my surprise, however, these boxes left no impression of their special properties as time-capsules – a characterisation that Amalie and I developed during our conversation. However, looks can be deceiving and, although the boxes were made of cardboard, they were acid-free. If the boxes were not

16.1 Photograph from the collections at Medical Museion taken in 2019. Photo: Martin Grünfeld.

acid-free, they would degrade faster and, in the process, possibly cause harm to the objects they were intended to protect. Thus, the cardboard boxes are intended to create a neutral environment and a border between inside and outside, enabling objects to hibernate while being shielded from the outside world. This is an isolated environment characterised by a limited flow, breakdown and exchange of matter, to keep the objects in a permanent state of being.

Isolation is key here – objects must be stored (ideally) outside the metabolic world we inhabit. Or, as Maiken, another conservator I interviewed, vividly expressed it: 'the optimal [form of preservation] would be to fly every museum object into space and have them in zero-G in a lightly heated state' (interview with M. Ploug Risom, 14 March 2019). I think this statement tells us a lot about the ideal of isolation guiding preservation practices. When objects are stored in boxes, they may not see the light of day for years, decades, maybe centuries. This realisation led me to ask Amalie and Maiken what it feels like to pack away objects knowing that the boxes might not be opened for a long time. Maiken immediately provided a level-headed response, 'less handling, less damage', followed by fascination a few minutes later: 'there is something spectacular, grandiose about being the only one allowed to touch it, maybe the only one touching it for a hundred years' (interview with A. Suurballe Schjøtt-Wieth and M. Ploug Risom, 4 April 2019). To enable objects to touch future generations, not only do we need to isolate them from environmental factors but we must also keep them out of touch from ourselves. As Amalie added, we have 'the weird obligation to preserve for eternity' – something we are a little closer to realising 'if the object is allowed to rest in peace for 20 years without anyone taking an interest in it. Then, if somebody is suddenly interested in it, that is fantastic, because then we have saved it . . . and we can remove it from the time-capsule'. I must admit that I planted the idea of the 'time-capsule' in the conversation earlier on, but Amalie adopts the conception to describe the ultimate function of the boxes: 'I think time-capsule is a good word for our boxes . . . That is what we do . . . Organised time-capsules.' Who would have thought cardboard boxes could be used for time travel?

The conservators organise time-capsules to remove museum objects from sources of decay such as light, pests, climate, even humans – an isolation that is crucial for their preservation. However, when the conservators care for objects, isolation alone is not enough. Their work is largely oriented toward stabilising the states of being of museum objects. As Maiken explained, along with the predicate 'museum object' comes an obligation to preserve the object in its current state (interview with M. Ploug Risom, 14 March 2019). For Nanna, stabilisation involves both a macroenvironmental focus on storage and climate and a focus on singular objects and their states (interview with N. Gerdes, 10 May 2019). The focus on singular objects poses a challenge for the conservators because it can be difficult to distinguish between necessary and accidental wear and spots. This makes stabilising and cleaning a complex task because the necessary wear and spots are a crucial part of the object. They constitute its authenticity and identity, which Nanna works toward preserving in her practice. This aim resonates with an ambition expressed by Amalie: 'we wish to make sure that it is possible to open up the boxes after 25, 50, 100 years and still find the same content' (interview with A. Suurballe Schjøtt-Wieth and M. Ploug Risom, 4 April 2019). Ideally, museum objects must remain the same across large timespans. They must reside in a state of permanence – a hypometabolic state between life and death.

The life of objects: towards a state of conserved permanence

When conservators at the museum speak about life in the collections, their discourse traverses literal and metaphorical senses of 'life' located within the tension between the metabolic and the cultural. Ideally, museum objects rest in a permanent and stabilised state of identity and authenticity – a state that suppresses metabolic processes to secure an extension of the cultural life of objects – yet the metabolic always remains a potentially destructive force.

During our conversation, Amalie told an anecdote about a pest-infected object: 'and it was, well I've never seen so many different pests at once. It was just . . . it was alive' (interview with A. Suurballe Schjøtt-Wieth and M. Ploug Risom, 4 April 2019). In this sense, the object was alive when it was crawling with heritage-eaters consuming it. This, however, is precisely the kind of life that conservation practices aim to hinder. In contrast to this biological sense of aliveness, the proper life of a museum object is defined within a cultural-metaphorical sense. As Nanna explained: 'Objects come to life through their history' (interview with N. Gerdes, 10 May 2019). It is the connection to the past, the use of the object and its users that bless it with life. This connection, however, is deeply material. As Nanna explained, one cannot simply restore or clean an object, because wear and dirt are part of its history. Its state of being has been formed by exchanges – users handling it, using it, storing it – as well as by the environment. History is woven together with the object, which becomes an interface between past and present. Fingerprints, dirt and wear become part of the object's surfaces and grant it a capaciousness to tell its life story. However, as Maiken pointed out, the life of a museum object is defined not only by the history it carries but also its relation to the future. That is, the role of the conservator is also to consider 'how to make sure that an object lives as long as possible and that as many generations as possible can enjoy it in its current state' (interview with M. Ploug Risom, 14 March 2019). Just like living organisms, objects have a lifespan, and conservation practices are about extending their life expectancy.

To extend the life of museum objects, they must not be alive either literally or metabolically, yet life-processes constantly interfere with the work of conservation. While the literal sense of life is relegated to the metaphorical, the life of objects continuously transgresses the dichotomy. This transgression links with the tension between ideal and reality that the conservators are negotiating in their practices of care. For them, perpetuity is a regulative ideal. Collections care is marked by the role of the museum as a cultural guardian responsible for the long-term preservation and presenting of culture and community (see also Knell 1994, 2). However, the ideal of preserving objects for eternity is a 'weird obligation', as Amalie expressed it, because the conservators' material knowledge places them within a field of tension between ideal and reality. Nanna expresses this tension when she describes her desire to 'preserve the marks and wear an object carries within itself . . . and say that I would like to preserve it for the future, for the next 100 or 200 years or for perpetuity. . . . or as long as possible, because the materials deteriorate'. Ideally, we isolate objects from the flux of life and save them for the future but, metabolically speaking, objects transform over time. This orientation toward saving inscribes the museum within a temporal ideology drawing lines between past, present and future (Martinon 2006, 158). Museum objects may crop up from hibernation and be put into new contexts such as exhibitions and research, providing new openings. But such openings rely on the museum as a place of endings, where life-processes are halted (ideally, suspended) to stabilise things permanently in their original condition. Life-processes can be devastating and are thus suppressed by a cultural-metaphorical concept of life: things must be kept dead to gain life. Thus, we try to isolate objects from the flux of life and stabilise them in a state of *conserved permanence*.

Beyond conserved permanence: or, what can we learn from fly stock centres and bioart?

Now let us move outside the museum and the self-given value of preserving things in a state of permanence. Taking up Caitlin DeSilvey's invitation 'to think about what could be gained if we were to care for the past without pickling it' (DeSilvey 2017, 188), I intend to destabilise the taken-for-granted ideal of saving for perpetuity. In the rest of this chapter, I explore what would happen if we were to embrace impermanence as an existential condition at the museum. I begin my journey in this section by rethinking the life of an object beyond its cultural-metaphorical sense and correlative state of conserved permanence. First, I use a scientific collection of flies as a backdrop for distinguishing between *conserving* and *culturing*. Second, I explore Thomas Feuerstein's bioart, which pushes us beyond permanence as a regulative ideal. Drawing these two strands together, I will propose *cultured impermanence* as an alternative target state of being for museum objects that may lead to other openings.

Cultured permanence: trapped flies and living collections[4]

At first glance, fly stock centres are very different from museum collections. Yet, despite their differences, both are characterised by a striving for permanence. Both sites share a macroenvironmental focus on temperature, light, humidity, gatekeeping. Furthermore, both sites ideally work with pure units to control the metabolic processes of their collections. For example, most stock centres deal with just a single species of *Drosophila*, to keep standardised stock and their specific characteristics pure (Bangham 2019, 130). To maintain pure units requires that objects be kept in isolation in boxes, vials and jars – vessels of permanence intended to sustain a border between inside and outside and establish a neutral environment for their (organic or inorganic) inhabitants. This renders both museums and fly stock centres sites of controlled metabolism.

However, the processes inside the vessels differ radically. The museum object ideally resides in a hypometabolic state characterised by a subordination of the metabolic to the cultural-metaphorical sense of life. In contrast, a collection of flies is dynamic: the flies eat, digest, sleep, reproduce and pass away. Each fly is not an individual object in its own right but a mere substitutable part of a living culture of flies that depends precisely on their continuous substitution to persist. As Jenny Bangham points out, it has not been possible to suspend cultures by freezing embryos for future use (Bangham 2019, 127). In other words, *Drosophila* resist a state of conserved permanence. The flies are stored in vials that gradually become overpopulated, and stock-keepers flip flies onto new food every two weeks, discarding old food and dead flies (Bangham 2019, 128). Because the adult fly lives for about a month, it is an ongoing process of life and death that maintains the vitality of a collection. Fly stocks depend on maintaining life-processes in a constant flux of destruction and becoming.

While the museum and the fly stock centre both aim at permanence, their materials are radically different and, thus, what it takes to sustain their identities diverges.

Perhaps this divergence can be understood as resembling the difference between an engine and a metabolising system, as described by Jonas. For Jonas, an engine functions by way of machine parts giving passage to fuel (inflow) and waste (outflow) without participating in this flow (Jonas 2001, 76). The engine remains substantially untouched. In contrast, a metabolising system is, itself, the result of its own continuous metabolising activity (Jonas 2001, 76). Yet Jonas' description of the engine takes us back to a mechanistic view of machines characterised by routinised, unaffected activity. Furthermore, his distinction between the living organism and the machine does not adequately apply to the difference between flies and museum objects, because the latter do not remain substantially unaffected by their previous use. The museum object is touched by time and use – its history is adhered to it, which grants it a cultural life. However, Jonas' analogy hints at an important difference when it comes to the identity of the objects. To maintain their identity, living organisms exist in a continuous flux of passing contents. Meanwhile, the identity and authenticity of museum objects rest on stabilising a material state, and metabolic processes may entail loss.

Through our exploration of the fly stock centre, we can now contrast conserved permanence with cultured permanence. While the former seeks to save and limit the exchange of matter, the latter nurtures a sustained *exchange* of matter. In the case of fly stock centres, this culturing secures the permanence of stocks of flies, but, within a museum context, it would lead to unstable collections, deterioration and loss. In the two sites we, thus, see an inverse relationship between the metabolic and the metaphorical senses of life. This difference leads to two radically different practices of care, both attempting to preserve the identity of the objects in stock: *conserving* or *culturing* permanence.

From permanence to impermanence: fungi in Thomas Feuerstein's bioart

The life of objects in museum collections is defined within a cultural-metaphorical sense of life that suppresses the metabolic. This subordinate relationship is reversed in the fly stock centre, where it is precisely biological life that renders scientific-cultural products such as data, results or publications possible. Meanwhile, Thomas Feuerstein's bioart provides an opportunity to push our previous distinctions between the metabolic and the metaphorical senses of life to their limits and think about the radical Other of these collections – impermanence. Feuerstein's work 'One and No Chair' (Figure 16.2) provides an opportunity to reflect

16.2 Thomas Feuerstein, 'One and No Chair', 2002–8. Made of timber *Serpula lacrymans*, plexiglass, stainless steel and aluminium, 170 x 65 x 65 cm. Created with the support of Christian Ebner, Institute of Microbiology, University of Innsbruck.

on what the life of an object could look like beyond the constraints of conserved or cultured permanence. In this section, I explore the unspeakable abyss of impermanence and Feuerstein's practice of *culturing* through his work 'One and No Chair'.

In 'One and No Chair', a wooden chair is broken down by a fungus, *Serpula lacrymans*, that often grows undetected and spreads throughout buildings, destroying wood by breaking down cellulose (Feuerstein 2020). In a piece of personal correspondence, Feuerstein explained how he cultured the work beginning with the cultivation of the fungus in a liquid medium of glucose and malt, storing the parts of the chair in water to reach optimal moisture (Thomas Feuerstein, personal communication). After four months, he assembled the chair and drilled holes in the wood to inject the cell culture before placing it in a greenhouse to prevent it from drying out. While Feuerstein continuously cared for the chair by spraying the surfaces with tap water, nothing was visible to the naked eye for almost two years. Then everything changed rapidly, fruiting bodies sprouted, and the chair had to be supported statically to avoid it breaking into pieces (he had also cultivated a table, which broke overnight!). Finally, after bringing the chair to the brink of collapse, he let it dry out to stop the fungi from growing further before exhibiting it. Consequently, his work transgresses our neatly assembled distinctions of conservation/culturing, metaphorical/metabolic and permanence/impermanence. The metabolic becomes the symbolic, accentuating the fragility of life itself in between permanence and impermanence, and challenging our sense of stability and control in our struggle against entropy.

With 'One and No Chair', Feuerstein is culturing impermanence – he sets in motion an uncontrollable growth within *an aesthetic of entropy*. An aesthetic that follows the dissolution of things and emphasises matter in transition (Feuerstein 2020). This lack of control and predictability is inscribed in the origin of the work. While *Serpula lacrymans* has never been able to form fruiting bodies under artificial lab conditions, in 'One and No Chair' they sprouted. Feuerstein speculates that this probably happened due to the non-sterile conditions in his studio and the changing temperatures of the seasons (T. Feuerstein, pers. comm.). Following Mainländer's description of the *cadaverisation of the world* that 'accepts the entropic flow of all that exists and sweeps aside all conservatisms and retarding moments in order to pave the way for a free flow of decomposition' (Feuerstein 2020), Feuerstein embraces the existential condition of impermanence. As he explains: 'The chair, containing within itself the possibility of not being a chair anymore, becomes a transitional object of decay. It refers to a universal logic of life and eludes the categorical orders of classic philosophy – possession, identity and ontology being subjected to a composting' (Feuerstein 2020). 'One and No Chair' gestures toward the end of the world. Not just the end of the chair but the movement from a state of being to non-being. Consequently, the work confronts our notions of stability, identity and authenticity. This may be frightening – nay, repulsive – for some. This is *cultured impermanence*.

Culturing impermanence at the museum

Now let us return to the museum with a broadened sense of what it means to care. By moving from *conserving* to *culturing*, I have shown how caring does not necessarily entail conserving but can also be associated with nurturing. This is a kind of *caring beyond saving* that responds to DeSilvey's invitation to think of 'care beyond conservation' and remove ourselves from the instinct to 'save at all costs' (DeSilvey 2017, 184). Yet, within a museum collection, caring as nurturing would inevitably lead to loss. This points to a turn from authenticity toward entropy as a culturing of impermanence that no longer aims for an unbroken link of *sameness* between past and present but accentuates the passing of time and the uncertainty of the future. In this section, I discuss this turn in more detail, first, by exploring the conceptual shift from authenticity and identity to difference and entropy, and second, by sketching out the 'Living Room' as an experimental site that embodies this turn in practice.

The turn: from authenticity to entropy

At the museum, the practice of conservation takes place within a tension between permanence and impermanence in an impulse toward stabilising objects in an authentic state. Thus, the 'weird obligation' to preserve for perpetuity is directly linked to authenticity. This is not surprising, because authenticity is a key concept in the museum, often associated with the original material fabric of objects (Mairesse and Peters 2019, 9–10). Sometimes, the material identity is expressed as the 'true nature' or the 'target state' of an object, which carries the evidence of its origin and information on its makers and users and the technology used to manufacture it (Ashley-Smith 1994, 14; Muñoz Viñas 2005, 90). But while the ascription of authenticity plays a key role, when determining the target state of objects to be stabilised, it imports a series of problems. For example, Salvador Muñoz Viñas argues that authenticity is meaningless because one cannot claim that something exists in a non-authentic state: the 'present condition is the only actually authentic condition' (Muñoz Viñas 2005, 94).

However, Muñoz Viñas' critique of the concept of authenticity remains within an overly simplistic binary. Rather, authenticity is what J. L. Austin called a *dimension word*, the meaning of which depends on what dimension of its referent is being described (Dutton 2003, 258). In preservation practices, the ascription of authenticity entails a redefinition of the 'true nature' of objects worth preserving that rests on a privileging of the cultural life of objects while suppressing the metabolic as a disruptive force in collections. Or, as Susan Crane explains, 'objects are frozen in the moment of their most emblematic value, . . . and denied their natural, or intended, decadent lifespan' (Crane 2011, 99). This is where the concept of authenticity pairs up with the striving for permanence and sameness in the maintaining of the identity of the objects. Avoiding loss entails stabilising the physical integrity of the object in a state of permanence deemed authentic.

Yet our conception of loss depends on the ontological frame within which it is thought. As Pip Laurenson explains, when objects are classified and described as authentic within an ontological framework that focuses on material identity, material transformations entail loss (Laurenson 2006). Drawing on the philosophy of difference, however, we soon come to realise that identity is an empty promise. For Heidegger, even the simplest sense of identity as expressed in the principle of identity as $A=A$, the two 'A's are separated spatially by the 'equals' sign, and temporally by the promise that they may coincide (Itzkowitz 1978, 128). While we can talk about time-capsules and future visitors, impermanence is always already trespassing on our sacred ground. Stabilising museum objects relies on mediation, synthesis and unification across time (for example, in registers) and space (for example, in boxes) to resist change. However, as we have seen in the example of the fly stock centres, change can also be a crucial premise for avoiding loss. And, in Feuerstein's 'One and No Chair', the fungus gradually alters the chair; yet, simultaneously, a work grows out of it – a processual sculpture literally acquiring a life of its own. At the museum, bacteria and fungi are usually perceived as agents of destruction affecting museum collections negatively (Gutarowska et al. 2012, 15). Such microorganisms can cause serious damage to heritage objects that may start to deteriorate due to the impact of specific enzymes, cellulases and the like (Valentín 2007, 1). Yet microorganisms play a crucial role in the constant becoming of the world. Moving from authenticity and identity toward entropy and difference entails an ontological reframing of our thinking about the life of objects at the museum, redeeming the literal/metabolic sense of the life of objects and obscuring our notion of consumers (not just people but also, for example, fungi and bacteria). Drawing on Heidegger's unravelling of the verb 'to save', Jean-Paul Martinon describes a different kind of saving that no longer aspires to snatch things from danger but rather lets something become its own nature (Martinon 2019). This is a kind of saving that, perhaps, reverses the privileging of the cultural over the metabolic.

When we move from authenticity to entropy, change no longer means loss. Rather, it becomes a productive force in the constant becoming of the objects. This might sound surprising. Think, for example, of Robert Smithson's explanation of entropy: 'Perhaps a nice succinct definition of entropy would be Humpty Dumpty. Like Humpty Dumpty sat on a wall, Humpty Dumpty had a great fall, all the king's horses and all the king's men couldn't put Humpty Dumpty back together again' (Smithson 1996, 301). This picture of Humpty Dumpty scattered all over the place is disorderly and disturbing. It is in direct opposition to our efforts to conserve or culture permanence. This is entropy – 'the more entropy, the more disorder' (Alberts et al. 2010, G:8). Yet, it can also be seen as proliferation and multiplication. Instead of aiming for a dubious authentic state, culturing impermanence entails nurturing the objects to unfold their otherness temporally. Rather than folding time, which Adrian Van Allen has described as a weaving together of disciplinary histories, transformed specimens and visions for the future in collections through practices of delay (Van Allen 2020), culturing impermanence entails the unfolding of time right before our eyes. Perhaps we can enable other openings at the museum if we diversify our engagement with the life of objects, not restricted to conserving identity and authenticity but also culturing, nurturing, re-growing difference and entropy.

The museum as host: a sketch of 'The Living Room'

At the Medical Museion, we are currently developing 'The Living Room' as an experimental site, where we attempt to establish a truly metabolic collection. Within the 'Living Room', we will explore the lives of objects from frozen hibernation and hypometabolic states to accelerated ageing and deterioration, at different levels. From the microscopic world of fungi, bacteria and microbiota to macro-environmental factors such as temperature, humidity and light; and across the organic/inorganic divide – diverse materials and their variable lives and deaths. Such explorations will revolve around processual installations and experiments in constant

CULTURING IMPERMANENCE AT THE MUSEUM   287

flux, accelerating or extending life-processes, exchanging and transforming, growing and de-growing. In the following, I will briefly sketch out our idea to develop a composting box that nurtures decomposition and the proliferation of things into multiple modes of existence.[5]

Imagine a sealed glass box containing objects: deaccessioned objects from the museum collections, defective and disposable objects used in labs, and objects that did not make it into the museum collections but were kept in storage. They are made of plastic, rubber, steel, paper, aluminium or wood. Objects in the box are not to be sealed off from the elements but rather exposed to them inside the box – *the inside becomes the outside*. In an exposure that the museum would usually do everything to prevent from the inside environment, this is a box that breaks all the rules. Now you might expect that conservators at the museum would be hostile toward this idea but, perhaps because of their working within the tension between the metaphorical and metabolic senses of life, they have a deep fascination with material processes and are eager to contribute to the project with their knowledge of processes of decay. In a collaboration between conservators, scientists and artists, we will carefully design a microclimate within the box to accelerate processes of deterioration. The performance of deterioration in the ageing of objects is accelerated by climatic and microbial agents such as heat, cold, humidity and light as well as microbes such as fungi and bacteria. Microbes thus act as heritage-eaters, turning the box into a metabolic time-machine and making the passing of time visible. The box is intended to expose objects and visitors to a time passing – accelerating its difference-making effects on things that seem more solid than our bodies – and gestures toward the inevitable end of everything.

Hosting life within the box turns into an aesthetic incarnation of the passing of time itself. Perhaps paradoxically, the items exposed in the box acquire a second life. However, even in its accelerated form, decomposition develops slowly. To increase the difference-making effect, the installation could be supported by time-lapse photography, sound recordings of deterioration processes and surreal lab protocols as multi-sensory methods. Through such methods, the objects in the box would proliferate into multiple *modes of existence* – for example, as food, habitat, images, sounds and stories. These states of being enable the objects to transgress the dichotomy between permanence and impermanence, simultaneously acquiring permanent and impermanent forms. The end also becomes a beginning. This proliferation, however, would not accommodate the sense of loss expressed by the tragic 'Æv!!' in the case of the strawberry-coloured wig. But if the wig had entered 'The Living Room', we could have done more with it. More than just a nutritive habitat for the maggots, it could have proliferated into multiple modes of existence. The de-growth of an object through accelerated metabolic processes also turns into a *re-growth* and a proliferation of states of being. Culturing becomes preservation. The objects become part of the pervasive entanglement of the (im)permanent cycle of life and death, establishing a metabolic connection.

Multiplying the lives of objects at the museum

Collections are always more metabolic than we like to think. Yet, at the museum, the metabolic life of objects is usually suppressed by a metaphorical sense of their rich cultural (after)life. In this chapter, I have challenged this self-given inclination to save at all costs and explored what might happen if we no longer aimed at suppressing the life-processes in collections. Instead of automatically pairing caring with saving, I have called for a multiplication of our practices of care, including a kind of caring closer to nurturing. Within our usual ontological framework, this reframing will appear troubling because material change entails loss. However, I propose we rethink this framework, with its inherent resistance to change, and realise the potential in redeeming the metabolic from its suppression under the reign of permanence. What I suggest is to multiply practices of caring for collections in ways that do not prejudge life-processes as destructive within the pre-given temporal ideology of permanence – an ideology that rests on the significance of identity and authenticity and resists difference and entropy. But I must stress that my intention here is precisely to argue for a *multiplication* of practices of caring and, correlatively, a proliferation of modes of existence of objects. Thus, my aim is not to expose and replace our traditional values of preservation but rather to develop a reparative critique that offers more – multiplying our senses of the lives of objects at the museum, beyond the ideal of stasis.[6] What I propose, then, is not to work toward the end of our collections but to show how the multiplication of the modes of existence of museum objects does not necessarily entail loss but can lead to proliferation and re-growth. Or, if we return to the strawberry-coloured wig, I believe it exemplifies something we could have done differently: we could have cared for it with an attitude other than 'preserving' and 'saving'. For the lost wig is not merely a story of a patient in pain with the added dimension of conservation practices. It is also a story about how our conservation practices may become destructive in our attempt to preserve our collections. Because of a temporal ideology of permanence, it ended up as garbage, whereas it could perhaps have become a new opening, offering a heightened sense of materiality and vulnerability. Presence and distance of the past. Permanence, ephemerality and temporality. Life and death.

Notes

1 Thanks to Niels Jakob, a historian working at the Medical Museion, for unearthing the example with the wig (object no. 10340) from the archives.
2 My development of a 'metabolic analytic' in this chapter is indebted to ongoing conversations with Adam Bencard, Jens Hauser and Louise Whiteley. See Bencard et al. 2020 for a first manifestation of our collaboration and a sketch of what we have tentatively called *metabolic humanities*.
3 A special thanks to Amalie, Anders, Maiken and Nanna for participating in the interviews. The interviews were conducted in Danish in the collections at the Medical Museion, Copenhagen. All translations are mine.
4 I wish to thank Ole Kjærulff, leader of the Drosophila lab at Neuroscience at the University of Copenhagen, for commenting on this section.
5 The idea of composting originated in a conversation with Caitlin DeSilvey during the 'Inevitable Ends' conference held in Aarhus, 2–4 May 2019.
6 For more on this alternative form of critique, see, for instance, Sedgwick 1997 and Latour 2004.

References

Alberts, Bruce, Dennis Bray, Karen Hopkin and Alexander Johnson. 2010. *Essential Cell Biology*. New York and London: Garland Science.
Ashley-Smith, Jonathan. 1994. 'The ethics of conservation'. In *Care of Collections*, edited by Simon Knell, 11–20. London: Routledge.
Bangham, Jenny. 2019. 'Living collections: Care and curation at drosophila stock centres', *BJHS Themes* 4: 123–47.
Barad, Karen. 2007. *Meeting the Universe Halfway: Quantum physics and the entanglement of matter and meaning*. Durham, NC: Duke University Press.
Bencard, Adam, Martin Grünfeld, Jens Hauser and Louise Whiteley, eds. 2020. *Stofsk(r)ifter: Metabolic machines*. Copenhagen: Medical Museion.
Bennett, Jane. 2010. *Vibrant Matter: A political ecology of things*. Durham, NC: Duke University Press.
Bing, Franklin C. 1971. 'The history of the word "metabolism"', *Journal of the History of Medicine and Allied Sciences* 26(2): 158–80.
Crane, Susan A. 2011. 'The conundrum of ephemerality: Time, memory, and museums'. In *A Companion to Museum Studies*, edited by Sharon Macdonald, 98–109. Chichester: Wiley-Blackwell.
DeSilvey, Caitlin. 2017. *Curated Decay*. Minneapolis, MN: University of Minnesota Press.
Dupré, John, and Maureen A. O'Malley. 2009. 'Varieties of living things: Life at the intersection of lineage and metabolism', *Philosophy, Theory, and Practice in Biology* 1(3). http://dx.doi.org/10.3998/ptb.6959004.0001.003.
Dutton, Denis. 2003. 'Authenticity in art'. In *The Oxford Handbook of Aesthetics*, edited by Jerrold Levinson, 258–74. Oxford and New York: Oxford University Press.
Feuerstein, Thomas. 2020. 'The aesthetics of entropy'. http://www.myzel.net/Myzel/index.en.html (last accessed 20 October 2021).
Gerdes, Nanna. 2019. Interview by Martin Grünfeld. 10 May. Medical Museion's collections.

Grünfeld, Martin. 2020a. 'Pancreas'. In *Stofsk(r)ifter: Metabolic machines*, edited by Adam Bencard, Martin Grünfeld, Jens Hauser and Louise Whiteley, 27–48. Copenhagen: Medical Museion.

Grünfeld, Martin. 2020b. *Writing and Thinking in Contemporary Academia: The poetics of clarity*. London: Routledge.

Gutarowska, Beata, Justyna Skora, Katarzyna Zduniak and Daria Rembisz. 2012. 'Analysis of the sensitivity of microorganisms contaminating museums and archives to silver nanoparticles', *International Biodeterioration & Biodegradation* 68: 7–17.

Itzkowitz, Kenneth. 1978. 'Differance and identity', *Research in Phenomenology* 8: 127–43.

Jonas, Hans. 2001. *The Phenomenon of Life: Toward a philosophical biology*. Evanston, IL: Northwestern University Press.

Knell, Simon, ed. 1994. *Care of Collections*. London: Routledge.

Landecker, Hannah. 2013. 'The metabolism of philosophy, in three parts'. In *Dialectic and Paradox: Configurations of the third in modernity*, edited by Ian Cooper and Bernhard Malkmus, 193–224. Bern: Peter Lang.

Latour, Bruno. 2004. 'Why has critique run out of steam? From matters of fact to matters of concern', *Critical Inquiry* 30(2): 225–48.

Laurenson, Pip. 2006. 'Authenticity, change and loss in the conservation of time-based media installations', *Tate Papers* 6. https://www.tate.org.uk/research/publications/tate-papers/06/authenticity-change-and-loss-conservation-of-time-based-media-installations (last accessed 20 October 2021).

Mairesse, François, and Renata F. Peters, eds. 2019. *What Is the Essence of Conservation? Materials for a discussion*. Paris: ICOFOM.

Martinon, Jean-Paul. 2006. 'Museums, plasticity, temporality', *Museum Management and Curatorship* 21(2): 157–67.

Martinon, Jean-Paul. 2019. 'Saved! The Future of Museums', unpublished conference paper, Collections, Knowledge and Time, Medical Museion, Copenhagen, 9 November 2019.

Maturana, Humberto R., and Francisco J. Varela. 1980. *Autopoiesis and Cognition: The realization of the living*. Dordrecht and London: Reidel.

Merleau-Ponty, Maurice. 1968. *The Visible and the Invisible*. Evanston, IL: Northwestern University Press.

Morgan, Jennie, and Sharon Macdonald. 2018. 'De-growing museum collections for new heritage futures', *International Journal of Heritage Studies* 15(1): 1–15.

Muñoz Viñas, Salvador. 2005. *Contemporary Theory of Conservation*. Oxford: Butterworth-Heinemann.

Otero-Pailos, Jorge. 2016. 'Experimental preservation: The potential of not-me creations'. In *Experimental Preservation*, edited by Jorge Otero-Pailos, Erik Langdalen and Thordis Arrhenius, 11–39. Zürich: Lars Müller.

Pearce, Susan M. 1999. *On Collecting*. London: Routledge.

Ploug Risom, Maiken. 2019. Interview by Martin Grünfeld, March 14. Medical Museion's collections.

Sedgwick, Eve Kosofsky. 1997. 'Paranoid reading and reparative reading: Or, you're so paranoid, you probably think this introduction is about you'. In *Novel Gazing: Queer readings in fiction*, edited by Eve K. Sedgwick, 1–40. Durham, NC, and London: Duke University Press.

Smithson, Robert. 1996. 'Entropy made visible'. In *Robert Smithson: The collected writings*, edited by Jack Flam, 301–9. Berkeley, CA: University of California Press.

Suurballe Schjøtt-Wieth, Amalie, and Maiken Ploug Risom. 2019. Interview by Martin Grünfeld, April 4. Medical Museion's collections.

Valentín, Nieves. 2007. 'Microbial contamination in archives and museums: Health hazards and preventive strategies using air ventilation systems'. Contribution to the experts' roundtable on sustainable climate management strategies (Tenerife, Spain, April 2007).

Van Allen, Adrian. 2020. 'Folding time: Practices of preservation, temporality and care in making bird specimens'. In *Deterritorializing the Future: Heritage in, of and after the Anthropocene*, edited by Rodney Harrison and Colin Sterling, 120–54. London: Open Humanities Press.

17
Screenshooting impermanence

Winnie Soon and Sarah Schorr

Images were being appropriated
Images were being uploaded
Images were being censored
Images were being leaked
Images were being stored
Images were being circulated
Images were being reproduced
Images were being formatted
Images were being displayed
Images were being erased
Images were being traced
Images were cherished
Images were detested and banned
Images were being found
Images were being captured
Images disappeared
Images were being wanted
Images were being queried
Images were being datafied
Images were being organised
Images were being sorted
Images were being computed
Images were being selected
Images were being timed
Images were being collaged
Images were being exhibited
Images were being seen

Images were on our skin
Images have different and multiple stages
Images have different versions
Images have different status
Images have different affordances
Images do not have a single author
Images are hardly captured
Images are materials
Images are unpredictable
Images are always changing
Images are performative

..

Post-digital image practice

Images are not still. Printed images fade. Operative images perform (Farocki 2004). 'Poor images' circulate (Steyel 2009). Coded images are constantly being updated, and the list goes on. How does the lens of impermanence alter how we frame our thinking about images? We explore this question via two art installations, 'Unerasable Images' (Soon 2019) and 'Saving Screens: Temporary Tattoos and Other Methods' (Schorr 2019), each of which explores the realm of hybrid post-digital image practices.

Rather than focusing on the technological advancement and innovation that are imposed on images, we position this chapter within the wider post-digital culture to reflect on the imperfections and ruptures that the imposition of technology can bring. The post-digital perspective is a genre of study in the areas of contemporary art, aesthetics and digital culture (Cramer 2014; Berry and Dieter 2015; Betancourt 2016; Menkman 2011). The term *post-digital* does not describe the end of the digital but rather refers to what Florian Cramer describes as 'more subtle cultural shifts and ongoing mutations' that are 'caused by the computerization and global digital networking of communication, technical infrastructures, markets and geopolitics' (Cramer 2014, 13). More specifically, the term 'post-digital' embraces the imperfections, such as glitches and failures, as opposed to only the changes wrought by high-speed production and 'high-tech and high-fidelity cleanness' (Cramer 2014, 14). This perspective of image practice as simultaneously both analogue and digital is present in our artwork. Using (wo)manual application and vintage projection (Schorr's attention to the tactile application of tattoos and Soon's focus on physical materials of a carousel projector/slides), the projects intersect at the juncture of disruption, altering image flow and image production to create space for reflection on the impermanence of capture and the impossibility of perfection.

Screenshooting is the act of digitalisation and presentation on a physical screen that captures 'life online' (Schorr and Soon 2020). We intentionally use the term *screenshooting* over *screenshotting* to connote an act of capturing computer screens. It alludes to the contemporary photo-shooting practice and we acknowledge that the term *shooting* has a violent metaphorical association similar to 'grab' and 'capture', for instance (Schorr and Soon 2020). When we use the screenshot command (which includes keyboard variations allowing full or selected partial image capture and is often accompanied by a shutter sound), we enact a set of physical gestures that create a recognisable sound – igniting, for many, a memory or association: the click of a camera. These human gestures produce a tangible digital image in a near-to-perfect representation of the screen content. However, capturing any dirt or dust on a screen (see Figure 17.1) is impossible with these commands as screenshooting operates beyond software. The act of screenshooting gives preference to a polished and (near-) perfect representation and makes us forget the physicality and materiality of a digital image, unlike analogue practices such as printed photographs, physical slides and cassette tapes, which allow for accidental imperfections (such as concrete noises/glitches/dust) to be highlighted as part of the experience.

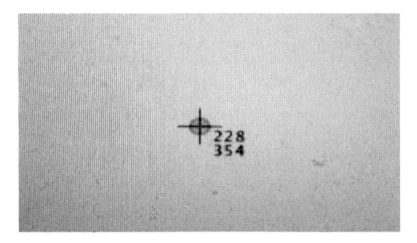

17.1 The screenshot of a dirty screen with a mobile phone, 2017. © Winnie Soon.

Softening 'fixed time' in an image

Tracing the connections between photographic practices is a non-linear pursuit. Why use photographic practices to reflect on impermanence and time slippage? In the Introduction, the editors of this volume reflect on the conflict they face as curators of an exhibition about impermanence; they are both collecting objects to care for while pursuing the theory of how all of the collections decay and change. In the field of photography, those same tensions exist, and, through tracing methods back to the painting practices that preceded photography practices, it is evident that photographic modes have been preoccupied with the subject of time passing. Susan Sontag once claimed that photographs could possess the past (1977). André Bazin (1960) and Roland Barthes (1980) likened photo practices to funeral embalming practices. John Berger wrote, in *Ways of Seeing*, that 'it became evident that an image could outlast what it represented' (Berger 1973, 10).

The realisation that images have the capacity to outlast what they originally represented includes the tacit acknowledgement that there are infinite ways in which images themselves mutate. Photographic images change from the very moment of their creation, with alterations of context, exchange and material deterioration. Even as the mechanics of image-production advance, photographers active in the field note that each new improvement holds its own imperfections. Just as dust invaded and altered the sanctuary of darkroom practices, digital files are vulnerable to electronic degradation and glitches.

In the context of the screenshot, a notable attribute is the speed of the inherent changes taking place within the file. For instance, JPEGs have a narrower range of features than RAW files, so it is expected that a generated JPEG on-screen will be no better than the original RAW file. However, depending on what features were used to record the original RAW data, it is still possible to notice issues in the Colour Depth (Sampling) or Colour Space (Gamut) or Image Data Compression, especially when printing. These files are both active and changing in different ways: they are certainly not still, even if they appear to be on the screen surface. And, as noted by Hoelzl and Marie, 'as a tentative view of networked databases, the image is constantly updated and refreshed' (2015, 3). This constant change and circulation of digital images enable countless adaptations and reappropriations (Steyel 2009).

Portability, or the relative immediacy of each image-exchange, is another quality that is particular to a screenshot image: in a screenshot, the file size is so small that the proximity of sharing is nearly instantaneous. In addition to the actual sharing, partial screenshot selection tools enable the image recipient to *crop* pictures with options that are extremely malleable. This makes the screenshot akin to a pencil gesture drawing – the loose form of sketching in which an artist attempts to capture a subject's basic form and express movement by allowing the hand to sketch, capturing what is seen with the eye without looking down at the paper. We consider how photographic images in the post-digital era can be altered not only when they are networked or printed or moistened and applied to the skin but also when they are considered in light of their context, portability and malleability. As such, we consider screenshooting as both an example of post-digital practice as well as a departure point for post-digital image practices, reflecting on the imperfections by printing the screenshots as tattoos that are applied to the human body and by developing photographic slides that are then viewed via a carousel projector. The following will introduce the two artworks that were exhibited in 'ScreenShots: Desire and Automated Image', curated by Magdalena Tyżlik-Carver in 2019 at Galleri Image in Denmark (Galleri Image 2019).

Winnie Soon: 'Unerasable Images' (2019)

This installation (see Figure 17.2) involved chronologically ordered slides that were placed in the two wooden boxes and a continuously looped carousel projector projecting one image at a time, per second. The slide images were a collection of screenshots taken almost every day in 2017 using the same keywords search: *6* and *4* in Chinese characters. This is a reference to the date *June Fourth* in 1989. These words as characters are also considered to be *sensitive keywords*, referring commonly to the incident of the student-led protest as well as the Tiananmen Square Massacre in Beijing. The search was specifically designed to find the Lego re-creation of the famous 'tank man' scene (see Figure 17.3). This image was originally published on a Chinese web portal in 2013 but was erased within 24 hours by censoring machines. However, this low resolution of 'poor image' (Steyel 2009) was still searchable outside of China after four years. It continued to be identified by the Google image-search platform following its erasure, occasionally appearing on the first few rows of results. The process of searching for (and recording the search for) this image illustrates the nature of post-digital images, in which they can be seen/unseen, revered/censored,

17.2 The installation view of 'Unerasable Images', 2019. © Winnie Soon.

17.3 The Lego reconstruction of the 'tank man' scene, 2018. © Winnie Soon.

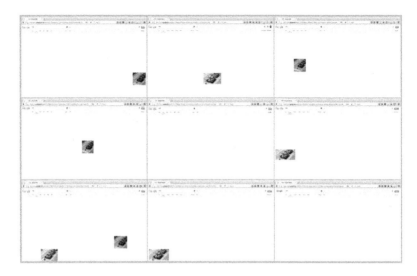

17.4 Nine selected images from 'Unerasable Images', 2018. © Winnie Soon.

stored/deleted, (re)produced/erased, leaked/circulated and, more importantly, regulated, governed, prioritised and controlled algorithmically via digital infrastructures, such as a firewall, software and grid interface design.

To exemplify the ever-changing status of the image, the collected screenshots were reappropriated to erase all the other image results from the search, leaving only the Lego 'tank man'. Such repetitive screenshooting and image reappropriation allowed for observation and contemplation of the constant changes. The presence/absence of the image is reminiscent of the memorial event as an ongoing resistance practice to remember and not to forget. Perhaps we can refer to this as 'presence in absence' (Runia 2006, 20), in which resistance is still there even though the image is absent from the representational search interface. To screenshoot the impermanence of the image-search is to also capture the ephemerality of images persistently regarding geopolitical sites, networked relationalities and the unknowable algorithmic processes that are operationalised within and beyond the screenshot frames. As a result, the collected and reappropriated screenshots were manifested as a 'slow' animation of moving images, projecting monumentalising loops of poor images on the gallery wall (see Figure 17.2).

Following the installation setup, the screenshots were transformed into physical slides to create a deeper reflection on image generation and reproduction across digital and analogue media, such as images that are uploaded in the East that are censored, that are leaked to the West, that are reproduced as thumbnails, that are moved, that appeared and disappeared from the grid, that are captured digitally as screenshots, that are developed as slides, and that are projected on the wall. The use of a post-digital device for presentation – slides illuminated by a carousel projector – slowed things down and reoriented viewers from the crisp, quiet representation format of PowerPoint-driven digital presentation to the visual imperfections and noisy interruptions of slides made from film and run by a timing device that prompts a very mechanical process (and the accompanying audible rattling) for the up/down slide changes and the off/on lamp switch. The entirety of the audio-visual experience investigates what has been remembered, forgotten and transformed in post-digital culture as well as what has been taken for granted in digital media.

This installation highlights the cultural influence of the digital materiality of screenshots and the desire to produce polished and perfect images that resist degradation. After prolonged use, the mechanical parts of the projector produced an audibly irritating, high-pitched sound, requiring disassembly, dust removal and lubricant application. Additionally, many individual slides had scratches and/or dust on the surface; it is simply impossible to present a perfect representation of the digital screenshots at any moment in time but the use of post-digital slides exemplifies disruptive moments of degradation. I argue that acknowledging the imperfection is part of the ontological condition of continuous change (introduction to this volume). In this way, impermanence was inherently present in the gallery space via the relationalities of images, including the networked images, digital and manipulated screenshots, photographic slides, and projected and moving images, that are always changing but also foster remembering. The title of the work 'Unerasable Images' calls attention to what can (and cannot) be erased and invites speculation on the potential transformational force that is generated across space and time from the original censored image.

Sarah Schorr: 'Saving Screens: Temporary Tattoos and Other Methods' (2019)

Set under a garish blinking LED light announcing 'TATTOO' that was reminiscent of 1970s ink parlours, gallery visitors were offered the opportunity to participate in my performance work, 'Sharing Screens:

17.5 Sarah Schorr applies a tattoo during a performance and exhibition at Galleri Image in Aarhus, Denmark, 2019. © Sarah Schorr.

Temporary Tattoos and Other Methods'. In this pre-COVID-19 installation, each visitor was personally invited to receive a digitally stitched tattoo that was created from screenshots from my recently deceased father's digital life. My father, Mark Schorr, was a poet whose work was captured in print, on the Web, in emails, through texts and in song. After his passing, collecting a great deal of source material and screenshots became a method for recording the pieces of his digital life that held affective resonance for me. These observed visual moments captured parts of his personality that were not recordable in words: they functioned as micro-observations of the pieces and elements of his creative process. The collections of screenshots grew into collages of digital life that were facilitated by the ease and speed of the screenshot. I cut each tattoo out by hand and tested all the ink levels by hand. Due to the particular printer used, the first print of the tattoos appeared more indigo than the screen rendering: this printer glitch caused me to reflect on a particular wistful beauty of this process of sorting and capturing, and I printed the rest of the tattoos with a bluish cast. The tattoos featured scraps of my father's poems, songs and messages framed by digital images of his Apple Watch or embedded in the shape of a butterfly, likening the capture process to the old-fashioned pastime of butterfly-catching (see Figure 17.6).

17.6 Sarah Schorr's screenshot temporary tattoos are installed in the gallery to mimic the practice of putting butterflies in cases, 2019. © Sarah Schorr.

My method for this performance developed because I had realised that something of my father's essence remained in his devices and I was resistant to erasing them totally after he passed away. However, saving the data felt limiting. How to save what could not easily be described? This process was about combing through what José van Dijk called 'the shoebox and the desktop' (2007, 15). My impulse to screenshoot was not just about preserving the memory of my father: through screenshooting his online presence and scanning his devices, my knowledge of my dad was remembered and (already) evolving.

I discovered three salient components to honouring the release of my father through this installation. First, the temporary tattoos highlighted the temporal nature of practices that seem (or purport) to be permanent. All tattoos fade. Tattoo artists make mistakes, they misspell. And live, interactive public performance cannot prescribe perfection. Ideas of making homage to importance often miss the mark. All things are impermanent. Second, even though screenshots are easily and quickly taken, I sought to slow the photographic process down by employing a hybrid post-digital process. The exercise was grounded in a deep

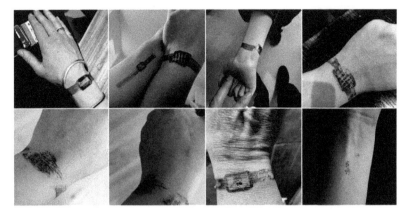

17.7 Participants record their tattoos as they fade and email them to Sarah Schorr to be included in the exhibition, 2019. © Sarah Schorr.

appreciation for photographic methods, from the photogram to the networked screenshot, to reflect on post-digital practices. The creation of an interactive performance created space for reflection on how these lens and screen practices informed each other. Finally, the installation served as a platform for externalising all of the tiny but potent images that had been collected; a conversation was thus started about how complex images fade.

Everyone experiences loss

Every interested visitor was invited to sit with me (see Figure 17.5). Each tattoo application involved cotton swabs and conversation as I held wrists, biceps or forearms in my hands. Not only did visitors physically hold photos in their hands but images were also affixed to their skin. In each application process, I resisted the urge to rush. Participants were given time to reflect on what screenshots capture and how they capture. I also invited them to send photographs (see Figure 17.7) to me as the tattoos faded, leaving trace elements of expression from the experience.

In the Introduction to this volume, loss is recognised as the condition of the entire world. Although this project was conceived during a period of bereavement, the project focus has been less about loss and more about the practice of learning how to let go, even as that process is permeated with the impulse to save.

Afterword

Capturing practices often walk the line between resisting impermanence and being inherently impermanent. Soon and Schorr's installations used screenshots to address impermanence and to further understand digital practices by engaging with low-tech materials and devices.

Both the material nature of images as well as the images themselves are impermanent. We share an interest in the process of capturing the ephemerality of objects on a computer screen as images that then serve as source 'poor materials' for further composition, remixing and reappropriation (Steyel 2009). This mixed-method approach also opens a pathway to further reflection on the nature of captured objects as instances of time and moments of operation in our digital culture with the observation that these objects and the images are also constantly changing, mutating and evolving, like the various devices we used to create the installation. Our smartphones, tablets and computers are static devices, yet, when left on but unused, can still continue actively scanning for Wi-Fi signals, updates and other autonomous functions. In other words, we are exploring ways to expose the impermanent nature of images and devices that merely *appear* to be still inactive.

Though we, as artists, each have a distinct perspective, our two artworks depart from collective and individual memorial events and further create a dialogue based on post-digital image practice in which to produce different forms of resistance and memorials. Through reflection, manipulation and sense-making of screenshots, we examine the impermanence of the image through externalisation of theoretical/ technological observation: for this process, we attempt to perform impermanence in a gallery setting. Screenshooting has the potential to be overlooked as a method of enquiry; however, through the emotive connection to the subject matter (the resonant poetry of a father, the unsettling nature of political dissonance), we explore the screenshot as a mode of expression that has a distinct, multifaceted and fluidly changing position in post-digital culture.

References

Barthes, Roland. [1980] 1981. *Camera Lucida: Reflections on photography*. New York: Hill and Wang.

Bazin, André, and Hugh Gray. 1960. 'The ontology of the photographic image', *Film Quarterly* 13: 4–9.

Berger, John. 1973. *Ways of Seeing*. New York: Viking Press.

Berry, David M., and Michael Dieter. 2015. 'Thinking postdigital aesthetics: Art, computation and design'. In *Postdigital Aesthetics: Art, computation and design*, edited by David M. Berry and Michael Dieter, 1–11. London: Palgrave Macmillan.

Betancourt, Michael. 2016. *Glitch Art in Theory and Practice: Critical failures and post-digital aesthetics*. New York: Routledge.

Cramer, Florian. 2014. 'What is 'post-digital?" *A Peer Reviewed Journal About Research Refusal* 3(1). https://doi.org/10.7146/aprja.v3i1.116068.

Farocki, Harun. 2004. 'Phantom images', *PUBLIC* 29: 12–22.

Hoelzl, Ingrid, and Remi Marie. 2015. *Softimage: Towards a new theory of the digital image*. Bristol and Chicago: Intellect.

Galleri Image. 2019. 'Screenshots: Desire and automated image'. http://www.galleriimage.dk/index.php/en/upcoming/event/257 (last accessed 29 October 2021).

Menkman, Rosa. 2011. *The Glitch Moment (um)*. Amsterdam: Network Notebooks.

Runia, Eelco. 2006. 'Presence', *History and Theory* 45(1): 1–29.

Schorr, Sarah. 2019. 'Saving Screens: Temporary Tattoos and Other Methods' (installation). https://www.sarahschorr.com/Artist.asp?ArtistID=49550&Akey=48347V9L&ajx=1#!Group1_Pf193725 (last accessed 30 October 2021).

Schorr, Sarah, and Winnie Soon. 2020. 'Screenshooting Life Online: Two artworks'. In *Metaphors of Internet: Ways of being in the age of ubiquity,* edited by Annette N. Markham and Katrin Tiidenberg. New York: Peter Lang.

Sontag, Susan. 1977. *On Photography*. London: Penguin Books.

Soon, Winnie. 2018. 'Unerasable images', *Technoculture* 8. https://tcjournal.org/vol8/soon (last accessed 22 October 2021).

Soon, Winnie. 2019. 'Unerasable Images' (installation). http://siusoon.net/unerasable-images/ (last accessed 22 October 2021).

Steyel, Hito. 2009. 'In defense of the poor image', *e-flux* 10. https://www.e-flux.com/journal/10/61362/in-defense-of-the-poor-image/ (last accessed 22 October 2021).

van Dijck, José. 2007. *Mediated Memories in the Digital Age*. Redwood City, CA: Stanford University Press.

18
'Museum of Impermanence': the making of an exhibition

Ulrik Høj Johnsen, Ton Otto and Cameron David Warner

On 9 February 2019, Moesgaard Museum in Aarhus, Denmark, opened the exhibition 'Museum of Impermanence: Stories from Nepal, Papua New Guinea and Tibet', which lasted until 19 May 2019. The exhibition was curated by Ton Otto, Cameron David Warner and Ulrik Høj Johnsen, all from Aarhus University and participants in the research project 'Precious Relics: Materiality and Value in the Practice of Ethnographic Collection', of which this exhibition was an integral part.[1] In the following, we introduce our reflections on the exhibition, including its collaborative ambitions and design concepts. We present how we endeavoured to make impermanence tangible, and think through the results of our collaborations in the places we conducted our field projects and within Moesgaard Museum itself.

Nothing lasts forever: in our lives, we experience the decay and loss of precious possessions and we witness the disappearance of cherished ways of life. We suffer from illness, ageing and death. But change can also be freeing. New art-forms rush to fill the spaces iconoclasm leaves behind. Some seeds only sprout after a devastating fire. The experience that everything inevitably changes and the self-conscious struggle with that realisation is what we wished to capture by naming the exhibition 'Museum of Impermanence'. As humans, we often try to find ways *to keep impermanence at bay*. We hold on to things by repairing and preserving them. We maintain our traditions or even reinvent them. And we spend so much effort and money to extend our lives. But, alternatively, we can also appreciate slow change as progress, celebrate innovation and even pursue radical transformation. The different reactions to the challenge of impermanence lead to different kinds of temporalities, orientations in time that may range from an obsessive fixation on continuity to a reckless embrace of change. A certain type of temporality may become dominant in the cultural traditions of groups and societies, and we may identify such a situation as characterised by a specific historicity (Hartog 2015; and see Introduction to this volume).

Museums are institutions that specialise in the preservation of objects and audio-visual materials they deem valuable. By keeping things that otherwise would have vanished or will disappear in the future, *museums respond to impermanence by attempting to secure a source of knowledge for future use.* In our exhibition, we took another approach: we wished to create an experience and appreciation of impermanence among our visitors. To this end, we mixed old and new collections to sensorially and intellectually evoke how different people – in Nepal, Papua New Guinea and the Tibetan diaspora – deal with impermanence. Some try to counter impermanence through repetitive rituals, the employment of long-lasting materials and the re-use of traditional forms of expression. Others believe that impermanence is unavoidable and therefore ought to be reconfigured as the positive potential embedded in processes of change. In this exhibition, we endeavoured to begin a dialogue on impermanence with visitors through Buddhist lamas making and unmaking a sand maṇḍala, young people from Tibet and Papua New Guinea embracing life by creatively mixing old and new into their own forms of expression, and Newar Buddhists and Hindus placing the emphasis in cultural preservation on process, over attachment to material expressions of their culture.

Exhibition-making is not just a means of communicating research results. It is also, and to a large extent, a means of conducting collaborative research. Obviously, collaboration begins in the field among artists, performers, villagers and urbanites, ritual specialists, curators, preservationists, activists, students, librarians and many others. At some stage, we find ourselves nearing the dissemination phase of a research project, where collaboration brings together architects, carpenters, scenographers, photographers, videographers, marketers, security guards, conservators, and us, the curators. In all of those meetings, the potential museumgoer loiters, silent, and yet half-visible. Ideally, the museum visitors figure as our final, essential, collaborators, for what is an exhibition without them? Therefore, as we searched for common ground to connect our various subprojects, the idea of a 'Museum of Impermanence' emerged as not only an innovative way to work visually but also to engage the predominantly Danish audience that visits the Moesgaard Museum.

New museology and collaboration

One of the central objectives of museums is to preserve objects and knowledge from, and about, the past for future generations (Ginsburch and Mairesse 1997). As such, museums are institutions that aspire to continuity of knowledge through their collections. Nevertheless, the museum as an institution is in a state of regular change. Since the birth of the 'modern museum' in the eighteenth century (Bennett 1995), the aims and trajectories of museums as institutions have taken several twists and turns. This applies, not least, to ethnographic museums. A major turn unfolded from the 1980s with the advent of the *new museology* (Vergo 1989; Lavine and Karp 1991; Peers and Brown 2003; Philips 2005; Coombes and Philips 2015; Thomas 2016). This new museology, or *critical museology*, set novel standards for how to conceptualise ethnographic museums and the potential of their collections. Ethnographic museums increasingly became conceptualised as contact zones (Clifford 1997), whose significance and potential are anchored less in retrospective understandings through artefacts than in the idea of museums as ongoing historical, political and moral relationships. What the museum collections represent, in other words, became less important than the relationships they afford, and ethnographic museums have been conceptualised as sites of 'reconciliation and social change' (Allen and Hamby 2011), 'dialogue, debate, healing and advocacy for social justice' (Coombes and Philips 2015), 'mediation, in-betweenness, brokerage and compromise' (Basu 2017), as well as 'sites of analysis' (Thomas 2016). As such, museums have been sites of contested histories, claims of restitution and repatriation, even pain and suffering.

In particular, the new museological winds induced an increased sensitivity among ethnographic museum curators and museum anthropologists toward the descendants of the people from whom the collections were obtained, the so-called originating communities or source communities (Thomas 2016; Peers and Brown 2003; Curtis 2006). From the 1990s, ethnographic museums in the Global North increasingly engaged themselves in collaborative and participatory engagements with members of originating communities in the Global South (Peers and Brown 2003; Philips 2005; Macdonald 2006). It became a trend in ethnographic museums to invite people, mostly artists, from these originating communities to perform their various arts in the ethnographic museums. This attentiveness toward the originating communities reached beyond a need for more engaging exhibitions; it also constituted a broadening of the horizons, in view of which the artefacts could and should be exhibited, represented and explained. New ways of understanding the artefacts, new epistemologies and new ontologies came to the fore based on the idea of collaboration, sharing of curatorial authority and co-creation of knowledge. This reflects broader tendencies in anthropology suggesting an experimental, collaborative and engaged approach to the generation of anthropological knowledge (Marcus 2010, 2012, 2013).

Taking our exhibition as a site of analysis (Thomas 2016), the three researchers in the Precious Relics project have explored the co-generation of knowledge through an experimental approach to exhibition-making (Basu and Macdonald 2006). Each researcher committed to the same method wherein artefacts were first virtually repatriated through photographs and videos, followed by discussions and co-curated exhibitions in our fieldsites, which contributed to decisions regarding the acquisition of new artefacts and subsequent representation in 'Museum of Impermanence'. During this process, we followed three overall strategies: 1) taking existing museum collections in the Global North as our points of departure; 2) curating exhibitions as material and social interventions in the places from where these collections originated; and 3) co-curating these exhibitions with local partners. In effect, we aimed for a movement of global comparison, self-aware of starting from and returning to a Danish 'centre'. In at least one crucial aspect, the three subprojects within Precious Relics differ from many other studies based on collaborative, experimenting engagements between ethnographic museums and originating communities. The three subprojects have unfolded as processes of knowledge-production through exhibition-making in the country or region where the collections were acquired in the Global South. The ambition of geographical *outreach* was fulfilled – if not materially (in all three cases, the museum artefacts were introduced photographically), then at least conceptually. Moreover, a central ambition in the research project has been to collect new artefacts with the aim of contextualising the existing museum collections.

Beginning with exhibitions abroad, we endeavoured first to decentre Europe (Denmark) as the inherent site of comparison and as the inherent mediator of the terms of collaboration and engagement. In full knowledge of the impossibility of neutralising existing power imbalances between us and our chosen partners, we also engaged our partners directly in our collecting practices. We asked our partners how they wanted to be represented to Danish audiences, and how the materiality of their life today related to the artefacts in our older collections. For example, Nyema Droma selected her photograph for the exhibition based on the jewellery in Prince Peter's collection; Bekha Maharjan carved his Green Tara in response to the one in Werner Jacobsen's collection; and Baluan carvers identified the artefacts from the collections that represented key social institutions from the past and that they produce again today.

In 'Museum of Impermanence', the project participants synthesised insights gained through these exhibitions in Dharamshala (India), the Kathmandu Valley of Nepal, and Manus (Papua New Guinea), respectively, as anthropological reflections on the concept of impermanence. The choice of impermanence as the guiding concept for the combined exhibition emerged from the three researchers-cum-curators bringing back our experiences from the exhibitions and discussions in the field. Comparing the different temporalities and valuations connected with the objects in the three fieldsites, we found that our informants, who were sometimes also our local exhibition partners, often spoke of the existential anxiety but also solace produced through witnessing cultural change. Even where our informants and partners spoke of indifference, their thoughts connected with impermanence. For example, in a discussion of the Prince Peter collection and the preservation practices of the National Museum, one group of Tibetan government workers commented, 'Why invest so much effort in preserving these things? You know they are impermanent, right?' Though the connection between artefacts and impermanence was suggested most explicitly in the Tibetan Buddhist material, it was surprisingly relevant for the other fieldsites as well.

Before the exhibition and afterward, as we discussed the collaborative process that had led to 'Museum of Impermanence', we found that two notions challenged our assumptions about the politics of collaboration: autopoiesis and sympoiesis – two terms from biology that had recently influenced the different branches of the social sciences. Autopoiesis refers to a living being's ability to maintain and reproduce itself in an environment, which is its particular 'world', that it produces in the act of living – in other words, the result of its 'worlding' activity. In the case of our work, it recognises how human actors create the cultural worlds in which their actions and products have meaning and effect. Sympoiesis, on the other hand, is, at first, a deceptively simple word that means 'to make with'. Drawn out from biologists, who focus on how certain species of organisms co-reproduce each other, such as Hawaiian bobtail squid and the bacteria that live with them sympoietically, Donna Haraway suggests that sympoiesis points toward 'worlding-with' in the company of others (2016, 58). We tentatively suggest that sympoiesis encapsulates the collaborative process of working together (with so many others) to make 'Museum of Impermanence', both in terms of the exhibition as a whole and in terms of how some of the artefacts came to be.

To truly collaborate in the design of an exhibition means to come into interdependent, evolving configurations of people and materials. This involves a kind of engagement that the colonial reference-frame in James Clifford's influential museums-as-contact-zones theory only partially, but not sufficiently, brings forward (Clifford 1997). Not only the exhibition design but also (even) particular artefacts and videos embody unique worlds, which, themselves, only came into being through worlding-with activities. By itself, collaboration seems to signify the voluntary act of working with someone else, whereas sympoiesis recognises the inherent and inescapable dependency on the other in the creative act. Whereas collaboration points to a hoped-for equality between two or more separate actors, sympoiesis places an emphasis on *contingent* assemblages, where actors cannot create alone but only come together in very particular circumstances. Biologists term sympoietic assemblages 'holobionts' and analyse combinations of multiple species, each with their own genetic material, as discrete ecological units. In nature, holobionts form when one species fully encapsulates the other morphologically. Often, one of those species already encapsulated another species in an earlier phase of evolution. Sometimes, as in the case of the diminutive Hawaiian bobtail squid and its bacterial symbionts, they must come together at a crucial moment in the juvenile squid's development.

For social science, sympoiesis can metaphorically be a recognition of the unequal power relations that exist within the contingent assemblages of relatively wealthy researchers and museum curators who are dependent upon less wealthy but potentially otherwise empowered others to bring an exhibition to fruition. Following the squid example, in particular, sympoiesis also places a crucial emphasis on the timing of when researchers, curators, artists and practitioners become dependent on each other. The same process seen in exhibition-making can be said to be at work in the collecting or commissioning of particular artefacts for an exhibition. Like biological sympoiesis, the type of relationship that produces the exhibition comes to resemble the type of relationship that produced the artefact. However, unlike sympoietic holobionts that can never disengage from each other, we recognised that the interdependent co-creative worlds that come into existence in the making of an exhibition are, themselves, fleeting. Therefore, artefact production and exhibition-making differ from the sympoietic theory of evolutionary biology in that autopoietic (self-creating) individuals come together into a sympoietic (creating-with) temporary period, before separating once again. The fragility and momentariness, both solemn and joyous, of sympoietic artefact- and exhibition-making inspired and constituted the ethos of *a* and *the* 'Museum of Impermanence'.

Background to the exhibition and its overall design ideas

Our aim with the 'Museum of Impermanence' exhibition at Moesgaard Museum was to entice our visitors to consider the idea of impermanence and what this could mean for them in their own lives. We came up with four main ideas to pursue this aim. First, we wanted to formulate some questions that directly addressed the audience on entering the exhibition.[2] Thus prepared, the visitors would then wander through different exhibited scenes representing diverse cultural engagements with impermanence in the three regions where we had conducted our collaborations. In addition, we undertook to commission artwork and, sympoietically, collaborate with artists in the three regions to articulate perspectives that were relevant for understanding impermanence. Finally, we reasoned that the organisation of events and especially ritualised happenings in the museum space could forcefully contribute to an experience of impermanence for our visitors. Here, we thought in particular of the Tibetan ritual of making and unmaking a sand maṇḍala.

One major design consideration was whether we should freely mix elements of the three regions according to themes and associative links or keep the regional scenes together as recognisable sections in the exhibition. Although there were arguments for both options, we decided to keep the regional material together as we were concerned that, otherwise, the diversity would be too overwhelming and difficult to decode. As a result of our attempts to mix information from the three regions associatively, we became aware that it made more sense to see the regional materials as elements of different cultural worlds – not fully coherent, and consisting of different local traditions and global influences, but nevertheless representing a kind of aesthetic and ideational whole.

Taking regional cultural worlds as the foundation for our representation created another problem of coherence, though – that of the exhibition itself. How could we avoid its falling apart into three smaller, regionally based exhibitions? The solution was provided by architects from the design department. They suggested we use ceiling-high panels to demarcate different sections while allowing a view of the whole room from every position (see Figures 18.1 and 18.2). Apart from their function as space-creating devices, the panels were also used to carry monitors, information boards or artwork. Finally, by adding decorative patterns pertaining to elements from the exhibits, the panels also contributed to the atmosphere of the exhibit as a whole. A second design concept to emphasise the integration of the exhibition as a whole was to have the sound, connected with light effects, move from one section to the other, in three-minute intervals. All other atmospheric sound was subdued or muted; but, if connected to video presentations,

18.1 View from the Tibet section. Photo: Media Moesgaard, Søren Vestergaard, 2019.

18.2 View from the Papua New Guinea section. Photo: Media Moesgaard, Søren Vestergaard, 2019.

sound could still be heard through headphones. The rhythmic movement of sound and light throughout the whole exhibit had the effect of connecting the scenes and encouraging the visitors to explore what was happening elsewhere in the space, in another cultural setting.

Another key design concept was to construct scenes, such as a shopping mall or a temple entrance, that could combine different elements we wished to exhibit, for example fashion clothes and jewellery from the Tibetan past and present. Among the centrally visual elements of the scenes were the scenographic built-ups, such as a shop-front and artefacts from old and new collections, often presented in juxtaposition, to show continuity in change. In some cases, we used replicas to make the scene more visually attractive, as the original old artefacts would have required special (intrusive) security measures. Different kinds of video material formed a very important part of the visual design. These included explanatory presentations by the researchers/collectors (Figure 18.3) but also video installations as bearing elements of the scenes, such as life-sized projected morning prayers in a Kathmandu temple (Figure 18.4) and a double-screen projection evoking a cultural show in Manus, Papua New Guinea.

Overall, the exhibition came across as a multifaceted, multimodal and lively whole that inspired our visitors to contemplate their own

18.3 People watching a video presentation. Moesgaard Museum. Photo: Ton Otto, 2019.

18.4 Morning *puja* in the Kwa Bahal temple in Patan. Photo: Media Moesgaard, Søren Vestergaard, 2019.

experiences. In our reflections afterwards, we discussed how exhibitions not only come into being through the interdependent relationships of those who work behind the scenes but also in relation to the audience itself. Curators base decisions on previous experiences with audiences. Artists who perform in spaces think in relation to their audience. The audience's attendance and actions impact the course of the present exhibition and future ones. Therefore, we came to the realisation that, in our debates over the exhibition design, we anticipated drawing the audience into our sympoietic assemblage. Some of the comments from our visitor book:

> This is an exciting and attractive exhibition that provided a lot of stuff for reflection. I am particularly enthusiastic about the videos with experts. That created a lovely quiet space to absorb and focus on their words. I am also enthusiastic about the multimodality of the exhibition. Please make more exhibitions in which you ask questions to the audience about their own life and culture (Kirsten, 18 April 2019, translated from Danish).

> This is such a fresh perspective and way of looking at things. Even questioning if a museum should be/its function in society is smart.

I am glad I got to see it. This is a new perspective . . . and I will now take in and consider it in my own life (Mallow, 22 April 2019).

This exhibition is one of the most interesting and best-framed ethnographic/historical exhibitions I have seen. Stories about the objects and the time and conditions they were collected in make them fantastically alive. The permanence, which is museums' task to safeguard, can sometimes freeze things in time and make them not fitting and irrelevant. This exhibition does exactly the opposite. Thanks! (Anonymous, n.d., translated from Danish).

The interdependent but unequal relationships – between curators, artefact creators and the audience – that we term a 'sympoietic assemblage' are poignantly demonstrated through the performed impermanence of the sand maṇḍala.

Sand maṇḍala as performed impermanence

For Buddhists, maṇḍalas are symbolic depictions of an entire universe from the perspective of the Buddhist deity or deities that reside in the centre of the maṇḍala. They are typically used as aids to memory for advanced meditators or as one important component of a set of connected ritual actions honouring a particular deity, which we can term a 'ritual cycle'. Each aspect of a maṇḍala is representative of multiple levels of symbolism, explained in detail in ritual texts. Across Asia, there are many different types of temporary paintings made of coloured flour or sand. In Tibet, the practice of temporary paintings and Buddhist maṇḍalas merged to create the distinctive artistic and ritual practice of sand maṇḍalas (*rdul mtshon dkyil 'khor*). Sand maṇḍalas are, by design, temporary. Toward the end of the ritual cycle, lamas deconstruct the sand maṇḍala by putting the sand into a local body of water in the understanding that the sand carries blessings (*byin rlabs*), which, via water, will enter the ocean and bless the entire world. Devotees often gather to collect blessed maṇḍala sand (or lamas formally distribute it) for use on home shrines.

When Buddhist lamas began constructing sand maṇḍalas in public venues outside of Asia, their fragility and ephemerality naturally led to frequent dialogues about their embodiment of the Buddhist view on impermanence. Sand maṇḍalas, as a form of cultural performance for secular or religiously pluralistic audiences at museums and on university campuses, became something more akin to mild missionary devices appropriate for introducing Buddhist concepts to the uninitiated, rather than esoteric meditation devices for highly trained yogis. It is in that spirit that Tenzin Lhawang, the General Secretary of the Library of Tibetan Works and Archives, explained to Warner the sand maṇḍala preserved under a glass case in the permanent exhibition at the Library. Tenzin wanted to include a sand maṇḍala as a new form of Tibetan art. And yet, how can a ritual be an art form? How can a temporary construction be part of a museum exhibition? Tenzin explained that it was important that the sand maṇḍala not become part of the permanent collection. But it was possible to *pause* the ritual in the middle, while the sand maṇḍala was intact, as long as the ritual would be completed someday.

Tenzin's innovation, pausing a ritual in the middle to temporarily, not permanently, preserve something became one of the key concepts in the design of 'Museum of Impermanence'. Conceptually, there is a stark difference between preserving an artefact for the sake of keeping it for future generations of researchers and visitors versus caring for a transient artefact so that museum visitors can interact with it during a limited period of time. We decided to build on Tenzin's idea and use a sand maṇḍala to deliberately confront our visitors with the threat of impermanence. We asked a group of lamas to construct a sand maṇḍala beginning on the first day of our exhibition but to leave it in place under glass for three months (Figure 18.5), the duration of the exhibition, and then return to complete the ritual – that is, deconstruct the maṇḍala on the final day of the exhibition. In a sense, there would be two rituals performed simultaneously. Over the course of the exhibition, the lamas would perform the complete Buddhist ritual cycle of their choice including prayers, offerings and construction and deconstruction of the maṇḍala,

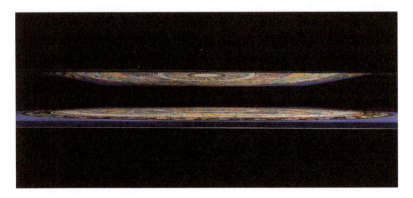

18.5 The sand maṇḍala under glass. Photo: Media Moesgaard, Michael Johansen, 2019.

but we curators would also collaborate with the lamas in performing the ritual of the opening of an exhibition at an ethnographic museum, including speeches, a reception and talks by the lamas and ourselves. The sand maṇḍala would serve as a linchpin to both rituals because not only is the maṇḍala impermanent but so are temporary exhibitions like ours.

On the first day of the exhibition, the lamas began a ritual cycle called 'The Sixteen Arhāts', which includes the Sixteen Arhāts sand maṇḍala. To ensure that as many visitors as possible could see the work in progress, we asked the lamas to spend a week building the maṇḍala instead of the usual one or two days. Three months later, the lamas returned to finish the ritual.

On the closing day, hundreds of people gathered very closely around the maṇḍala, many of whom arrived very early to secure the best view. This is where the ritual of closing a temporary museum exhibition and the end of a Buddhist ritual cycle differ dramatically. For visitors, the last day of an exhibition does not differ from the rest. The act of taking down the exhibition happens out of their view. By contrast, the deconstruction of the sand maṇḍala was an inherently participatory, and somewhat collaborative, event. The lamas began with concluding prayers that lasted over an hour. Despite their length, and the fact that the prayers were chanted only in Tibetan, all of the participants waited patiently and many even tried to chant Tibetan using copies of the prayers the lamas handed out. When the lamas had swept up the sand, hundreds of people followed in a procession down the hill from the museum, at times silent and reflective, at times boisterous and excited, to a small creek behind the Moesgaard Manor house where the lamas poured a small, symbolic portion of the sand into the water (Figure 18.6). Visitors described the experience in ecstatic terms such as profound, joyous, moving or essential. Some spoke of their perception that contemporary Danish culture is bereft of rituals and the transformative experiences they can convey. At the water's edge, Khenpo Pema invited the crowd to come forward and gave to every person in attendance some of the consecrated sand for use at home. Over the course of the exhibition, the sand maṇḍala, in effect, became a kind of museum artefact but one whose size, shape and meaning were explicitly impermanent and were eventually distributed across countless kilometres to unknown locales across Jutland. The deconstruction of the sand maṇḍala became a world unto itself, made in the sympoietic, yet fleeting, interdependencies between the lamas-as-performance-artists, the visitors and we curators. The normal rules of decorum in the museum, the means of engagement between staff and visitors, and even the geographical layout

18.6 Visitors and lamas collaboratively finishing the sand maṇḍala and closing the exhibit. Photo: Sarah Schorr, 2019.

of inner and external spaces, all changed, often spontaneously, as the sand maṇḍala 'holobiont' lived out its brief life.

The 1376 'Museum of Impermanence' Store

The Tibetan section of 'Museum of Impermanence' featured three interrelated stories displaying the diversity and complexity of perspectives on impermanence among contemporary Tibetans: the 2018 Jokhang Fire, Tibetan Art and Artistic Preservation in Exile (Figure 18.7 a–b), and the 1376 'Museum of Impermanence' Store. '1376' is the name of a new clothing brand, which has also become a new Tibetan expression (explained in detail in Chapter 10) meaning 'do what you think about'. From the point of view of exhibition design, the 1376 Store served as the visible anchor for the Tibetan section of 'Museum of Impermanence' (Figure 18.8). The Store worked as our own playful interpretation of how Tibetan fashion designers and musicians have responded to the impermanence of Tibetan ways of life and material culture through remixing globalised urban clothing and music styles with ancient Tibetan instruments, fabrics and designs.

The inspiration for the Store came from Warner's fieldwork on the eastern edge of the Tibetan plateau and his interviews with leading

18.7a Silk appliqué *thangka* of Goddess Tara by Tenzin Nyima, 2019. Photo: Cameron David Warner.

18.7b Hand-painted *thangka* inspired by a mural in Lo Munthang by Dawa Thondup, 2019. Photo: Media Moesgaard, Søren Vestergaard.

18.8 The 1376 'Museum of Impermanence' store. Photo: Media Moesgaard, Søren Vestergaard, 2019.

Tibetan fashion designers such as Anu Ranglug (the region's most popular hip hop group) and Nyema Droma, the founder of the Hima Ālaya lifestyle brand. Warner and the fashion designers discussed which items of clothing and contemporary artwork, such as Nyema Droma's chosen photograph, would work well, first with an exile Tibetan audience in India, and later with a Danish audience. Even after the exhibition opened, we edited the selection of clothing on display as Warner chatted with one of the designers over the social media platform WeChat. Upon seeing the clothes on display, one of the designers thought one of the shirts could be misconstrued over social media by museum visitors and therefore we replaced it with a different shirt. Our store featured clothing from the actual 1376 Store in Xining, China, as well as other popular Tibetan brands such as Hima Ālaya and Rewa (Warner 2019) (for photographs of items in the store and their ethnographical background, see Chapter 10 in this volume), popular Tibetan-language books on contemporary culture, contemporary art, and three Tibetan music videos displayed on loop. At the centre of our store, we showcased the amulet case (*ga'u*), neckband and coral headdress (*mu tig spa phrug*) of Pema Dolkar, one of the wealthiest Tibetan women in 1950 (Figures 18.9a–b). Collected for the National Museum of Denmark by HRH Prince Peter of Greece and Denmark (1908–1980), Pema Dolkar's jewellery intersected with many Tibetan stories of impermanence: the loss of political independence, iconoclasm, massive and rapid cultural upheaval, secularisation, and the fragility of some materials such as silk, but also the stubborn persistence

18.9a Pema Dolkar's amulet case. Photo: Media Moesgaard, Michael Johansen, 2019. Courtesy of the National Museum of Denmark.

18.9b Pema Dolkar's coral headdress and other jewellery. Photo: Ton Otto, 2019. Courtesy of the National Museum of Denmark.

of some forms and styles of Tibetan adornment, the continued value of authenticity to Tibetan society, the analogical resilience of gems and the malleability of gold.

The beauty and historical value of the clothing and jewellery collected by Prince Peter served as the origin of the Tibetan part of the Precious Relics research project and, for a long time, served as one anchor of our design plan. We endeavoured to display four complete Tibetan robes and accoutrements in 'Museum of Impermanence'. Warner's research interest in these items drew his attention to Tibetan fashion and, eventually, the desire to build a collection of Tibetan clothing to parallel Prince Peter's collection from 65 years earlier. Though the National Museum of Denmark originally acceded to our proposal, we were eventually forced to redesign the exhibition around the contemporary clothing as the National Museum heightened its demands over handling, proper display, climate control, lighting and security. In a sense, the Prince Peter collection is so valuable to the Museum as to be almost impossible to display to the public anywhere outside of the Museum itself. Paradoxically, visitors to 'Museum of Impermanence' expressed much more enthusiasm and interest toward the recently acquired artefacts than the older ones, such as asking to buy the clothing, mirroring the response of Tibetans to a previous exhibition that Warner co-curated, 'The Value and Impermanence of Tibetan Culture', at India's Library of Tibetan Works.

Tibetan designers inspired his decision to feature new clothing alongside the items in Prince Peter's collection as they did not find the latter collection of aristocratic garments nearly as captivating as their own creations. Due to the inevitability of impermanence, designers pointed to items of contemporary clothing with authentically ancient Tibetan symbols, such as a hooded sweatshirt embroidered with a Tibetan opera mask as both an act of creation and an act of preservation. The 1376 'Museum of Impermanence' Store invited the audience to reflect on the interaction of globalisation, Chinese market forces and creative inspiration between Tibetans, and between them and non-Tibetan worlds. For example, the hooded sweatshirt embodies twenty-first-century Tibetan hip hop's dependency on fourteenth-century Tibetan opera, which is encapsulated within the new musical style. The choice of items in the store brought together the interests of people in contemporary Tibet and exile settlements in India within an exhibition funded and designed in Aarhus, Denmark. And, finally, the success of the Store itself depended on visitors directly engaging with it as an ersatz site of exchange where heterogeneous 'species' depended on each other in unequal arrangements resulting in a complex, unique and impermanent world.

Newar juxtapositions

In the Nepalese section of the exhibition, two carved wooden Green Taras from Nepal were exhibited facing each other (Figures 18.10a–b):

18.10a The old Green Tara. Photo: Media Moesgaard, Søren Vestergaard, 2019.

18.10b Bekha Maharjan's new Green Tara. Photo: Media Moesgaard, Søren Vestergaard, 2019.

Seated on high pedestals and protected behind glass domes, they sit at eye level gazing at each other approximately 3 metres apart. Although the two Green Taras depict the same Buddhist deity with its particular characteristics, they differ in crucial ways. The first is scarred by time; the toes on the right foot are missing and the paint is flaked. Before the Danish archaeologist Werner Jacobsen acquired her in the Kathmandu Valley in the late 1950s, we presume Newar Buddhists worshipped this Green Tara as a manifestation of the goddess in a monastery in Kathmandu. In contrast, the second Green Tara embodies a youthful freshness; Bekha Maharjan had carved it specifically for the Precious Relics project two years prior to the exhibition in the Moesgaard Museum. Around its feet, Maharjan's tools and piles of woodchips, which he had painstakingly cut away with his wooden hammer and chisels, covered the bottom of the exhibition case.

Ulrik Johnsen had encountered the works of Bekha Maharjan in an art gallery in Patan. They developed a dialogue on the making of a contemporary counterpart to the Green Tara that Jacobsen had collected in the 1950s. Carving the new Green Tara, Maharjan was eager to study photographs of the one collected by Jacobsen to ensure it was in accordance with Buddhist iconography, and yet insisted on his own

18.11   The Nepalese section in bird's-eye perspective. Photo: Moesgaard Museum, Ulrik Høj Johnsen, 2019.

personal touch. In opposition to the old Green Tara, Maharjan's version is more richly ornamented and it is not painted.

The way we exhibited this second Green Tara along with the woodchips and tools accentuated one of the central insights in the Nepalese section of the exhibition, namely that repetition of particular material forms (such as the form of the Green Tara) contributes to cultural and religious continuity. So, too, do repetitions of particular actions such as rituals. The backdrop to the installation with the two versions of Tara was a life-sized video projection of the entrance to the Buddhist monastery Kwa Bahal in Patan, where worshippers were going into and coming out from their daily morning *puja* (ritual offering) (Figure 18.11).

Here, the two Green Taras were engaged in a silent conversation, which we as curators invited the audience to be a part of – intellectually, but also physically on the floor between them. We designed this installation as a *juxtaposition*, which is a powerful methodological and analytical tool to explore anthropological questions and to generate knowledge (Vium 2018). The juxtaposition of the two versions opened a space designed to explore temporal relations over a timespan of 60 years. The 'divine conversation', which the museum audience could follow, focused on the *reproduction* of particular forms and actions in Nepal, reflecting broader cultural, social and religious continuities and changes in the Kathmandu Valley from the 1950s to the present day. Despite profound changes in the social life in the Valley, the handicraft and the production of particular forms are still alive – albeit in different ways than in the 1950s. Newar artisans carved the older version of Green Tara, which Jacobsen collected, with the same basic tools as those on display; using the same techniques, Maharjan carved this new version – but for very different purposes. Undoubtedly, artisans made the 'old' Green Tara for worship in a temple in Kathmandu. Those among the audience who studied the two versions of Tara closely could see that, while the rear side of the old Green Tara was not beautifully ornamented (the craftsmen intended for her to be seen and interacted with exclusively from the front, during worship), the new interpretation had elaborate woodcarving at the back, too. Bekha Maharjan and Johnsen never intended for it to be worshipped in a temple. Rather, it constitutes an instantiation of another complex process of world-making, based on contributions of heterogeneous sympoietic elements dependent on each other for the sake of reaching their own goals, but where Bekha Maharjan's creation will always be encapsulated by Moesgaard Museum.

Innovation, materiality and ancestors in Papua New Guinea

The Papua New Guinea section has two main stories to tell about impermanence: one exuberant, the other more composed. The first deals with how young Baluan adults hark back to lost traditions to assert and celebrate their particular identity in the modern world. This exhibition scene consists of a dual-screen life-sized installation and some large artefacts evoking a cultural festival that was staged on Baluan Island, Manus, Papua New Guinea in 2006. Here, we see young women dressed as traditional brides walk on stage in a Western-style fashion show. As part of their performance, they sit down on a miniature version of a traditional wedding bed, carry out a traditional dance and pronounce, in front of a microphone, that they want to maintain their unique culture for future generations and display it for tourists. Dancing on a horizontal, 6-metre-long beam, the traditional leader says the same thing. The festival celebrates both the impermanence and the revitalisation of culture.

One striking example is the log drum and its music, which was nearly lost but is now flourishing again (Figure 18.12). The new culture, realised at and through the festival, is the sympoietic creation of local people with different personal trajectories, knowledge and interests: those who had grown up and stayed in the village and those who became immersed in Western cultural institutions through their education and work in urban environments, both in Papua New Guinea and abroad. Otto, together with his colleagues, anthropologist-filmmakers Christian Suhr and Steffen Dalsgaard, was invited to participate in the festival and film it. The production of this film and its later use became part of the ongoing sympoietic relationships between anthropologists and their local partners (Otto 2013). The rendering of the festival and its key material artefacts in 'Museum of Impermanence' was strongly impacted by workshops and exhibition preparations on Baluan between local carvers, dancers and Otto, but also by the input of Moesgaard Museum designers and AV technicians: in a sympoietic fashion, different points of view, oppositions and agreements, existing forms and innovations came together into a new temporary formation of an effervescent world of material artefacts, dance, music and the celebration of continuity within change.

The second story in the Papua New Guinea section relates how people's concerns about their dead have changed but also stayed the

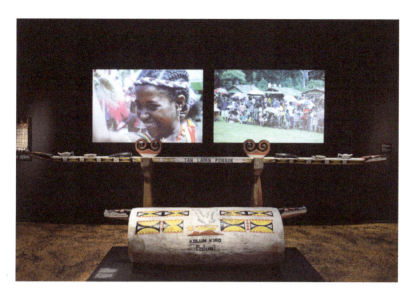

18.12 The festival scene with video installation, dancing beam and large log drum. Photo: Media Moesgaard, Søren Vestergaard, 2019.

same. This is a story about ancestral spirits, traditional and modern. In 1932, a man from the village of Patusi on Manus gave or sold the skull of his ancestor – probably his father or elder brother – to Alfred Bühler, a Swiss anthropologist, who was collecting for the Museum of Ethnology in Basel (Ohnemus 1998). The question of why he did this becomes even more urgent if one realises that this skull was the embodiment of the ancestral spirit who provided him with good fortune and protection (Fortune 1935). How could he discard his local god? A plausible answer, corroborated by historical information about the region, is that he had recently converted to Christianity and thus subscribed to a more powerful god, who – as claimed by the European missionaries – did not tolerate competition from local spirits (Otto 1998). The skull had been kept in the owner's house, carefully placed in a wooden bowl hanging from the rafters. Since 1933, both bowl and skull have been meticulously preserved in the storerooms of the Museum of Cultures in Basel (formerly called Museum of Ethnology), only to be displayed on rare occasions.

The serene but commanding expression of the skull in the bowl had made a strong impression on Otto when he first saw it as presented in Basel (Figure 18.13a). When he worked in Manus in the 2010s, he discovered that people had fully returned to their veneration of the spirits of the dead without discarding their Christian beliefs. In this period, people had begun to build small houses on the graves of leading men (and some women), where they would go to ask the spirits for assistance. Struck by the persistence of the beliefs in ancestral presence and fascinated by the way new materials, such as concrete and iron, were used to underline the continuing existence of the spirits, he wanted to make this into an installation within 'Museum of Impermanence'.

18.13a Original Manus skull in wooden bowl. Courtesy of Museum of Cultures, Basel.

18.13b Replica of the Manus skull in another wooden bowl, Moesgaard Museum. Photo: Media Moesgaard, Michael Johansen, 2019.

But this was not without its challenges, due to the preservative regime of museums. The Basel Museum had generously agreed to loan the original skull to Moesgaard Museum, but the costs of guarded transport, insurance and protective display were simply so high that we decided to find a different solution: that of the replica (Figure 18.13b). One important consideration was that this allowed us more freedom in making the scene as we envisaged it. And we also thus avoided provoking ethical sensitivities concerning the display of human remains.

The key idea behind the installation was to juxtapose the old way of ancestor worship with the new way, thus highlighting both the persistence of the belief and the radical transformation of its material rendering (Figure 18.14). In the installation of the modern grave, we showed the materials used, including concrete and roofing iron, and screened a video about a woman standing next to such a grave explaining the importance of talking to the ancestors in the present day. The video included a slideshow of other gravesites, emphasising the importance of their materiality in a tropical environment that defies permanence. Spiritual tenacity and material durability went hand in hand to assert some form of continuity in a world overwhelmingly characterised by change.

18.14 Two houses, two different graves. Photo: Media Moesgaard, Søren Vestergaard, 2019.

Concluding considerations

The research conducted under the auspices of the Precious Relics project produced a bevy of results and revealed different kinds of temporalities and historicities that are produced in dealing with impermanence. We studied how new Tibetan fashion in China took inspiration from old forms of Tibetan clothing and jewellery that can be seen in our museum collections, thus creating continuity in change. We also found how the reproduction of religious practices and forms in Newar temples in Kathmandu created a sense of continuity in a world impacted by global transformations. In Manus, Papua New Guinea, we encountered a surprising persistence of beliefs and practices concerning ancestral spirits that was amplified by the use of new durable materials, which defied the continuous decay and transformation of tropical environments. And we discovered how the Tibetan practice of making and using sand maṇḍalas to meditate on impermanence could be adapted to the temporality of temporary exhibitions by pausing the ritual, so that the maṇḍala could serve as a temporary museum artefact.

'Museum of Impermanence' focused on visualising impermanence with our audience as a provocative and perhaps innovative discussion for contemporary Denmark. We invited and prompted our audience into a dialogue with us: what kinds of insights reveal themselves when we come to terms with the fact that material artefacts, rituals and customs are, themselves, always subject to change? How can researchers and the public find value in something after we realise it is only temporary? And when thinking cross-culturally, what can Danish society, which has a certain predilection for permanence, learn from societies that live in political, ritual and natural ecologies more cognisant of change? We wanted to display visually the contrast between the kind of impermanence that happens steadily at a pace almost invisible to an observer and the more punctual, where impermanence seems to happen rapidly in bursts after long periods of stasis. We also wanted to disturb the fallacy that change continues along a consistent trajectory from the past to the present. Rather, impermanence as both moments of death and rebirth allows for recursive movements where styles, motifs and practices, long believed dead and forgotten, can suddenly reappear in unexpected places and novel configurations.

Sympoiesis as a means of conceptualising 'making with' speaks to the polytemporal, polyspatial, contingent and dynamic interdependencies we worked to make visual in 'Museum of Impermanence', in ways that the term 'collaboration' alone does not. For example, the Venerable Lekshey Chhotar Bista drew our attention to the impermanence of the sand maṇḍala even in the time between its making and unmaking: 'See, we worked hard to construct high ridges in the sand for the sake of the audience. But even in a seismically peaceful place like Aarhus, those ridges will settle over time. The mountains of sand will slowly crumble.' We placed the two Green Taras facing each other, one with signs of wear and tear, the other newly emergent from her block of wood, to fashion an intra-active relationship between the two of them and the audience. Throughout the history of biological life and artistic creativity, truly new things only ever emerge when strangers (whether they be persons, nonhuman beings, things or ideas) become sympoietically dependent, such as Hima Ālaya fashioning a pseudo-sheepskin coat out of only plant-based materials – in effect, redesigning an ancient article of clothing in a newly invented material – or the people of Manus inventing a cultural festival to display their authenticity to tourists (and to preserve and recover it for themselves). Sympoiesis puts to words the complicated dynamics and unequal politics of lamas from Nepal, hundreds of local Danes and the curators working together on a cloudy and slightly rainy day in the unmaking of our/their sand maṇḍala, our/their 'Museum of Impermanence'.

Acknowledgements

The authors would like to acknowledge the essential contributions of our fieldsite partners. In Tibet we thank Tenzin Lhawang, Nyema Dronma, Anu Ranglug, Tenzin Nyima and Dawa Thondup. We are further indebted to the lamas from Pema Ts'al Sakya Monastic Institute: Venerable Tashi Wangyal Bista, Venerable Lhekshey Chhotar Bista, Venerable Dhundup Gurung, Venerable Ngawang Tashi Gurung, their junior abbot Venerable Jampa Dhakpa Gurung and their monastery's patron and co-founder, Venerable Khenpo Pema Wangdak. We also acknowledge the collaboration of Papua New Guinean artist Joe Nalo, the late Soanin Kilangit and the other organisers of the Balopa Cultural Festival, Selvia Maron, and the Nurunan Paluai-Baluan Design group, also from Papua New Guinea. Further, we acknowledge the collaboration of Swosti Kayastha Rajbhandari, lecturer at Lumbini Buddhist University, and the woodcarver Bekha Maharjan from Bungamati, Nepal. Last but not least we are grateful for the generous support from members of staff at Moesgaard Museum, the National Museum of Denmark and the Museum of Cultures, Basel.

Notes

1 The project entitled 'Precious Relics: Materiality and Value in the Practice of Ethnographic Collection' was financially supported by the Danish Council for Independent Research, Culture and Communication (grant no. DFF 4180-00326), for which we express our deep gratitude and appreciation. Cameron Warner was the grant holder and principal investigator, while Ton Otto, as head of the Museum's Ethnographic Department, was primarily responsible for the collaboration with the museum and the realisation of the exhibition. We owe a great thank-you to all the staff at Moesgaard Museum who were involved in this project and especially Ditte Lyngkær Pedersen, who was appointed as coordinator and was assisted by student-in-practice Amanda Vásquez.

2 This was the first text for the visitors to encounter:
Impermanence means that everything inevitably changes.
What do you experience as impermanent in your own life?
Should we hang on to our cherished possessions and way of life?
Why should museums collect and preserve things?

References

Allen, Lindy, and Louise Hamby. 2011. 'Pathways to knowledge: Research, agency and power relations in the context of collaborations between museums and source communities'. In *Unpacking the Collection: Networks of material and social agency in the museum*, edited by Sarah Byrne, Anne Clarke, Rodney Harrison and Robin Torrence, 209–29. London: Springer.

Basu, Paul. 2017. 'The inbetweenness of things'. In *The Inbetweenness of Things: Materializing mediation and movement between worlds*, edited by Paul Basu, 1–20. London: Bloomsbury.

Basu, Paul, and Sharon Macdonald. 2006. 'Introduction: Experiments in exhibition, ethnography, art and science'. In *Exhibition Experiments*, edited by Paul Basu and Sharon Macdonald, 1–24. Hoboken, NJ: Wiley-Blackwell.

Bennett, Tony. 1995. *The Birth of the Museum: History, theory, politics*. London: Routledge.

Clifford, James. 1997. 'Museums as contact zones'. In *Routes: Travel and translation in the late twentieth century*, edited by James Clifford, 188–219. Cambridge, MA: Harvard University Press.

Coombes, Annie E., and Ruth B. Philips. 2015. 'Introduction: Museums in transformation. Dynamics of democratization and decolonization'. In *Museum Transformations: Decolonization and democratization*, edited by Annie E. Coombes and Ruth Philips, xxv–lv. Hoboken, NJ: Wiley-Blackwell.

Curtis, Neil G.W. 2006. 'Universal museums, museum objects and repatriation: The tangled stories of things', *Museum Management and Curatorship* 21: 117–27.

Fortune, Reo F. 1935. *Manus Religion: An ethnological study of the Manus natives of the Admiralty Islands*. Lincoln, NE: University of Nebraska Press.

Ginsburch, Victor, and François Mairesse. 1997. 'Defining a museum: Suggestions for an alternative approach', *Museum Management and Curatorship* 16(1): 15–33.

Haraway, Donna J. 2016. *Staying with the Trouble: Making kin in the Chthulucene*. Durham, NC: Duke University Press.

Hartog, François. 2015. *Regimes of Historicity: Presentism and experiences of time* (translated by Saskia Brown). New York: Columbia University Press.

Lavine, Steven D., and Ivan Karp. 1991. *Exhibiting Cultures: The poetics and politics of museum display*. Washington, DC: Smithsonian Institution Press.

Macdonald, Sharon, ed. 2006. *A Companion to Museum Studies*. Malden, MA: Blackwell.

Marcus, George E. 2010. 'Contemporary fieldwork aesthetics in art and anthropology: Experiments in collaboration and intervention', *Visual Anthropology* 23: 263–77.

Marcus, George E. 2012. 'Classic fieldwork, critique and engaged anthropology: Into the new century', *Anthropological Journal of European Cultures* 21(2): 35–42.

Marcus, George E. 2013. 'Experimental forms for the expression of norms in the ethnography of the contemporary', *HAU: Journal of Ethnographic Theory* 3 (2): 197–217.

Ohnemus, Sylvia. 1998. *An Ethnology of the Admiralty Islanders: The Alfred Bühler Collection, Museum der Kulturen, Basel*. Bathurst, NSW: Crawford House Publishing.

Otto, Ton. 1998. 'Local narratives of a great transformation: Conversion to Christianity in Manus, Papua New Guinea', *FOLK: Journal of the Danish Ethnographic Society* 40: 71–97.

Otto, Ton. 2013. 'Ethnographic film as exchange', *The Asia Pacific Journal of Anthropology* 14(2): 195–205.

Peers, Laura, and Alison K. Brown, eds. 2003. *Museums and Source Communities*. London and New York: Routledge.

Philips, Ruth B. 2005. 'Re-placing objects: Historical practices for the second museum age', *The Canadian Historical Review* 86(1): 83–110.

Thomas, Nicholas. 2016. *The Return of Curiosity: What museums are good for in the 21st century*. London: Reaktion Books.

Vergo, Peter. 1989. *The New Museology*. London: Reaktion Books.

Vium, Christian. 2018. 'Temporal dialogues: Collaborative photographic re-enactments as a form of cultural critique', *Visual Anthropology* 31(4–5): 355–75.

Warner, Cameron David. 2019. 'Tibetan heritage in urban China', *Volume* 55(1): 30–3.

19
Epilogue: self unhinged

Caitlin DeSilvey

When we gathered in Aarhus in May 2019 to talk about 'impermanence' at the Inevitable Ends conference, the concept was comfortably abstract, intellectually stimulating and – for the most part – at a safe remove from the lived experience of the assembled academics and artists. Impermanence was good to think with, we agreed. As I write this Epilogue in January 2021 and reflect on a set of chapters grounded in the certainties of the before-time, the conference's exploration of the claim that impermanence could offer a 'poignant hermeneutic for our time' seems prescient. A year and a half later, and almost a year into the COVID-19 pandemic, we are living impermanence daily, and I cannot offer these reflections from any position other than the state of bewilderment and instability that has become commonplace, and pervasive, for many of us. In this chapter, I want to let some of that openness and instability in, and to allow the moment we are living through (which will, of course, have passed by the time this appears in print) to work back on some of the ideas presented in the preceding chapters.

In her 1997 essay 'Time unhinged', Ann Game writes about moments of rupture and collapse, when catastrophe 'draws attention to impermanence' and prompts us to acknowledge: 'I did not anticipate this; I could not control, master it' (Game 1997, 124). She writes about how such moments disrupt a 'project-driven, future-oriented life' (122), in which our sense of self is anchored in a projected future. When that future is taken away, she observes, we experience a 'loss of self'– but also open up the possibility of accessing other selves. During the pandemic we have all been coping with the abandonment of our future-oriented selves in various ways, as it has successively derailed and deferred our plans and projects. Occasionally, we may have been able to let go of our frustration about the situation to achieve a heightened awareness of our present moment and an openness to other forms of self, attuned to connection rather than momentum: 'In the moment of suspension, everything is contingent. And possible' (Game 1997, 127).

Game's reflections on the relation between the self and perceptions of impermanence will frame my discussion here, but first I want to offer a little more reflection on the 'moment of suspension' we are living through. For those reading this on the far side of the pandemic – a place difficult for us to imagine now – it's worth noting that the recognition of impermanence is currently working in the world in two quite distinct ways. With COVID-19, we have an awareness of the fundamental fragility and vulnerability of our bodies, but also the precarity of wider structures and systems. The illusion of stability has been stripped away and we are contending with the impermanence of small things – plans, projects – and much larger ones – industries, economies. Many of the institutional arrangements we believed to be relatively stable and enduring – education, worship, work – have been suspended or significantly slowed, and when they return they will be altered, either subtly or radically. The inverse revelation saturating this moment is around awareness of our impact on the earth's climate and ecological systems. Damage that had seemed provisional and perhaps repairable is now understood as permanent and irreversible, and the evidence mounts about the lasting harm caused by our casual consumption, accumulating in deposits of microplastics, greenhouse gases and forever chemicals.

The current moment of uncertainty, instability and precarity, on the one hand, and recognition of indelible damage, on the other, perhaps reveals some of the strangeness that characterises thinking through, and about, impermanence. As many of the authors in this volume observe, impermanence is a concept formed of contradictions. Contemplation of impermanence, as noted in the Introduction, 'allows us to sit within the uncomfortable tensions and paradoxes that emerge from our lived experiences': impermanence can be an opportunity for obliteration as well as innovation, erasure as well as renewal, transience as well as transmutation. Precarity may, paradoxically, produce resilience, and the threat of social (and environmental) change may provide an opportunity for the creation of new cultural and ecological forms. The accounts shared in this book reveal some of this ambivalence and ambiguity. In many of the case studies, impermanence is framed as something aspired to, a cultural ideal or practice that promises transcendence and release. Buddhism's framing of impermanence as liberation, and its ethics of ephemerality, are stitched throughout many of the chapters. But impermanence also emerges quite clearly, at times, as something to be resisted or denied, through strategies of conservation and protection. In several chapters, the positive and the negative framings of impermanence exist in tandem and in tension with each other.

In the rest of this chapter, I will explore how the apparently paradoxical qualities of impermanence can be understood, in part, through reference to conceptions of self and identity. Impermanence can threaten a sense of self as coherent and bounded, or it can enable the realisation of a more porous and relational sense of self. The editors, and some of the authors, make reference to recent thinking around 'worlding' and *autopoeisis*, in which biological concepts are borrowed to propose a model of the self as generated through continual interface with a changing environment. While these ideas are clearly relevant, the authors perhaps overlook older alternative traditions in social theory and the relational and vitalist thinking that emerged in the early part of the twentieth century. In Game's aforementioned essay, she draws attention to philosophies that 'value flux and change over solidity and stasis' (1997, 118), including the work of Henri Bergson and William James, setting them in relation to Buddhist understandings of self and time. She writes: 'my interest is in developing an understanding of "ways of being" that acknowledge the impermanence of things including the self' (1997, 116).

Key to her argument is the assertion that cultural analysis needs to encompass both abstract/conceptual and lived/embodied aspects of experience, and accommodate a 'multiplicity of selves': '[D]ifferent selves and temporalities co-exist: a self that is coherent and produced through narrative . . . and another self that is mobile and heterogeneous, a self that changes, living the time of contingency' (Game 1997, 116). Critically, Game resists the impulse to place these different expressions of the self in opposition. She argues that the reification of such an opposition risks 'reinventing the very singularity that would be undone' (Game 1997, 116). While Game is warning against approaches that would fix and privilege 'movement' over 'stasis' specifically in relation to understandings of the self (a position she identifies with Bergson), this insight applies equally to conceptions of impermanence. An insistence on the ubiquity of 'impermanence' may unintentionally result in the calcification of the concept. For the most part, the authors in this volume resist a simple opposition between 'permanence' and 'impermanence', but they but also at times rely on it, or identify its expression in the social worlds they are exploring. Following Game, a rigid and dualist interpretation assumes that impermanence excludes permanence, but a perspective anchored in contingency and co-existence understands that, in lived experience, it is possible to hold both in relation: 'in lived experience, supposedly mutually exclusive elements coexist' (Game 1997, 122).

Several of the chapters in this volume engage directly with the workings of multiple selves, simultaneously and in tension, exposing how 'different selves and temporalities coexist' (Game 1997, 116). McGranahan's reflection on 'social death' in an exiled Tibetan Buddhist family narrates the experience of individuals who attempt to align abstract, cultural perceptions of inevitable impermanence with an acute sense of personal loss, as they mourn the selves associated with former ways of living and relating. McGranahan describes how these people experience 'culture as a series of lived contradictions', with the concept of impermanence lived as a practice and a process on a continuum that acknowledges that things – including selves – are never whole or stable. A similar theme, in a radically different context, appears in Llewellyn's chapter, where he articulates the tension between two different versions of self: the self as anchored in a narrative of recovery and continuation, and the self as released, through death, into the unknown and the uncertain. He describes how the 'death-denying environment' of cancer care can lead people to hold onto their former, stable sense of self for too long, not leaving them enough time to make the transition to palliative care and to face their passing intentionally. He comments that his case studies reveal a 'fundamental ambivalence around human impermanence in Western thought and culture'. Louw's chapter also centres on an exploration of the relation between self and death, as neo-atheists assert their alternative conception of self through anticipatory protest, their self-definition in the present hinging on self-annihilation in the future.

In her essay, Game explores how Bergson's theory of 'duration' relies on a conception of 'a self that lives in and acknowledges transformation and change' (Game 1997, 120) rather than a coherent and bounded self. She aligns Bergson's ideas with the Buddhist embrace of 'emptiness' and a conception of self that is 'constituted in a net of traces, connections: a self that in its emptiness is open to all possibilities' (Game 1997, 119), quoting Nhat Hanh: 'Emptiness is impermanence, it is change'. This sense of an 'empty' self, receptive to, and renewed by, exchange with a wider environment is one that emerges in several of the chapters. Hermkens and Timmer, in their discussion of Melanesian Asmat artefacts, describe a permeable boundary between self, artefact and environment, in which balance is maintained through continual exchange, enabled by generative processes of decay and renewal. When artefacts are accessioned into museums, the 'ontology of permanence eradicates objects' life force and agency, reducing Asmat carvings and the

Asmat peoples themselves to mere emblems'. In the collection, the objects 'die' a sterile death, and this death also works back on the identities of the people connected to them. Geismar's story of the displaced, and then replaced, G'psgolox totem pole reveals a similar insight. The curators from Stockholm's Ethnographic Museum, operating with the 'ontology of permanence', struggle to understand that cultural persistence is achieved, in part, through the material *impermanence* of the pole and a state of continual ecological and cultural exchange and transformation, in situ. Otto's chapter addresses the question of self most explicitly, asking 'how theories of world-making, autopoiesis and sympoiesis might help articulate the relation between culture as a conservative force and as a factor of change'. In his discussion of the latent temporalities associated with the revival of a traditional ceremony, he posits a relation between self and world in which the self works back on the world, rather than the other way round: 'if there cease to be selves that identify with a certain world, then that world ceases to exist.' In all of these examples, the self is maintained through exchange with the world, and attempts to shut down or arrest this exchange threaten both cultural and individual identity.

As discussed in the opening to this chapter, moments of rupture and suspension can provide opportunities for radical reconfiguration of the self, as continuity is broken or arrested, and transformation becomes possible. The forced abandonment of a projected future and associated plans can initially trigger 'a terrifying loss of self' (Game 1997, 123). But the recognition of impermanence can emerge as an opportunity for reinvention and reorientation – a theme that emerges strongly in Cassaniti's chapter. Using the example of a Thai Buddhist struggling with alcohol addiction, she describes how a close encounter with death allowed him to transition to a more 'positive orientation to impermanence' and, paradoxically, come to value his own persistence. She unravels the complex workings of 'moral personhood' in this case, as embracing change lays 'the groundwork for an alternative ontological approach to time and self' – achieved through a moment of rupture and collapse. A similar discovery of potential in rupture and discontinuity comes through in Warner's discussion of a young, urban community of displaced Tibetan Buddhists. Among these individuals, displacement produces the conditions of possibility for the creation of new cultural forms, and new expressions of self, in India: 'This is where impermanence can play a key role because it points to both the impossibility of preserving forms (because of inevitable ends) and also the creative potential unleashed as endings become beginnings.' In this case, instability facilitates continuity – of self, as well as of intangible Tibetan heritage and culture.

In the pause, the swerve, the suspension, one opens oneself to other ways of seeing and being with impermanence. 'An impermanent, empty self is a self that can be "present" now,' writes Game (1997, 123) – and open to perceiving other capacities and connections. Close attention to the qualities and properties of these connections can lead to new insights and new understandings of the relation between self and object. Grünfeld writes about how a 'metabolic analytic' – applied to the curation of the complex biochemical lives of museum objects – opens up the possibility of exploring the 'dynamic between permanence and impermanence always already at work'. He contrasts a state of 'conserved permanence' with that of 'cultured impermanence', echoing some of the work of his co-authors by pointing out how the preservation of *life* in a 'cultural-metaphorical' sense requires its suppression in a 'metabolic-literal' sense. I'm prompted to wonder what a 'metabolic analytic' would bring to the case study explored by Pallesen, in which Indians living in Tanzania struggle with social impermanence as a condition of their existence in an adopted country – and as they confront the material impermanence of the concrete, physical structures that symbolise their successful settlement. These structures, in their decay, exacerbate feelings of existential instability but they also display a metabolic potentiality that might provide an opening to other responses and resonances. The expats' former homes, as with Grünfeld's wig, are 'compounded phenomena', contingent rather than coherent, and can potentially be understood through a lens that, in Warner's terms, finds 'positivity in relational dependence, co-origination, instability'.

The final theme I wish to draw out of the work assembled in this volume concerns the mediation and presentation of impermanence. Several chapters touch on this theme and discuss how difficult it can be to frame and interpret entities whose defining property is one of transience and transformation. Extending this to Game's argument, one can see how the attempt to craft a singular, legible narrative can lead to the marginalisation of mobile and multiple meanings and plural – potentially contradictory – selves. This comes across powerfully in McAtackney's discussion of the residual materiality of Ireland's Magdalene Laundries. Reflecting on evidence of theft and vandalism at one of the sites, she notes how destructive acts can serve a 'performative social justice function', expressing collective anger and sorrow about a difficult past. For the women who lived and worked in these spaces, the impermanence of these material remainders can be both welcomed (as aligned with their own rejection of their personal pasts in these places) and resisted (to the extent that they are concerned this collective history may be erased or denied). Individuals are capable of holding both orientations at once, and of living with the contradiction this implies, but this is much more difficult for the institutions that seek to memorialise and exhibit these troubled histories. A similar challenge faces the curators tasked with caring for Gustav Metzger's auto-destructive art, as documented by Laurenson and Bayley. In this case, it is the artist who appears to be divided within himself, desiring both for his art to be 'represented within the museum and campaign[ing] for its destruction' and disintegration. The curators must negotiate these apparently contradictory desires while also remaining faithful to their own professional practice and the expectations of the institution within which they work. The authors write: 'There is something about this imperfect and paradoxical representation of auto-destructive art that demonstrates the museum's potential to recreate its narratives and realities' – a theme also eloquently addressed in Geismar's chapter about how impermanence, and also intangible practice, can be managed through alternative processes of care. Finally, in their chapter about the exhibition that inspired the 'Inevitable Ends' conference, Johnsen, Otto and Warner explore in detail the challenges of curating and communicating diverse cultural expressions of impermanence in an institution oriented to achieving its very opposite.

In closing, I bring us back to this unhinged moment and the fundamental awareness of instability and impermanence that underlies our pandemic days. Can a volume like this help us find the resources to face moments like this critically and creatively, to describe what is happening to, and around, us in more precise and careful language? Can we cultivate an openness to the lessons that are there to be learned in change and transience, and let go of our predilection for stability and stasis? These are skills – lived and abstract – that we are likely to need in the decades to come as we cope with accelerating change and disruption. As with COVID-19, we will struggle to control and contain much of this change, but we will have some agency over how we respond and how we choose to apprehend and interpret impermanence. In the process, we will have an opportunity to find and form different versions of our selves – and, in fact, this may be necessary.

On 7 January 2021, while the United States Capitol building recovered from its incursion and as England's third COVID-19 lockdown entered its third day, I walked with my family down to the head of the nearby tidal creek. We roasted frankfurters over a fire in a patch of rare winter sun, the ground boggy with the just-receded tide. My children explored the properties of ice, and fell in the mud. I walked home with my older son up shadowed lanes still edged with morning frost while my husband and younger son held a home-learning session by the fire. I could have been – should have been? – at my desk preparing the following week's online learning, or writing this epilogue (multiple deadlines already deferred). But instead, I leaned into the moment of suspension and the connections I might find there. Impermanence became an 'opening to otherness' and an opportunity for the emergence of something else (Game 1997, 125).

References

Game, Ann. 1997. 'Time unhinged'. *Time & Society* 6(2/3): 115–29.

Index

Abramović, Marina:
'Seven Easy Pieces', 257
'Rhythm O', 252–253, *253*f15.2, 261
Allerton, Catherine, 100
Al-Mohammad, Hayder, on the with of being, 48
Almond, Philip C., 81n4
Anu Ranglug (*a nu ring lugs*):
'1376 Rap of Tibet Cypher' video, 169–170, *170*f10.4
popularity in China, 176
Tibetan heritage preserved through the music of, 166–167, 168, 175, 318, 320
Arendt, Hannah, on 'the right to have rights', 103–104
Asmat Museum of Culture and Progress:
consciousness-raising mission of, 118
founding by the Catholic Church, 117, 119, 124
Asmat society, 114–115
bisj poles used for transporting souls to the realm of the dead, 112–113, *112*f8.1, 126
emblematising (*lambang*) of the Asmat and their art, 113, 116–119, 123–125
interviews with two Asmat men. *See* Jimanipits, David; Tijup, Martinus
atheism:
Facebook used for networking by Kyrgyzstani atheists, 60, 61
restricted by government policy in the Soviet Union, 62n3
self-definition of Kyrgyz neo-atheists hinged on self-annihilation in the future, 1, 13, 47–48, 53, 61–62, 337
Austin, J. L., 286
autopoiesis:
defined as 'changing to stay the same' (Margulis and Sagan), 9, 132–133, 141
defined in terms of three fundamental processes necessary for the organisation of life, 142
and the dynamics of cultural and social change, 135, 142, 338
key processes of autopoiesis identified by Thompson, 9, 142
Sakumai's autopoietic world-making in the *yiwan kup* ritual, 147
sympoiesis as a necessary corollary of (according to Haraway), 150, 151, 309–310

world-making/worlding related to, 10, 142, 309
Azoulay, Ariella Aisha, 126, 269n40

Bangham, Jenny, 281–282
Barad, Karen, 174, 275
Barthes, Roland, 295
Bayley, Lucy and Pip Laurenson, on strategies for the representation of Gustav Metzger's auto-destructive art, 18, 251–272, 340
Bazin, André, 295
Bennett, Jane, conception of *vibrant matter*, 276
Bennett, Tony, 210, 307
Berger, John, 295
Biehl, João, and Peter Locke, on the anthropology of becoming, 12, 173
Blanchot, Maurice, 58
Bourdieu, Pierre, 101, 133
Boym, Svetlana, 94
Britton, Willoughby B. and colleagues, 81n5
Buddhist practices. *See* emptiness (Skt. *śūnyatā*, Tib. *stong pa nyid*); impermanence as a Buddhist teaching; Theravāda Buddhism; Tibetan Buddhist practice

Cacho, Lisa Marie, 37
Card, Claudia, on social death in the context of genocide, 37, 38
care and practices of care:
as a commentary on impermanence, 16
attention to impermanence as an alternative therapeutic intervention for addiction, 81n5
care as unsettled and full of ambivalence, 16, 209
of the dead. See death and dying
destructive potential of, 15, 58–60, 114, 125–126, 203, 337
feminist ethics of care, 15, 183–184, 191, 219
Llewellyn on care and the medical imaginary among people with cancer, 16, 183–204, 337
politics and ethics of care as top-down forms of governmentality, 15–16, 126, 219

processes of artistic creativity underpinned by the language of care, 219

world-building and world-repairing associated with, 59–60

Carsten, Janet, and Stephen Hugh-Jones, 101

Cassaniti, Julia, on attachment and alcoholism in Thailand, 14, 65–82, 338

Christianity and the Bible:

Asmat culture collected and conserved by the Catholic Church, 113, 114–115, 117–120, 124–129

belief in an immortal soul, 81n2

impact of conversion on Manus, Papua New Guinea, 133–134, 148

Jimanipits's carving of the corpus of Jesus and the Last Supper, 120–124, *121*f8.2

Magdalene Laundries in Ireland, 16, 226–243, *235*f13.1, *239*f13.2, 339–340

phrases referring to uncertainty and impermanence of life corresponding to *anicca*, 81n3

Clifford, James:

on erasure due to curatorial decisions in Western museums, 263

museums-as-contact-zones theory, 307, 310

colonialism:

British colonial administration of Tanzania, 85, 86

development of ethnographic museums directed by, 125–126

pacification policies in Netherlands New Guinea, 111, 115–116, 121

postcolonial citizenship politics in Tanzania, 85–87

shared colonial history stressed by proponents of the New Melanesian History, 134–135

Conrad, Tony, 'Ten Years Alive on the Infinite Plain', 262

conservation and conservators:

conservation as a social activity, 211

conserved permanence contrasted with cultured permanence, 281, 284–285, 287

long-term perception of flux and transformation explored in the work of ephemeral objects by Soon and Schorr, 17–18, 292–304

politics and ethics of care as top-down forms of governmentality, 15–16, 126, 219

'post-preservation' and the positivity of instability explored by Caitlin DeSilvey, 11–12, 208, 281, 285

subject position of, 210–211, 219

Cook, Joanna, and Catherine Trundle, on care practices as 'unsettled', 16, 209

COVID-19 and coping with impermanence, 79, 334, 340–341

Cramer, Florian, 293

Crane, Susan A., 286

Dalai Lama XIII, and the Pangdatsang family, 33–34

Dalai Lama XIV:

escape to exile in India, 29, 34

flight to Yatung, 160, 177n7

meditation on impermanence by, 6

Mind Life Institute co-founded with Varela and Engle, 10

older brother of. *See* Gyalo Thondup

toys sent to him by Pangda Yamphel, 35, 44n4

vision of Tibet as an environmental utopia, 169, 172

death and dying:

beliefs and practices related to *arbak*, 54–55

care and the medical imaginary among people with cancer, 16, 183–204, 337

disputes over how to care for the dead, 56–57

and Heidegger's concept of *having-been* (*da-gewesen*), 49, 56, 62n6

Kisāgotamī's struggle to accept impermanence, 3–4, 6

learning to let go explored by Schorr, 299–302

lifecycle rituals and ritual cycles of headhunting aimed at securing life force (*ji* or *ti*), 110–111, 113

Melanesian mortuary rituals, 112

of non-totalized communities, 57

objects transformed from 'life' to 'death' by museum accessioning, 15, 110–111, 114, 117, 123–126, 273, 337–338

reincarnation in Tibetan Buddhism, 28, 30–31

self-definition of Kyrgyz neo-atheists hinged on self-annihilation in the future, 1, 13, 47–48, 53, 58, 61–62, 337

See also social death

de la Cadena, Marisol, and Mario Blaser, pluriversal cosmopolitics of, 30, 141, 174

Deleuze, Gilles, 12

DeSilvey, Caitlin:

'Epilogue: self unhinged', 334–341

on 'post-preservation' and the positivity of instability, 11–12, 208, 281, 285

deterioration and decay:

creative destruction and renewal of Asmat artefacts, 15, 110–111, 337

impermanence and time-slippage as a subject of photography, 295

long-term perception of flux and transformation explored in the work of ephemeral objects by Soon and Schorr, 17–18, 292–304

'post-preservation' and the positivity of instability explored by Caitlin DeSilvey, 11–12, 208, 281, 285

the regenerative potential of, 43

See also environments and environmental crises

DiMaggio, Paul, 263

Domínguez Rubio, Fernando:
  on the museum as an artwork-
    maintaining machine, 259
  on the museum as an objectification
    machine, 206, 221
Dubuisson, Eva-Marie, 55

emptiness (Skt. śūnyatā, Tib. *stong pa nyid*):
  as a core concept of Buddhism, 4–5
  of the five aggregates (Skt. *skandha*, Tib.
    phyng po lnga), 174
  identified as impermanence by Thich
    Nhat Hanh on, 337
environments and environmental crises:
  biodegradable urns for cremation, 47,
    60
  continuous change in, 2
  contribution of Escobar's ontology of
    design to alternative world-making, 10
  the Dalai Lama's vision of Tibet as an
    environmental utopia, 169, 172
  interdependence theorised in Uexküll's
    concept of *Umwelt*, 9, 142
  Nalo's vision of impermanence, *109*f7.1
  and the regenerative potential of
    deterioration and decay, 43
  stewardship of the environment as a
    focus of the Tibetan social
    entrepreneurship movement, 172
  sustainability focused on life itself, 175
Eriksen, Thomas Hylland, 11
Escobar, Arturo, interdependence/
  co-origination incorporated into his
  manifesto for the future of design, 10,
    142, 157, 174–174, 177n17
ethnographic museums:
colonialism directing the development of, 125
Stockholm Ethnographic Museum, 208–209,
  338
ethnographic theory:
  and the challenge of anthropology of
    impermanence, 41–43, 335–337
  social death as an ethnographic and
    analytic category, 29–30

Fabian, Johannes, on the notion of coevalness
  in historical time, 42, 152n2
Feuerstein, Thomas, 'One and No Chair',
  *283*f16.2
Foster, Robert J., New Melanesian
  Anthropology proposed by, 134–135
Foucault, Michel, 187

Game, Ann:
  Bergson's ideas aligned with the
    Buddhist embrace of emptiness,
    336–337
  on the relation between self and
    perceptions of impermanence, 334–335,
    338–339, 341
Gaton Lekpa Rinpoché (1864–1941), 6
Geertz, Clifford, semiotic understanding of
  cultural processes, 141, 152n2
Geismar, Haidy, on caring for the social (in
  museums), 16, 205–224, 338, 340
gifts and gift-giving:

during mortuary rites as a Baluan
  cultural practice, 144
as part of Kyrgyz funeral rituals, 54
personhood constituted by things
  transacted as gifts, 111
Good, Byron, on medicine's soteriological
  vision, 187
G'psgolox totem pole, 208, 209, 338
Gyalo Thondup (the Dalai Lama's elder
  brother), dispute with Pangda Yampel,
  29, 35

Hallisey, Charles, 81n4
Hansen, Thomas Blom, 98
Haraway, Donna, 219
  the concept 'worlding' adopted by, 141,
    309–310
  on sympoiesis as a necessary corollary of
    autopoiesis, 150, 151
Hardenberg, Rola, 54
Hartog, François, regimes of historicity
  identified by, 8–9
Hatoum, Mona, 'Performance Still', 251,
  252–253, 252f15.1
Hegel:
  idea of *Aufhebung*, 269n40
  tragedy of Antigone recounted by, 56
Heidegger, Martin:
  concept of *having-been*, 49, 62n6
  principle of identity as A=A, 286
  the term 'world' rooted in the
    phenomenological philosophy of, 9, 140
  unravelling of the verb 'to save', 286
Hermkens, Anna-Karina and Jaap Timmer, on
  the permeable boundary between self,
  artefact and environment of Asmat
  carvings, 9, 15, 110–130, 338–339
Hertz, Robert, 48
Hinduism and Hindus:
  social death of Dalit/untouchable status,
    37
  Upaniṣadic conceptions of *ātman*, 81n2
Hoelzl, Ingrid, and Remi Marie, 295
Hoogerbrugge, Jacques, 118–119
Husserl, Edmund, 9, 140
Hutcheon, Linda, 90

identity. *See* self and identity
impermanence as a Buddhist teaching:
  and a cornerstone of most Buddhist
    ontologies, 4–5
  meditation on impermanence, 5, 6, 32,
    41–42
  mi rtag pa practices in Tibetan Buddhist
    practice, 31–32, 39
  the Pali term *anicca*, 67, 72, 77, 79, 81n3
  shifting intersubjective factors
    associated with one's present identity, 5,
    20n5
  suffering (*dukkha*) associated with, 5,
    74, 78
impermanence lived as a practice, 337
  anicca as an emic concept for a Thai
    Buddhist struggling with alcohol
    addiction, 14, 72–80, 338

attention to impermanence as an alternative therapeutic intervention for addiction, 81n5
awareness of change in popular culture in Thailand, 66f5.1, 67
capitalist expectations of productivity challenged by, 43
chants about impermanence from the Mahā Parinibāṇa Sutta at Thai funerals, 67–68
the circle of revolving life force in Asmat cosmology, 110–111, 113, 327–328
conceptualisation of an Asmat 'museum of impermanence', 126–127
Khenpo Pema Wangdak on suffering related to, 172–173
Kisāgotamī's struggle to accept impermanence, 3–4, 6
'material memory' of Ireland's derelict Magdelene Laundries, 16, 229–230, 233–238, 235f13.1, 239f13.2, 242–243, 339–340
the process of cultural loss and preservation experienced by Tanzanian Indians, 14, 93–94, 101–102, 103, 306, 339
in Tibetan society and culture. *See* Tibetan heritage
world-making as, 142
Indonesia, permeability of Manggarai houses as a positive feature, 100
interdependence:
  finding positivity in relational dependence compared with, 174, 339
  incorporation into Escobar's manifesto for the future of design, 10, 142, 157, 174–174, 177n17
  interdependence between an organism and its world theorised in Uexküll's concept of *Umwelt*, 9, 142
  of the interface between inside and outside of metabolism, 274
  Puig de la Bellacasa on human interconnection, 59
Islam and Muslim practices:
  afterlife beliefs of Kyrgyz Muslims, 48, 54–55, 62
  beliefs and practices related to *arbak*, 54–55
  Qur'anic teaching about the dangers of clinging to worldly permanence, 81n3
  restricted by government policy in the Soviet Union, 62n3
  restrictions on women, 50

Jackson, Steven J., on the language of care, 219
Jains:
  the process of cultural preservation emphasized by Tanzanian Indians, 14, 93–94, 101–102
  settlement of Gujarati merchants in East Africa, 85
  story of emigration by displaced Tanzanian Indians (Manu and Deepa), 84, 89, 94, 95–98, 99, 103

story of the persistence of Tanzanian Indians (Karan and Bhavana), 84, 87, 90–92, 95–99, 101, 102–103
Jeudy-Ballini, Monique, 126
Jimanipits, David, carving of the corpus of Jesus and the Last Supper, 120–124, 121f8.2
Johnsen, Ulrik Høj, Ton Otto and Cameron David Warner, 'Museum of Impermanence', 305–333, 340
Jonas, Hans, 282
Jónasson, Pétur, typology of touch explored by, 215–216

Kesby, Alison, on finding a 'place in the world', 104
Kleinman, Arthur, and Sjaak van der Geest, 59
Koselleck, Reinhart, on 'horizons of expectations', 88

Landecker, Hannah, metabolism defined by, 274
Latour, Bruno:
  'matters of concern', 15
  and the plasticity of the anthropology of becoming, 173
Laurenson, Pip, on loss entailed by material identity, 286
Laurenson, Pip and Haidy Gesmar, 'Finding Photography', 205, 212–215, 219–220, 221
Laurenson, Pip and Lucy Bayley, on strategies for the representation of Gustav Metzger's auto-destructive art, 18, 251–272, 340
Leach, James, 111–112
Levinas, Emmanuel, 56, 59
Lévi-Strauss, Claude, 101
Lewis, Sara, 43
Llewellyn, Henry, on care and the medical imaginary among people with cancer, 16, 183–204, 337
Lock, Margaret, on social death in the medical field, 37–38
loss:
  destruction of self at the end of one's world as an act of world-building, 49, 58–62
  entailed by material identity and metabolic processes, 282, 286–287
  entropy as an alternative to change as loss, 287, 289
  and learning to let go explored by Schorr, 299–302
  loss of self experienced in moments of rupture and collapse, 334, 338
  sense of loss expressed by 'Æv!' in the case of the strawberry-coloured wig, 272–273, 276, 288–290, 339
  symbolic cultural loss expressed in Nyedron's photograpy, 163, 163f10.2
  See also death and dying; nostalgia
Louw, Maria, on atheist endings in contemporary Kyrgystan, 13, 47–64, 337
Luhmann, Niklas, 141
Lyons, Kristina, 43

McAtackney, Laura, on Ireland's derelict
Magdalene Laundries, 16, 226–244,
235f13.1, 239f13.2, 339–340
McGranahan, Carole, on social death, 28–46,
337
Margulis, Lynn, and Dorion Sagan, autopoiesis
defined as 'changing to stay the same', 9,
132–133, 141
Martinon, Jean-Paul, 286
Maturana, Humberto and Francisco Varela,
understanding of living systems as
autopoietic, 10, 141–142, 275
Medical Museion:
collections at, 277f16.1
interviews with conservators, 276–280
interview with Amalie Suurballe
Schjøtt-Wieth and Maiken Ploug Risom
(4 April 2019), 277, 278–279
interview with Maiken Ploug Risom (14
March 2019), 278, 279, 280
interview with Nanna Gerdes (10 May
2019), 279–280
practices of conserved permanence at,
273
strawberry-coloured wig donated to,
272–273, 276, 289–290, 339
'The Living Room' being developed at,
287–289
Mendieta, Ana, 'Untitled (Blood and Feathers
#2)', 251–253
Merleau-Ponty, Maurice, 274
Metzger, Gustav:
auto-destructive practice of, 259–261
cross-disciplinary collaboration featured
in, 263–264
obsession with matter, materiality and
documentation, 263, 265
'Recreation of First Public Demonstration
of Auto-Destructive Art', 6, 18, 254–257,
254f15.3, 258f15.3, 258f15.4,
258f15.5, 259, 262, 263,
265–266, 340
Miller, Daniel, 176n2
Morgan, Jennie, and Sharon Macdonald, on
de-growth practices, 273
museological and curatorial practice:
conceptualisation of an Asmat 'museum
of impermanence', 126–127
cultural fragility (impermanence) and
nostalgia for a more authentic past
(tradition) as driving forces behind,
220–221
erasure due to curatorial decisions in
Western museums, 263
museums-as-contact-zones theory of
James Clifford, 307, 310
museums as objectification machines,
206, 207, 221
sympoietic artefact- and exhibition-
making, 309–311
worlds embodied by exhibition designs,
310
See also conservation and conservators
Muñoz Viñas, Salvador, critique of the concept
of authenticity, 285–286

museological impermanence, the displaced
and then replaced G'psgolox totem pole,
208–209, 338
museological impermanence–CULTURING
IMPERMANENCE, 273–274, 278, 281,
284–287
Museum of Cultures (formerly Museum of
Ethnology) in Basel, Manus skull and its
replica at, 327–329, 328f18.13a–b
Museum of Impermanence, 18, 305–333, 340
1376 'Museum of Impermanence' Store,
318–322
designing of, 305–307, 311–315
explanatory videos, 313, 313f18.3,
314f18.4, 329, 329f18.14
Manus skull replica displayed at,
327–329, 328f18.13a–b
Nepalese section, 323–325
old Green Tara and new Green Tara at,
309, 323f18.10a–b, 324–325
Papua New Guinea section, 312f18.2,
326–329, 32718.12
sand maṇḍala at, 2, 39, 306, 311,
315–318, 316f18.5, 318f18.6,
330–331
sympoietic assemblage of, 309, 311,
314–315, 317, 325–326, 330–331,
331
tangka inspired by a mural in Lo,
318f18.7b
tangka of Goddess Tara by Tenzin
Nyima, 319f18.7
Tibetan music videos featured in the
Store, 320
view from the Tibet section, 312f18.1

Nagar, Richa, 99
Nalo, Joe, vision of impermanence, 109f7.1
Nancy, Jean-Luc, 57–58
nationalised housing in Tanzania, 93f6.2
the Acquisition of Buildings Act of 1971,
83–84, 93f6.2
and the right to a place in the world,
84–85, 90–92, 95–97, 101–102,
104
nostalgia:
inaccessibility of the past as part of its
power, 90, 94
the invention of ethnographic collection
driven by, 220
Nyema Droma (Nyedron):
fake amulet case, 163f10.2, 169
Hima Ālaya fashion label, 162–165,
163f10.3
Munsel criticised by, 164
photography by, 162–163, 163f10.2
reinterpretation of Tibetan heritage
emphasized by, 164, 175

Oonk, Gijsbert, 104n1
Otto, Ton:
Manus skull encountered in the Museum
of Cultures in Basel, 327–328
on reinventing ritual on Baluan Island,
Papua New Guinea, 14, 131–154, 338

Otto, Ton, Ulrik Høj Johnsen and Cameron David Warner, 'Museum of Impermanence', 18, 305–333, 340

Paliau Movement, traditional ceremonies and rituals abolished, 131, 133–134, 147–148, 151
Pallesen, Cecil Marie Schou, on Tanzanian Indians' responses to impermanence, 14, 83–105, 339
Pangdatsang family:
    close relations with the Dalai Lama's family, 34–35, 38
    luck and *las* (karma) of, 33–34, 39
    patronage of major monasteries of Tibet, 38–39
    social death of, 13, 29–30, 35–36, 38
    and the thirteenth Dalai Lama, 33–34
    trading business in Kham, 29, 33
Pangdatsang family–PANGDA NYIGYAL:
    friendship with the thirteenth Dalai Lama, 33
    murder of, 33, 39–40, 41
Pangdatsang family–PANGDA RAPGA:
    death of, 39
    Gyalo Thondup's lodging paid for by, 35, 44n5
    impact of social death on, 34–35, 39
    intellectual interests of, 39
    revolt against Tibetan Government troops led by, 34
Pangdatsang family–PANGDA TOBGYAL:
    as a regional power figure, 33
    revolt against Tibetan Government troops led by, 34
    torturing of, 39
Pangdatsang family–PANGDA WANGMO (PANGDA YAMPEL'S DAUGHTER):
    impact of social death on, 35–36, 43
    social rebirth accomplished by reclaiming of her name and some of the family property, 43–44
    story of the Pangdatsang family related to McGranahan, 28–29
Pangdatsang family–PANGDA YAMPEL:
    accussed of being a communist sympathiser, 35, 39
    death of, 39
    dispute with Gyalo Thondup (the Dalai Lama's elder brother), 29, 35
    trade monopoly of, 34
Patterson, Orlando, on the social death of African slaves, 29, 37
Pearce, Susan M., objects entering a museum described as a transformation from 'life' to 'death', 273
Petryna, Adriana, 183
photography:
    impermanence and time-slippage as a subject of, 295
    post-digital image culture and practice, 293
    screenshotting as a post-digital practice explored by Soon and Schorr, 17–18, 292–304
Puig de la Bellacasa, María:

on human interconnection and interdependency, 59
    the negotiation of permanence and impermanence by care, 15–16, 219
    on the potentially destructive power of acts of care, 59

Rinpoche, Lama Zopa, 32
Ruin, Hans, 49, 56–57, 62n6
Runia, Eelco, 298

Sakumai Yêp, *yiwan kup* ritual performed by, 131, 135–140, *136*f9.1, *138*f9.2, *139*f9.3, 143–151, 152n6
Schneebaum, Tobias, 119
Schorr, Sarah:
    'Saving Screens: Temporary Tattoos and Other Methods', 299–303, *300*f17.5, *301*f17.6, *302*f17.7, 303
    'screenshotting' technique, 17–18, 294, 298, *302*f17.7, 303
Schorr, Sarah and Winnie Soon, 'Screenshooting impermanence', 17–18, 292–304
Schutz, Alfred, 9, 140
self and identity:
    cultural and social identity entangled with 'things' by Melanesians, 111
    culture as a conservative force and as a factor of change, 14, 131, 133–134, 147–148, 151, 338
    emblematising (*lambang*) of the Asmat and their art, 113, 116–119, 123–125
    houses constructed as images of, 101–102
    loss of. See loss; social death
    permanence associated with identity in social theory, 2
    permeable boundary between self, artefact and environment in Melanesian Asmat artefacts, 112–113, 119, 123, 126, 337–338
    personhood constituted by things transacted as gifts, 111
    and the potentially destructive power of acts of care, 58–60
    the relation between self and world explored in the revival of ritual on Baluan Island, 131–154, 338
    sameness (as a continuing identity) accomplished through change, 9
    self-definition of Kyrgyz neo-atheists hinged on self-annihilation in the future, 13, 48, 53, 61–62, 337
    shifting intersubjective factors associated with (*anatta*), 5, 20n5, 78
    social death defined in terms of loss of social identity, 37
    and subject–object duality, 7
    See also autopoiesis; social death
Sen (Chiang Mai Buddhist resident):
    conceptions of change in Thailand, 66, 67
    struggles with attachment and alcohol, 67
Smithson, Robert, 287

social death:
of African slaves, 29, 37
anthropology of impermanence
challenged by, 41–43, 337
in the context of genocide, 37, 38
in ethnographic theory, 29–30, 43–43
inflicted on certain individuals within
neoliberal, heteropatriarchal society, 37
and the loss of social identity, 37
in the medical field, 37–38
overcoming by social rebirth, 6, 43–44
of the Pangdatsang family, 13, 29–30,
35–36, 38
and the potentially destructive power of
acts of care, 58–60
shame (*ngo tsha*) associated with, 40
social impermanence as a condition of
the existence of Tanzanian Indians, 14,
92–94, 101–102, 306, 339
as an unnamed but known practice in
Tibet, 36
Sontag, Susan, 295
Soon, Winnie:
Lego reconstruction of the 'tank man'
scene, 17, 296, 297f17.3, 298
'screenshotting' technique, 17–18,
294–296, 294f17.1, 298, 303
'Unerasable Images', 17, 296–297,
297f17.2, 298f17.4, 299
Soon, Winnie and Sarah Schoor,
'Screenshooting impermanence', 17–18,
292–304
souls and afterlife beliefs:
Asmat *bisj* poles used for transporting
souls to the realm of the dead, 112–113,
*112*f8.1, 126
Buddhist meanings of impermanence
contrasted with, 78
of Kyrgyz Muslims, 54–55, 62
Spivak, Gayatri, the concept 'worlding'
adopted by, 141
Stair, Julian, typology of touch explored by,
215–216
Stanley, Nick, 119, 123
Stengers, Isabelle, 42
Stevenson, Lisa, 203
Steyel, Hito, 293, 295, 296, 303
Stockholm Ethnographic Museum, the
displaced and then replaced G'psgolox
totem pole of, 208–209, 338
Strathern, Marilyn, 111
Strecker, Ivo, and Stephen Tyler, 141
sympoiesis:
and the dynamics of cultural and social
change, 135, 326, 331, 338
the Museum of Impermanence as a
sympoietic assemblage, 309, 311,
314–315, 317, 325–326, 330–331
sympoietic artefact- and exhibition-
making, 309–311
sympoietic theory of evolutionary
biology, 310–311
as 'worlding-with' in the company of
others according to Haraway, 309–310

Theravāda Buddhism:

chants about impermanence from the
Mahā Parinibāṇa Sutta, 67–68
the constructed nature of global
representations of, 81n4
emptiness as a core concept of, 4–5
impermanence (*anicca*) as an emic
concept for a Thai Buddhist struggling
with alcohol addition, 14, 72–80, 338
Northern Thai monk Khruba Siwichai,
75f5.3
Thomas, Nicholas, 114, 124
Thompson, Evan, key processes of autopoiesis
identified by, 9, 142
Tibetan Buddhist practice:
mi rtag pa (meditation on
impermanence), 5, 6, 31–32, 39, 41–43
reincarnation, 28, 30–31, 43
ritual making and unmaking of sand
maṇḍalas, 2, 15, 39, 306, 311, 315–318,
316f18.5, 318f18.6, 330–331
Tibetan heritage:
continuity facilitated by instability,
175–176, 339
and the creative potential of Tibetan
fashion, 168, 171–172, 174–176, 318,
322
and the impermanence of Tibetan
society and culture, 155–157
preserved and transformed in musical
expression, 156–157, 166–167, 168,
175–176, 177n13, 318, 320, 322
trukcha, 162, 162f10.1ab, 164, 172
See also Anu Ranglug (*a nu ring lugs*);
Nyema Droma (Nyedron)
Tijup, Martinus, reflections on Asmat culture,
114, 116–117, 124
Timmer, Jaap and Anna-Karina Hermkens, on
the permeable boundary between self,
artefact and environment of Asmat
carvings, 9, 15, 110–130, 338–339
Toren, Christina, and João de Pina-Cabral, 141
Tronto, Joan C., feminist ethics of care, 15,
183–184, 191, 219
Tsering Woeser, 'Heavy curtains and deep
sleep within darkness', 25–26
Tsing, Anna:
the concept 'worlding' adopted by, 141
on the friction between global capitalism
and local 'nature', 11

Valeri, Valerio, *mana* defined by, 110
Van Allen, Adrian, 287
Varela, Francisco, Mind Life Institute
co-founded by, 10
Varela, Francisco and Humberto Maturana,
understanding of living systems as
autopoietic, 10, 141–142, 275
Verdery, Katherine, 57
von Uexküll, Jakob, concept of *Umwelt*, 9, 142

Warner, Cameron David, fashionable
responses to the end of Tibet, 6, 15,
155–179, 330
Warner, Cameron David, Ulrik Høj Johnsen
and Ton Otto, 'Museum of
Impermanence', 18, 305–333, 340

Weiner, Annette, B., 111
Western philosophical tradition:
    the concept of 'world' or 'lifeworld' as an
    analytical tool in, 9, 140
    impermanence elaborated in, 81n3
    See also Hegel; Heidegger, Martin;
    Varela, Francisco
Wharton, Glenn, on the museum as an
    objectification machine, 221
wig donated to Copenhagen's Medical
    Museion:
    existential instability evoked by, 339
    sense of loss expressed by 'Æv!',
        272–273, 276, 288–290
worlds and world-making:
    assertion of the right to a place in the
    world by Tanzanian Indians, 14, 93–94,
    101–104
    and the concept of 'world' or 'lifeworld'
    as an analytical tool in the Western
    philosophical tradition, 9, 140
    cultural world creation attempted by the
    Paliau Movement, 131, 133–134,
        147–148, 151
    destruction of self at the end of one's
    world as an act of, 49, 58–62
    and the dynamics of cultural and social
    change, 135, 174, 338
    effected by the creative destruction in
    ritual of Asmat artefacts, 15
    and the exploration of cultural practices
    involved in engendered worlds, 142
    'horizons of expectations' constituting
    the possibilities and limits for Tanzanian
    Indians, 88–89, 93, 103
    multiple worlds transversed by the rise
    and fall of the Pangdatsang family, 30,
        41
    pluriversal cosmopolitics of de la Cadena
    and Blaser, 30, 141, 174
    reclaiming of nationalised housing by
    Tanzanian Indians. *See* nationalised
    housing in Tanzania
    in Sakumai Yêp's performance of the
    yiwan kup ritual, 131, 135–140, *136*f9.1,
        *138*f9.2, 137f9.3, 143–151, 152n6
    'worlding' as a term, 141, 152n8, 336
    See also autopoiesis

Younger, Paul, 88

Zigon, Jarrett, 57–58

Ingram Content Group UK Ltd.
Milton Keynes UK
UKHW051254170523
421899UK00009B/40